ACCA

FUNDAMENTALS LEVEL

PAPER F7

FINANCIAL REPORTING
(INTERNATIONAL)

PRACTICE & REVISION KIT

In this January 2010 new edition

- We discuss the **best strategies** for revising and taking your ACCA exams

- We show you how to be **well prepared** for your exam

- We give you **lots of great guidance** on tackling questions

- We show you how you can **build your own exams**

- We provide you with **three** mock exams including the **December 2009 exam**

- We provide the **ACCA examiner's answers** as well as our own to the June and December 2009 exams as an additional revision aid

Our **i-Pass** product also supports this paper.

FOR EXAMS IN 2010

D1335723

LEARNING MEDIA

First edition 2007
Fourth edition January 2010

ISBN 9780 7517 8054 3
(previous ISBN 9780 7517 6661 5)

e-ISBN 9780 7517 7627 0

British Library Cataloguing-in-Publication Data
A catalogue record for this book
is available from the British Library

Published by

BPP Learning Media Ltd
BPP House, Aldine Place
London W12 8AA

www.bpp.com/learningmedia

Printed in the United Kingdom

We are grateful to the Association of Chartered Certified
Accountants for permission to reproduce past
examination questions. The suggested solutions in the
exam answer bank have been prepared by BPP Learning
Media Ltd, except where otherwise stated.

Your learning materials, published by BPP Learning
Media Ltd, are printed on paper sourced from
sustainable, managed forests.

Contents

Question index

The headings in this checklist/index indicate the main topics of questions, but questions are expected to cover several different topics. Questions marked 2.5 were examination questions under the previous syllabus.

Examiner's answers. For the June and December 2009 exams the examiner's answers can be found at the end of this kit.

Planning your question practice

Our guidance from page (xvii) shows you how to organise your question practice, either by attempting questions from each syllabus area or **by building your own exams** – tackling questions as a series of practice exams.

ACCA examiner's answers

The ACCA examiner's answers to questions marked Pilot papers to 12/08 can be found on the BPP website at the following link: www.bpp.com/acca/examiner-solutions

Additional question guidance

Additional guidance to certain questions can be found on the BPP website at the following link:

www.bpp.com/acca/extra-question-guidance

Using your BPP Learning Media products

This Kit gives you the question practice and guidance you need in the exam. Our other products can also help you pass:

- **Learning to Learn Accountancy** gives further valuable advice on revision

- **Passcards** provide you with clear topic summaries and exam tips

- **Success CDs** help you revise on the move

- **i-Pass CDs** offer tests of knowledge against the clock

You can purchase these products by visiting www.bpp.com/mybpp.

Using your BPP Learning Media Practice and Revision Kit

Tackling revision and the exam

You can significantly improve your chances of passing by tackling revision and the exam in the right ways. Our advice is based on feedback from ACCA examiners.

- We look at the dos and don'ts of revising for, and taking, ACCA exams
- We focus on Paper F7; we discuss revising the syllabus, what to do (and what not to do) in the exam, how to approach different types of question and ways of obtaining easy marks

Selecting questions

We provide signposts to help you plan your revision.

- A full **question index**
- **BPP's question plan** highlighting the most important questions and explaining why you should attempt them
- **Build your own exams**, showing how you can practise questions in a series of exams

Making the most of question practice

At BPP Learning Media we realise that you need more than just questions and model answers to get the most from your question practice.

- Our **Top tips** included for certain questions provide essential advice on tackling questions, presenting answers and the key points that answers need to include
- We show you how you can pick up **Easy marks** on some questions, as we know that picking up all readily available marks often can make the difference between passing and failing
- We include **marking guides** to show you what the examiner rewards
- We include **examiners' comments** to show you where students struggled or performed well in the actual exam
- We refer to the **2009 BPP Study Text** (for exams in December 2009 and June 2010) for detailed coverage of the topics covered in questions
- In a bank at the end of this Kit we include the **examiner's answers** to the June and December 2009 papers. Used in conjunction with our answers they provide an indication of all possible points that could be made, issues that could be covered and approaches to adopt.

Attempting mock exams

There are three mock exams that provide practice at coping with the pressures of the exam day. We strongly recommend that you attempt them under exam conditions. **Mock exams 1 and 2** reflect the question styles and syllabus coverage of the exam; **Mock exam 3** is the December 2009 paper.

Revising F7

General exam support from BPP Learning Media

BPP Learning Media is committed to giving you the best possible support in your quest for exam success. With this in mind, we have produced **guidance** on how to revise and techniques you can apply to **improve your chances of passing** the exam. This guidance can be found on the BPP Learning Media web site at the following link:

www.bpp.com/acca/examtips/revising-for-ACCA-exams.doc

A paper copy of this guidance is available by emailing learningmedia@BPP.com

Topics to revise

What we do know about F7 is that Question 1 will be a consolidation question. This can be a statement of financial position or income statement or both, and it will probably include an associate, so be prepared for all of this. Therefore you must revise all the consolidation workings, and you must know how to account for an associate. All questions are compulsory.

Question 2 will be a single company accounts preparation question. This allows the examiner to bring in more complex issues that he would not test in the consolidation question. Make sure you can deal with finance leases, deferred tax, calculating finance costs using the effective interest rate, prior period adjustments, discontinued operations and construction contracts.

Question 3 will be on statements of cash flow or interpretation of accounts. You have studied both of these at 1.1, so make sure you can do them well. Other recent questions have involved non-current assets and impairment, intangible assets, EPS, provisions and regulatory issues. These are all likely topics for questions 4 and 5.

There will be a certain amount of discussion in some of the questions, so be prepared to write about financial reporting topics, such as the *Framework* or specific accounting standards.

Question practice

This is the most important thing to do if you want to get through. All of the most up-to-date exam questions from the previous syllabus and all the F7 questions to date are in this kit. Practice doing them under timed conditions, then go through the answers and go back to the study text for any topic you are really having trouble with. Come back to a question week later and try it again – you will be surprised at how much better you are getting. Be very ruthless with yourself at this stage – you have to do the question in the time, without looking at the answer. This will really sharpen your wits and make the exam experience less worrying. Just keep doing this and you will get better at doing questions and you will really find out what you know and what you don't know.

Passing the F7 exam

If you have honestly done your revision then you can pass this exam. What you must do is remain calm and tackle it in a professional manner. The examiner stresses a number of points which you should bear in mind.

- You must read the question properly. Students often fail to read the question properly and miss some of the information. Time spent reading the question a second time would be time well spent. Make yourself do this, don't just rush into it in a panic.

- Workings must be clear and cross-referenced. If the marker can read and understand your workings they can give you credit for using the right method, even if your answer is wrong. If your answer is wrong and there are no workings, or they are illegible and incomprehensible, you will get no marks for that part of the question.

- Stick to the timings and answer all questions. Do not spend too long on one question at the expense of others. The number of extra marks you will gain on that question will be minimal, and you could have at least obtained the easy marks on the next question.

- Do not neglect the short parts of the question. If you get a 20-mark consolidation with a 5-mark discussion topic at the end, leave time for that last part. You can't afford to throw away 5 marks.

- Make sure you get the easy marks. If an accounts preparation question contains something that you are unable to do, just ignore it and do the rest. You will probably only lose a few marks and if you start trying to puzzle it out you might waste a lot of minutes.

- Answer the question. In a discussion-type question you may be tempted to just write down everything you know about the topic. This will do you no good. The marking parameters for these questions are quite precise. You will only get marks for making points that answer the question exactly as it has been set. So don't waste your time waffling – you could be scoring marks somewhere else.

Note that you have 15 minutes reading time at the start of this exam, during which you are allowed to make notes on the question paper. Use this to read the questions carefully and underline important points. Make note of any points that occur to you which you may otherwise forget. Get really familiar with the paper and focus on what you can do, not the bits you think you can't do.

Gaining the easy marks

The first point to make is that you do not get any marks for just writing down the formats for a financial statement. But, once you have put the formats down, you are then in a position to start filling in the numbers and getting the easy marks. Also, correct formats will give you a guide so that you don't miss things. For instance, it's easy to forget about the minority interest in a group income statement. So that's a good place to start.

Having put down the formats, then go through the workings and slot in the figures. Make sure you get in all the ones you can do easily. Complicated parts are well worth doing if you are able to do them – there will be marks for those. Complicated parts which you don't know how to do are best left alone.

If you have an interpretation question, you will not get many marks for just producing lots of ratios or restating information you have already been given in the question. You have to be able to evaluate the information and see what judgements can be made. So go through the information critically and see which ratios are actually relevant. Then calculate them and say something sensible about them.

Exam information

Format of the exam

All questions are compulsory.

	Number of marks
Questions 1-3; 25 marks each	75
Question 4	15
Question 5	10
	100

Time allowed: 3 hours plus 15 minutes reading time

Additional information

The Study Guide provides more detailed guidance on the syllabus.

December 2009

		Marks
1	Consolidated income statement including associate	25
2	Single company statement of comprehensive income and statement of financial position	25
3	Mixed question on non-current assets, cash flows and ROCE	25
4	Scenario question on assets	15
5	Scenario question on EPS	10
		100

June 2009

		Marks
1	Consolidated statement of financial position including associate	25
2	Prepare income statement and statement of financial position from trial balance	25
3	Statement of cash flows and comment on ratios	25
4	IAS 10 scenario question	15
5	Financial statement extracts for complex asset	10
		100

Examiner's comment. The overall performance of candidates in this paper was poor. A significant number of candidates did not attempt either or both of Questions 4 and 5. Answers to sections of the paper requiring written comment, interpretation or analysis were weak or non-existent.

December 2008

		Marks
1	Consolidated income statement and statement of financial position	25
2	Single company statement of comprehensive income, statement of changes in equity and statement of financial position	25
3	Ratio analysis and comparison of performance for two companies	25
4	Discussion and scenario on provisions	15
5	Non current asset and depreciation – financial statement extracts	10
		100

June 2008

		Marks
1	Consolidated income statement plus calculate goodwill on acquisition and discuss treatment of associate	25
2	Redraft financial statements	25
3	Statement of cash flows and comment on cash flow management	25
4	Explain qualitative characteristics and apply to inventory	15
5	Accounting for convertible loan note	10
		100

December 2007

		Marks
1	Consolidated statement of financial position including associate	25
2	Single company accounts preparation question	25
3	Performance appraisal including calculation of ratios	25
4	Discussion of 'faithful representation' and leasing scenario	15
5	Discussion and scenario on development expenditure	10
		100

Pilot paper

Analysis of past papers

Below provides an overview of the syllabus and details of when each element has have been examined. Further details are included in the relevant chapter of the knowledge bank.

Covered in text chapter	Pilot paper	Dec 2007	June 2008	Dec 2008	June 2009	Dec 2009
A CONCEPTUAL FRAMEWORK FOR FINANCIAL REPORTING						
1 The need for a conceptual framework						
1 Understandability, relevance, reliability and comparability						
– Framework qualitative characteristics	Q4(a)(b)	Q4(a)(b)	Q4(a)(b)	Q4(a)		
– Accounting policies, changes in accounting estimates and errors	Q4(b)	Q5(b)	Q2			
1 Recognition and measurement				Q4(a)		Q4
15 The legal versus the commercial view of accounting			Q2		Q2	
22 Alternative models and practices (accounting for inflation)	Q4(b)					
1 The concept of 'faithful representation' ('true and fair view')		Q4(a)				
A REGULATORY FRAMEWORK FOR FINANCIAL REPORTING						
2 Reasons for the existence of a regulatory framework						
2 The standard setting process						
23 Specialised, not-for-profit and public sector entities						
FINANCIAL STATEMENTS						
21 Statements of cash flows			Q3		Q3	Q3
4 Tangible non-current assets						
– Property, plant and equipment	Q2	Q2	Q2	Q2, Q5	Q2, Q5	Q2, Q4
– Investment properties	Q2					
– Government grants						
– Borrowing costs						
5 Intangible assets		Q5(a)(b)		Q2		Q4
12 Inventories and construction contracts	Q2, Q5		Q4(b)		Q2, Q4(b)	
14 Financial assets and financial liabilities						
– Fair value through profit or loss		Q1(a)	Q2			
– Amortised cost	Q2	Q2		Q2	Q2	Q2
– Convertible debt			Q5			
16 Leases	Q2, Q4(b)	Q4(b)			Q2	
13 Provisions, contingent liabilities and contingent assets				Q2, Q4		Q2
6 Impairment of assets						
– Group accounting	Q1(b)	Q1(a)				
– Other						

	Pilot paper	Dec 2007	June 2008	Dec 2008	June 2009	De 20
C **FINANCIAL STATEMENTS (CONT'D)**						
C9 Taxation						
– Current tax	Q2	Q2	Q2	Q2	Q2	Q
– Deferred tax	Q2	Q2	Q2	Q2	Q2, Q4(b)	
C10 Regulatory requirements relating to the preparation of financial statements						
– Income statement	Q2	Q2(a)	Q2(a)			
– Statement of comprehensive income				Q2(a)	Q2(a)	Q
– Statement of financial position	Q2	Q2(b)	Q2(c)	Q2(c)	Q2(b)	Q
– Statement of changes in equity	Q2		Q2(b)	Q2(b)		
C11 Reporting financial performance						
– Discontinued operations						
– Non-current assets held for sale						
– Earnings per share		Q2(c)				Q5
D **BUSINESS COMBINATIONS**						
D1 The concept and principles of a group	Q1(a)		Q1(c)			
D2 The concept of consolidated financial statements		Q1(b)				
D3 Preparation of consolidated financial statements:						
– Consolidated income statement			Q1(b)	Q1(a)		Q
– Consolidated statement of comprehensive income						
– Consolidated statement of financial position	Q1(b)	Q1(a)		Q1(b)	Q1	Q
– Associates	Q1(b)		Q1(b)		Q1	Q
E **ANALYSING AND INTERPRETING FINANCIAL STATEMENTS**						
E1 Limitations of financial statements						
E2 Calculation and interpretation of accounting ratios and trends to address users' and stakeholders' needs	Q3(a)(b)	Q3(a)(b)	Q3(b)	Q3(a)(b)	Q3(b)	Q3
E3 Limitations of interpretation techniques				Q3(c)	Q4	
E4 Specialised, not-for-profit and public sector entities	Q3(c)					

Planning your question practice

We have already stressed that question practice should be right at the centre of your revision. Whilst you will spend some time looking at your notes and Paper F7 Passcards, you should spend the majority of your revision time practising questions.

We recommend two ways in which you can practise questions.

- Use **BPP Learning Media's question plan** to work systematically through the syllabus and attempt key and other questions on a section-by-section basis

- **Build your own exams** – attempt questions as a series of practice exams

These ways are suggestions and simply following them is no guarantee of success. You or your college may prefer an alternative but equally valid approach.

BPP Learning Media's question plan

The BPP Learning Media plan below requires you to devote a **minimum of 30 hours** to revision of Paper F7. Any time you can spend over and above this should only increase your chances of success.

Step 1   **Review your notes** and the chapter summaries in the Paper F7 **Passcards** for each section of the syllabus.

Step 2   **Answer the key questions** for that section. These questions have boxes round the question number in the table below and you should answer them in full. Even if you are short of time you must attempt these questions if you want to pass the exam. You should complete your answers without referring to our solutions.

Step 3   **Attempt the other questions** in that section.

Step 4   Attempt **Mock exams 1, 2 and 3** under strict exam conditions.

Syllabus section	2010 Passcards chapters	Questions in this Kit	Comments	Done ☑
The conceptual framework	1	1, 2, 3	Peterlee is a straightforward question on the *Framework* and Derringdo gets you to apply the *Framework* to the issue of revenue recognition. Make sure you do Porto from the pilot paper.	☐
The regulatory framework	2	4	This question covers a lot of material and is good revision.	☐
Presentation of published financial statements	3	12 13	All of these questions are good. Candel and Pricewell are the most recent.	☐
Non-current assets	4	15 16	Broadoak is a full question on IAS 16, so make sure you do it. The other questions reflect what you may see for a 10 or 15-mark question.	☐
Intangible assets	5	19, 20	Dexterity is a 25-mark on goodwill and intangible assets, so it covers a lot of ground. Emerald is a recent question.	☐
Impairment of assets	6	22	Wilderness is an excellent question on impairment. See if you can do it in the time.	☐
Reporting financial performance	7	26	Partway is a recent question on discontinued operations.	☐
Introduction to groups	8	27, 28	Question 27 is a good preparation question on the basics. Question 28 looks at the effect of related parties on group accounts. This is the context within which the examiner will examine related parties.	☐
The consolidated statement of financial position	9	29, 30, 31	Highveldt does not require the whole position statement, but gets you to produce the key workings. Pedantic is from the December 2008 paper.	☐
The consolidated income statement	10	32, 33, 34, 35	Start with the preparation question, and then do Hydan, which is a recent question.	☐
Accounting for associates	11	36, 37 40 43	Do the two preparation questions first and then Patronic and Pacemaker, which are the latest exam questions.	☐
Inventories and construction contracts	12	44, 47, 48	Start with the preparation question and make sure you also do Torrent and Beetie.	☐
Provisions, contingent liabilities and contingent assets	13	49 51	Make sure you do Bodyline, which is a full question on provisions. Promoil is a good example of a 15-mark question from the December 2008 paper.	☐
Financial assets and financial liabilities	14	53 54	Both of these questions cover calculation of interest costs. Make sure you can do them.	☐
The legal versus the commercial view of accounting	15	55 57	These are good questions on the application of substance over form. Do both of them.	☐
Leasing	16	59, 60, 61	These are all short questions. Do them all.	☐

Syllabus section	2010 Passcards chapters	Questions in this Kit	Comments	Done ✓
Accounting for taxation	17	62 64	Do the preparation question. Question 63 is good practice for a question on deferred tax.	☐
Earnings per share	18	65, 67	Question 67 is part of a recent exam question, so good practice.	☐
Analysing and interpreting financial statements	19	70 71	You must do Greenwood and Victular, which are recent questions.	☐
Limitations of financial statements and interpretation techniques	20	72 75	Waxwork and Harbin are the most recent questions.	☐
Statements of cash flows	21	76, 81 82	Do the preparation question and Pinto and Coaltown, which are the most recent questions.	☐
Alternative models and practices	22	84	Update is a typical question on this area.	☐
Specialised, not-for-profit and public sector entities	23	85	You will not get a full question on this. The examiner has stated that this part-question in the pilot paper is typical of how it will be examined.	☐

Build your own exams

Having revised your notes and the BPP Passcards, you can attempt the questions in the Kit as a series of practice exams. This is our suggestion:

	Practice exams					
	1	2	3	4	5	6
1	43	38	39	40	41	42
2	7	8	9	10	11	6
3	69	70	73	78	79	80
4	3	1	48	50	61	66
5	19	45	16	17	47	54

We have selected these questions on the following basis:

- Question 1 will be a consolidation
- Question 2 will be an accounts preparation question
- Question 3 will be a statement of cash flows or an interpretation of accounts question
- Questions 4 and 5 will test other areas of the syllabus

December 2008 Paper: 12, 17, 31, 51, 71
June 2009 Paper: 13, 18, 43, 75, 81

Questions

ACCA examiner's answers

Remember that you can access the ACCA examiner's solutions to questions marked '**Pilot paper**' or '**12/07**'on the BPP website using the following link:

www.bpp.com/acca/examiner-solutions

Additional question guidance

Remember that you can find additional guidance to certain questions on the BPP website using the following link:

www.bpp.com/acca/extra-question-guidance

1 Peterlee (2.5 6/06)

23 mins

(a) The IASB's *Framework for the preparation and presentation of financial statements* (Framework) sets out the concepts that underlie the preparation and presentation of financial statements that external users are likely to rely on when making economic decisions about an entity.

Required

Explain the purpose and authoritative status of the *Framework*. **(5 marks)**

(b) Of particular importance within the *Framework* are the definitions and recognition criteria for assets and liabilities.

Required

Define assets and liabilities and explain the important aspects of their definitions. Explain why these definitions are of particular importance to the preparation of an entity's statement of financial position and income statement. **(8 marks)**

(Total = 13 marks)

2 Derringdo (2.5 6/03 part)

20 mins

Revenue recognition is the process by which companies decide when and how much income should be included in the income statement. It is a topical area of great debate in the accounting profession. The IASB looks at revenue recognition from conceptual and substance points of view. There are occasions where a more traditional approach to revenue recognition does not entirely conform to the IASB guidance; indeed neither do some International Accounting Standards.

Required

(a) Explain the implications that the IASB's *Framework for the Preparation and Presentation of Financial Statements (Framework)* and the application of substance over form have on the recognition of income. Give examples of how this may conflict with traditional practice and some accounting standards. **(6 marks)**

(b) Derringdo sells goods supplied by Gungho. The goods are classed as A grade (perfect quality) or B grade, having slight faults. Derringdo sells the A grade goods acting as an agent for Gungho at a fixed price calculated to yield a gross profit margin of 50%. Derringdo receives a commission of 12·5% of the sales it achieves for these goods. The arrangement for B grade goods is that they are sold by Gungho to Derringdo and Derringdo sells them at a gross profit margin of 25%. The following information has been obtained from Derringdo's financial records:

		$'000
Inventory held on premises 1 April 20X2	– A grade	2,400
	– B grade	1,000
Goods from Gungho year to 31 March 20X3	– A grade	18,000
	– B grade	8,800
Inventory held on premises 31 March 20X3	– A grade	2,000
	– B grade	1,250

Required

Prepare the income statement extracts for Derringdo for the year to 31 March 20X3 reflecting the above information. **(5 marks)**

(Total = 11 marks)

3 Porto (pilot paper amended)

23 mins

(a)   The qualitative characteristics of relevance, reliability and comparability identified in the IASB's *Framework or the preparation and presentation of financial statements* (Framework) are some of the attributes that make financial information useful to the various users of financial statements.

Required

Explain what is meant by relevance, reliability and comparability and how they make financial information useful.

(9 marks)

(b)   During the year ended 31 March 20X6, Porto experienced the following transactions or events:

   (i)   Entered into a finance lease to rent an asset for substantially the whole of its useful economic life.

   (ii)   The company's income statement prepared using historical costs showed a loss from operating its hotels, but the company is aware that the increase in the value of its properties during the period far outweighed the operating loss.

Required

Explain how you would treat the items above in Porto's financial statements and indicate on which of the Framework's qualitative characteristics your treatment is based.

(4 marks)

(Total = 13 marks)

4 Regulatory framework (2.5 12/04)

45 mins

Historically financial reporting throughout the world has differed widely. The International Accounting Standards Committee Foundation (IASCF) is committed to developing, in the public interest, a single set of high quality, understandable and enforceable global accounting standards that require transparent and comparable information in general purpose financial statements. The various pronouncements of the IASCF are sometimes collectively referred to as International Financial Reporting Standards (IFRS) GAAP.

Required

(a)   Describe the functions of the various internal bodies of the IASCF, and how the IASCF interrelates with other national standard setters.

(10 marks)

(b)   Describe the IASCF's standard setting process including how standards are produced, enforced and occasionally supplemented.

(10 marks)

(c)   Comment on whether you feel the move to date towards global accounting standards has been successful.

(5 marks)

(Total = 25 marks)

5 Winger (2.5 pilot paper amended)   45 mins

The following list of account balances relates to Winger at 31 March 20X1.

	$'000	$'000
Sales revenue (note a)		358,450
Cost of sales	185,050	
Distribution costs	28,700	
Administration expenses	15,000	
Lease rentals (note b)	20,000	
Loan interest paid	2,000	
Dividend paid	12,000	
Property at cost (note c)	200,000	
Plant and equipment cost	154,800	
Depreciation 1 April 20X0 - plant and equipment		34,800
Development expenditure (note d)	30,000	
Profit on disposal of non-current assets		45,000
Trade accounts receivable	55,000	
Inventories: 31 March 20X1	28,240	
Cash and bank	10,660	
Trade accounts payable		29,400
Taxation: over provision in year to 31 March 20X0		2,200
Equity shares of 25c each		150,000
8% loan notes (issued in 20W8)		50,000
Retained earnings 1 April 20X0		71,600
	741,450	741,450

The following notes are relevant.

(a)   Included in sales revenue is $27 million, which relates to sales made to customers under sale or return agreements. The expiry date for the return of these goods is 30 April 20X1. Winger has charged a mark-up of 20% on cost for these sales.

(b)   A lease rental of $20 million was paid on 1 April 20X0. It is the first of five annual payments in advance for the rental of an item of equipment that has a cash purchase price of $80 million. The auditors have advised that this is a finance lease and have calculated the implicit interest rate in the lease as 12% per annum. Leased assets should be depreciated on a straight-line basis over the life of the lease.

(c)   On 1 April 20X0 Winger acquired a new property at a cost of $200 million. For the purpose of calculating depreciation only, the asset has been separated into the following elements.

Separate asset	Cost	Life
	$'000	
Land	50,000	freehold
Heating system	20,000	10 years
Lifts	30,000	15 years
Building	100,000	50 years

The depreciation of the elements of the property should be calculated on a straight-line basis. The new property replaced an existing one that was sold on the same date for $95 million. It had cost $50 million and had a carrying value of $80 million at the date of sale. The profit on this property has been calculated on the original cost. It had not been depreciated on the basis that the depreciation charge would not be material.

Plant and machinery is depreciated at 20% on the reducing balance basis.

(d)   The figure for development expenditure in the list of account balances represents the amounts deferred in previous years in respect of the development of a new product. Unfortunately, during the current year, the government has introduced legislation which effectively bans this type of product. As a consequence of this the project has been abandoned. The directors of Winger are of the opinion that writing off the development expenditure, as opposed to its previous deferment, represents a change of accounting policy and therefore wish to treat the write off as a prior period adjustment.

(e) A provision for income tax for the year to 31 March 20X1 of $15 million is required.

Required

(a) Prepare Winger's income statement for the year to 31 March 20X1, along with the changes in retained earnings from the statement of changes in equity. **(9 marks)**

(b) Prepare a statement of financial position as at 31 March 20X1 in accordance with International Financial Reporting Standards as far as the information permits. **(11 marks)**

(c) Discuss the acceptability of the company's previous policy in respect of non-depreciation of property.
(5 marks)

(Total = 25 marks)

6 Harrington (2.5 6/05 amended)   45 mins

Reproduced below are the draft financial statements of Harrington, a public company, for the year to 31 March 20X5:

INCOME STATEMENT - YEAR TO 31 MARCH 20X5

	$'000
Sales revenue (note (i))	13,700
Cost of sales (note (ii))	(9,200)
Gross profit	4,500
Operating expenses	(2,400)
Loan note interest paid (refer to statement of financial position)	(25)
Profit before tax	2,075
Income tax expense (note (vi))	(55)
Profit for the year	2,020

STATEMENT OF FINANCIAL POSITION AS AT 31 MARCH 20X5	$'000	$'000
Property, plant and equipment (note (iii))		6,270
Investments (note (iv))		1,200
		7,470
Current assets		
Inventory	1,750	
Trade receivables	2,450	
Bank	350	
		4,550
Total assets		12,020
Equity and liabilities:		
Ordinary shares of 25c each (note (v))		2,000
Reserves:		
Share premium		600
Retained earnings – 1 April 20X4	2,990	
– Year to 31 March 20X5	2,020	
– dividends paid	(500)	
		4,510
		7,110
Non-current liabilities		
10% loan note (issued 20X2)	500	
Deferred tax (note (vi))	280	
		780
Current liabilities		
Trade payables		4,130
		12,020

The company policy for ALL depreciation is that it is charged to cost of sales and a full year's charge is made in the year of acquisition or completion and none in the year of disposal.

The following matters are relevant:

(i)   Included in sales revenue is $300,000 being the sale proceeds of an item of plant that was sold in January 20X5. The plant had originally cost $900,000 and had been depreciated by $630,000 at the date of its sale. Other than recording the proceeds in sales and cash, no other accounting entries for the disposal of the plant have been made. All plant is depreciated at 25% per annum on the reducing balance basis.

(ii)   On 31 December 20X4 the company completed the construction of a new warehouse. The construction was achieved using the company's own resources as follows:

	$'000
Purchased materials	150
Direct labour	800
Supervision	65
Design and planning costs	20

Included in the above figures are $10,000 for materials and $25,000 for labour costs that were effectively lost due to the foundations being too close to a neighbouring property. All the above costs are included in cost of sales. The building was brought into immediate use on completion and has an estimated life of 20 years (straightline depreciation).

(iii)   Details of the other property, plant and equipment at 31 March 20X5 are:

	$'000	$'000
Land at cost		1,000
Buildings at cost	4,000	
Less accumulated depreciation at 31 March 20X4	(800)	3,200
Plant at cost	5,200	
Less accumulated depreciation at 31 March 20X4	(3,130)	
		2,070
		6,270

At the beginning of the current year (1 April 20X4), Harrington had an open market basis valuation of its properties (excluding the warehouse in note (ii) above). Land was valued at $1·2 million and the property at $4·8 million. The directors wish these values to be incorporated into the financial statements. The properties had an estimated remaining life of 20 years at the date of the valuation (straight-line depreciation is used). Harrington makes a transfer to realised profits in respect of the excess depreciation on revalued assets. Note: depreciation for the year to 31 March 20X5 has not yet been accounted for in the draft financial statements.

(iv)   The investments are in quoted companies that are carried at their stock market values with any gains and losses recorded in the income statement. The value shown in the statement of financial position is that at 31 March 20X4 and during the year to 31 March 20X5 the investments have risen in value by an average of 10%. Harrington has not reflected this increase in its financial statements.

(v)   On 1 October 20X4 there had been a fully subscribed rights issue of 1 for 4 at 60c. This has been recorded in the above statement of financial position.

(vi)   Income tax on the profits for the year to 31 March 20X5 is estimated at $260,000. The figure in the income statement is the underprovision for income tax for the year to 31 March 20X4. The carrying value of Harrington's net assets is $1·4 million more than their tax base at 31 March 20X5. The income tax rate is 25%.

Required

(a)   Prepare a restated statement of comprehensive income for the year to 31 March 20X5 reflecting the information in notes (i) to (vi) above.   **(9 marks)**

(b)   Prepare a statement of changes in equity for the year to 31 March 20X5.   **(6 marks)**

(c)   Prepare a restated statement of financial position at 31 March 20X5 reflecting the information in notes (i) to (vi) above.   **(10 marks)**

(Total = 25 marks)

7 Llama (12/07)

45 mins

The following trial balance relates to Llama, a listed company, at 30 September 2007:

	$'000	$'000
Land and buildings – at valuation 1 October 2006 (note (i))	130,000	
Plant – at cost (note (i))	128,000	
Accumulated depreciation of plant at 1 October 2006		32,000
Investments – at fair value through profit or loss (note (i))	26,500	
Investment income		2,200
Cost of sales (note (i))	89,200	
Distribution costs	11,000	
Administrative expenses	12,500	
Loan interest paid	800	
Inventory at 30 September 2007	37,900	
Income tax (note (ii))		400
Trade receivables	35,100	
Revenue		180,400
Equity shares of 50 cents each fully paid		60,000
Retained earnings at 1 October 2006		25,500
2% loan note 2009 (note (iii))		80,000
Trade payables		34,700
Revaluation reserve (arising from land and buildings)		14,000
Deferred tax		11,200
Suspense account (note (iv))		24,000
Bank		6,600
	471,000	471,000

The following notes are relevant:

(i)   Llama has a policy of revaluing its land and buildings at each year end. The valuation in the trial balance includes a land element of $30 million. The estimated remaining life of the buildings at that date (1 October 2006) was 20 years. On 30 September 2007, a professional valuer valued the buildings at $92 million with no change in the value of the land. Depreciation of buildings is charged 60% to cost of sales and 20% each to distribution costs and administrative expenses.

During the year Llama manufactured an item of plant that it is using as part of its own operating capacity. The details of its cost, which is included in cost of sales in the trial balance, are:

	$'000
Materials cost	6,000
Direct labour cost	4,000
Machine time cost	8,000
Directly attributable overheads	6,000

The manufacture of the plant was completed on 31 March 2007 and the plant was brought into immediate use, but its cost has not yet been capitalised.

All plant is depreciated at 12½% per annum (time apportioned where relevant) using the reducing balance method and charged to cost of sales. No non-current assets were sold during the year.

The fair value of the investments held at fair value through profit or loss at 30 September 2007 was $27·1 million.

(ii)   The balance of income tax in the trial balance represents the under/over provision of the previous year's estimate. The estimated income tax liability for the year ended 30 September 2007 is $18·7 million. At 30 September 2007 there were $40 million of taxable temporary differences. The income tax rate is 25%. Note: you may assume that the movement in deferred tax should be taken to profit or loss (income statement).

(iii) The 2% loan note was issued on 1 April 2007 under terms that provide for a large premium on redemption in 2009. The finance department has calculated that the effect of this is that the loan note has an effective interest rate of 6% per annum.

(iv) The suspense account contains the corresponding credit entry for the proceeds of a rights issue of shares made on 1 July 2007. The terms of the issue were one share for every four held at 80 cents per share. Llama's share price immediately before the issue was $1. The issue was fully subscribed.

Required

Prepare for Llama:

(a)	A statement of comprehensive income for the year ended 30 September 2007.	**(9 marks)**
(b)	A statement of financial position as at 30 September 2007.	**(13 marks)**
(c)	A calculation of the earnings per share for the year ended 30 September 2007.	**(3 marks)**

Note. a statement of changes in equity is not required.

(Total = 25 marks)

8 Tadeon (2.5 12/06)   45 mins

The following trial balance relates to Tadeon, a publicly listed company, at 30 September 20X6:

	$'000	$'000
Revenue		277,800
Cost of sales	118,000	
Operating expenses	40,000	
Loan interest paid (note (i))	1,000	
Rental of vehicles (note (ii))	6,200	
Investment income		2,000
25 year leasehold property at cost (note (iii))	225,000	
Plant and equipment at cost	181,000	
Investments at amortised cost	42,000	
Accumulated depreciation at 1 October 20X5 – leasehold property		36,000
– plant and equipment		85,000
Equity shares of 20 cents each fully paid		150,000
Retained earnings at 1 October 20X5		18,600
2% Loan note (note (i))		50,000
Deferred tax balance 1 October 20X5 (note (iv))		12,000
Trade receivables	53,500	
Inventories at 30 September 20X6	33,300	
Bank		1,900
Trade payables		18,700
Suspense account (note (v))		48,000
	700,000	700,000

The following notes are relevant:

(i) The loan note was issued on 1 October 20X5. It is redeemable on 30 September 20Y0 at a large premium (in order to compensate for the low nominal interest rate). The finance department has calculated that the effective interest rate on the loan is 5.5% per annum.

(ii) The rental of the vehicles relates to two separate contracts. These have been scrutinised by the finance department and they have come to the conclusion that $5 million of the rentals relate to a finance lease. The finance lease was entered into on 1 October 20X5 (the date the $5 million was paid) for a four year period. The vehicles had a fair value of $20 million (straight-line depreciation should be used) at 1 October 20X5 and the lease agreement requires three further annual payments of $6 million each on the anniversary of the lease. The interest rate implicit in the lease is to be taken as 10% per annum. (Note: you are not required to calculate the present value of the minimum lease payments.) The other contract is an operating lease and should be charged to operating expenses.

Other plant and equipment is depreciated at 12 1/2% per annum on the reducing balance basis.

All depreciation of property, plant and equipment is charged to cost of sales.

(iii)   On 30 September 20X6 the leasehold property was revalued to $200 million. The directors wish to incorporate this valuation into the financial statements.

(iv)   The directors have estimated the provision for income tax for the year ended 30 September 20X6 at $38 million. At 30 September 20X6 there were $74 million of taxable temporary differences, of which $20 million related to the revaluation of the leasehold property (see (iii) above). The income tax rate is 20%.

(v)   The suspense account balance can be reconciled from the following transactions:

The payment of a dividend in October 20X5. This was calculated to give a 5% yield on the company's share price of 80 cents as at 30 September 20X5.

The net receipt in March 20X6 of a fully subscribed rights issue of one new share for every three held at a price of 32 cents each. The expenses of the share issue were $2 million and should be charged to share premium.

Note. The cash entries for these transactions have been correctly accounted for.

Required

Prepare for Tadeon:

(a)   A statement of comprehensive income for the year ended 30 September 20X6; and   **(8 marks)**
(b)   A statement of financial position as at 30 September 20X6.   **(17 marks)**

Note. A statement of changes in equity is not required. Disclosure notes are not required.   **(Total = 25 marks)**

9 Kala (pilot paper amended)   45 mins

The following trial balance relates to Kala, a publicly listed company, at 31 March 20X6:

	$'000	$'000
Land and buildings at cost (note (i))	270,000	
Plant – at cost (note (i))	156,000	
Investment properties – valuation at 1 April 20X5 (note (i))	90,000	
Purchases	78,200	
Operating expenses	15,500	
Loan interest paid	2,000	
Rental of leased plant (note (ii))	22,000	
Dividends paid	15,000	
Inventory at 1 April 20X5	37,800	
Trade receivables	53,200	
Revenue		278,400
Income from investment property		4,500
Equity shares of $1 each fully paid		150,000
Retained earnings at 1 April 20X5		119,500
8% (actual and effective) loan note (note (iii))		50,000
Accumulated depreciation at 1 April 20X5 – buildings		60,000
– plant		26,000
Trade payables		33,400
Deferred tax		12,500
Bank		5,400
	739,700	739,700

The following notes are relevant:

(i)   The land and buildings were purchased on 1 April 20W0. The cost of the land was $70 million. No land and buildings have been purchased by Kala since that date. On 1 April 20X5 Kala had its land and buildings professionally valued at $80 million and $175 million respectively. The directors wish to incorporate these values into the financial statements. The estimated life of the buildings was originally 50 years and the remaining life has not changed as a result of the valuation.

Later, the valuers informed Kala that investment properties of the type Kala owned had increased in value by 7% in the year to 31 March 20X6.

Plant, other than leased plant (see below), is depreciated at 15% per annum using the reducing balance method. Depreciation of buildings and plant is charged to cost of sales.

(ii)   On 1 April 20X5 Kala entered into a lease for an item of plant which had an estimated life of five years. The lease period is also five years with annual rentals of $22 million payable in advance from 1 April 20X5. The plant is expected to have a nil residual value at the end of its life. If purchased this plant would have a cost of $92 million and be depreciated on a straight-line basis. The lessor includes a finance cost of 10% per annum when calculating annual rentals. (Note: you are not required to calculate the present value of the minimum lease payments.)

(iii)   The loan note was issued on 1 July 20X5 with interest payable six monthly in arrears.

(iv)   The provision for income tax for the year to 31 March 20X6 has been estimated at $28.3 million. The deferred tax provision at 31 March 20X6 is to be adjusted to a credit balance of $14.1 million.

(v)   The inventory at 31 March 20X6 was valued at $43.2 million.

Required, Prepare for Kala:

(a)   A statement of comprehensive income for the year ended 31 March 20X6.   **(10 marks)**

(b)   A statement of changes in equity for the year ended 31 March 20X6.   **(4 marks)**

(c)   A statement of financial position as at 31 March 20X6.   **(11 marks)**

(Total = 25 marks)

10 Wellmay (2.5 6/07 amended)   45 mins

The summarised draft financial statements of Wellmay are shown below.

INCOME STATEMENT YEAR ENDED 31 MARCH 20X7

	$'000
Revenue (note (i))	4,200
Cost of sales (note (ii))	(2,700)
Gross profit	1,500
Operating expenses	(470
Investment property rental income	20
Finance costs	(55)
Profit before tax	995
Income tax	(360)
Profit for the year	635

STATEMENT OF FINANCIAL POSITION AS AT 31 MARCH 20X7

	$'000	$'000
Assets		
Non-current assets		
Property, plant and equipment (note (iii))		4,200
Investment property (note (iii))		400
		4,600
Current assets		1,400
Total assets		6,000
Equity and liabilities		
Equity		
Equity shares of 50 cents each (note (vii))		1,200
Reserves:		
Retained earnings (note (iv))	2,850	
Revaluation reserve	350	3,200
		4,400
Non-current liabilities		
8% convertible loan note (20Y0) (note (v))	600	
Deferred tax (note (vi))	180	780
Current liabilities		820
Total equity and liabilities		6,000

The following information is relevant to the draft financial statements:

(i) Revenue includes $500,000 for the sale on 1 April 20X6 of maturing goods to Westwood. The goods had a cost of $200,000 at the date of sale. Wellmay can repurchase the goods on 31 March 20X8 for $605,000 (based on achieving a lender's return of 10% per annum) at which time the goods are estimated to have a value of $750,000.

(ii) Past experience shows that after the end of the reporting period the company often receives unrecorded invoices for materials relating to the previous year. As a result of this an accrued charge of $75,000 for contingent costs has been included in cost of sales and as a current liability.

(iii) Non-current assets:

Wellmay owns two properties. One is a factory (with office accommodation) used by Wellmay as a production facility and the other is an investment property that is leased to a third party under an operating lease. Wellmay revalues all its properties to current value at the end of each year and uses the fair value model in IAS 40 *Investment property*. Relevant details of the fair values of the properties are:

	Factory	Investment property
	$'000	$'000
Valuation 31 March 20X6	1,200	400
Valuation 31 March 20X7	1,350	375

The valuations at 31 March 20X7 have not yet been incorporated into the financial statements. Factory depreciation for the year ended 31 March 20X7 of $40,000 was charged to cost of sales. As the factory includes some office accommodation, 20% of this depreciation should have been charged to operating expenses.

(iv) The balance of retained earnings is made up of:

	$'000
Balance b/f 1 April 20X6	2,615
Profit for the year	635
Dividends paid during year ended 31 March 20X7	(400)
	2,850

(v) 8% convertible loan note (20Y0)

On 1 April 20X6 an 8% convertible loan note with a nominal value of $600,000 was issued at par. It is redeemable on 31 March 20Y0 at par or it may be converted into equity shares of Wellmay on the basis of 100 new shares for each $200 of loan note. An equivalent loan note without the conversion option would have carried an interest rate of 10%. Interest of $48,000 has been paid on the loan and charged as a finance cost.

The present value of $1 receivable at the end of each year, based on discount rates of 8% and 10% are:

	8%	10%
End of year 1	0·93	0·91
2	0·86	0·83
3	0·79	0·75
4	0·73	0·68

(vi) The carrying amounts of Wellmay's net assets at 31 March 20X7 are $600,000 higher than their tax base. The rate of taxation is 35%. The income tax charge of $360,000 does not include the adjustment required to the deferred tax provision which should be charged in full to the income statement.

(vii) Bonus/scrip issue:

On 15 March 20X7, Wellmay made a bonus issue from retained earnings of one share for every four held. The issue has not been recorded in the draft financial statements.

Required

Redraft the financial statements of Wellmay, including a statement of comprehensive income and a statement of changes in equity, for the year ended 31 March 20X7 reflecting the adjustments required by notes (i) to (vii) above.

Note: Calculations should be made to the nearest $'000.

(25 marks)

11 Dexon (6/08) 45 mins

Below is the summarised draft statement of financial position of Dexon, a publicly listed company, as at 31 March 2008.

	$'000	$'000	$'000
Assets			
Non-current assets			
Property at valuation (land $20,000; buildings $165,000 (note (ii))			185,000
Plant (note (ii))			180,500
Investments at fair value through profit and loss at 1 April 2007 (note (iii))			12,500
			378,000
Current assets			
Inventory		84,000	
Trade receivables (note (iv))		52,200	
Bank		3,800	140,000
Total assets			518,000
Equity and liabilities			
Equity			
Ordinary shares of $1 each			250,000
Share premium		40,000	
Revaluation reserve		18,000	
Retained earnings – at 1 April 2007	12,300		
– for the year ended 31 March 2008	96,700	109,000	167,000
			417,000
Non-current liabilities			
Deferred tax – at 1 April 2007 (note (v))			19,200
Current liabilities			81,800
Total equity and liabilities			518,000

The following information is relevant:

(i) Dexon's income statement includes $8 million of revenue for credit sales made on a 'sale or return' basis. At 31 March 2008, customers who had not paid for the goods, had the right to return $2·6 million of them. Dexon applied a mark up on cost of 30% on all these sales. In the past, Dexon's customers have sometimes returned goods under this type of agreement.

(ii) The non-current assets have not been depreciated for the year ended 31 March 2008.

Dexon has a policy of revaluing its land and buildings at the end of each accounting year. The values in the above statement of financial position are as at 1 April 2007 when the buildings had a remaining life of fifteen years. A qualified surveyor has valued the land and buildings at 31 March 2008 at $180 million.

Plant is depreciated at 20% on the reducing balance basis.

(iii) The investments at fair value through profit and loss are held in a fund whose value changes directly in proportion to a specified market index. At 1 April 2007 the relevant index was 1,200 and at 31 March 2008 it was 1,296.

(iv) In late March 2008 the directors of Dexon discovered a material fraud perpetrated by the company's credit controller that had been continuing for some time. Investigations revealed that a total of $4 million of the trade receivables as shown in the statement of financial position at 31 March 2008 had in fact been paid and the money had been stolen by the credit controller. An analysis revealed that $1·5 million had been stolen in the year to 31 March 2007 with the rest being stolen in the current year. Dexon is not insured for this loss and it cannot be recovered from the credit controller, nor is it deductible for tax purposes.

(v) During the year the company's taxable temporary differences increased by $10 million of which $6 million related to the revaluation of the property. The deferred tax relating to the remainder of the increase in the temporary differences should be taken to the income statement. The applicable income tax rate is 20%.

(vi) The above figures do not include the estimated provision for income tax on the profit for the year ended 31 March 2008. After allowing for any adjustments required in items (i) to (iv), the directors have estimated the provision at $11·4 million (this is in addition to the deferred tax effects of item (v)).

(vii) On 1 September 2007 there was a fully subscribed rights issue of one new share for every four held at a price of $1·20 each. The proceeds of the issue have been received and the issue of the shares has been correctly accounted for in the above statement of financial position.

(viii) In May 2007 a dividend of 4 cents per share was paid. In November 2007 (after the rights issue in item (vii) above) a further dividend of 3 cents per share was paid. Both dividends have been correctly accounted for in the above statement of financial position.

Required

Taking into account any adjustments required by items (i) to (viii) above

(a) Prepare a statement showing the recalculation of Dexon's profit for the year ended 31 March 2008.

(8 marks)

(b) Prepare the statement of changes in equity of Dexon for the year ended 31 March 2008.   **(8 marks)**

(c) Redraft the statement of financial position of Dexon as at 31 March 2008.   **(9 marks)**

Note. notes to the financial statements are NOT required.

(Total = 25 marks)

12 Candel (12/08)

The following trial balance relates to Candel at 30 September 2008:

	$'000	$'000
Leasehold property – at valuation 1 October 2007 (note (i))	50,000	
Plant and equipment – at cost (note (i))	76,600	
Plant and equipment – accumulated depreciation at 1 October 2007		24,600
Capitalised development expenditure – at 1 October 2007 (note (ii))	20,000	
Development expenditure – accumulated amortisation at 1 October 2007		6,000
Closing inventory at 30 September 2008	20,000	
Trade receivables	43,100	
Bank		1,300
Trade payables and provisions (note (iii))		23,800
Revenue (note (i))		300,000
Cost of sales	204,000	
Distribution costs	14,500	
Administrative expenses (note (iii))	22,200	
Preference dividend paid	800	
Interest on bank borrowings	200	
Equity dividend paid	6,000	
Research and development costs (note (ii))	8,600	
Equity shares of 25 cents each		50,000
8% redeemable preference shares of $1 each (note (iv))		20,000
Retained earnings at 1 October 2007		24,500
Deferred tax (note (v))		5,800
Leasehold property revaluation reserve		10,000
	466,000	466,000

The following notes are relevant:

(i)   Non-current assets – tangible:

The leasehold property had a remaining life of 20 years at 1 October 2007. The company's policy is to revalue its property at each year end and at 30 September 2008 it was valued at $43 million. Ignore deferred tax on the revaluation.

On 1 October 2007 an item of plant was disposed of for $2·5 million cash. The proceeds have been treated as sales revenue by Candel. The plant is still included in the above trial balance figures at its cost of $8 million and accumulated depreciation of $4 million (to the date of disposal).

All plant is depreciated at 20% per annum using the reducing balance method.

Depreciation and amortisation of all non-current assets is charged to cost of sales.

(ii) Non-current assets – intangible:

In addition to the capitalised development expenditure (of $20 million), further research and development costs were incurred on a new project which commenced on 1 October 2007. The research stage of the new project lasted until 31 December 2007 and incurred $1·4 million of costs. From that date the project incurred development costs of $800,000 per month. On 1 April 2008 the directors became confident that the project would be successful and yield a profit well in excess of its costs. The project is still in development at 30 September 2008.

Capitalised development expenditure is amortised at 20% per annum using the straight-line method. All expensed research and development is charged to cost of sales.

(iii) Candel is being sued by a customer for $2 million for breach of contract over a cancelled order. Candel has obtained legal opinion that there is a 20% chance that Candel will lose the case. Accordingly Candel has provided $400,000 ($2 million × 20%) included in administrative expenses in respect of the claim. The unrecoverable legal costs of defending the action are estimated at $100,000. These have not been provided for as the legal action will not go to court until next year.

(iv)   The preference shares were issued on 1 April 2008 at par. They are redeemable at a large premium which gives them an effective finance cost of 12% per annum.

(v)   The directors have estimated the provision for income tax for the year ended 30 September 2008 at $11·4 million. The required deferred tax provision at 30 September 2008 is $6 million.

Required

(a)   Prepare the statement of comprehensive income for the year ended 30 September 2008.   **(12 marks)**
(b)   Prepare the statement of changes in equity for the year ended 30 September 2008.   **(3 marks)**
(c)   Prepare the statement of financial position as at 30 September 2008.   **(10 marks)**

Note: notes to the financial statements are not required.

(Total = 25 marks)

13 Pricewell (6/09)   45 mins

The following trial balance relates to Pricewell at 31 March 2009:

	$'000	$'000
Leasehold property – at valuation 31 March 2008 (note (i))	25,200	
Plant and equipment (owned) – at cost (note (i))	46,800	
Plant and equipment (leased) – at cost (note (i))	20,000	
Accumulated depreciation at 31 March 2008		
Owned plant and equipment		12,800
Leased plant and equipment		5,000
Finance lease payment (paid on 31 March 2009) (note (i))	6,000	
Obligations under finance lease at 1 April 2008 (note (i))		15,600
Construction contract (note (ii))	14,300	
Inventory at 31 March 2009	28,200	
Trade receivables	33,100	
Bank	5,500	
Trade payables		33,400
Revenue (note (iii))		310,000
Cost of sales (note (iii))	234,500	
Distribution costs	19,500	
Administrative expenses	27,500	
Preference dividend paid (note (iv))	2,400	
Equity dividend paid	8,000	
Equity shares of 50 cents each		40,000
6% redeemable preference shares at 31 March 2008 (note (iv))		41,600
Retained earnings at 31 March 2008		4,900
Current tax (note (v))	700	
Deferred tax (note (v))		
		8,400
	471,700	471,700

The following notes are relevant:

(i)   Non-current assets:

The 15 year leasehold property was acquired on 1 April 2007 at cost $30 million. The company policy is to revalue the property at market value at each year end. The valuation in the trial balance of $25·2 million as at 31 March 2008 led to an impairment charge of $2·8 million which was reported in the income statement of the previous year (ie year ended 31 March 2008). At 31 March 2009 the property was valued at $24·9 million.

Owned plant is depreciated at 25% per annum using the reducing balance method.

The leased plant was acquired on 1 April 2007. The rentals are $6 million per annum for four years payable in arrears on 31 March each year. The interest rate implicit in the lease is 8% per annum. Leased plant is depreciated at 25% per annum using the straight-line method.

No depreciation has yet been charged on any non-current assets for the year ended 31 March 2009. All depreciation is charged to cost of sales.

(ii) On 1 October 2008 Pricewell entered into a contract to construct a bridge over a river. The agreed price of the bridge is $50 million and construction was expected to be completed on 30 September 2010. The $14·3 million in the trial balance is:

	$'000
Materials, labour and overheads	12,000
Specialist plant acquired 1 October 2008	8,000
Payment from customer	(5,700)
	14,300

The sales value of the work done at 31 March 2009 has been agreed at $22 million and the estimated cost to complete (excluding plant depreciation) is $10 million. The specialist plant will have no residual value at the end of the contract and should be depreciated on a monthly basis. Pricewell recognises profits on uncompleted contracts on the percentage of completion basis as determined by the agreed work to date compared to the total contract price.

(iii) Pricewell's revenue includes $8 million for goods it sold acting as an agent for Trilby. Pricewell earned a commission of 20% on these sales and remitted the difference of $6·4 million (included in cost of sales) to Trilby.

(iv) The 6% preference shares were issued on 1 April 2007 at par for $40 million. They have an effective finance cost of 10% per annum due to a premium payable on their redemption.

(v) The directors have estimated the provision for income tax for the year ended 31 March 2009 at $4·5 million. The required deferred tax provision at 31 March 2009 is $5·6 million; all adjustments to deferred tax should be taken to the income statement. The balance of current tax in the trial balance represents the under/over provision of the income tax liability for the year ended 31 March 2008.

Required

(a) Prepare the statement of comprehensive income for the year ended 31 March 2009. **(12 marks)**
(b) Prepare the statement of financial position as at 31 March 2009. **(13 marks)**

Note: a statement of changes in equity and notes to the financial statements are not required. **(Total = 25 marks)**

14 Derringdo II (2.5 6/03 part) 16 mins

Derringdo acquired an item of plant at a gross cost of $800,000 on 1 October 20X2. The plant has an estimated life of 10 years with a residual value equal to 15% of its gross cost. Derringdo uses straight-line depreciation on a time apportioned basis. The company received a government grant of 30% of its cost price at the time of its purchase. The terms of the grant are that if the company retains the asset for four years or more, then no repayment liability will be incurred. If the plant is sold within four years a repayment on a sliding scale would be applicable. The repayment is 75% if sold within the first year of purchase and this amount decreases by 25% per annum. Derringdo has no intention to sell the plant within the first four years. Derringdo's accounting policy for capital based government grants is to treat them as deferred credits and release them to income over the life of the asset to which they relate.

Required

(a) Discuss whether the company's policy for the treatment of government grants meets the definition of a liability in the IASB's Framework; and **(3 marks)**

(b) Prepare extracts of Derringdo's financial statements for the year to 31 March 20X3 in respect of the plant and the related grant:

- applying the company's policy;
- in compliance with the definition of a liability in the Framework. Your answer should consider whether the sliding scale repayment should be used in determining the deferred credit for the grant.

(6 marks)

(Total = 9 marks)

15 Broadoak (2.5 12/01)   45 mins

The broad principles of accounting for property, plant and equipment involve distinguishing between capital and revenue expenditure, measuring the cost of assets, determining how they should be depreciated and dealing with the problems of subsequent measurement and subsequent expenditure. IAS 16 *Property, plant and equipment* has the intention of improving consistency in these areas.

Required

(a) Explain:

(i) How the initial cost of property, plant and equipment should be measured **(4 marks)**

(ii) The circumstances in which subsequent expenditure on those assets should be capitalised

(3 marks)

(b) Explain IAS 16's requirements regarding the revaluation of non-current assets and the accounting treatment of surpluses and deficits on revaluation and gains and losses on disposal. **(8 marks)**

(c) (i) Broadoak has recently purchased an item of plant from Plantco, the details of this are:

	$	$
Basic list price of plant		240,000
Trade discount applicable to Broadoak		12.5% on list price
Ancillary costs:		
Shipping and handling costs		2,750
Estimated pre-production testing		12,500
Maintenance contract for three years		24,000
Site preparation costs:		
electrical cable installation	14,000	
concrete reinforcement	4,500	
own labour costs	7,500	
		26,000

Broadoak paid for the plant (excluding the ancillary costs) within four weeks of order, thereby obtaining an early settlement discount of 3%.

Broadoak had incorrectly specified the power loading of the original electrical cable to be installed by the contractor. The cost of correcting this error of $6,000 is included in the above figure of $14,000.

The plant is expected to last for 10 years. At the end of this period there will be compulsory costs of $15,000 to dismantle the plant and $3,000 to restore the site to its original use condition.

Required

Calculate the amount at which the plant will be measured at recognition. (Ignore discounting.)

(5 marks)

(ii) Broadoak acquired a 12 year lease on a property on 1 October 20X0 at a cost of $240,000. The company policy is to revalue its properties to their market values at the end of each year. Accumulated amortisation is eliminated and the property is restated to the revalued amount. Annual amortisation is calculated on the carrying values at the beginning of the year. The market values of the property on 30 September 20X1 and 20X2 were $231,000 and $175,000 respectively. The existing balance on the revaluation surplus at 1 October 20X0 was $50,000. This related to some non-depreciable land whose value had not changed significantly since 1 October 20X0.

Prepare extracts of the financial statements of Broadoak (including the movement on the revaluation reserve) for the years to 30 September 20X1 and 20X2 in respect of the leasehold property.

(5 marks)

(Total = 25 marks)

16 Elite Leisure (2.5 12/05 part)   22 mins

Elite Leisure is a private limited liability company that operates a single cruise ship. The ship was acquired on 1 October 20W6. Details of the cost of the ship's components and their estimated useful lives are:

Component	Original cost ($ million)	Deprecation basis
Ship's fabric (hull, decks etc)	300	25 years straight–line
Cabins and entertainment area fittings	150	12 years straight–line
Propulsion system	100	Useful life of 40,000 hours

At 30 September 20X4 no further capital expenditure had been incurred on the ship.

In the year ended 30 September 20X4 the ship had experienced a high level of engine trouble which had cost the company considerable lost revenue and compensation costs. The measured expired life of the propulsion system at 30 September 20X4 was 30,000 hours. Due to the unreliability of the engines, a decision was taken in early October 20X4 to replace the whole of the propulsion system at a cost of $140 million. The expected life of the new propulsion system was 50,000 hours and in the year ended 30 September 20X5 the ship had used its engines for 5,000 hours.

At the same time as the propulsion system replacement, the company took the opportunity to do a limited upgrade to the cabin and entertainment facilities at a cost of $60 million and repaint the ship's fabric at a cost of $20 million. After the upgrade of the cabin and entertainment area fittings it was estimated that their remaining life was five years (from the date of the upgrade). For the purpose of calculating depreciation, all the work on the ship can be assumed to have been completed on 1 October 20X4. All residual values can be taken as nil.

Required

Calculate the carrying amount of Elite Leisure's cruise ship at 30 September 20X5 and its related expenditure in the income statement for the year ended 30 September 20X5. Your answer should explain the treatment of each item.

(12 marks)

17 Dearing (12/08)   18 mins

On 1 October 2005 Dearing acquired a machine under the following terms:

	Hours	$
Manufacturer's base price		1,050,000
Trade discount (applying to base price only)		20%
Early settlement discount taken (on the payable amount of the base cost only)		5%
Freight charges		30,000
Electrical installation cost		28,000
Staff training in use of machine		40,000
Pre-production testing		22,000
Purchase of a three-year maintenance contract		60,000
Estimated residual value		20,000
Estimated life in machine hours	6,000	
Hours used – year ended 30 September 2006	1,200	
– year ended 30 September 2007	1,800	
– year ended 30 September 2008 (see below)	850	

On 1 October 2007 Dearing decided to upgrade the machine by adding new components at a cost of $200,000. This upgrade led to a reduction in the production time per unit of the goods being manufactured using the machine. The

upgrade also increased the estimated remaining life of the machine at 1 October 2007 to 4,500 machine hours and its estimated residual value was revised to $40,000.

Required

Prepare extracts from the income statement and statement of financial position for the above machine for each of the three years to 30 September 2008. **(10 marks)**

18 Flightline (6/09)   18 mins

Flightline is an airline which treats its aircraft as complex non-current assets. The cost and other details of one of its aircraft are:

	$'000	*Estimated life*
Exterior structure – purchase date 1 April 1995	120,000	20 years
Interior cabin fittings – replaced 1 April 2005	25,000	5 years
Engines (2 at $9 million each) – replaced 1 April 2005	18,000	36,000 flying hours

No residual values are attributed to any of the component parts.

At 1 April 2008 the aircraft log showed it had flown 10,800 hours since 1 April 2005. In the year ended 31 March 2009, the aircraft flew for 1,200 hours for the six months to 30 September 2008 and a further 1,000 hours in the six months to 31 March 2009.

On 1 October 2008 the aircraft suffered a 'bird strike' accident which damaged one of the engines beyond repair. This was replaced by a new engine with a life of 36,000 hours at cost of $10·8 million. The other engine was also damaged, but was repaired at a cost of $3 million; however, its remaining estimated life was shortened to 15,000 hours. The accident also caused cosmetic damage to the exterior of the aircraft which required repainting at a cost of $2 million. As the aircraft was out of service for some weeks due to the accident, Flightline took the opportunity to upgrade its cabin facilities at a cost of $4·5 million. This did not increase the estimated remaining life of the cabin fittings, but the improved facilities enabled Flightline to substantially increase the air fares on this aircraft

Required:

Calculate the charges to the income statement in respect of the aircraft for the year ended 31 March 2009 and its carrying amount in the statement of financial position as at that date.

Note: the post accident changes are deemed effective from 1 October 2008. **(10 marks)**

19 Emerald (12/07)   18 mins

Product development costs are a material cost for many companies. They are either written off as an expense or capitalised as an asset.

Required

(a) Discuss the conceptual issues involved and the definition of an asset that may be applied in determining whether development expenditure should be treated as an expense or an asset.

(4 marks)

(b) Emerald has had a policy of writing off development expenditure to the income statement as it was incurred. In preparing its financial statements for the year ended 30 September 2007 it has become aware that, under IFRS rules, qualifying development expenditure should be treated as an intangible asset. Below is the qualifying development expenditure for Emerald:

	$'000
Year ended 30 September 2004	300
Year ended 30 September 2005	240
Year ended 30 September 2006	800
Year ended 30 September 2007	400

All capitalised development expenditure is deemed to have a four year life. Assume amortisation commences at the beginning of the accounting period following capitalisation. Emerald had no development expenditure before that for the year ended 30 September 2004.

Required

Treating the above as the correction of an error in applying an accounting policy, calculate the amounts which should appear in the income statement and statement of financial position (including comparative figures), and statement of changes in equity of Emerald in respect of the development expenditure for the year ended 30 September 2007.

Note. Ignore taxation.

(6 marks)

(Total = 10 marks)

20 Dexterity (2.5 6/04)   45 mins

(a)   During the last decade it has not been unusual for the premium paid to acquire control of a business to be greater than the fair value of its tangible net assets. This increase in the relative proportions of intangible assets has made the accounting practices for them all the more important. During the same period many companies have spent a great deal of money internally developing new intangible assets such as software and brands. IAS 38 '*Intangible assets*' was issued in September 1998 and prescribes the accounting treatment for intangible assets.

Required

In accordance with IAS 38, discuss whether intangible assets should be recognised, and if so how they should be initially recorded and subsequently amortised in the following circumstances:

(i)   When they are purchased separately from other assets

(ii)   When they are obtained as part of acquiring the whole of a business

(iii)   When they are developed internally.   (10 marks)

Note. Your answer should consider goodwill separately from other intangibles.

(b)   Dexterity is a public listed company. It has been considering the accounting treatment of its intangible assets and has asked for your opinion on how the matters below should be treated in its financial statements for the year to 31 March 20X4.

(i)   On 1 October 20X3 Dexterity acquired Temerity, a small company that specialises in pharmaceutical drug research and development. The purchase consideration was by way of a share exchange and valued at $35 million. The fair value of Temerity's net assets was $15 million (excluding any items referred to below). Temerity owns a patent for an established successful drug that has a remaining life of 8 years. A firm of specialist advisors, Leadbrand, has estimated the current value of this patent to be $10 million, however the company is awaiting the outcome of clinical trials where the drug has been tested to treat a different illness. If the trials are successful, the value of the drug is then estimated to be $15 million. Also included in the company's statement of financial position is $2 million for medical research that has been conducted on behalf of a client.   (4 marks)

(ii)   Dexterity has developed and patented a new drug which has been approved for clinical use. The costs of developing the drug were $12 million. Based on early assessments of its sales success, Leadbrand have estimated its market value at $20 million.   (3 marks)

(iii)   Dexterity's manufacturing facilities have recently received a favourable inspection by government medical scientists. As a result of this the company has been granted an exclusive five-year licence to manufacture and distribute a new vaccine. Although the licence had no direct cost to Dexterity, its directors feel its granting is a reflection of the company's standing and have asked Leadbrand to value the licence. Accordingly they have placed a value of $10 million on it.   (3 marks)

(iv)   In the current accounting period, Dexterity has spent $3 million sending its staff on specialist training courses. Whilst these courses have been expensive, they have led to a marked improvement in production quality and staff now need less supervision. This in turn has led to an increase in revenue and cost reductions. The directors of Dexterity believe these benefits will continue for at least three years and wish to treat the training costs as an asset.   (2 marks)

(v)   In December 20X3, Dexterity paid $5 million for a television advertising campaign for its products that will run for 6 months from 1 January 20X4 to 30 June 20X4. The directors believe that increased sales as a result of the publicity will continue for two years from the start of the advertisements.

(3 marks)

Required

Explain how the directors of Dexterity should treat the above items in the financial statements for the year to 31 March 20X4.   **(15 marks as indicated)**

Note. The values given by Leadbrand can be taken as being reliable measurements. You are not required to consider depreciation aspects.   **(Total = 25 marks)**

21 Advent (2.5 12/04 amended)   23 mins

Advent is a publicly listed company.

Details of Advent's non-current assets at 1 October 20X8 were:

	Land and building $m	Plant $m	Telecommunications licence $m	Total $m
Cost/valuation	280	150	300	730
Accumulated depreciation/amortisation	(40)	(105)	(30)	(175)
Net book value	240	45	270	555

The following information is relevant:

(i)   The land and building were revalued on 1 October 20X3 with $80 million attributable to the land and $200 million to the building. At that date the estimated remaining life of the building was 25 years. A further revaluation was not needed until 1 October 20X8 when the land and building were valued at $85 million and $180 million respectively. The remaining estimated life of the building at this date was 20 years.

(ii)   Plant is depreciated at 20% per annum on cost with time apportionment where appropriate. On 1 April 20X9 new plant costing $45 million was acquired. In addition, this plant cost $5 million to install and commission. No plant is more than four years old.

(iii)   The telecommunications licence was bought from the government on 1 October 20X7 and has a 10 year life. It is amortised on a straight line basis. In September 20X9, a review of the sales of the products related to the licence showed them to be very disappointing. As a result of this review the estimated recoverable amount of the licence at 30 September 20X9 was estimated at only $100 million.

There were no disposals of non-current assets during the year to 30 September 20X9.

Required

(a)   Prepare extracts from the statement of financial position relating to Advent's non-current assets as at 30 September 20X9 (including comparative figures), together with any disclosures (other than those of the accounting policies) under current International Financial Reporting Standards.   **(9 marks)**

(b)   Explain the usefulness of the above disclosures to the users of the financial statements.   **(4 marks)**

(Total = 13 marks)

22 Wilderness (2.5 12/05)   45 mins

(a)   IAS 36 *Impairment of assets* was issued in June 1998 and subsequently amended in March 2004. Its main objective is to prescribe the procedures that should ensure that an entity's assets are included in its statement of financial position at no more than their recoverable amounts. Where an asset is carried at an amount in excess of its recoverable amount, it is said to be impaired and IAS 36 requires an impairment loss to be recognised.

Required

(i)   Define an impairment loss explaining the relevance of fair value less costs to sell and value in use; and state how frequently assets should be tested for impairment;   **(6 marks)**

Note: your answer should NOT describe the possible indicators of an impairment.

(ii)   Explain how an impairment loss is accounted for after it has been calculated.   **(5 marks)**

(b)   The assistant financial controller of the Wilderness group, a public listed company, has identified the matters below which she believes may indicate an impairment to one or more assets:

(i)   Wilderness owns and operates an item of plant that cost $640,000 and had accumulated depreciation of $400,000 at 1 October 20X4. It is being depreciated at $12\frac{1}{2}$% on cost. On 1 April 20X5 (exactly half way through the year) the plant was damaged when a factory vehicle collided into it. Due to the unavailability of replacement parts, it is not possible to repair the plant, but it still operates, albeit at a reduced capacity. Also it is expected that as a result of the damage the remaining life of the plant from the date of the damage will be only two years. Based on its reduced capacity, the estimated present value of the plant in use if $150,000. The plant has a current disposal value of $20,000 (which will be nil in two years' time), but Wilderness has been offered a trade–in value of $180,000 against a replacement machine which has a cost of $1 million (there would be no disposal costs for the replaced plant). Wilderness is reluctant to replace the plant as it is worried about the long–term demand for the produce produced by the plant. The trade–in value is only available if the plant is replaced.

Required

Prepare extracts from the statement of financial position and income statement of Wilderness in respect of the plant for the year ended 30 September 20X5. Your answer should explain how you arrived at your figures.   **(7 marks)**

(ii)   On 1 April 20X4 Wilderness acquired 100% of the share capital of Mossel, whose only activity is the extraction and sale of spa water. Mossel had been profitable since its acquisition, but bad publicity resulting from several consumers becoming ill due to a contamination of the spa water supply in April 20X5 has led to unexpected losses in the last six months. The carrying amounts of Mossel's assets at 30 September 20X5 are:

	$'000
Brand (Quencher – see below)	7,000
Land containing spa	12,000
Purifying and bottling plant	8,000
Inventories	5,000
	32,000

The source of the contamination was found and it has now ceased.

The company originally sold the bottled water under the brand name of 'Quencher', but because of the contamination it has rebranded its bottled water as 'Phoenix'. After a large advertising campaign, sales are now starting to recover and are approaching previous levels. The value of the brand in the statement of financial position is the depreciated amount of the original brand name of 'Quencher'.

The directors have acknowledged that $1.5 million will have to be spent in the first three months of the next accounting period to upgrade the purifying and bottling plant.

Inventories contain some old 'Quencher' bottled water at a cost of $2 million; the remaining inventories are labeled with the new brand 'Phoenix'. Samples of all the bottled water have been tested by the health authority and have been passed as fit to sell. The old bottled water will have to be relabelled at a cost of $250,000, but is then expected to be sold at the normal selling price of (normal) cost plus 50%.

Based on the estimated future cash flows, the directors have estimated that the value in use of Mossel at 30 September 20X5, calculated according to the guidance in IAS 36, is $20 million. There is no reliable estimate of the fair value less costs to sell of Mossel.

Required

Calculate the amounts at which the assets of Mossel should appear in the consolidated statement of financial position of Wilderness at 30 September 20X5. Your answer should explain how you arrive at your figures. **(7 marks)**

(Total = 25 marks)

23 Derringdo III (2.5 6/03 amended part)   9 mins

Derringdo sells carpets from several retail outlets. In previous years the company has undertaken responsibility for fitting the carpets in customers' premises. Customers pay for the carpets at the time they are ordered. The average length of time from a customer ordering a carpet to its fitting is 14 days. In previous years, Derringdo had not recognised a sale in income until the carpet had been successfully fitted as the rectification costs of any fitting error would be expensive. From 1 April 20X2 Derringdo changed its method of trading by sub-contracting the fitting to approved contractors. Under this policy the sub-contractors are paid by Derringdo and they (the subcontractors) are liable for any errors made in the fitting. Because of this Derringdo is proposing to recognise sales when customers order and pay for the goods, rather than when they have been fitted. Details of the relevant sales figures are:

	$'000
Sales made in retail outlets for the year to 31 March 20X3	23,000
Sales value of carpets fitted in the 14 days to 14 April 20X2	1,200
Sales value of carpets fitted in the 14 days to 14 April 20X3	1,600

Note: the sales value of carpets fitted in the 14 days to 14 April 20X2 are not included in the annual sales figure of $23 million, but those for the 14 days to 14 April 20X3 are included.

Required

Discuss whether the above represents a change of accounting policy, and, based on your discussion, calculate the amount that you would include in sales revenue for carpets in the year to 31 March 20X3. **(5 marks)**

24 Telenorth (2.5 12/01)

45 mins

The following trial balance relates to Telenorth at 30 September 20X1.

	$'000	$'000
Sales revenue		283,460
Inventory 1 October 20X0	12,400	
Purchases	147,200	
Distribution expenses	22,300	
Administration expenses	34,440	
Loan note interest paid	300	
Interim dividends: ordinary	2,000	
preference	480	
Investment income		1,500
25 year leasehold building – cost	56,250	
Plant and equipment – cost	55,000	
Computer system – cost	35,000	
Investments at valuation	34,500	
Depreciation 1 October 20X0 (note (b))		
Leasehold building		18,000
Plant and equipment		12,800
Computer system		9,600
Trade accounts receivable (note (c))	35,700	
Bank overdraft		1,680
Trade accounts payable		17,770
Deferred tax (note (d))		5,200
Ordinary shares of $1 each		20,000
Suspense account (note (e))		26,000
6% loan notes (issued 1 October 20X0)		10,000
8% preference shares (redeemable)		12,000
Revaluation surplus (note (d))		3,400
Retained earnings 1 October 20X0		14,160
	435,570	435,570

The following notes are relevant.

(a)   An inventory count was not conducted by Telenorth until 4 October 20X1 due to operational reasons. The value of the inventory on the premises at this date was $16 million at cost. Between the year-end and the inventory count the following transactions have been identified.

	$
Normal sales at a mark up on cost of 40%	1,400,000
Sales on a sale or return basis at a mark up on cost of 30%	650,000
Goods received at cost	820,000

All sales and purchases had been correctly recorded in the period in which they occurred.

(b)   Telenorth has the following depreciation policy.

Leasehold building – straight-line

Plant and equipment – five years straight line with residual values estimated at $5,000,000

Computer system – 40% per annum reducing balance

Depreciation of the leasehold building and plant is treated as cost of sales; depreciation of the computer system is an administration cost.

(c)   The outstanding account receivable of a major customer amounting to $12 million was factored to Kwikfinance on 1 September 20X1. The terms of the factoring were as follows.

(i)   Kwikfinance paid 80% of the outstanding account to Telenorth immediately

(ii) The balance will be paid (less the charges below) when the account is collected in full. Any amount of the account outstanding after four months will be transferred back to Telenorth at its full book value.

(iii) Kwikfinance will charge 1.0% per month of the net amount owing from Telenorth at the beginning of each month. Kwikfinance had not collected any of the amounts receivable by the year end.

Telenorth debited the cash from Kwikfinance to its bank account and removed the account receivable from its sales ledger. It has prudently charged the difference as an administration cost.

(d) A provision for income tax of $23.4 million for the year to 30 September 20X1 is required. The deferred tax liability is to be increased by $2.2 million, of which $1 million is to be charged direct to the revaluation surplus.

(e) The suspense account contains the proceeds of two share issues.

(i) The exercise of all the outstanding directors' share options of four million shares on 1 October 20X0 at $2 each

(ii) A fully subscribed rights issue on 1 July 20X1 of 1 for 4 held at a price of $3 each. The stock market price of Telenorth's shares immediately before the rights issue was $4.

(f) The finance charge relating to the preference shares is equal to the dividend payable.

Required

(a) (i) The income statement of Telenorth for the year to 30 September 20X1 **(8 marks)**

(ii) A statement of financial position as at 30 September 20X1 in accordance with International Financial Reporting Standards as far as the information permits. **(12 marks)**

Notes to the financial statements are not required.

(b) Calculate the earnings per share in accordance with IAS 33 for the year to 30 September 20X1 (ignore comparatives). **(5 marks)**

(Total = 25 marks)

25 Tourmalet (2.5 12/03) 45 mins

The following extracted balances relate to Tourmalet at 30 September 20X4:

	$000	$000
Ordinary shares of 20 cents each		50,000
Retained earnings at 1 October 20X3		47,800
Revaluation reserve at 1 October 20X3		18,500
6% Redeemable preference shares 20X6		30,000
Trade accounts payable		35,300
Tax		2,100
Land and buildings – at valuation (note (iii))	150,000	
Plant and equipment – cost (note (v))	98,600	
Investment property – valuation at 1 October 20X3 (note (iv))	10,000	
Depreciation 1 October 20X3 – land and buildings		9,000
Depreciation 1 October 20X3 – plant and equipment		24,600
Trade accounts receivable	31,200	
Inventory – 1 October 20X3	26,550	
Bank	3,700	
Sales revenue (note (i))		313,000
Investment income (from properties)		1,200
Purchases	158,450	
Distribution expenses	26,400	
Administration expenses	23,200	
Interim preference dividend	900	
Ordinary dividend paid	2,500	
	531,500	531,500

The following notes are relevant:

(i)   Sales revenue includes $50 million for an item of plant sold on 1 June 20X4. The plant had a book value of $40 million at the date of its sale, which was charged to cost of sales. On the same date, Tourmalet entered into an agreement to lease back the plant for the next five years (being the estimated remaining life of the plant) at a cost of $14 million per annum payable annually in arrears. An arrangement of this type is deemed to have a financing cost of 12% per annum. No depreciation has been charged on the item of plant in the current year.

(ii)   The inventory at 30 September 20X4 was valued at cost of $28·5 million. This includes $4·5 million of slow moving goods. Tourmalet is trying to sell these to another retailer but has not been successful in obtaining a reasonable offer. The best price it has been offered is $2 million.

(iii)   On 1 October 20X0 Tourmalet had its land and buildings revalued by a firm of surveyors at $150 million, with $30 million of this attributed to the land. At that date the remaining life of the building was estimated to be 40 years. These figures were incorporated into the company's books. There has been no significant change in property values since the revaluation. $500,000 of the revaluation reserve will be realised in the current year as a result of the depreciation of the buildings and should be transferred to retained earnings.

(iv)   Details of the investment property are:

Value – 1 October 20X3 $10 million
Value – 30 September 20X4 $9·8 million

The company adopts the fair value method in IAS 40 'Investment Property' of valuing its investment property.

(v)   Plant and equipment (other than that referred to in note (i) above) is depreciated at 20% per annum on the reducing balance basis. All depreciation is to be charged to cost of sales.

(vi)   The above balances contain the results of Tourmalet's car retailing operations which ceased on 31 December 20X3 due to mounting losses. The results of the car retailing operation, which is to be treated as a discontinued operation, for the year to 30 September 20X4 are:

	$000
Sales	15,200
Cost of sales	16,000
Operating expenses (4,000 less 800 tax repayment due)	3,200

The operating expenses are included in administration expenses in the trial balance. Tourmalet is still paying rentals for the lease of its car showrooms. The rentals are included in operating expenses. Tourmalet is hoping to use the premises as an expansion of its administration offices. This is dependent on obtaining planning permission from the local authority for the change of use, however this is very difficult to obtain. Failing this, the best option would be early termination of the lease which will cost $1·5 million in penalties. This amount has not been provided for.

(vii)   The balance on the taxation account in the trial balance is the result of the settlement of the previous year's tax charge. The directors have estimated the provision for income tax for the year to 30 September 20X4 at $9·2 million.

(viii) The preference shares will be redeemed at par. The finance cost is equivalent to the annual dividend.

Required

(a)   Comment on the substance of the sale of the plant and the directors' treatment of it.   **(5 marks)**

(b)   Prepare the income statement.   **(17 marks)**

(c)   A statement of changes in equity for Tourmalet for the year to 30 September 20X4 in accordance with current International Accounting Standards.   **(3 marks)**

Note. A statement of financial position is NOT required. Disclosure notes are NOT required.   **(Total = 25 marks)**

26 Partway (2.5 12/06)

45 mins

(a) (i) State the definition of both non-current assets held for sale and discontinued operations and explain the usefulness of information for discontinued operations. **(4 marks)**

Partway is in the process of preparing its financial statements for the year ended 31 October 20X6. The company's main activity is in the travel industry mainly selling package holidays (flights and accommodation) to the general public through the Internet and retail travel agencies. During the current year the number of holidays sold by travel agencies declined dramatically and the directors decided at a board meeting on 15 October 20X6 to cease marketing holidays through its chain of travel agents and sell off the related high-street premises. Immediately after the meeting the travel agencies' staff and suppliers were notified of the situation and an announcement was made in the press. The directors wish to show the travel agencies' results as a discontinued operation in the financial statements to 31 October 20X6. Due to the declining business of the travel agents, on 1 August 20X6 (three months before the year end) Partway expanded its Internet operations to offer car hire facilities to purchasers of its Internet holidays.

The following are Partway's summarised income statement results – years ended:

	Internet $'000	31 October 20X6 travel agencies $'000	car hire $'000	total $'000	31 October 20X5 Total $'000
Revenue	23,000	14,000	2,000	39,000	40,000
Cost of sales	(18,000)	(16,500)	(1,500)	(36,000)	(32,000)
Gross profit/(loss)	5,000	(2,500)	500	3,000	8,000
Operating expenses	(1,000)	(1,500)	(100)	(2,600)	(2,000)
Profit/(loss) before tax	4,000	(4,000)	400	400	6,000

The results for the travel agencies for the year ended 31 October 20X5 were: revenue $18 million, cost of sales $15 million and operating expenses of $1.5 million.

Required

(ii) Discuss whether the directors' wish to show the travel agencies' results as a discontinued operation is justifiable. **(4 marks)**

(iii) Assuming the closure of the travel agencies is a discontinued operation, prepare the (summarised) income statement of Partway for the year ended 31 October 20X6 together with its comparatives.

Note. Partway discloses the analysis of its discontinued operations on the face of its income statement. **(6 marks)**

(b) (i) Describe the circumstances in which an entity may change its accounting policies and how a change should be applied. **(5 marks)**

The terms under which Partway sells its holidays are that a 10% deposit is required on booking and the balance of the holiday must be paid six weeks before the travel date. In previous years Partway has recognised revenue (and profit) from the sale of its holidays at the date the holiday is actually taken. From the beginning of November 20X5, Partway has made it a condition of booking that all customers must have holiday cancellation insurance and as a result it is unlikely that the outstanding balance of any holidays will be unpaid due to cancellation. In preparing its financial statements to 31 October 20X6, the directors are proposing to change to recognising revenue (and related estimated costs) at the date when a booking is made. The directors also feel that this change will help to negate the adverse effect of comparison with last year's results (year ended 31 October 20X5) which were better than the current year's.

Required

(ii) Comment on whether Partway's proposal to change the timing of its recognition of its revenue is acceptable and whether this would be a change of accounting policy. **(6 marks)**

(Total = 25 marks)

27 Preparation question with helping hands: Simple consolidation

Boo has owned 80% of Goose's equity since its incorporation. On 31 December 20X8 it despatched goods which cost $80,000 to Goose, at an invoiced cost of $100,000. Goose received the goods on 2 January 20X9 and recorded the transaction then. The two companies' draft accounts as at 31 December 20X8 are shown below.

INCOME STATEMENT FOR THE YEAR ENDED 31 DECEMBER 20X8

	Boo	Goose
	$'000	$'000
Revenue	5,000	1,000
Cost of sales	2,900	600
Gross profit	2,100	400
Other expenses	1,700	320
Profit before tax	400	80
Income tax expense	130	25
Profit for the year	270	55

STATEMENTS OF FINANCIAL POSITION AT 31 DECEMBER 20X8

	$'000	$'000
Assets		
Non-current assets	2,000	200
Current assets		
Inventories	500	120
Trade receivables	650	40
Bank and cash	390	35
	1,540	195
Total assets	3,540	395
	$'000	$'000
Equity and liabilities		
Equity		
Share capital	2,000	100
Retained earnings	500	240
	2,500	340
Current liabilities		
Trade payables	910	30
Tax	130	25
	1,040	55
Total equity and liabilities	3,540	395

Required

Prepare a draft consolidated statement of financial position and income statement. It is the group policy to value the non-controlling interest at acquisition at its proportionate share of the fair value of the subsidiary's identifiable net assets.

Helping hands

1   This is a very easy example to ease you into the technique of preparing consolidated accounts. There are a number of points to note.

2   Inventory in transit should be included in the statement of financial position and deducted from cost of sales at cost to the group.

3   Similarly, the intra-group receivable and sale should be eliminated as a consolidation adjustment.

4   Boo Co must have included its inter-company account in trade receivables as it is not specifically mentioned elsewhere in the accounts.

5   Remember that only the parent's issued share capital is shown in the group accounts.

---

6   The non-controlling interest in the income statement is easily calculated as 20% of post-tax profit for the
     year as shown in Goose's accounts. In the statement of financial position, the non-controlling interest
     represents the non-controlling interest in retained earnings and share capital only.

7   Don't forget that Boo's accounts must somewhere contain a balance for its investment in Goose (its holding
     of shares in Goose, at par value since no share premium is shown in Goose's books). Non- current assets
     must therefore be reduced by this amount to correspond to the cancellation of Goose's share capital.

28 Hideaway (2.5 12/05 amended)   18 mins

Related party relationships are a common feature of commercial life. The objective of IAS 24 *Related party
disclosures* is to ensure that financial statements contain the necessary disclosures to make users aware of the
possibility that financial statements may have been affected by the existence of related parties.

Required

(a) Explain why the disclosure of related party relationships and transactions may be important.   **(4 marks)**

(b) Hideaway is a public listed company that owns two subsidiary company investments. It owns 100% of the
     equity shares of Benedict and 55% of the equity shares of Depret. During the year ended 30 September
     20X5 Depret made several sales of goods to Benedict. These sales totaled 415 million and had cost Depret
     $14 million to manufacture. Depret made these sales on the instruction of the Board of Hideaway. It is
     known that one of the directors of Depret, who is not a director of Hideaway, is unhappy with the parent
     company's instruction as he believes the goods could have been sold to other companies outside the group
     at the far higher price of $20 million. All directors within the group benefit from a profit sharing scheme.

     Required

     Describe the financial effect that Hideaway's instruction may have on the financial statements of the
     companies within the group and the implications this may have for other interested parties.   **(6 marks)**

                                                                                        (Total = 10 marks)

29 Highveldt (2.5 6/05)   45 mins

Highveldt, a public listed company, acquired 75% of Samson's ordinary shares on 1 April 20X4. Highveldt paid an
immediate $3·50 per share in cash and agreed to pay a further amount of $108 million on 1 April 20X5. Highveldt's
cost of capital is 8% per annum. Highveldt has only recorded the cash consideration of $3·50 per share.

The summarised statements of financial position of the two companies at 31 March 20X5 are shown below:

	Highveldt		Samson	
	$m	$m	$m	$m
Tangible non-current assets (note (i))		420		320
Development costs (note (iv))		nil		40
Investments (note (ii))		300		20
		720		380
Current assets		133		91
Total assets		853		471

	Highveldt		Samson	
	$m	$m	$m	$m
Equity and liabilities				
Ordinary shares of $1 each		270		80
Reserves:				
Share premium		80		40
Revaluation surplus		45		nil
Retained earnings – 1 April 20X4	160		134	
– year to 31 March 20X5	190		76	
		350		210
		745		330
Non-current liabilities				
10% inter company loan (note (ii))		nil		60
Current liabilities		108		81
Total equity and liabilities		853		471

The following information is relevant:

(i) Highveldt has a policy of revaluing land and buildings to fair value. At the date of acquisition Samson's land and buildings had a fair value $20 million higher than their book value and at 31 March 20X5 this had increased by a further $4 million (ignore any additional depreciation).

(ii) Included in Highveldt's investments is a loan of $60 million made to Samson at the date of acquisition. Interest is payable annually in arrears. Samson paid the interest due for the year on 31 March 20X5, but Highveldt did not receive this until after the year end. Highveldt has not accounted for the accrued interest from Samson.

(iii) Samson had established a line of products under the brand name of Titanware. Acting on behalf of Highveldt, a firm of specialists, had valued the brand name at a value of $40 million with an estimated life of 10 years as at 1 April 20X4. The brand is not included in Samson's statement of financial position.

(iv) Samson's development project was completed on 30 September 20X4 at a cost of $50 million. $10 million of this had been amortised by 31 March 20X5. Development costs capitalised by Samson at the date of acquisition were $18 million. Highveldt's directors are of the opinion that Samson's development costs do not meet the criteria in IAS 38 'Intangible Assets' for recognition as an asset.

(v) Samson sold goods to Highveldt during the year at a profit of $6 million, one-third of these goods were still in the inventory of Highveldt at 31 March 20X5.

(vi) An impairment test at 31 March 20X5 on the consolidated goodwill concluded that it should be written down by $22 million. No other assets were impaired.

(vii) It is the group policy to value the non-controlling interest at acquisition at its proportionate share of the fair value of the subsidiary's identifiable net assets.

Required

(a) Calculate the following figures as they would appear in the consolidated statement of financial position of Highveldt at 31 March 20X5:

(i) Goodwill **(8 marks)**

(ii) Non-controlling interest **(4 marks)**

(iii) The following consolidated reserves
share premium, revaluation surplus and retained earnings. **(8 marks)**
Note. Show your workings

(b) Explain why consolidated financial statements are useful to the users of financial statements (as opposed to just the parent company's separate (entity) financial statements). **(5 marks)**

(Total = 25 marks)

30 Parentis (2.5 6/07)

45 mins

Parentis, a public listed company, acquired 600 million equity shares in Offspring on 1 April 20X6. The purchase consideration was made up of:

- A share exchange of one share in Parentis for two shares in Offspring
- The issue of $100 10% loan note for every 500 shares acquired; and
- A deferred cash payment of 11 cents per share acquired payable on 1 April 20X7.

Parentis has only recorded the issue of the loan notes. The value of each Parentis share at the date of acquisition was 75 cents and Parentis has a cost of capital of 10% per annum.

The statements of financial position of the two companies at 31 March 20X7 are shown below:

	Parentis		Offspring	
	$ m	$ m	$ m	$ m
Assets				
Property, plant and equipment (note (i))		640		340
Investments		120		nil
Intellectual property (note (ii))		nil		30
		760		370
Current assets				
Inventory (note (iii))	76		22	
Trade receivables (note (iii))	84		44	
Bank	nil	160	4	70
Total assets		920		440
Equity and liabilities				
Equity shares of 25 cents each		300		200
Retained earnings – 1 April 20X6	210		120	
– year ended 31 March 20X7	90	300	20	140
		600		340
Non-current liabilities				
10% loan notes		120		20
Current liabilities				
Trade payables (note (iii))	130		57	
Current tax payable	45		23	
Overdraft	25	200	nil	80
Total equity and liabilities		920		440

The following information is relevant:

(i)   At the date of acquisition the fair values of Offspring's net assets were approximately equal to their carrying amounts with the exception of its properties. These properties had a fair value of $40 million in excess of their carrying amounts which would create additional depreciation of $2 million in the post acquisition period to 31 March 20X7. The fair values have not been reflected in Offspring's statement of financial position.

(ii)   The intellectual property is a system of encryption designed for internet use. Offspring has been advised that government legislation (passed since acquisition) has now made this type of encryption illegal. Offspring will receive $10 million in compensation from the government.

(iii)   Offspring sold Parentis goods for $15 million in the post acquisition period. $5 million of these goods are included in the inventory of Parentis at 31 March 20X7. The profit made by Offspring on these sales was $6 million. Offspring's trade payable account (in the records of Parentis) of $7 million does not agree with Parentis's trade receivable account (in the records of Offspring) due to cash in transit of $4 million paid by Parentis.

(iv)   Due to the impact of the above legislation, Parentis has concluded that the consolidated goodwill has been impaired by $27 million.

(v) It is the group policy to value the non-controlling interest at acquisition at its proportionate share of the fair value of the subsidiary's identifiable net assets.

Required

Prepare the consolidated statement of financial position of Parentis as at 31 March 20X7. **(25 marks)**

31 Pedantic (12/08)   45 mins

On 1 April 2008, Pedantic acquired 60% of the equity share capital of Sophistic in a share exchange of two shares in Pedantic for three shares in Sophistic. The issue of shares has not yet been recorded by Pedantic. At the date of acquisition shares in Pedantic had a market value of $6 each. Below are the summarised draft financial statements of both companies.

Income statements for the year ended 30 September 2008

	Pedantic	Sophistic
	$'000	$'000
Revenue	85,000	42,000
Cost of sales	(63,000)	(32,000)
Gross profit	22,000	10,000
Distribution costs	(2,000)	(2,000)
Administrative expenses	(6,000)	(3,200)
Finance costs	(300)	(400)
Profit before tax	13,700	4,400
Income tax expense	(4,700)	(1,400)
Profit for the year	9,000	3,000

Statements of financial position as at 30 September 2008

	Pedantic	Sophistic
Assets		
Non-current assets		
Property, plant and equipment	40,600	12,600
Current assets	16,000	6,600
Total assets	56,600	19,200
Equity and liabilities		
Equity shares of $1 each	10,000	4,000
Retained earnings	35,400	6,500
	45,400	10,500
Non-current liabilities		
10% loan notes	3,000	4,000
Current liabilities	8,200	4,700
Total equity and liabilities	56,600	19,200

The following information is relevant:

(i) At the date of acquisition, the fair values of Sophistic's assets were equal to their carrying amounts with the exception of an item of plant, which had a fair value of $2 million in excess of its carrying amount. It had a remaining life of five years at that date [straight-line depreciation is used]. Sophistic has not adjusted the carrying amount of its plant as a result of the fair value exercise.

(ii) Sales from Sophistic to Pedantic in the post acquisition period were $8 million. Sophistic made a mark up on cost of 40% on these sales. Pedantic had sold $5·2 million (at cost to Pedantic) of these goods by 30 September 2008.

(iii) Other than where indicated, income statement items are deemed to accrue evenly on a time basis.

(iv) Sophistic's trade receivables at 30 September 2008 include $600,000 due from Pedantic which did not agree with Pedantic's corresponding trade payable. This was due to cash in transit of $200,000 from Pedantic to Sophistic. Both companies have positive bank balances.

(v)   Pedantic has a policy of accounting for any non-controlling interest at fair value. For this purpose the fair value of the goodwill attributable to the non-controlling interest in Sophistic is $1·5 million. Consolidated goodwill was not impaired at 30 September 2008.

Required

(a)   Prepare the consolidated income statement for Pedantic for the year ended 30 September 2008.   **(9 marks)**

(b)   Prepare the consolidated statement of financial position for Pedantic as at 30 September 2008.   **(16 marks)**

Note: a statement of changes in equity is not required.

(Total = 25 marks)

32 Preparation question: Acquisition during the year

Port has many investments, but before 20X4 none of these investments met the criteria for consolidation as a subsidiary. One of these older investments was a $2.3m 12% loan to Alfred which was made in 20W1 and is not due to be repaid until 20Y6.

On 1st November 20X4 Port purchased 75% of the equity of Alfred for $650,000. The consideration was 35,000 $1 equity shares in Port with a fair value of $650,000.

Noted below are the draft income statements and movement in retained earnings for Port and its subsidiary Alfred for the year ending 31st December 20X4 along with the draft statements of financial position as at 31st December 20X4.

INCOME STATEMENTS FOR THE YEAR ENDING 31 DECEMBER 20X4

	Port	Alfred
	$'000	$'000
Revenue	100	996
Cost of sales	(36)	(258)
Gross profit	64	738
Interest on loan to Alfred	276	–
Other investment income	158	–
Operating expenses	(56)	(330)
Finance costs	–	(276)
Profit before tax	442	132
Income tax expense	(112)	(36)
Profit for the year	330	96

STATEMENTS OF FINANCIAL POSITION AS AT 31 DECEMBER 20X4

	Port	Alfred
	$'000	$'000
Assets		
Non-current assets		
Property, plant and equipment	100	3,000
Investments		
Loan to Alfred	2,300	–
Other investments	600	–
	3,000	3,000
Current assets	800	139
Total assets	3,800	3,139

	Port $'000	Alfred $'000
Equity and liabilities		
Equity		
$1 Equity shares	200	100
Share premium	500	85
Retained earnings	2,900	331
	3,600	516
Non-current liabilities		
Loan from Port	–	2,300
Current liabilities		
Sundry	200	323
Total equity and liabilities	3,800	3,139

Notes

(a) Port has not accounted for the issue of its own shares or for the acquisition of the investment in Alfred.

(b) There has been no impairment in the value of the goodwill.

(c) It is the group policy to value the non-controlling interest at acquisition at its proportionate share of the fair value of the subsidiary's identifiable net assets.

Required

Prepare the income statement for the Port Group for the year ending 31 December 20X4 and a statement of financial position at that date.

Approaching the question

1 Establish the **group structure**, noting for how long Alfred was a subsidiary.

2 Adjust Port's statement of financial position for the issue of its own shares and the cost of the investment in Alfred.

3 Sketch out the **format** of the group income statement and statement of financial position, and then fill in the amounts for each company directly from the question. (Note, sub-totals are not normally needed when you do this.)

4 **Time apportion** the income, expenditure and taxation for the subsidiary acquired.

5 Calculate the **goodwill**.

6 Remember to time-apportion the non-controlling interest in Alfred.

33 Hillusion (2.5 6/03)   45 mins

In recent years Hillusion has acquired a reputation for buying modestly performing businesses and selling them at a substantial profit within a period of two to three years of their acquisition. On 1 July 20X2 Hillusion acquired 80% of the ordinary share capital of Skeptik at a cost of $10,280,000. On the same date it also acquired 50% of Skeptik's 10% loan notes at par. The summarised draft financial statements of both companies are:

INCOME STATEMENTS: YEAR TO 31 MARCH 20X3

	Hillusion $'000	Skeptik $'000
Sales revenue	60,000	24,000
Cost of sales	(42,000)	(20,000)
Gross profit	18,000	4,000
Operating expenses	(6,000)	(200)
Loan interest received (paid)	75	(200)
Profit before tax	12,075	3,600
Income tax expense	(3,000)	(600)
Profit for the year	9,075	3,000

STATEMENTS OF FINANCIAL POSITION: AS AT 31 MARCH 20X3

	Hillusion $'000	Skeptik $'000
Assets		
Tangible non-current Assets	19,320	8,000
Investments	11,280	Nil
	30,000	8,000
Current assets	15,000	8,000
Total assets	45,600	16,000
Equity and liabilities		
Equity		
Ordinary shares of $1 each	10,000	2,000
Retained earnings	25,600	8,400
	35,600	10,400
Non-current liabilities		
10% loan notes	Nil	2,000
Current liabilities	10,000	3,600
Total equity and liabilities	45,600	16,000

The following information is relevant:

(i) The fair values of Skeptik's assets were equal to their book values with the exception of its plant, which had a fair value of $3·2 million in excess of its book value at the date of acquisition. The remaining life of all of Skeptik's plant at the date of its acquisition was four years and this period has not changed as a result of the acquisition. Depreciation of plant is on a straight-line basis and charged to cost of sales. Skeptik has not adjusted the value of its plant as a result of the fair value exercise.

(ii) In the post acquisition period Hillusion sold goods to Skeptik at a price of $12 million. These goods had cost Hillusion $9 million. During the year Skeptik had sold $10 million (at cost to Skeptik) of these goods for $15 million.

(iii) Hillusion bears almost all of the administration costs incurred on behalf of the group (invoicing, credit control etc). It does not charge Skeptik for this service as to do so would not have a material effect on the group profit.

(iv) Revenues and profits should be deemed to accrue evenly throughout the year.

(v) The current accounts of the two companies were reconciled at the year-end with Skeptik owing Hillusion $750,000.

(vi) The goodwill was reviewed for impairment at the end of the reporting period and had suffered an impairment loss of $300,000, which is to be treated as an operating expense.

(vii) Hillusion's opening retained earnings were $16,525,000 and Skeptik's were $5,400,000. No dividends were paid or declared by either entity during the year.

(viii) It is the group policy to value the non-controlling interest at acquisition at fair value. The directors valued the non-controlling interest at $2.5m at the date of acquisition.

Required

(a) Prepare a consolidated income statement and statement of financial position for Hillusion for the year to 31 March 20X3. **(20 marks)**

(b) Explain why it is necessary to eliminate unrealised profits when preparing group financial statements; and how reliance on the entity financial statements of Skeptik may mislead a potential purchaser of the company. **(5 marks)**

(Total = 25 marks)

34 Hydan (2.5 6/06)

45 mins

On 1 October 20X5 Hydan, a publicly listed company, acquired a 60% controlling interest in Systan paying $9 per share in cash. Prior to the acquisition Hydan had been experiencing difficulties with the supply of components that it used in its manufacturing process. Systan is one of Hydan's main suppliers and the acquisition was motivated by the need to secure supplies. In order to finance an increase in the production capacity of Systan, Hydan made a non-dated loan at the date of acquisition of $4 million to Systan that carried an actual and effective interest rate of 10% per annum. The interest to 31 March 20X6 on this loan has been paid by Systan and accounted for by both companies. The summarised draft financial statements of the companies are:

INCOME STATEMENTS FOR THE YEAR ENDED 31 MARCH 20X6

	Hydan	Systan pre-acquisition	Systan post-acquisition
	$'000	$'000	$'000
Revenue	98,000	24,000	35,200
Cost of sales	(76,000)	(18,000)	(31,000)
Gross profit	22,000	6,000	4,200
Operating expenses	(11,800)	(1,200)	(8,000)
Interest income	350	nil	nil
Finance costs	(420)	nil	(200)
Profit/(loss) before tax	10,130	4,800	(4,000)
Income tax (expense)/relief	(4,200)	(1,200)	1,000
Profit/(loss) for the year	5,930	3,600	(3,000)

STATEMENTS OF FINANCIAL POSITION AS AT 31 MARCH 20X6

	Hydan $'000	Systan $'000
Non-current assets		
Property, plant and equipment	18,400	9,500
Investments (including loan to Systan)	16,000	nil
	34,400	9,500
Current assets	18,000	7,200
Total assets	52,400	16,700
Equity and liabilities		
Ordinary shares of $1 each	10,000	2,000
Share premium	5,000	500
Retained earnings	20,000	6,300
	35,000	8,800
Non-current liabilities		
7% Bank loan	6,000	nil
10% loan from Hydan	nil	4,000
Current liabilities	11,400	3,900
Total equity and liabilities	52,400	16,700

The following information is relevant:

(i) At the date of acquisition, the fair values of Systan's property, plant and equipment were $1·2 million in excess of their carrying amounts. This will have the effect of creating an additional depreciation charge (to cost of sales) of $300,000 in the consolidated financial statements for the year ended 31 March 20X6. Systan has not adjusted its assets to fair value.

(ii) In the post acquisition period Systan's sales to Hydan were $30 million on which Systan had made a consistent profit of 5% of the selling price. Of these goods, $4 million (at selling price to Hydan) were still in the inventory of Hydan at 31 March 20X6. Prior to its acquisition Systan made all its sales at a uniform gross profit margin.

(iii) Included in Hydan's current liabilities is $1 million owing to Systan. This agreed with Systan's receivables ledger balance for Hydan at the year end.

(iv) An impairment review of the consolidated goodwill at 31 March 20X6 revealed that its current value was $375,000 less than its carrying amount.

(v) Neither company paid a dividend in the year to 31 March 20X6.

(vi) It is group policy to value the non-controlling interest at acquisition at full (or fair) value. Just prior to acquisition by Hydan, Systan's shares were trading at $7.

Required

(a) Prepare the consolidated income statement for the year ended 31 March 20X6 and the consolidated statement of financial position at that date. **(20 marks)**

(b) Discuss the effect that the acquisition of Systan appears to have had on Systan's operating performance.

(5 marks)

(Total = 25 marks)

35 Hydrate (2.5 12/02 amended)   36 mins

Hydrate is a public company operating in the industrial chemical sector. In order to achieve economies of scale, it has been advised to enter into business combinations with compatible partner companies. As a first step in this strategy Hydrate acquired all of the ordinary share capital of Sulphate by way of a share exchange on 1 April 20X2. Hydrate issued five of its own shares for every four shares in Sulphate. The market value of Hydrate's shares on 1 April 20X2 was $6 each. The share issue has not yet been recorded in Hydrate's books. The summarised financial statements of both companies for the year to 30 September 20X2 are:

INCOME STATEMENT – YEAR TO 30 SEPTEMBER 20X2

	Hydrate $'000	Sulphate $'000
Sales revenue	24,000	20,000
Cost of sales	(16,600)	(11,800)
Gross profit	7,400	8,200
Operating expenses	(1,600)	(1,000)
Profit before tax	5,800	7,200
Taxation	(2,000)	(3,000)
Profit for the year	3,800	4,200

STATEMENT OF FINANCIAL POSITION – AS AT 30 SEPTEMBER 20X2

	$'000	$'000	$'000	$'000
Non-current assets				
Property, plant and equipment		64,000		35,000
Investment		nil		12,800
		64,000		47,800
Current assets				
Inventory	22,800		23,600	
Trade receivables	16,400		24,200	
Bank	500	39,700	200	48,000
Total assets		103,700		95,800
Equity and liabilities				
Ordinary shares of $1 each		20,000		12,000
Reserves:				
Share premium	4,000		2,400	
Retained earnings	57,200	61,200	42,700	45,100
		81,200		57,100
Non-current liabilities				
8% loan rate		5,000		18,000
Current liabilities				
Trade payables	15,300		17,700	
Taxation	2,200		3,000	
		17,500		20,700
		103,700		95,800

The following information is relevant.

- The fair value of Sulphate's investment was $5 million in excess of its book value at the date of acquisition. The fair values of Sulphate's other net assets were equal to their book values.
- Goodwill was reviewed at 30 September 20X2. A $3m impairment loss is to be recognised.
- No dividends have been paid or proposed by either company.

Required

Prepare the consolidated income statement, statement of changes in equity, and statement of financial position of Hydrate for the year to 30 September 20X2. **(20 marks)**

36 Preparation question: Laurel

CONSOLIDATED STATEMENT OF FINANCIAL POSITION

Laurel acquired 80% of the ordinary share capital of Hardy for $160,000 and 40% of the ordinary share capital of Comic for $70,000 on 1 January 20X7 when the retained earnings balances were $64,000 in Hardy and $24,000 in Comic. Laurel, Comic and Hardy are public limited companies.

The statements of financial position of the three companies at 31 December 20X9 are set out below:

	Laurel $'000	Hardy $'000	Comic $'000
Non-current assets			
Property, plant and equipment	220	160	78
Investments	230		
	450	160	78
Current assets			
Inventories	384	234	122
Trade receivables	275	166	67
Cash at bank	42	10	34
	701	410	223
	1,151	570	301
Equity			
Share capital – $1 ordinary shares	400	96	80
Share premium	16	3	-
Retained earnings	278	128	97
	694	227	177
Current liabilities			
Trade payables	457	343	124
	1,151	570	301

You are also given the following information:

1 On 30 November 20X9 Laurel sold some goods to Hardy for cash for $32,000. These goods had originally cost $22,000 and none had been sold by the year-end. On the same date Laurel also sold goods to Comic for cash for $22,000. These goods originally cost $10,000 and Comic had sold half by the year end.

2 On 1 January 20X7 Hardy owned some items of equipment with a book value of $45,000 that had a fair value of $57,000. These assets were originally purchased by Hardy on 1 January 20X5 and are being depreciated over 6 years.

3 Group policy is to measure non-controlling interests at acquisition at fair value. The fair value of the non-controlling interests in Hardy on 1 January 20X7 was calculated as $39,000.

4 Cumulative impairment losses on recognised goodwill amounted to $15,000 at 31 December 20X9. No impairment losses have been necessary to date relating to the investment in the associate.

Required

Prepare a consolidated statement of financial position for Laurel and its subsidiary as at 31 December 20X9, incorporating its associate in accordance with IAS 28.

SOLUTION

Laurel Group – Consolidated statement of financial position as at 31 December 20X9

	$'000
Non-current assets	
Property, plant and equipment	
Goodwill	
Investment in associate	
Current assets	
Inventories	
Trade receivables	
Cash	
Equity attributable to owners of the parent	
Share capital – $1 ordinary shares	
Share premium	
Retained earnings	
Non-controlling interests	
Current liabilities	
Trade payables	

Workings

37 Preparation question: Tyson

CONSOLIDATED STATEMENT OF COMPREHENSIVE INCOME

Below are the statements of comprehensive income of Tyson, its subsidiary Douglas and associate Frank at 31 December 20X8. Tyson, Douglas and Frank are public limited companies.

	Tyson $'000	Douglas $'000	Frank $'000
Revenue	500	150	70
Cost of sales	(270)	(80)	(30)
Gross profit	230	70	40
Other expenses	(150)	(20)	(15)
Finance income	15	10	–
Finance costs	(20)	–	(10)
Profit before tax	75	60	15
Income tax expense	(25)	(15)	(5)
PROFIT FOR THE YEAR	50	45	10
Other comprehensive income:			
Gains on property revaluation, net of tax	20	10	5
TOTAL COMPREHENSIVE INCOME FOR THE YEAR	70	55	15

You are also given the following information:

1 Tyson acquired 80,000 shares in Douglas for $188,000 3 years ago when Douglas had a credit balance on its reserves of $40,000. Douglas has 100,000 $1 ordinary shares.

2 Tyson acquired 40,000 shares in Frank for $60,000 2 years ago when that company had a credit balance on its reserves of $20,000. Frank has 100,000 $1 ordinary shares.

3 During the year Douglas sold some goods to Tyson for $66,000 (cost $48,000). None of the goods had been sold by the year end.

4 Group policy is to measure non-controlling interests at acquisition at fair value. The fair value of the non-controlling interests in Douglas at acquisition was $40,000. An impairment test carried out at the year end resulted in $15,000 of the recognised goodwill relating to Douglas being written off and recognition of impairment losses of $2,400 relating to the investment in Frank.

Required

Prepare the consolidated statement of comprehensive income for the year ended 31 December 20X8 for Tyson, incorporating its associate.

SOLUTION

Tyson Group - Consolidated statement of comprehensive income for the year ended 31 December 20X8

	$'000
Revenue	
Cost of sales	
Gross profit	
Other expenses	
Finance income	
Finance costs	
Share of profit of associate	
Profit before tax	
Income tax expense	
PROFIT FOR THE YEAR	
Gains on property revaluation net of tax	
Share of other comprehensive income of associates	
Other comprehensive income for the year net of tax	
TOTAL COMPREHENSIVE INCOME FOR THE YEAR	
Profit attributable to:	
Owners of the parent	
Non-controlling interests	
Total comprehensive income attributable to:	
Owners of the parent	
Non-controlling interests	

Workings

38 Plateau (12/07)

On 1 October 2006 Plateau acquired the following non-current investments:

- 3 million equity shares in Savannah by an exchange of one share in Plateau for every two shares in Savannah plus $1.25 per acquired Savannah share in cash. The market price of each Plateau share at the date of acquisition was $6 and the market price of each Savannah share at the date of acquisition was $3.25.
- 30% of the equity shares of Axle at a cost of $7·50 per share in cash.

Only the cash consideration of the above investments has been recorded by Plateau. In addition $500,000 of professional costs relating to the acquisition of Savannah are also included in the cost of the investment.

The summarised draft statements of financial position of the three companies at 30 September 2007 are:

	Plateau $'000	Savannah $'000	Axle $'000
Assets			
Non-current assets			
Property, plant and equipment	18,400	10,400	18,000
Investments in Savannah and Axle	13,250	nil	nil
Available-for-sale investments	6,500	nil	Nil
	38,150	10,400	18,000
Current assets			
Inventory	6,900	6,200	3,600
Trade receivables	3,200	1,500	2,400
Total assets	48,250	18,100	24,000
Equity and liabilities			
Equity shares of $1 each	10,000	4,000	4,000
Retained earnings			
– at 30 September 2006	16,000	6,000	11,000
– for year ended 30 September 2007	9,250	2,900	5,000
	35,250	12,900	20,000
Non-current liabilities			
7% Loan notes	5,000	1,000	1,000
Current liabilities	8,000	4,200	3,000
Total equity and liabilities	48,250	18,100	24,000

The following information is relevant:

(i)   At the date of acquisition Savannah had five years remaining of an agreement to supply goods to one of its major customers. Savannah believes it is highly likely that the agreement will be renewed when it expires. The directors of Plateau estimate that the value of this customer based contract has a fair value of £1 million and an indefinite life and has not suffered any impairment.

(ii)   On 1 October 2006, Plateau sold an item of plant to Savannah at its agreed fair value of $2·5 million. Its carrying amount prior to the sale was $2 million. The estimated remaining life of the plant at the date of sale was five years (straight-line depreciation).

(iii)   During the year ended 30 September 2007 Savannah sold goods to Plateau for $2·7 million. Savannah had marked up these goods by 50% on cost. Plateau had a third of the goods still in its inventory at 30 September 2007. There were no intra-group payables/receivables at 30 September 2007.

(iv)   Impairment tests on 30 September 2007 concluded that neither consolidated goodwill nor the value of the investment in Axle were impaired.

(v)   The available-for-sale investments are included in Plateau's statement of financial position (above) at their fair value on 1 October 2006, but they have a fair value of $9 million at 30 September 2007.

(vi)   No dividends were paid during the year by any of the companies.

(vii)   It is the group policy to value non-controlling interest at acquisition at full (or fair) value. For this purpose the share price of Savannah at this date should be used.

Required

(a)   Prepare the consolidated statement of financial position for Plateau as at 30 September 2007.   **(20 marks)**

(b)   A financial assistant has observed that the fair value exercise means that a subsidiary's net assets are included at acquisition at their fair (current) values in the consolidated statement of financial position. The assistant believes that it is inconsistent to aggregate the subsidiary's net assets with those of the parent because most of the parent's assets are carried at historical cost.

Required

Comment on the assistant's observation and explain why the net assets of acquired subsidiaries are consolidated at acquisition at their fair values.   **(5 marks)**

(Total = 25 marks)

39 Holdrite (2.5 12/04)   45 mins

Holdrite purchased 75% of the issued share capital of Staybrite and 40% of the issued share capital of Allbrite on 1 April 20X4.

Details of the purchase consideration given at the date of purchase are:

Staybrite: a share exchange of 2 shares in Holdrite for every 3 shares in Staybrite plus an issue to the shareholders of Staybrite 8% loan notes redeemable at par on 30 June 20X6 on the basis of $100 loan note for every 250 shares held in Staybrite.

Allbrite: a share exchange of 3 shares in Holdrite for every 4 shares in Allbrite plus $1 per share acquired in cash. The market price of Holdrite's shares at 1 April 20X4 was $6 per share.

The summarised income statements for the three companies for the year to 30 September 20X4 are:

	Holdrite	Staybrite	Allbrite
	$000	$000	$000
Revenue	75,000	40,700	31,000
Cost of Sales	(47,400)	(19,700)	(15,300)
Gross Profit	27,600	21,000	15,700
Operating expenses	(10,480)	(9,000)	(9,700)
Operating Profit	17,120	12,000	6,000
Interest expense	(170)		
Profit before tax	16,950	12,000	6,000
Income tax expense	(4,800)	(3,000)	(2,000)
Profit for year	12,150	9,000	4,000

The following information is relevant:

(i)   A fair value exercise was carried out for Staybrite at the date of its acquisition with the following results:

	Book value	Fair value
	$'000	$'000
Land	20,000	23,000
Plant	25,000	30,000

The fair values have not been reflected in Staybrite's financial statements. The increase in the fair value of the plant would create additional depreciation of $500,000 in the post acquisition period in the consolidated financial statements to 30 September 20X4.

Depreciation of plant is charged to cost of sales.

(ii)   The details of each company's share capital and reserves at 1 October 20X3 are:

	Holdrite $'000	Staybrite $'000	Allbrite $'000
Equity shares of $1 each	20,000	10,000	5,000
Share premium	5,000	4,000	2,000
Retained earnings	18,000	7,500	6,000

(iii)   In the post acquisition period Holdrite sold goods to Staybrite for $10 million. Holdrite made a profit of $4 million on these sales. One-quarter of these goods were still in the inventory of Staybrite at 30 September 20X4.

(iv)   Impairment tests on the goodwill of Staybrite and Allbrite at 30 September 20X4 resulted in the need to write down Staybrite's goodwill by $750,000.

(v)   Holdrite paid a dividend of $5 million on 20 September 20X4. Staybrite and Allbrite did not make any dividend payments.

(vi)   It is the group policy to value the non-controlling interest at acquisition at its proportionate share of the fair value of the subsidiary's identifiable net assets.

Required

(a)   Calculate the goodwill arising on the purchase of the shares in Staybrite and the carrying value of Allbrite at 1 April 20X4.

(8 marks)

(b)   Prepare a consolidated income statement for the Holdrite Group for the year to 30 September 20X4.

(15 marks)

(c)   Show the movement on the consolidated retained earnings attributable to Holdrite for the year to 30 September 20X4.

(2 marks)

(Total = 25 marks)

Note. The additional disclosures in IFRS 3 *Business combinations* relating to a newly acquired subsidiary are not required.

40 Patronic (6/08)   45 mins

On 1 August 2007 Patronic purchased 18 million of a total of 24 million equity shares in Sardonic. The acquisition was through a share exchange of two shares in Patronic for every three shares in Sardonic. Both companies have shares with a par value of $1 each. The market price of Patronic's shares at 1 August 2007 was $5·75 per share. Patronic will also pay in cash on 31 July 2009 (two years after acquisition) $2·42 per acquired share of Sardonic. Patronic's cost of capital is 10% per annum. The reserves of Sardonic on 1 April 2007 were $69 million.

Patronic has held an investment of 30% of the equity shares in Acerbic for many years.

The summarised income statements for the three companies for the year ended 31 March 2008 are:

	Patronic $'000	Sardonic $'000	Acerbic $'000
Revenue	150,000	78,000	80,000
Cost of sales	(94,000)	(51,000)	(60,000)
Gross profit	56,000	27,000	20,000
Distribution costs	(7,400)	(3,000)	(3,500)
Administrative expenses	(12,500)	(6,000)	(6,500)
Finance costs (note (ii))	(2,000)	(900)	nil
Profit before tax	34,100	17,100	10,000
Income tax expense	(10,400)	(3,600)	(4,000)
Profit for the period	23,700	13,500	6,000

The following information is relevant:

(i) The fair values of the net assets of Sardonic at the date of acquisition were equal to their carrying amounts with the exception of property and plant. Property and plant had fair values of $4·1 million and $2·4 million respectively in excess of their carrying amounts. The increase in the fair value of the property would create additional depreciation of $200,000 in the consolidated financial statements in the post acquisition period to 31 March 2008 and the plant had a remaining life of four years (straight-line depreciation) at the date of acquisition of Sardonic. All depreciation is treated as part of cost of sales.

The fair values have not been reflected in Sardonic's financial statements.

No fair value adjustments were required on the acquisition of Acerbic.

(ii) The finance costs of Patronic do not include the finance cost on the deferred consideration.

(iii) Prior to its acquisition, Sardonic had been a good customer of Patronic. In the year to 31 March 2008, Patronic sold goods at a selling price of $1·25 million per month to Sardonic both before and after its acquisition. Patronic made a profit of 20% on the cost of these sales. At 31 March 2008 Sardonic still held inventory of $3 million (at cost to Sardonic) of goods purchased in the post acquisition period from Patronic.

(iv) An impairment test on the goodwill of Sardonic conducted on 31 March 2008 concluded that it should be written down by $2 million. The value of the investment in Acerbic was not impaired.

(v) All items in the above income statements are deemed to accrue evenly over the year.

(vi) Ignore deferred tax.

(vii) It is the group policy to value the non-controlling interest at its proportionate share of the fair value of the subsidiary's identifiable net assets.

Required

(a) Calculate the goodwill arising on the acquisition of Sardonic at 1 August 2007. **(6 marks)**

(b) Prepare the consolidated income statement for the Patronic Group for the year ended 31 March 2008.

Note. assume that the investment in Acerbic has been accounted for using the equity method since its acquisition. **(15 marks)**

(c) At 31 March 2008 the other equity shares (70%) in Acerbic were owned by many separate investors. Shortly after this date Spekulate (a company unrelated to Patronic) accumulated a 60% interest in Acerbic by buying shares from the other shareholders. In May 2008 a meeting of the board of directors of Acerbic was held at which Patronic lost its seat on Acerbic's board.

Required

Explain, with reasons, the accounting treatment Patronic should adopt for its investment in Acerbic when it prepares its financial statements for the year ending 31 March 2009. **(4 marks)**

(Total = 25 marks)

41 Hedra (2.5 12/05)   45 mins

Hedra, a public listed company, acquired the following investments:

(i) On 1 October 20X4, 72 million shares in Salvador for an immediate cash payment of $195 million. Hedra agreed to pay further consideration on 30 September 20X5 of $49 million if the post acquisition profits of Salvador exceeded an agreed figure at that date (ignore discounting). Hedra has not yet accounted for this $49 million which is regarded as being at fair value. Salvador also accepted a $50 million 8% loan from Hedra at the date of its acquisition.

(ii) On 1 April 20X5, 40 million shares in Aragon by way of a share exchange of two shares in Hedra for each acquired share in Aragon. The share market value of Hedra 's shares at the date of this share exchange was $2.50. Hedra has not yet recorded the acquisition of the investment in Aragon.

The summarised statements of financial position of the three companies as at 30 September 20X5 are:

	Hedra $m	Hedra $m	Salvador $m	Salvador $m	Aragon $m	Aragon $m
Non–current assets						
Property, plant and equipment		358		240		270
Investments – in Salvador		245		nil		nil
– other		45		nil		nil
		648		240		270
Current assets						
Inventories	130		80		110	
Trade receivables	142		97		70	
Cash and bank	nil		4		20	
		272		181		200
		920		421		470
Equity and liabilities						
Ordinary share capital ($1 each)		400		120		100
Reserves:						
Share premium	40		50		nil	
Revaluation surplus	15		nil		nil	
Retained earnings	240		60		300	
		295		110		300
		695		230		400
Non–current liabilities						
8% loan note	nil		50		nil	
Deferred tax	45	45	nil	50	nil	nil
Current liabilities						
Trade payables	118		141		40	
Bank overdraft	12		nil		nil	
Current tax payable	50		nil		30	
		180		141		70
Total equity and liabilities		920		421		470

The following information is relevant.

(a) Fair value adjustments and revaluations:

   (i) Hedra's accounting policy for land and buildings is that they should be carried at their fair values. The fair value of Salvador's land at the date of acquisition was $20 million in excess of its carrying value. By 30 September 20X5 this excess had increased by a further $5 million. Salvador's buildings did not require any fair value adjustments. The fair value of Hedra's own land and buildings at 30 September 20X5 was $12 million in excess of its carrying value in the above statement of financial position.

   (ii) The fair value of some of Salvador's plant at the date of acquisition was $20 million in excess of its carrying value and had a remaining life of four years (straight–line depreciation is used).

   (iii) At the date of acquisition Salvador had unrelieved tax losses of $40 million from previous years. Salvador had not accounted for these as a deferred tax asset as its directors did not believe the company would be sufficiently profitable in the near future. However, the directors of Hedra were confident that these losses would be utilised and accordingly they should be recognised as a deferred tax asset. By 30 September 20X5 the group had not yet utilised any of these losses. The income tax rate is 25%.

(b) The retained earnings of Salvador and Aragon at 1 October 20X4, as reported in their separate financial statements, were $20 million and $200 million respectively. All profits are deemed to accrue evenly throughout the year.

(c) An impairment test on 30 September 20X5 showed that consolidated goodwill should be written down by $20million. Hedra has applied IFRS 3 Business combinations since the acquisition of Salvador.

(d) The investment in Aragon has not suffered any impairment.

(e)   It is the group policy to value non-controlling interest at acquisition at full (or fair) value. The directors value the goodwill attributable to the non-controlling interest at acquisition at $10m.

Required

Prepare the consolidated statement of financial position of Hedra as at 30 September 20X5.   **(25 marks)**

42 Hosterling (2.5 12/06)   **45 mins**

Hosterling purchased the following equity investments:

On 1 October 20X5: 80% of the issued share capital of Sunlee. The acquisition was through a share exchange of three shares in Hosterling for every five shares in Sunlee. The market price of Hosterling's shares at 1 October 20X5 was $5 per share.

On 1 July 20X6: 6 million shares in Amber paying $3 per share in cash and issuing to Amber's shareholders 6% (actual and effective rate) loan notes on the basis of $100 loan note for every 100 shares acquired.

The summarised income statements for the three companies for the year ended 30 September 20X6 are:

	Hosterling	Sunlee	Amber
	$'000	$'000	$'000
Revenue	105,000	62,000	50,000
Cost of sales	(68,000)	(36,500)	(61,000)
Gross profit/(loss)	37,000	25,500	(11,000)
Other income (note (i))	400	nil	nil
Distribution costs	(4,000)	(2,000)	(4,500)
Administrative expenses	(7,500)	(7,000)	(8,500)
Finance costs	(1,200)	(900)	nil
Profit/(loss) before tax	24,700	15,600	(24,000)
Income tax (expense)/credit	(8,700)	(2,600)	4,000
Profit/(loss) for the year	16,000	13,000	(20,000)

The following information is relevant:

(i)   The other income is a dividend received from Sunlee on 31 March 20X6.

(ii)   The details of Sunlee's and Amber's share capital and reserves at 1 October 20X5 were:

	Sunlee	Amber
	$'000	$'000
Equity shares of $1 each	20,000	15,000
Retained earnings	18,000	35,000

(iii) A fair value exercise was carried out at the date of acquisition of Sunlee with the following results:

	Carrying amount	Fair value	Remaining life (straight line)
	$'000	$'000	
Intellectual property	18,000	22,000	still in development
Land	17,000	20,000	not applicable
Plant	30,000	35,000	five years

The fair values have not been reflected in Sunlee's financial statements.

Plant depreciation is included in cost of sales.

No fair value adjustments were required on the acquisition of Amber.

(iv)   In the year ended 30 September 20X6 Hosterling sold goods to Sunlee at a selling price of $18 million. Hosterling made a profit of cost plus 25% on these sales. $7.5 million (at cost to Sunlee) of these goods were still in the inventories of Sunlee at 30 September 20X6.

(v)   Impairment tests for both Sunlee and Amber were conducted on 30 September 20X6. They concluded that the goodwill of Sunlee should be written down by $1.6 million and, due to its losses since acquisition, the investment in Amber was worth $21.5 million.

(vi)   All trading profits and losses are deemed to accrue evenly throughout the year.

(vii)   It is group policy to value the non-controlling interest at acquisition at its proportionate share of the fair value of the subsidiary's identifiable net assets.

Required

(a)   Calculate the goodwill arising on the acquisition of Sunlee at 1 October 20X5.   **(5 marks)**

(b)   Calculate the carrying amount of the investment in Amber at 30 September 20X6 under the equity method prior to the impairment test.   **(4 marks)**

(c)   Prepare the consolidated income statement for the Hosterling Group for the year ended 30 September 20X6.
                    (16 marks)

                    (Total = 25 marks)

43 Pacemaker (6/09)   45 mins

Below are the summarised statements of financial position for three companies as at 31 March 2009:

	Pacemaker		Syclop		Vardine	
Assets	$ million	$ million	$ million	$ million	$ million	$ million
Non-current assets						
Property, plant and equipment		520		280		240
Investments		345		40		nil
		865		320		240
Current assets						
Inventory	142		160		120	
Trade receivables	95		88		50	
Cash and bank	8	245	22	270	10	180
Total assets		1,110		590		420
Equity and liabilities						
Equity shares of $1 each		500		145		100
Share premium	100		nil		nil	
Retained earnings	130	230	260	260	240	240
		730		405		340
Non-current liabilities						
10% loan notes		180		20		nil
Current liabilities		200		165		80
Total equity and liabilities		1,110		590		420

Notes

Pacemaker is a public listed company that acquired the following investments:

(i)   Investment in Syclop

        On 1 April 2007 Pacemaker acquired 116 million shares in Syclop for an immediate cash payment of $210 million and issued at par one 10% $100 loan note for every 200 shares acquired. Syclop's retained earnings at the date of acquisition were $120 million.

(ii)   Investment in Vardine

        On 1 October 2008 Pacemaker acquired 30 million shares in Vardine in exchange for 75 million of its own shares. The stock market value of Pacemaker's shares at the date of this share exchange was $1·60 each. Pacemaker has not yet recorded the investment in Vardine.

(iii)   Pacemaker's other investments, and those of Syclop, are available-for-sale investments which are carried at their fair values as at 31 March 2008. The fair value of these investments at 31 March 2009 is $82 million and $37 million respectively.

Other relevant information:

(iv)   Pacemaker's policy is to value non-controlling interests at their fair values. The directors of Pacemaker assessed the fair value of the non-controlling interest in Syclop at the date of acquisition to be $65 million.

There has been no impairment to goodwill or the value of the investment in Vardine.

(v)   At the date of acquisition of Syclop owned a recently built property that was carried at its (depreciated) construction cost of $62 million. The fair value of this property at the date of acquisition was $82 million and it had an estimated remaining life of 20 years.

For many years Syclop has been selling some of its products under the brand name of 'Kyklop'. At the date of acquisition the directors of Pacemaker valued this brand at $25 million with a remaining life of 10 years. The brand is not included in Syclop's statement of financial position.

(vi)   The inventory of Syclop at 31 March 2009 includes goods supplied by Pacemaker for $56 million (at selling price from Pacemaker). Pacemaker adds a mark-up of 40% on cost when selling goods to Syclop. There are no intra-group receivables or payables at 31 March 2009.

(vii)   Vardine's profit is subject to seasonal variation. Its profit for the year ended 31 March 2009 was $100 million. $20 million of this profit was made from 1 April 2008 to 30 September 2008.

(viii)   None of the companies have paid any dividends for many years.

Required

Prepare the consolidated statement of financial position of Pacemaker as at 31 March 2009.

(25 marks)

44 Preparation question: Contract

The following details are as at the 31 December 20X5.

	Contract 1	Contract 2	Contract 3	Contract 4
Contract value	$120,000	$72,000	$240,000	$500,000
Costs to date	$48,000	$8,000	$103,200	$299,600
Estimated costs to completion	$48,000	$54,000	$160,800	$120,400
Progress payments received and receivable	$50,400	–	$76,800	$345,200
Date started	1.3.20X5	15.10.20X5	1.7.20X5	1.6.20X4
Estimated completion date	30.6.20X6	15.9.20X6	30.11.20X6	30.7.20X6
% complete	45%	10%	35%	70%

You are to assume that profit accrues evenly over the contract.

The income statement for the previous year showed revenue of $225,000 and expenses of $189,000 in relation to contract 4.

The company considers that the outcome of a contract cannot be estimated reliably until a contract is 25% complete. It is, however, probable that the customer will pay for costs incurred so far.

Required

Calculate the amounts to be included in the income statement for the year ended 31 December 20X5 and the statement of financial position as at that date.

	Contract 1 $	Contract 2 $	Contract 3 $	Contract 4 $

Income statement

Revenue
Expenses
Expected loss
Recognised profit/(loss)

Contract costs incurred
Recognised profits less recognised losses

Less: progress billings to date

Trade receivables

Progress billings to date
Less: cash received

Workings

45 Concepts (6/08)   27 mins

(a)   The IASB's Framework for the Preparation and Presentation of Financial Statements requires financial
       statements to be prepared on the basis that they comply with certain accounting concepts, underlying
       assumptions and (qualitative) characteristics. Five of these are:

       Matching/accruals
       Substance over form
       Prudence
       Comparability
       Materiality

(b)   For most entities, applying the appropriate concepts/assumptions in accounting for inventories is an important element in preparing their financial statements.

Required

Illustrate with examples how each of the concepts/assumptions in (a) may be applied to accounting for inventory. **(10 marks)**

(Total = 15 marks)

46 Linnet (2.5 6/04)   23 mins

(a)   Linnet is a large public listed company involved in the construction industry. Revenue on construction contracts is normally recognised by reference to the stage of completion of the contract. However, in certain circumstances, revenue is only recognised to the extent that it does not exceed recoverable contract costs.

Required

Discuss the principles that underlie each of the two methods and describe the circumstances in which their use is appropriate. **(5 marks)**

(b)   Linnet is part way through a contract to build a new football stadium at a contracted price of $300 million. Details of the progress of this contract at 1 April 20X3 are shown below:

	$ million
Cumulative sales revenue recognised	150
Cumulative cost of sales to date	112
Profit to date	38

The following information has been extracted from the accounting records at 31 March 20X4:

	$ million
Total progress payment received for work certified at **29 February 20X4**	180
Total costs incurred to date (excluding rectification costs below)	195
Rectification costs	17

Linnet has received progress payments of 90% of the work certified at 29 February 20X4. Linnet's surveyor has estimated the sales value of the further work completed during March 20X4 was $20 million.

At 31 March 20X4 the estimated remaining costs to complete the contract were $45 million.

The rectification costs are the costs incurred in widening access roads to the stadium. This was the result of an error by Linnet's architect when he made his initial drawings.

Linnet calculates the percentage of completion of its contracts as the proportion of sales value earned to date compared to the contract price.

All estimates can be taken as being reliable.

Required

Prepare extracts of the financial statements for Linnet for the above contract for the year to 31 March 20X4. **(8 marks)**

(Total = 13 marks)

47 Torrent (2.5 6/06)

Torrent is a large publicly listed company whose main activity involves construction contracts. Details of three of its contracts for the year ended 31 March 20X6 are:

Contract Date commenced	Alfa 1 April 20X4	Beta 1 October 20X5	Ceta 1 October 20X5
Estimated duration	3 years	18 months	2 years
	$m	$m	$m
Fixed contract price	20	6	12
Estimated costs at start of contract	15	7.5 (note (iii))	10
Cost to date:			
At 31 March 20X5	5	Nil	Nil
At 31 March 20X6	12.5 (note (ii))	2	4
Estimated costs at 31 March 20X6 to complete	3.5	5.5 (note (iii))	6
Progress payments received at 31 March 20X5 (note (i))	5.4	Nil	Nil
Progress payments received at 31 March 20X6 (note (i))	12.6	1.8	nil

Notes

(i) The company's normal policy for determining the percentage completion of contracts is based on the value of work invoiced to date compared to the contract price. Progress payments received represent 90% of the work invoiced. However, no progress payments will be invoiced or received from contract Ceta until it is completed, so the percentage completion of this contract is to be based on the cost to date compared to the estimated total contract costs.

(ii) The cost to date of $12·5 million at 31 March 20X6 for contract Alfa includes $1 million relating to unplanned rectification costs incurred during the current year (ended 31 March 20X6) due to subsidence occurring on site.

(iii) Since negotiating the price of contract Beta, Torrent has discovered the land that it purchased for the project is contaminated by toxic pollutants. The estimated cost at the start of the contract and the estimated costs to complete the contract include the unexpected costs of decontaminating the site before construction could commence.

Required

Prepare extracts of the income statement and statement of financial position for Torrent in respect of the above construction contracts for the year ended 31 March 20X6. **(12 marks)**

48 Beetie (pilot paper)

IAS 11 *Construction contracts* deals with accounting requirements for construction contracts whose durations usually span at least two accounting periods.

Required

(a) Describe the issues of revenue and profit recognition relating to construction contracts. **(4 marks)**

(b) Beetie is a construction company that prepares its financial statements to 31 March each year. During the year ended 31 March 20X6 the company commenced two construction contracts that are expected to take more than one year to complete. The position of each contract at 31 March 20X6 is as follows:

Contract	1	2
	$'000	$'000
Agreed contract price	5,500	1,200
Estimated total cost of contract at commencement	4,000	900
Estimated total cost at 31 March 20X6	4,000	1,250
Agreed value of work completed at 31 March 20X6	3,300	840
Progress billings invoiced and received at 31 March 20X6	3,000	880
Contract costs incurred to 31 March 20X6	3,900	720

The agreed value of the work completed at 31 March 20X6 is considered to be equal to the revenue earned in the year ended 31 March 20X6. The percentage of completion is calculated as the agreed value of work completed to the agreed contract price.

Required

Calculate the amounts which should appear in the income statement and statement of financial position of Beetie at 31 March 20X6 in respect of the above contracts. **(6 marks)**

(Total = 10 marks)

49 Bodyline (2.5 12/03) 45 mins

IAS 37 *Provisions, contingent liabilities and contingent assets* sets out the principles of accounting for these items and clarifies when provisions should and should not be made. Prior to its issue, the inappropriate use of provisions had been an area where companies had been accused of manipulating the financial statements and of creative accounting.

Required

(a) Describe the nature of provisions and the accounting requirements for them contained in IAS 37. **(6 marks)**

(b) Explain why there is a need for an accounting standard in this area. Illustrate your answer with three practical examples of how the standard addresses controversial issues. **(6 marks)**

(c) Bodyline sells sports goods and clothing through a chain of retail outlets. It offers customers a full refund facility for any goods returned within 28 days of their purchase provided they are unused and in their original packaging. In addition, all goods carry a warranty against manufacturing defects for 12 months from their date of purchase. For most goods the manufacturer underwrites this warranty such that Bodyline is credited with the cost of the goods that are returned as faulty. Goods purchased from one manufacturer, Header, are sold to Bodyline at a negotiated discount which is designed to compensate Bodyline for manufacturing defects. No refunds are given by Header, thus Bodyline has to bear the cost of any manufacturing faults of these goods.

Bodyline makes a uniform mark up on cost of 25% on all goods it sells, except for those supplied from Header on which it makes a mark up on cost of 40%. Sales of goods manufactured by Header consistently account for 20% of all Bodyline's sales.

Sales in the last 28 days of the trading year to 30 September 20X3 were $1,750,000. Past trends reliably indicate that 10% of all goods are returned under the 28-day return facility. These are not faulty goods. Of these 70% are later resold at the normal selling price and the remaining 30% are sold as 'sale' items at half the normal retail price.

In addition to the above expected returns, an estimated $160,000 (at selling price) of the goods sold during the year will have manufacturing defects and have yet to be returned by customers. Goods returned as faulty have no resale value.

Required

Describe the nature of the above warranty/return facilities and calculate the provision Bodyline is required to make at 30 September 20X3:

(i) For goods subject to the 28 day returns policy
(ii) For goods that are likely to be faulty **(8 marks)**

(d) Rockbuster has recently purchased an item of earth moving plant at a total cost of $24 million. The plant has an estimated life of 10 years with no residual value, however its engine will need replacing after every 5,000 hours of use at an estimated cost of $7.5 million. The directors of Rockbuster intend to depreciate the plant at $2.4 million ($24 million/10 years) per annum and make a provision of $1,500 ($7.5 million/5,000 hours) per hour of use for the replacement of the engine.

Required

Explain how the plant should be treated in accordance with International Financial Reporting Standards and comment on the Directors' proposed treatment. **(5 marks)**

(Total = 25 marks)

50 Tentacle (2.5 6/07)   27 mins

After the end of the reporting period, prior to authorising for issue the financial statements of Tentacle for the year ended 31 March 20X7, the following material information has arisen.

(i) The notification of the bankruptcy of a customer. The balance of the trade receivable due from the customer at 31 March 20X7 was $23,000 and at the date of the notification it was $25,000. No payment is expected from the bankruptcy proceedings. **(3 marks)**

(ii) Sales of some items of product W32 were made at a price of $5·40 each in April and May 20X7. Sales staff receive a commission of 15% of the sales price on this product. At 31 March 20X7 Tentacle had 12,000 units of product W32 in inventory included at cost of $6 each. **(4 marks)**

(iii) Tentacle is being sued by an employee who lost a limb in an accident while at work on 15 March 20X7. The company is contesting the claim as the employee was not following the safety procedures that he had been instructed to use. Accordingly the financial statements include a note of a contingent liability of $500,000 for personal injury damages. In a recently decided case where a similar injury was sustained, a settlement figure of $750,000 was awarded by the court. Although the injury was similar, the circumstances of the accident in the decided case are different from those of Tentacle's case. **(4 marks)**

(iv) Tentacle is involved in the construction of a residential apartment building. It is being accounted for using the percentage of completion basis in IAS 11 *Construction contracts*. The recognised profit at 31 March 20X7 was $1·2 million based on costs to date of $3 million as a percentage of the total estimated costs of $6 million. Early in May 20X7 Tentacle was informed that due to very recent industry shortages, building materials will cost $1·5 million more than the estimate of total cost used in the calculation of the percentage of completion. Tentacle cannot pass on any additional costs to the customer. **(4 marks)**

Required

State and quantify how items (i) to (iv) above should be treated when finalising the financial statements of Tentacle for the year ended 31 March 20X7.

Note. The mark allocation is shown against each of the four items above.

(Total = 15 marks)

51 Promoil (12/08)   27 mins

(a) The definition of a liability forms an important element of the International Accounting Standards Board's *Framework for the Preparation and Presentation of Financial Statements* which, in turn, forms the basis for IAS 37 *Provisions, Contingent Liabilities and Contingent Assets*.

Required

Define a liability and describe the circumstances under which provisions should be recognised. Give two examples of how the definition of liabilities enhances the reliability of financial statements. **(5 marks)**

(b) On 1 October 2007, Promoil acquired a newly constructed oil platform at a cost of $30 million together with the right to extract oil from an offshore oilfield under a government licence. The terms of the licence are that Promoil will have to remove the platform (which will then have no value) and restore the sea bed to an environmentally satisfactory condition in 10 years' time when the oil reserves have been exhausted. The estimated cost of this on 30 September 2017 will be $15 million. The present value of $1 receivable in 10 years at the appropriate discount rate for Promoil of 8% is $0·46.

Required

(i) Explain and quantify how the oil platform should be treated in the financial statements of Promoil for the year ended 30 September 2008; **(7 marks)**

(ii) Describe how your answer to (b)(i) would change if the government licence did not require an environmental clean up. **(3 marks)**

(Total = 15 marks)

52 Peterlee II (2.5 6/06 part)   22 mins

Peterlee is preparing its financial statements for the year ended 31 March 20X6. The following items have been brought to your attention:

(a) Peterlee acquired the entire share capital of Trantor during the year. The acquisition was achieved through a share exchange. The terms of the exchange were based on the relative values of the two companies obtained by capitalising the companies' estimated future cash flows. When the fair value of Trantor's identifiable net assets was deducted from the value of the company as a whole, its goodwill was calculated at $2·5 million. A similar exercise valued the goodwill of Peterlee at $4 million. The directors wish to incorporate both the goodwill values in the companies' consolidated financial statements. **(4 marks)**

(b) During the year Peterlee acquired an iron ore mine at a cost of $6 million. In addition, when all the ore has been extracted (estimated in 10 years time) the company will face estimated costs for landscaping the area affected by the mining that have a present value of $2 million. These costs would still have to be incurred even if no further ore was extracted. The directors have proposed that an accrual of $200,000 per year for the next ten years should be made for the landscaping. **(4 marks)**

(c) On 1 April 20X5 Peterlee issued an 8% $5 million convertible loan at par. The loan is convertible in three years time to ordinary shares or redeemable at par in cash. The directors decided to issue a convertible loan because a non-convertible loan would have required an interest rate of 10%. The directors intend to show the loan at $5 million under non-current liabilities. The following discount rates are available:

	8%	10%
Year 1	0·93	0·91
Year 2	0·86	0·83
Year 3	0·79	0·75

(4 marks)

Required

Describe (and quantify where possible) how Peterlee should treat the items in (a) to (b) in its financial statements for the year ended 31 March 20X6 commenting on the directors' views where appropriate.

The mark allocation is shown against each of the three items above. **(Total = 12 marks)**

53 Jedders   27 mins

Your assistant at Jedders, a small listed company, has been preparing the financial statements for the year ended 31 December 20X0 and has raised the following queries.

(a) The company has three long leasehold properties in different parts of the region. The leases were acquired at different times, and the lease terms are all for fifty years. As at 1 January 20X0, their original cost, accumulated depreciation to date and carrying (book) values were as follows.

	Cost	Depreciation	Carrying value 1.1.20X0
	$'000	$'000	$'000
Property in North	3,000	1,800	1,200
Property in Central	6,000	1,200	4,800
Property in South	3,750	1,500	2,250

On 1 January an independent surveyor provided valuation information to suggest that the value of the South property was the same as book value, the North property had fallen against carrying value by 20% and the Central property had risen by 40% in value against the carrying value.

The directors of the company wish to include the revaluation of the Central property in the accounts to 31 December 20X0, whilst leaving the other properties at their depreciated historical cost.

The directors believe that this treatment of the North property is prudent and can be justified because property prices are expected to recover within the next few years so that this fall in value will be entirely reversed.

Required

(i)   Advise the directors whether their proposal is acceptable, assuming they are committed to the use of current value for the Central property.   **(2 marks)**

(ii)   Assuming that all of the properties are revalued, calculate the income statement charges and the non-current asset statement of financial position extracts for all the properties for the year ended 31 December 20X0. You should follow the requirements of IAS 16 *Property, plant and equipment*.
                                                                                                  (3 marks)

(b)   On 1 October 20X0, Jedders signed a receivable factoring agreement with a company Fab Factors. Jedders' trade receivables are to be split into three groups, as follows.

●   *Group A* receivables will not be factored or administered by Fab Factors under the agreement, but instead will be collected as usual by Jedders.

●   *Group B* receivables are to be factored and collected by Fab Factors on a 'with recourse' basis. Fab Factors will charge a 1% per month finance charge on the balance outstanding at the beginning of the month. Jedders will reimburse in full any individual balance outstanding after three months.

●   *Group C* receivables will be factored and collected by Fab Factors 'without recourse'; Fab Factors will pay Jedders 95% of the book value of the debtors.

Jedders has a policy of making a receivables allowance of 20% of a trade receivable balance when it becomes three months old.

The receivables groups have been analysed as follows.

	Balance @ 1 Oct 20X0	% of 1 October 20X0 balance collected in: October	November	December
	$'000			
Group A	1,250	30%	30%	20%
Group B	1,500	40%	30%	20%
Group C	2,000	50%	25%	22%

Required

For the accounts of Jedders, calculate the finance costs and receivables allowance for each group of trade receivables for the period 1 October - 31 December 20X0 and show the financial position values for those trade receivables as at 31 December 20X0.   **(5 marks)**

(c)   On 1 January 20X0, Jedders issued $15m of 7% convertible loan notes at par. The loan notes are convertible into equity shares in the company, at the option of the note holders, five years after the date of issue (31 December 20X4) on the basis of 25 shares for each $100 of loan stock. Alternatively, the loan notes will be redeemed at par.

Jedders has been advised by Fab Factors that, had the company issued similar loan notes without the conversion rights, then it would have had to pay interest of 10%; the rate is thus lower because the conversion rights are favourable.

Fab Factors also suggest that, as some of the loan note holders will choose to convert, the loan notes are, in substance, equity and should be treated as such on Jedders' statement of financial position. Thus, as well as a reduced finance cost being achieved to boost profitability, Jedders' gearing has been improved compared to a straight issue of debt.

The present value of $1 receivable at the end of each year, based on discount rates of 7% and 10% can be taken as:

End of year	7%	10%
1	0.93	0.91
2	0.87	0.83
3	0.82	0.75
4	0.76	0.68
5	0.71	0.62

Required

In relation to the 7% convertible loan notes, calculate the finance cost to be shown in the income statement and the statement of financial position extracts for the year to 31 December 20X0 for Jedders and comment on the advice from Fab Factors. **(5 marks)**

(Total = 15 marks)

54 Pingway (6/08)   18 mins

Pingway issued a $10 million 3% convertible loan note at par on 1 April 2007 with interest payable annually in arrears. Three years later, on 31 March 2010, the loan note is convertible into equity shares on the basis of $100 of loan note for 25 equity shares or it may be redeemed at par in cash at the option of the loan note holder. One of the company's financial assistants observed that the use of a convertible loan note was preferable to a non-convertible loan note as the latter would have required an interest rate of 8% in order to make it attractive to investors. The assistant has also commented that the use of a convertible loan note will improve the profit as a result of lower interest costs and, as it is likely that the loan note holders will choose the equity option, the loan note can be classified as equity which will improve the company's high gearing position.

The present value of $1 receivable at the end of the year, based on discount rates of 3% and 8% can be taken as:

		3%	8%
		$	$
End of year	1	0.97	0.93
	2	0.94	0.86
	3	0.92	0.79

Required

Comment on the financial assistant's observations and show how the convertible loan note should be accounted for in Pingway's income statement for the year ended 31 March 2008 and statement of financial position as at that date. **(10 marks)**

55 Triangle (2.5 6/05)   45 mins

Triangle, a public listed company, is in the process of preparing its draft financial statements for the year to 31 March 20X5. The following matters have been brought to your attention:

(i)   On 1 April 20X4 the company brought into use a new processing plant that had cost $15 million to construct and had an estimated life of ten years. The plant uses hazardous chemicals which are put in containers and shipped abroad for safe disposal after processing. The chemicals have also contaminated the plant itself which occurred as soon as the plant was used. It is a legal requirement that the plant is decontaminated at the end of its life. The estimated present value of this decontamination, using a discount rate of 8% per annum, is $5 million. The financial statements have been charged with $1·5 million ($15 million/10 years) for plant depreciation and a provision of $500,000 ($5 million/10 years) has been made towards the cost of the decontamination. **(8 marks)**

(ii)   On 15 May 20X5 the company's auditors discovered a fraud in the material requisitions department. A senior member of staff who took up employment with Triangle in August 20X4 had been authorising payments for goods that had never been received. The payments were made to a fictitious company that cannot be traced. The member of staff was immediately dismissed. Calculations show that the total amount of the fraud to the date of its discovery was $240,000 of which $210,000 related to the year to 31 March 20X5. (Assume the fraud is material). **(5 marks)**

(iii) The company has contacted its insurers in respect of the above fraud. Triangle is insured for theft, but the insurance company maintains that this is a commercial fraud and is not covered by the theft clause in the insurance policy. Triangle has not yet had an opinion from its lawyers. **(4 marks)**

(iv) On 1 April 20X4 Triangle sold maturing inventory that had a carrying value of $3 million (at cost) to Factorall, a finance house, for $5 million. Its estimated market value at this date was in excess of $5 million. The inventory will not be ready for sale until 31 March 20X8 and will remain on Triangle's premises until this date. The sale contract includes a clause allowing Triangle to repurchase the inventory at any time up to 31 March 20X8 at a price of $5 million plus interest at 10% per annum compounded from 1 April 20X4. The inventory will incur storage costs until maturity. The cost of storage for the current year of $300,000 has been included in trade receivables (in the name of Factorall). If Triangle chooses not to repurchase the inventory, Factorall will pay the accumulated storage costs on 31 March 20X8. The proceeds of the sale have been debited to the bank and the sale has been included in Triangle's sales revenue. **(8 marks)**

Required

Explain how the items in (i) to (iv) above should be treated in Triangle's financial statements for the year to 31 March 20X5 in accordance with current international accounting standards. Your answer should quantify the amounts where possible.

The mark allocation is shown against each of the four matters above. **(Total = 25 marks)**

56 Atkins (2.5 12/02) 27 mins

The principle of recording the substance or economic reality of transactions rather than their legal form lies at the heart of the *Framework for Preparation and Presentation of Financial Statements* and several International Financial Reporting Standards. The development of this principle was partly in reaction to a minority of public interest companies entering into certain complex transactions. These transactions sometimes led to accusations that company directors were involved in 'creative accounting'.

(i) Atkins's operations involve selling cars to the public through a chain of retail car showrooms. It buys most of its new vehicles directly from the manufacturer on the following terms:

- Atkins will pay the manufacturer for the cars on the date they are sold to a customer or six months after they are delivered to its showrooms whichever is the sooner.

- The price paid will be 80% of the retail list price as set by the manufacturer at the date that the goods are delivered.

- Atkins will pay the manufacturer 1·5% per month (of the cost price to Atkins) as a 'display charge' until the goods are paid for.

- Atkins may return the cars to the manufacturer any time up until the date the cars are due to be paid for. Atkins will incur the freight cost of any such returns. Atkins has never taken advantage of this right of return.

- The manufacturer can recall the cars or request them to be transferred to another retailer any time up until the time they are paid for by Atkins.

Required

Discuss which party bears the risks and rewards in the above arrangement and come to a conclusion on how the transactions should be treated by each party. **(6 marks)**

(ii) Atkins bought five identical plots of development land for $2 million in 20X0. On 1 October 20X2 Atkins sold three of the plots of land to an investment company, Landbank, for a total of $2·4 million. This price was based on 75% of the fair market value of $3·2 million as determined by an independent surveyor at the date of sale. The terms of the sale contained two clauses:

- Atkins can re-purchase the plots of land for the full fair value of $3·2 million (the value determined at the date of sale) any time until 30 September 20X5; and

–   On 1 October 20X5, Landbank has the option to require Atkins to re-purchase the properties for $3·2 million. You may assume that Landbank seeks a return on its investments of 10% per annum.

Required

Discuss the substance of the above transactions; and **(3 marks)**

Prepare extracts of the income statement and statement of financial position (ignore cash) of Atkins for the year to 30 September 20X3:

–   If the plots of land are considered as sold to Landbank; and **(2 marks)**
–   Reflecting the substance of the above transactions. **(4 marks)**

(Total = 15 marks)

57 Angelino (2.5 12/06) 45 mins

(a)   Recording the substance of transactions, rather than their legal form, is an important principle in financial accounting. Abuse of this principle can lead to profit manipulation, non-recognition of assets and substantial debt not being recorded in the statement of financial position.

Required

Describe how the use of off balance sheet financing can mislead users of financial statements.

Note. Your answer should refer to specific user groups and include examples where recording the legal form of transactions may mislead them. **(9 marks)**

(b)   Angelino has entered into the following transactions during the year ended 30 September 20X6:

(i)   In September 20X6 Angelino sold (factored) some of its trade receivables to Omar, a finance house. On selected account balances Omar paid Angelino 80% of their book value. The agreement was that Omar would administer the collection of the receivables and remit a residual amount to Angelino depending upon how quickly individual customers paid. Any balance uncollected by Omar after six months will be refunded to Omar by Angelino. **(5 marks)**

(ii)   On 1 October 20X5 Angelino owned a freehold building that had a carrying amount of $7.5 million and had an estimated remaining life of 20 years. On this date it sold the building to Finaid for a price of $12 million and entered into an agreement with Finaid to rent back the building for an annual rental of $1.3 million for a period of five years. The auditors of Angelino have commented that in their opinion the building had a market value of only $10 million at the date of its sale and to rent an equivalent building under similar terms to the agreement between Angelino and Finaid would only cost $800,000 per annum. Assume any finance costs are 10% per annum. **(6 marks)**

(iii)   Angelino is a motor car dealer selling vehicles to the public. Most of its new vehicles are supplied on consignment by two manufacturers, Monza and Capri, who trade on different terms.

Monza supplies cars on terms that allow Angelino to display the vehicles for a period of three months from the date of delivery or when Angelino sells the cars on to a retail customer if this is less than three months. Within this period Angelino can return the cars to Monza or can be asked by Monza to transfer the cars to another dealership (both at no cost to Angelino). Angelino pays the manufacturer's list price at the end of the three month period (or at the date of sale if sooner). In recent years Angelino has returned several cars to Monza that were not selling very well and has also been required to transfer cars to other dealerships at Monza's request.

Capri's terms of supply are that Angelino pays 10% of the manufacturer's price at the date of delivery and 1% of the outstanding balance per month as a display charge. After six months (or sooner if Angelino chooses), Angelino must pay the balance of the purchase price or return the cars to Capri. If the cars are returned to the manufacturer, Angelino has to pay for the transportation costs and forfeits the 10% deposit. Because of this Angelino has only returned vehicles to Capri once in the last three years. **(5 marks)**

Required

Describe how the above transactions and events should be treated in the financial statements of Angelino for the year ended 30 September 20X6. Your answer should explain, where relevant, the difference between the legal form of the transactions and their substance.

Note. The mark allocation is shown against each of the three transactions above.   **(Total = 25 marks)**

58 Preparation question: Branch

Branch acquired an item of plant and equipment on a finance lease on 1 January 20X1. The terms of the agreement were as follows:

Deposit   : $1,150 (non-refundable)
Instalments   : $4,000 pa for seven years payable in arrears
Cash price   : $20,000

The asset has useful life of four years and the interest rate implicit in the lease is 11%.

Required

Prepare extracts from the income statement and statement of financial position for the year ending 31 December 20X1.

(Notes to the financial statements are not required.)

59 Evans   22 mins

On 1 October 20X3 Evans entered into a non-cancellable agreement whereby Evans would lease a new rocket booster. The terms of the agreement were that Evans would pay 26 rentals of $3,000 quarterly in advance commencing on 1 October 20X3, and that after this initial period Evans could continue, at its option, to use the rocket booster for a nominal rental which is not material. The cash price of this asset would have been $61,570 and the asset has a useful life of 10 years. Evans considers this lease to be a finance lease and charges a full year's depreciation in the year of purchase of an asset. The rate of interest implicit in the lease is 2% per quarter.

On 1 July 20X2 Evans entered into another non-cancellable agreement to lease a Zarkov rocket for a period of 10 years at a rental of $5,000 half-yearly to be paid in advance, commencing on 1 July 20X2. Evans considers this lease to be an operating lease.

Required

Show how these transactions would be reflected in the financial statements for the year ended 31 December 20X3.

(12 marks)

60 Bowtock (2.5 12/03 amended)   9 mins

Bowtock has leased an item of plant under the following terms:

Commencement of the lease was **1 January 20X2**

Term of lease 5 years

Annual payments in advance $12,000

Cash price and fair value of the asset – $52,000 at 1 January 20X2 – equivalent to the present value of the minimum lease payments.

Implicit interest rate within the lease (as supplied by the lessor) 8% per annum (to be apportioned on a time basis where relevant).

The company's depreciation policy for this type of plant is 20% per annum on cost (apportioned on a time basis where relevant).

Prepare extracts of the income statement and statement of financial position for Bowtock for the year to 30 September 20X3 for the above lease.

(5 marks)

61 Fino (12/07)

27 mins

(a) An important requirement of the IASB's *Framework for the Preparation and Presentation of Financial Statements* (*Framework*) is that in order to be reliable, an entity's financial statements should represent faithfully the transactions and events that it has undertaken.

Required

Explain what is meant by faithful representation and how it enhances reliability.

(5 marks)

(b) On 1 April 2007, Fino increased the operating capacity of its plant. Due to a lack of liquid funds it was unable to buy the required plant which had a cost of $350,000. On the recommendation of the finance director, Fino entered into an agreement to lease the plant from the manufacturer. The lease required four annual payments in advance of $100,000 each commencing on 1 April 2007. The plant would have a useful life of four years and would be scrapped at the end of this period. The finance director, believing the lease to be an operating lease, commented that the agreement would improve the company's return on capital employed (compared to outright purchase of the plant).

Required

(i) Discuss the validity of the finance director's comment and describe how IAS 17 *Leases* ensures that leases such as the above are faithfully represented in an entity's financial statements. **(4 marks)**

(ii) Prepare extracts of Fino's income statement and statement of financial position for the year ended 30 September 2007 in respect of the rental agreement assuming:

    (1)   It is an operating lease **(2 marks)**

    (2)   It is a finance lease (use an implicit interest rate of 10% per annum). **(4 marks)**

(Total = 15 marks)

62 Preparation question: Julian

Julian recognised a deferred tax liability for the year end 31 December 20X3 which related solely to accelerated tax depreciation on property, plant and equipment at a rate 30%. The net book value of the property, plant and equipment at that date was $310,000 and the tax written down value was $230,000.

The following data relates to the year ended 31 December 20X4:

(i) At the end of the year the carrying value of property, plant and equipment was $460,000 and their tax written down value was $270,000. During the year some items were revalued by $90,000. No items had previously required revaluation. In the tax jurisdiction in which Julian operates revaluations of assets do not affect the tax base of an asset or taxable profit. Gains due to revaluations are taxable on sale.

(ii) Julian began development of a new product during the year and capitalised $60,000 in accordance with IAS 38. The expenditure was deducted for tax purposes as it was incurred. None of the expenditure had been amortised by the year end.

(iii) Julian's income statement showed interest income receivable of $55,000, but only $45,000 of this had been received by the year end. Interest income is taxed on a receipts basis.

(iv) During the year, Julian made a provision of $40,000 to cover an obligation to clean up some damage caused by an environmental accident. None of the provision had been used by the year end. The expenditure will be tax deductible when paid.

The corporate income tax rate recently enacted for the following year is 30% (unchanged from the previous year).

The current tax charge was calculated for the year as $45,000.

Current tax is settled on a net basis with the national tax authority.

Required

(a) Prepare a table showing the carrying values, tax bases and temporary differences for each for the items above at 31 December 20X4.

(b) Prepare the income statement and statement of financial position notes to the financial statements relating to deferred tax for the year ended 31 December 20X4.

63 Deferred taxation

27 mins

(a) Explain, with examples, the nature and purpose of deferred taxation. **(10 marks)**

(b) The information below relates to G for the year ended 31 March 20X3.

The balance on the provision for deferred taxation account at 1 April 20X2 was $35,000. This represented taxation at 35% on cumulative timing differences of $100,000 at 1 April 20X2. Capital allowances (tax depreciation) and depreciation for the year ending 31 March 20X3 are as follows.

	Capital allowances $'000	Depreciation $'000
20X3 (actual)	100	90

The income tax rate for 20X3 is 30% and is expected to remain at this level for the for the foreseeable future.

Required

State, with reasons, how to account for deferred tax in the year ended 31 March 20X3. **(5 marks)**

(Total = 15 marks)

64 Bowtock II (2.5 12/03 amended)

18 mins

(a) IAS 12 *Income Taxes* was issued in 1996 and revised in 2000. It details the requirements relating to the accounting treatment of deferred taxes.

Required

Explain why it is considered necessary to provide for deferred tax and briefly outline the principles of accounting for deferred tax contained in IAS 12 *Income taxes*. **(4 marks)**

(b) Bowtock purchased an item of plant for $2,000,000 on 1 October 20X0. It had an estimated life of eight years and an estimated residual value of $400,000. The plant is depreciated on a straight-line basis. The tax authorities do not allow depreciation as a deductible expense. Instead a tax expense of 40% of the cost of this type of asset can be claimed against income tax in the year of purchase and 20% per annum (on a reducing balance basis) of its tax base thereafter. The rate of income tax can be taken as 25%.

Required

In respect of the above item of plant, calculate the deferred tax charge/credit in Bowtock's income statement for the year to 30 September 20X3 and the deferred tax balance in the statement of financial position at that date. **(6 marks)**

Note. Work to the nearest $'000. **(Total = 10 marks)**

65 Preparation question: Fenton

(a) Fenton had 5,000,000 ordinary shares in issue on 1 January 20X1.

On 31 January 20X1, the company made a rights issue of 1 for 4 at $1.75. The cum rights price was $2 per share.

On 30 June 20X1, the company made an issue at full market price of 125,000 shares.

Finally, on 30 November 20X1, the company made a 1 for 10 bonus issue.

Profit for the year was $2,900,000.

The reported EPS for year ended 31 December 20X0 was 46.4c.

Required

What was the earnings per share figure for year ended 31 December 20X1 and the restated EPS for year ended 31 December 20X0?

(b) Sinbad had the same 10 million ordinary shares in issue on both 1 January 20X1 and 31 December 20X1. On 1 January 20X1 the company issued 1,200,000 $1 units of 5% convertible loan stock. Each unit of stock is convertible into 4 ordinary shares on 1 January 20X9 at the option of the holder. The following is an extract from Sinbad's income statement for the year ended 31 December 20X1:

	$'000
Profit before interest and tax	980
Interest payable on 5% convertible loan stock	(60)
Profit before tax	920
Income tax expense (at 30%)	(276)
Profit for the year	644

Required

What was the basic and diluted earnings per share for the year ended 31 December 20X1?

(c) Talbot has in issue 5,000,000 50c ordinary shares throughout 20X3.

During 20X1 the company had given certain senior executives options over 400,000 shares exercisable at $1.10 at any time after 31 May 20X4. None were exercised during 20X3. The average market value of one ordinary share during the period was $1.60. Talbot had made a profit after tax of $540,000 in 20X3.

Required

What is the basic and diluted earnings per share for the year ended 31 December 20X3?

66 Savoir (2.5 6/06 part)   23 mins

(a) The issued share capital of Savoir, a publicly listed company, at 31 March 20X3 was $10 million. Its shares are denominated at 25 cents each. Savoir's earnings attributable to its ordinary shareholders for the year ended 31 March 20X3 were also $10 million, giving an earnings per share of 25 cents.

Year ended 31 March 20X4

On 1 July 20X3 Savoir issued eight million ordinary shares at full market value. On 1 January 20X4 a bonus issue of one new ordinary share for every four ordinary shares held was made. Earnings attributable to ordinary shareholders for the year ended 31 March 20X4 were $13,800,000.

Year ended 31 March 20X5

On 1 October 20X4 Savoir made a rights issue of shares of two new ordinary shares at a price of $1·00 each for every five ordinary shares held. The offer was fully subscribed. The market price of Savoir's ordinary shares immediately prior to the offer was $2·40 each. Earnings attributable to ordinary shareholders for the year ended 31 March 20X5 were $19,500,000.

Required

Calculate Savoir's earnings per share for the years ended 31 March 20X4 and 20X5 including comparative figures. **(9 marks)**

(b) On 1 April 20X5 Savoir issued $20 million 8% convertible loan stock at par. The terms of conversion (on 1 April 20X8) are that for every $100 of loan stock, 50 ordinary shares will be issued at the option of loan stockholders. Alternatively the loan stock will be redeemed at par for cash. Also on 1 April 20X5 the directors of Savoir were awarded share options on 12 million ordinary shares exercisable from 1 April 20X8 at $1·50 per share. The average market value of Savoir's ordinary shares for the year ended 31 March 20X6 was $2·50 each. The income tax rate is 25%. Earnings attributable to ordinary shareholders for the year ended 31 March 20X6 were $25,200,000. The share options have been correctly recorded in the income statement.

Required

Calculate Savoir's basic and diluted earnings per share for the year ended 31 March 20X6 (comparative figures are not required).

You may assume that both the convertible loan stock and the directors' options are dilutive. **(4 marks)**

(Total = 13 marks)

67 Niagara (2.5 6/03 part) 23 mins

Extracts of Niagara's consolidated statement of comprehensive income for the year to 31 March 20X3 are:

	$'000
Revenue	36,000
Cost of sales	(21,000)
Gross profit	15,000
Other operating expenses	(6,200)
Interest payable	(800)
Impairment of non-current assets	(4,000)
Share of profit of associates	1,500
Profit before tax	5,500
Income tax expense	(2,800)
Profit for the year	2,700
Profit attributable to:	
Owners of the parent	2,585
Non-controlling interest	115
	2,700

This draft income statement does **not** include any amounts in respect of the preference dividends or equity dividends for the year.

The impairment of non-current assets attracted tax relief of $1 million which has been included in the tax charge.

Niagara paid an interim ordinary dividend of 3c per share in June 20X2 and declared a final dividend on 25 March 20X3 of 6c per share.

The issued share capital of Niagara on **1 April 20X2** was:

Ordinary shares of 25c each	$3 million
8% Preference shares	$1 million

The preference shares are non-redeemable.

The company also had an issue $2 million 7% convertible loan stock dated 20X5. The loan stock will be redeemed at par in 20X5 or converted to ordinary shares on the basis of 40 new shares for each $100 of loan stock at the option of the stockholders. Niagara's income tax rate is 30%.

There are also in existence directors' share warrants (issued in 20X1) which entitle the directors to receive 750,000 new shares in total in 20X5 at no cost to the directors.

The following share issues took place during the year to 31 March 20X3:

- 1 July 20X2; a rights issue of 1 new share at $1·50 for every 5 shares held. The market price of Niagara's shares the day before the rights was $2·40.
- 1 October 20X2; an issue of $1 million 6% non-redeemable preference shares at par.

Both issues were fully subscribed.

Niagara's basic earnings per share in the year to 31 March 20X2 was correctly disclosed as 24c.

Required

Calculate for Niagara for the year to 31 March 20X3:

(a)	the dividend cover and explain its significance;	**(3 marks)**
(b)	the basic earnings per share including the comparative;	**(4 marks)**
(c)	the fully diluted earnings per share (ignore comparative); and advise a prospective investor of the significance of the diluted earnings per share figure.	**(6 marks)**
		(Total = 13 marks)

68 Rytetrend (2.5 6/03)   45 mins

Rytetrend is a retailer of electrical goods. Extracts from the company's financial statements are set out below:

INCOME STATEMENT FOR THE YEAR ENDED 31 MARCH

	20X3	20X3	20X2	20X2
	$'000	$'000	$'000	$'000
Sales revenue		31,800		23,500
Cost of sales		(22,500)		(16,000)
Gross profit		9,300		7,500
Other operating expense		(5,440)		(4,600)
Interest payable – loan notes	(260)		(500)	
– overdraft	(200)	(460)	Nil	(500)
Profit before taxation		3,400		2,400
Income tax expense		(1,000)		(800)
Profit for the year		2,400		1,600

STATEMENTS OF FINANCIAL POSITION AS AT 31 MARCH

	20X3	20X3	20X2	20X2
Assets	$'000	$'000	$'000	$'000
Non-current assets (note (i))		24,500		17,300
Current assts				
Inventory	2,650		3,270	
Receivables	1,100		1,950	
Bank	Nil	3,750	400	5,620
Total assets		28,250		22,920
Equity and liabilities				
Equity				
Ordinary capital ($1 shares)		11,500		10,000
Share premium		1,500		Nil
Retained earnings		8,130		6,160
		21,130		16,160
Non-current liabilities				
10% loan notes		Nil		4,000
6% loan notes		2,000		Nil
	20X3		20X2	

	$'000	$'000	$'000	$'000
Current liabilities				
Bank overdraft	1,050		Nil	
Trade payables	2,850		1,980	
Taxation	720		630	
Warranty provision (note (ii))	500	5,120	150	2,760
Total equity and liabilities		28,250		22,920

Notes

(i)   The details of the non-current assets are:

	Cost	Accumulated depreciation	Net book value
	$'000	$'000	$'000
At 31 March 20X2	27,500	10,200	17,300
At 31 March 20X3	37,250	12,750	24,500

During the year there was a major refurbishment of display equipment. Old equipment that had cost $6 million in September 20W8 was replaced with new equipment at a gross cost of $8 million. The equipment manufacturer had allowed Rytetrend a trade in allowance of $500,000 on the old display equipment. In addition to this Rytetrend used its own staff to install the new equipment. The value of staff time spent on the installation has been costed at $300,000, but this has not been included in the cost of the asset. All staff costs have been included in operating expenses. All display equipment held at the end of the financial year is depreciated at 20% on its cost. No equipment is more than five years old.

(ii)   Operating expenses contain a charge of $580,000 for the cost of warranties on the goods sold by Rytetrend. The company makes a warranty provision when it sells its products and cash payments for warranty claims are deducted from the provision as they are settled.

(iii)   Dividends paid in the year ended 31 March 20X3 were $430,000.

Required

(a)   Prepare a cash flow statement for Rytetrend for the year ended 31 March 20X3.   **(12 marks)**

(b)   Write a report briefly analysing the operating performance and financial position of Rytetrend for the years ended 31 March 20X2 and 20X3.   **(13 marks)**

Your report should be supported by appropriate ratios.   **(Total = 25 marks)**

69 Reactive (pilot paper part)   36 mins

Reactive is a publicly listed company that assembles domestic electrical goods which it then sells to both wholesale and retail customers. Reactive's management were disappointed in the company's results for the year ended 31 March 20X5. In an attempt to improve performance the following measures were taken early in the year ended 31 March 20X6:

−   A national advertising campaign was undertaken,

−   Rebates to all wholesale customers purchasing goods above set quantity levels were introduced,

−   The assembly of certain lines ceased and was replaced by bought in completed products. This allowed Reactive to dispose of surplus plant.

Reactive's summarised financial statements for the year ended 31 March 20X6 are set out below:

INCOME STATEMENT

	$million
Revenue (25% cash sales)	4,000
Cost of sales	(3,450)
Gross profit	550
Operating expenses	(370)
	180
Profit on disposal of plant (note (i))	40
Finance charges	(20)
Profit before tax	200
Income tax expense	(50)
Profit for the year	150

STATEMENT OF FINANCIAL POSITION

	$million	$million
Non-current assets		
Property, plant and equipment (note (i))		550
Current assets		
Inventory	250	
Trade receivables	360	
Bank	nil	610
Total assets		1,160
Equity and liabilities		
Equity shares of 25 cents each		100
Retained earnings		380
		480
Non-current liabilities		
8% loan notes		200
Current liabilities		
Bank overdraft	10	
Trade payables	430	
Current tax payable	40	480
Total equity and liabilities		1,160

Below are ratios calculated for the year ended 31 March 20X5.

Return on year end capital employed (profit before interest and tax over total assets less current liabilities)	28.1%
Net asset (equal to capital employed) turnover	4 times
Gross profit margin	17%
Net profit (before tax) margin	6.3%
Current ratio	1.6:1
Closing inventory holding period	46 days
Trade receivables' collection period	45 days
Trade payables' payment period	55 days
Dividend yield	3.75%
Dividend cover	2 times

Notes.

(i) Reactive received $120 million from the sale of plant that had a carrying amount of $80 million at the date of its sale.

(ii) The market price of Reactive's shares throughout the year averaged $3.75 each.

(iii) There were no issues or redemption of shares or loans during the year.

(iv) Dividends paid during the year ended 31 March 20X6 amounted to $90 million, maintaining the same dividend paid in the year ended 31 March 20X5.

Required

(a) Calculate ratios for the year ended 31 March 20X6 (showing your workings) for Reactive, equivalent to those provided above. **(10 marks)**

(b) Analyse the financial performance and position of Reactive for the year ended 31 March 20X6 compared to the previous year. **(10 marks)**

(Total = 20 marks)

70 Greenwood (2.5 6/07)   45 mins

Greenwood is a public listed company. During the year ended 31 March 20X7 the directors decided to cease operations of one of its activities and put the assets of the operation up for sale (the discontinued activity has no associated liabilities). The directors have been advised that the cessation qualifies as a discontinued operation and has been accounted for accordingly.

Extracts from Greenwood's financial statements are set out below.

Note: the income statement figures down to the profit for the period from continuing operations are those of the continuing operations only.

INCOME STATEMENTS FOR THE YEAR ENDED 31 MARCH

	20X7	20X6
	$'000	$'000
Revenue	27,500	21,200
Cost of sales	(19,500)	(15,000)
Gross profit	8,000	6,200
Operating expenses	(2,900)	(2,450)
	5,100	3,750
Finance costs	(600)	(250)
Profit before taxation	4,500	3,500
Income tax expense	(1,000)	(800)
Profit for the period from continuing operations	3,500	2,700
Profit/(loss) from discontinued operations	(1,500)	320
Profit for the year	2,000	3,020
Analysis of discontinued operations:		
Revenue	7,500	9,000
Cost of sales	(8,500)	(8,000)
Gross profit/(loss)	(1,000)	1,000
Operating expenses	(400)	(550)
Profit/(loss) before tax	(1,400)	450
Tax (expense)/relief	300	(130)
	(1,100)	320
Loss on measurement to fair value of disposal group	(500)	–
Tax relief on disposal group	100	–
Profit/(loss) from discontinued operations	(1,500)	320

STATEMENTS OF FINANCIAL POSITION AS AT 31 MARCH

	20X7		20X6	
	$'000	$'000	$'000	$'000
Non-current assets		17,500		17,600
Current assets				
Inventory	1,500		1,350	
Trade receivables	2,000		2,300	
Bank	nil		50	
Assets held for sale (at fair value)	6,000	9,500	nil	3,700
Total assets		27,000		21,300
Equity and liabilities				
Equity shares of $1 each		10,000		10,000
Retained earnings		4,500		2,500
		14,500		12,500
Non-current liabilities				
5% loan notes		8,000		5,000
Current liabilities				
Bank overdraft	1,150		nil	
Trade payables	2,400		2,800	
Current tax payable	950	4,500	1,000	3,800
Total equity and liabilities		27,000		21,300

Note: the carrying amount of the assets of the discontinued operation at 31 March 20X6 was $6·3 million.

Required

Analyse the financial performance and position of Greenwood for the two years ended 31 March 20X7.

Note: Your analysis should be supported by appropriate ratios (up to 10 marks available) and refer to the effects of the discontinued operation.

(25 marks)

71 Victular (12/08)   45 mins

Victular is a public company that would like to acquire (100% of) a suitable private company. It has obtained the following draft financial statements for two companies, Grappa and Merlot. They operate in the same industry and their managements have indicated that they would be receptive to a takeover.

Income statements for the year ended 30 September 2008

		Grappa		Merlot
	$'000	$'000	$'000	$'000
Revenue		12,000		20,500
Cost of sales		(10,500)		(18,000)
Gross profit		1,500		2,500
Operating expenses		(240)		(500)
Finance costs – loan		(210)		(300)
– overdraft		nil		(10)
– lease		nil		(290)
Profit before tax		1,050		1,400
Income tax expense		(150)		(400)
Profit for the year		900		1,000
Note: dividends paid during the year		250		700

Statements of financial position as at 30 September 2008

	$'000	Grappa $'000	$'000	Merlot $'000
Assets				
Non-current assets				
Freehold factory (note (i))		4,400		nil
Owned plant (note (ii))		5,000		2,200
Leased plant (note (ii))		nil		5,300
		9,400		7,500
Current assets				
Inventory	2,000		3,600	
Trade receivables	2,400		3,700	
Bank	600		nil	
		5,000		7,300
Total assets		14,400		14,800
Equity and liabilities				
Equity shares of $1 each		2,000		2,000
Property revaluation reserve	900		nil	
Retained earnings	2,600		800	
		3,500		800
		5,500		2,800
Non-current liabilities				
Finance lease obligations (note (iii))	nil		3,200	
7% loan notes	3,000		nil	
10% loan notes	nil		3,000	
Deferred tax	600		100	
Government grants	1,200		nil	
		4,800		6,300
Current liabilities				
Bank overdraft	nil		1,200	
Trade payables	3,100		3,800	
Government grants	400		nil	
Finance lease obligations (note (iii))	nil		500	
Taxation	600		200	
		4,100		5,700
Total equity and liabilities		14,400		14,800

Notes

(i)   Both companies operate from similar premises.

(ii) Additional details of the two companies' plant are:

	Grappa $'000	Merlot $'000
Owned plant – cost	8,000	10,000
Leased plant – original fair value	nil	7,500

There were no disposals of plant during the year by either company.

(iii) The interest rate implicit within Merlot's finance leases is 7·5% per annum. For the purpose of calculating ROCE and gearing, all finance lease obligations are treated as long-term interest bearing borrowings.

(iv)   The following ratios have been calculated for Grappa and can be taken to be correct:

Return on year end capital employed (ROCE)   14.8%
(capital employed taken as shareholders' funds plus long-term interest bearing
borrowings – see note (iii) above)
Pre-tax return on equity (ROE)   19.1%
Net asset (total assets less current liabilities) turnover   1.2 times
Gross profit margin   12.5%
Operating profit margin   10.5%
Current ratio   1.2:1
Closing inventory holding period   70 days
Trade receivables' collection period   73 days
Trade payables' payment period (using cost of sales)   108 days
Gearing (see note (iii) above)   35.3%
Interest cover   6 times
Dividend cover   3·6 times

Required

(a)   Calculate for Merlot the ratios equivalent to all those given for Grappa above.   **(8 marks)**

(b)   Assess the relative performance and financial position of Grappa and Merlot for the year ended 30
       September 2008 to inform the directors of Victular in their acquisition decision.   **(12 marks)**

(c)   Explain the limitations of ratio analysis and any further information that may be useful to the directors of
       Victular when making an acquisition decision.   **(5 marks)**

                                                                                        (Total = 25 marks)

72 Harbin (12/07)   **45 mins**

Shown below are the recently issued (summarised) financial statements of Harbin, a listed company, for the year
ended 30 September 2007, together with comparatives for 2006 and extracts from the Chief Executive's report that
accompanied their issue.

INCOME STATEMENT

	2007	2006
	$'000	$'000
Revenue	250,000	180,000
Cost of sales	(200,000)	(150,000)
Gross profit	50,000	30,000
Operating expenses	(26,000)	(22,000)
Finance costs	(8,000)	(nil)
Profit before tax	16,000	8,000
Income tax expense (at 25%)	(4,000)	(2,000)
Profit for the year	12,000	6,000

STATEMENT OF FINANCIAL POSITION

Non-current assets		
Property, plant and equipment	210,000	90,000
Goodwill	10,000	nil
	220,000	90,000
Current assets		
Inventory	25,000	15,000
Trade receivables	13,000	8,000
Bank	nil	14,000
	38,000	37,000
Total assets	258,000	127,000
Equity and liabilities		
Equity shares of $1 each	100,000	100,000
Retained earnings	14,000	12,000
	114,000	112,000
Non-current liabilities		
8% loan notes	100,000	nil
Current liabilities		
Bank overdraft	17,000	nil
Trade payables	23,000	13,000
Current tax payable	4,000	2,000
	44,000	15,000
Total equity and liabilities	258,000	127,000

Extracts from the Chief Executive's report:

'Highlights of Harbin's performance for the year ended 30 September 2007:

> an increase in sales revenue of 39%
> gross profit margin up from 16·7% to 20%
> a doubling of the profit for the period.

In response to the improved position the Board paid a dividend of 10 cents per share in September 2007 an increase of 25% on the previous year.'

You have also been provided with the following further information.

On 1 October 2006 Harbin purchased the whole of the net assets of Fatima (previously a privately owned entity) for $100 million. The contribution of the purchase to Harbin's results for the year ended 30 September 2007 was:

	$'000
Revenue	70,000
Cost of sales	(40,000)
Gross profit	30,000
Operating expenses	(8,000)
Profit before tax	22,000

There were no disposals of non-current assets during the year.

The following ratios have been calculated for Harbin for the year ended 30 September 2006:

Return on year-end capital employed	7.1%
(profit before interest and tax over total assets less current liabilities)	
Net asset (equal to capital employed) turnover	1.6
Net profit (before tax) margin	4.4%
Current ratio	2.5
Closing inventory holding period (in days)	37
Trade receivables' collection period (in days)	16
Trade payables' payment period (based on cost of sales) (in days)	32
Gearing (debt over debt plus equity)	nil

Required

(a)   Calculate ratios for Harbin for the year ended 30 September 2007 equivalent to those calculated for the year
       ended 30 September 2006 (showing your workings).   **(8 marks)**

(b)   Assess the financial performance and position of Harbin for the year ended 30 September 2007 compared to
       the previous year. Your answer should refer to the information in the Chief Executive's report and the impact
       of the purchase of the net assets of Fatima.   **(17 marks)**

(Total = 25 marks)

73 Breadline (2.5 6/02)   45 mins

You are the assistant financial controller of Judicious. One of your company's credit controllers has asked you to
consider the account balance of one of your customers, Breadline. He is concerned at the pattern of payments and
increasing size and age of the account balance. As part of company policy he has obtained the most recently filed
financial statements of Breadline and these are summarised below. A note to the financial statements of Breadline
states that it is a wholly owned subsidiary of Wheatmaster, and its main activities are the production and
distribution of bakery products to wholesalers. By coincidence your company's Chief Executive has been made
aware that Breadline may be available for sale. She has asked for your opinion on whether Breadline would make a
suitable addition to the group's portfolio.

BREADLINE
INCOME STATEMENT YEAR TO:

	31 December 20X1		31 December 20X0	
	$'000	$'000	$'000	$'000
Sales revenue		8,500		6,500
Cost of sales		(5,950)		(4,810)
Gross profit		2,550		1,690
Operating expenses		(560)		(660)
Finance costs: loan note	10		nil	
Overdraft	10		5	
		(20)		(5)
Profit before tax		1,970		1,025
Taxation		(470)		(175)
Profit for the year		1,500		850

STATEMENTS OF FINANCIAL POSITION AS AT:

	31 December 20X1		31 December 20X0	
	$'000	$'000	$'000	$'000
Non-current assets				
Freehold premises at valuation		nil		1,250
Leasehold premises		2,500		nil
Plant		1,620		750
		4,120		2,000
Current assets				
Inventory	370		240	
Accounts receivable	960		600	
Bank	nil		250	
		1,330		1,090
Total assets		5,450		3,090
Equity and liabilities				
Equity				
Ordinary shares of $1 each		500		100
Reserves				
Share premium	200		nil	
Revaluation surplus				
(re freehold premises)	nil		700	
Retained earnings	3,000		1,700	
		3,200		2,400
		3,700		2,500
Non-current liabilities				
2% loan note		500		nil
Current liabilities				
Accounts payable	1,030		590	
Overdraft	220		nil	
		1,250		590
Total equity and liabilities		5,450		3,090

From your company's own records you have ascertained that sales to Breadline for the year to 20X1 and 20X0 were $1,200,000 and $800,000 respectively and the year-end account balances were $340,000 and $100,000 respectively. Normal credit terms, which should apply to Breadline, are that payment is due 30 days after the end of the month of sale. You are also aware that the company has not changed its address and is trading from the same premises. A note to Breadline's financial statements says that the profit on the disposal of its freehold premises has been included in cost of sales as this is where the depreciation on the freehold was charged. Dividends of $900,000 were paid in 20X1. No dividends were paid in 20X0.

Note. a commercial rate of interest on the loan note of Breadline would be 8% per annum.

Required

(a)   Describe the matters that may be relevant when entity financial statements are used to assess the performance of a company that is a wholly owned subsidiary.   **(5 marks)**

   Note. Your answer should give attention to related party issues.

(b)   From the information above and with the aid of suitable ratios, prepare a report for your Chief Executive on the overall financial position of Breadline. Your answer should include reference to matters in the financial statements of Breadline that may give you cause for concern or require further investigation.   **(20 marks)**

(Total = 25 marks)

74 Toogood (2.5 6/07)   45 mins

(a)   A trainee accountant has been assisting in the preparation of the financial statements of Toogood for the
        year ended 31 March 20X7. He has observed that the corresponding figures (ie for the year ended 31 March
        20X6) in the financial statements for the year ended 31 March 20X7 do not agree in several instances with
        the equivalent figures that were published in the company's financial statements for year ended 31 March
        20X6. In particular:

            Non-current assets have been revised,
            The brought forward retained earnings have been restated and;
            Several income statement line items are also different.

        The trainee accountant has also noted that even when the revised earnings figure for the year ended 31
        March 20X6 is divided by the weighted average number of shares in issue during that year, it still does not
        agree with the comparative earnings per share figure (ie for the year ended 31 March 20X6) reported in the
        financial statements for the year ended 31 March 20X7.

        Required

        Explain three circumstances where accounting standards require previously reported financial statement
        figures to be amended when they are reproduced as corresponding amounts.

        Note. It may help to consider, among other things, the items mentioned by the trainee accountant.

                                                                                          (12 marks)

(b)   The trainee accountant has been reading some literature written by a qualified surveyor on the values of
        leasehold property located in the area where Toogood owns leasehold property. The main thrust is that
        historically, annual increases in property prices more than compensate for the fall in the carrying amount
        caused by annual amortisation until a leasehold property has less than 10 years of remaining life. Therefore
        the trainee accountant suggests that the company should adopt a policy of carrying its leasehold properties
        at cost until their remaining lives are 10 years and then amortising them on a straight-line basis over 10
        years. This would improve the company's reported profit and cash flows as well as showing a faithful
        representation of the value of the leasehold properties.

        Required

        Comment on the validity and acceptability of the trainee accountant's suggestion.   (7 marks)

(c)   The trainee accountant notes that Toogood acquired the Trilogy group during the year ended 31 March
        20X7. The Trilogy group consists of Trilogy itself and two wholly owned subsidiaries. Toogood has only
        consolidated Trilogy and one subsidiary with the other subsidiary being shown as a current asset. The
        trainee accountant wonders if this is because the non-consolidated subsidiary is making losses.

        Required

        Explain why the two subsidiaries may require the different treatments that Toogood has applied.   (6 marks)

                                                                                      (Total = 25 marks)

75 Waxwork (6/09)   27 mins

(a)   The objective of IAS 10 *Events After the Reporting Period* is to prescribe the treatment of events that occur
        after an entity's reporting period has ended.

        Required

        Define the period to which IAS 10 relates and distinguish between adjusting and non-adjusting events.

                                                                                           (5 marks)

(b)   Waxwork's current year end is 31 March 2009. Its financial statements were authorised for issue by its
        directors on 6 May 2009 and the AGM (annual general meeting) will be held on 3 June 2009. The following
        matters have been brought to your attention:

(i) On 12 April 2009 a fire completely destroyed the company's largest warehouse and the inventory it contained. The carrying amounts of the warehouse and the inventory were $10 million and $6 million respectively. It appears that the company has not updated the value of its insurance cover and only expects to be able to recover a maximum of $9 million from its insurers. Waxwork's trading operations have been severely disrupted since the fire and it expects large trading losses for some time to come. **(4 marks)**

(ii) A single class of inventory held at another warehouse was valued at its cost of $460,000 at 31 March 2009. In April 2009 70% of this inventory was sold for $280,000 on which Waxworks' sales staff earned a commission of 15% of the selling price. **(3 marks)**

(iii) On 18 May 2009 the government announced tax changes which have the effect of increasing Waxwork's deferred tax liability by $650,000 as at 31 March 2009. **(3 marks)**

Required

Explain the required treatment of the items (i) to (iii) by Waxwork in its financial statements for the year ended 31 March 2009.

Note: assume all items are material and are independent of each other. **(10 marks as indicated)**

(Total =15 marks)

76 Preparation question: Dickson

Below are the statements of financial position of Dickson as at 31 March 20X8 and 31 March 20X7, together with the income statement for the year ended 31 March 20X8.

	20X8 $'000	20X7 $'000
Non-current assets		
Property, plant and equipment	825	637
Goodwill	100	100
Development expenditure	290	160
	1,215	897
Current assets		
Inventories	360	227
Trade receivables	274	324
Investments	143	46
Cash	29	117
	806	714
	2,021	1,611
Equity		
Share capital – $1 ordinary shares	500	400
Share premium	350	100
Revaluation surplus	152	60
Retained earnings	237	255
	1,239	815
Non-current liabilities		
6% debentures	150	100
Finance lease liabilities	100	80
Deferred tax	48	45
	298	225
Current liabilities		
Trade payables	274	352
Finance lease liabilities	17	12
Current tax	56	153
Debenture interest	5	–
Bank overdraft	132	54
	484	571
	2,021	1,611

INCOME STATEMENT

	$'000
Revenue	1,476
Cost of sales	(962)
Gross profit	514
Other expenses	(157)
Finance costs	(15)
Profit before tax	342
Income tax expense	(162)
Profit for the year	180
Dividends paid during the period	156

Notes

(1)   Goodwill arose on the acquisition of unincorporated businesses. During 20X8 expenditure on development projects totalled $190,000.

(2)   During 20X8 items of property, plant and equipment with a net book value of $103,000 were sold for $110,000. Depreciation charged in the year on property, plant and equipment totalled $57,000. Dickson transfers extra depreciation on revalued property, plant and equipment to retained earnings as allowed by IAS 16. Depreciation based on historical cost in 20X8 is $49,000. Dickson purchased $56,000 of property, plant and equipment by means of finance leases, payments being made in arrears on the last day of each accounting period.

(3)   The current asset investments are government bonds and management has decided to class them as cash equivalents.

(4)   The new debentures were issued on 1.4.X7. Finance cost includes debenture interest and finance lease finance charges only.

(5)   During the year Dickson made a 1 for 8 bonus issue capitalising its retained earnings followed by a rights issue.

Required

(a)   Prepare a statement of cash flows for Dickson in accordance with IAS 7 using the indirect method.

(b)   Prepare (additionally) net cash from operating activities using the direct method.

(a)

DICKSON
STATEMENT OF CASH FLOWS FOR YEAR ENDED 31 MARCH 20X8

	$'000	$'000
Cash flows from operating activities		
Profit before taxation		
Adjustments for:		
Depreciation		
Amortisation		
Interest expense		
Profit on disposal of assets		
Movement in trade receivables		
Movement in inventories		
Movement in trade payables		
Cash generated from operations		
Interest paid		
Income taxes paid		
Net cash from operating activities		
Cash flows from investing activities		
Development expenditure		
Purchase of property, plant & equipment		
Proceeds from sale of property, plant & equipment		
Net cash used in investing activities		
Cash flows from financing activities		
Proceeds from issue of shares		
Proceeds from issue of debentures		
Payment of finance lease liabilities		
Dividends paid		
Net cash from financing activities		
Net decrease in cash and cash equivalents		
Cash and cash equivalents at beginning of period		
Cash and cash equivalent at end of period		

(b)   CASH FLOWS FROM OPERATING ACTIVITIES (Direct method)

$'000

Cash received from customers
Cash paid to suppliers and employees
Cash generated from operations
Interest paid
Income taxes paid
Net cash from operating activities

Workings

77 Bigwood (2.5 12/04)   **45 mins**

Bigwood, a public company, is a high street retailer that sells clothing and food. The managing director is very
disappointed with the current year's results. The company expanded its operations and commissioned a famous
designer to restyle its clothing products. This has led to increased sales in both retail lines, yet overall profits are
down.

Details of the financial statements for the two years to 30 September 20X4 are shown below.

INCOME STATEMENT:	Year to 30 September 20X4		Year to 30 September 20X3	
	$'000	$'000	$'000	$'000
Revenue – clothing	16,000		15,600	
– food	7,000	23,000	4,000	19,600
Cost of sales – clothing	14,500		12,700	
– food	4,750	(19,250)	3,000	(15,700)
Gross profit		3,750		3,900
Other operating expenses		(2,750)		(1,900)
Operating profit		1,000		2,000
Interest expense		(300)		(80)
Profit before tax		700		1,920
Income tax expense		(250)		(520)
Profit for the year		450		1,400

SUMMARISED CHANGES IN EQUITY:	Year to 30 September 20X4	Year to 30 September 20X3
	$'000	$'000
Retained profit b/f	1,900	1,100
Profit for the year	450	1,400
Dividends paid	(600)	(600)
Retained profit c/f	1,750	1,900

STATEMENTS OF FINANCIAL POSITION AS AT:	30 September 20X4		30 September 20X3	
	$'000	$'000	$'000	$'000
Property, plant and equipment at cost		17,000		9,500
Accumulated depreciation		(5,000)		(3,000)
		12,000		6,500
Current assets				
Inventory – clothing	2,700		1,360	
– food	200		140	
Trade receivables	100		50	
Bank	Nil	3,000	450	2,000
Total assets		15,000		8,500
Equity and liabilities				
Issued ordinary capital ($1 shares)		5,000		3,000
Share premium		1,000		Nil
Retained earnings		1,750		1,900
		7,750		4,900
Non-current liabilities				
Long-term loans		3,000		1,000
Current liabilities				
Bank overdraft	930		nil	
Trade payables	3,100		2,150	
Current tax payable	220	4,250	450	2,600
		15,000		8,500

Note. The directors have signalled their intention to maintain annual dividends at $600,000 for the foreseeable future.

The following information is relevant:

(i)   The increase in property, plant and equipment was due to the acquisition of five new stores and the refurbishment of some existing stores during the year. The carrying value of fixtures scrapped at the refurbished stores was $1.2 million; they had originally cost $3 million. Bigwood received no scrap proceeds from the fixtures, but did incur costs of $50,000 to remove and dispose of them. The losses on the refurbishment have been charged to operating expenses. Depreciation is charged to cost of sales apportioned in relation to floor area (see below).

(ii)   The floor sales areas (in square metres) were:

	30 September 20X4	30 September 20X3
Clothing	48,000	35,000
Food	6,000	5,000
	54,000	40,000

(iii)   The share price of Bigwood averaged $6.00 during the year to 30 September 20X3, but was only $3.00 at 30 September 20X4.

(iv)   The following ratios have been calculated:

	20X4	20X3
Return on capital employed	9.3%	33.9%
Net assets turnover	2.1 times	3.3 times
Gross profit margin		
– clothing	9.4%	18.6%
– food	32.1%	25%
Net profit (after tax) margin	2.0%	7.1%
Current ratio	0.71:1	0.77 :1
Inventory holding period		
– clothing	68 days	39 days
– food	15 days	17 days
Accounts payment period	59 days	50 days
Gearing	28%	17%
Interest cover	3.3 times	25 times

Required

(a)   Prepare, using the indirect method, a statement of cash flows for Bigwood for the year to 30 September 20X4   **(12 marks)**

(b)   Write a report analysing the financial performance and financial position of Bigwood for the two years ended 30 September 20X4.   **(13 marks)**

        Your report should utilise the above ratios and the information in your statement of cash flows. It should refer to the relative performance of the clothing and food sales and be supported by any further ratios you consider appropriate.

                                                                                        (Total = 25 marks)

78 Casino (2.5 6/05)

45 mins

(a) Casino is a publicly listed company. Details of its statements of financial position as at 31 March 20X5 and 20X4 are shown below together with other relevant information

STATEMENT OF FINANCIAL POSITION AS AT	31 March 20X5		31 March 20X4	
Non-current assets (note (i))	$m	$m	$m	$m
Property, plant and equipment		880		760
Intangible assets		400		510
		1,280		1,270
Current assets				
Inventory	350		420	
Trade receivables	808		372	
Interest receivable	5		3	
Short term deposits	32		120	
Bank	15	1,210	75	990
Total assets		2,490		2,260
Share capital and reserves				
Ordinary shares of $1 each		300		200
Reserves				
Share premium	60		Nil	
Revaluation reserve	112		45	
Retained earnings	1,098		1,165	
		1,270		1,210
		1,570		1,410
Non-current liabilities				
12% loan note	Nil		150	
8% variable rate loan note	160		Nil	
Deferred tax	90	250	75	225
Current liabilities				
Trade payables	530		515	
Bank overdraft	125		Nil	
Taxation	15		110	
		670		625
Total equity and liabilities		2,490		2,260

The following supporting information is available:

(i) Details relating to the non-current assets are:

Property, plant and equipment at:

	31 March 20X5			31 March 20X4		
	Cost/ valuation	Depreci- ation	Carrying value	Cost/ valuation	Depreci- ation	Carrying value
	$m	$m	$m	$m	$m	$m
Land & buildings	600	12	588	500	80	420
Plant	440	148	292	445	105	340
			880			760

Casino revalued the carrying value of its land and buildings by an increase of $70 million on 1 April 20X4. On 31 March 20X5 Casino transferred $3 million from the revaluation reserve to retained earnings representing the realisation of the revaluation reserve due to the depreciation of buildings.

During the year Casino acquired new plant at a cost of $60 million and sold some old plant for $15 million at a loss of $12 million.

There were no acquisitions or disposals of intangible assets.

(ii)   The following extract is from the draft income statement for the year to 31 March 20X5:

	$m	$m
Operating loss		(32)
Interest receivable		12
Finance costs		(24)
Loss before tax		(44)
Income tax repayment claim	14	
Deferred tax charge	(15)	
		(1)
Loss for the year		(45)

The finance costs are made up of:

Interest expense	(16)
Penalty cost for early redemption of fixed rate loan	(6)
Issue costs of variable rate loan	(2)
	(24)

(iii)   The short term deposits meet the definition of cash equivalents.

(iv)   Dividends of $25 million were paid during the year.

Required

As far as the information permits, prepare a statement of cash flows for Casino for the year to 31 March 20X5 in accordance with IAS 7 *Statement of cash flows*.   **(20 marks)**

(b)   In recent years many analysts have commented on a growing disillusionment with the usefulness and reliability of the information contained in some companies' income statements.

Required

Discuss the extent to which a company's statement of cash flows may be more useful and reliable than its income statement.   **(5 marks)**

(Total = 25 marks)

79 Tabba (2.5 12/05)   45 mins

The following draft financial statements relate to Tabba, a private company.

Statements of financial position as at:	30 September 20X5		30 September 20X4	
	$'000	$'000	$'000	$'000
Property, plant and equipment (note (ii))		10,600		15,800
Current assets				
Inventories	2,550		1,850	
Trade receivables	3,100		2,600	
Insurance claim (note (iii))	1,500		1,200	
Cash and bank	850		nil	
		8,000		5,650
Total assets		18,600		21,450
Equity				
Share capital ($1 each)		6,000		6,000
Reserves:				
Revaluation (note (ii))	nil		1,600	
Retained earnings	2,550		850	
		2,550		2,450
		8,550		8,450

Statements of financial position as at:	30 September 20X5		30 September 20X4	
	$'000	$'000	$'000	$'000
Non–current liabilities				
Finance lease obligations (note (ii))	2,000		1,700	
6% loan notes	800		nil	
10% loan notes	nil		4,000	
Deferred tax	200		500	
Government grants (note (ii))	1,400		900	
		4,400		7,100
Current liabilities				
Bank overdraft	nil		550	
Trade payables	4,050		2,950	
Government grants (note (ii))	600		400	
Finance lease obligations (note (ii))	900		800	
Current tax payable	100		1,200	
		5,650		5,900
Total equity and liabilities		18,600		21,450

The following additional information is relevant:

(i) Income statement extract for the year ended 30 September 20X5:

	$'000
Operating profit before interest and tax	270
Interest expense	(260)
Interest receivable	40
Profit before tax	50
Net income tax credit	50
Profit for the year	100

Note. The interest expense includes finance lease interest.

(ii) The details of the property, plant and equipment are:

	Cost $'000	Acc'd depreciation $'000	Carrying value $'000
At 30 September 20X4	20,200	4,400	15,800
At 30 September 20X5	16,000	5,400	10,600

During the year Tabba sold its factory for its fair value $12 million and agreed to rent it back, under an operating lease, for a period of five years at $1 million per annum. At the date of sale it had a carrying value of $7.4 million based on a previous revaluation of $8.6 million less depreciation of $1.2 million since the revaluation. The profit on the sale of the factory has been included in operating profit. The surplus on the revaluation reserve related entirely to the factory. No other disposals of non–current assets were made during the year.

Plant acquired under finance leases during the year was $1.5 million. Other purchases of plant during the year qualified for government grants of $950,000.

Amortisation of government grants has been credited to cost of sales.

(iii) The insurance claim related to flood damage to the company's inventories which occurred in September 20X4. The original estimate has been revised during the year after negotiations with the insurance company. The claim is expected to be settled in the near future.

Required

(a) Prepare a statement of cash flows using the indirect method for Tabba in accordance with IAS 7 *Statement of Cash Flows* for the year ended 30 September 20X5. **(17 marks)**

(b) Using the information in the question and your statement of cash flows, comment on the change in the financial position of Tabba during the year ended 30 September 20X5. **(8 marks)**

Note. You are not required to calculate any ratios.

(Total = 25 marks)

80 Minster (2.5 12/06)

45 mins

Minster is a publicly listed company. Details of its financial statements for the year ended 30 September 20X6, together with a comparative statement of financial position, are:

STATEMENT OF FINANCIAL POSITION AT

	30 September 20X6		30 September 20X5	
	$'000	$'000	$'000	$'000
Non-current assets (note (i))				
Property, plant and equipment		1,280		940
Software		135		nil
Investments at fair value through profit and loss		150		125
		1,565		1,065
Current assets				
Inventories	480		510	
Trade receivables	270		380	
Amounts due from construction contracts	80		55	
Bank	nil		35	
		830		980
Total assets		2,395		2,045
Equity and liabilities				
Equity shares of 25 cents each		500		300
Reserves				
Share premium (note (ii))	150		85	
Revaluation reserve	60		25	
Retained earnings	950		965	
		1,160		1,075
		1,660		1,375
Non-current liabilities				
9% loan note	120		nil	
Environmental provision	162		nil	
Deferred tax	18		25	
		300		25
Current liabilities				
Trade payables	350		555	
Bank overdraft	25		40	
Current tax payable	60		50	
Total equity and liabilities		435		645
		2,395		2,045

INCOME STATEMENT FOR THE YEAR ENDED 30 SEPTEMBER 20X6

	$'000
Revenue	1,397
Cost of sales	(1,110)
Gross profit	287
Operating expenses	(125)
	162
Finance costs (note (i))	(40)
Investment income and gain on investments	20
Profit before tax	142
Income tax expense	(57)
Profit for the year	85

The following supporting information is available:

(i) Included in property, plant and equipment is a coal mine and related plant that Minster purchased on 1 October 20X5. Legislation requires that in ten years' time (the estimated life of the mine) Minster will have to landscape the area affected by the mining. The future cost of this has been estimated and discounted at a rate of 8% to a present value of $150,000. This cost has been included in the carrying amount of the mine and, together with the unwinding of the discount, has also been treated as a provision. The unwinding of the discount is included within finance costs in the income statement.

Other land was revalued (upward) by $35,000 during the year.

Depreciation of property, plant and equipment for the year was $255,000.

There were no disposals of property, plant and equipment during the year.

The software was purchased on 1 April 20X6 for $180,000.

The market value of the investments had increased during the year by $15,000. There have been no sales of these investments during the year.

(ii) On 1 April 20X6 there was a bonus (scrip) issue of equity shares of one for every four held utilising the share premium reserve. A further cash share issue was made on 1 June 20X6. No shares were redeemed during the year.

(iii) A dividend of 5 cents per share was paid on 1 July 20X6.

Required

(a) Prepare a statement of cash flows for Minster for the year to 30 September 20X6 in accordance with IAS 7 *Statement of cash flows*.

(15 marks)

(b) Comment on the financial performance and position of Minster as revealed by the above financial statements and your statement of cash flows.

(10 marks)

(Total = 25 marks)

81 Pinto (6/08)

45 mins

Pinto is a publicly listed company. The following financial statements of Pinto are available:

STATEMENT OF COMPREHENSIVE INCOME FOR THE YEAR ENDED 31 MARCH 2008

	$'000
Revenue	5,740
Cost of sales	(4,840)
Gross profit	900
Income from and gains on investment property	60
Distribution costs	(120)
Administrative expenses (note (ii))	(350)
Finance costs	(50)
Profit before tax	440
Income tax expense	(160)
Profit for the year	280
Other comprehensive income	
Gains on property revaluation	100
Total comprehensive income	380

STATEMENTS OF FINANCIAL POSITION AS AT

	31 March 2008		31 March 2007	
	$'000	$'000	$'000	$'000
Assets				
Non-current assets (note (i))				
Property, plant and equipment		2,880		1,860
Investment property		420		400
		3,300		2,260
Current assets				
Inventory	1,210		810	
Trade receivables	480		540	
Income tax asset	nil		50	
Bank	10	1,700	nil	1,400
Total assets		5,000		3,660
Equity and liabilities				
Equity shares of 20 cents each (note (iii))		1,000		600
Share premium	600		nil	
Revaluation reserve	150		50	
Retained earnings	1,440	2,190	1,310	1,360
		3,190		1,960

	31 March 2008		31 March 2007	
	$'000	$'000	$'000	$'000
Non-current liabilities				
6% loan notes (note (ii))	nil		400	
Deferred tax	50	50	30	430
Current liabilities				
Trade payables	1,410		1,050	
Bank overdraft	nil		120	
Warranty provision (note (iv))	200		100	
Current tax payable	150	1,760	nil	1,270
Total equity and liabilities		5,000		3,660

The following supporting information is available:

(i) An item of plant with a carrying amount of $240,000 was sold at a loss of $90,000 during the year. Depreciation of $280,000 was charged (to cost of sales) for property, plant and equipment in the year ended 31 March 2008.

Pinto uses the fair value model in IAS 40 *Investment Property*. There were no purchases or sales of investment property during the year.

(ii) The 6% loan notes were redeemed early incurring a penalty payment of $20,000 which has been charged as an administrative expense in the income statement.

(iii) There was an issue of shares for cash on 1 October 2007. There were no bonus issues of shares during the year.

(iv) Pinto gives a 12 month warranty on some of the products it sells. The amounts shown in current liabilities as warranty provision are an accurate assessment, based on past experience, of the amount of claims likely to be made in respect of warranties outstanding at each year end. Warranty costs are included in cost of sales.

(v) A dividend of 3 cents per share was paid on 1 January 2008.

Required

(a) Prepare a statement of cash flows for Pinto for the year to 31 March 2008 in accordance with IAS 7 *Statement of cash flows*. **(15 marks)**

(b) Comment on the cash flow management of Pinto as revealed by the statement of cash flows and the information provided by the above financial statements.

Note. ratio analysis is not required, and will not be awarded any marks. **(10 marks)**

(Total = 25 marks)

82 Coaltown (6/09)

45 mins

(a) Coaltown is a wholesaler and retailer of office furniture. Extracts from the company's financial statements are set out below:

Statements of comprehensive income for the year ended:

	31 March 2009		31 March 2008	
	$'000	$'000	$'000	$'000
Revenue – cash	12,800		26,500	
– credit	53,000	65,800	28,500	55,000
Cost of sales		(43,800)		(33,000)
Gross profit		22,000		22,000
Operating expenses		(11,200)		(6,920)
Finance costs – loan notes	(380)		(180)	
– overdraft	(220)	(600)	nil	(180)
Profit before tax		10,200		14,900
Income tax expense		(3,200)		(4,400)
Profit for period		7,000		10,500
Other comprehensive income				
Gain on property revaluation		5,000		1,200
Total comprehensive income for the year		12,000		11,700

Statement of changes in equity for the year ended 31 March 2009:

	Equity shares	Share premium	Revaluation reserve	Retained earnings	Total
	$'000	$'000	$'000	$'000	$'000
Balances b/f	8,000	500	2,500	15,800	26,800
Share issue	8,600	4,300			12,900
Comprehensive income			5,000	7,000	12,000
Dividends paid				(4,000)	(4,000)
Balances c/f	16,600	4,800	7,500	18,800	47,700

Statements of financial position as at 31 March:

	2009		2008	
	$'000	$'000	$'000	$'000
Assets				
Non-current assets (see note)				
Cost		93,500		80,000
Accumulated depreciation		(43,000)		(48,000)
		50,500		32,000
Current assets				
Inventory	5,200		4,400	
Trade receivables	7,800		2,800	
Bank	nil	13,000	700	7,900
Total assets		63,500		39,900
Equity and liabilities				
Equity shares of $1 each		16,600		8,000
Share premium		4,800		500
Revaluation reserve		7,500		2,500
Retained earnings		18,800		15,800
		47,700		26,800
Non-current liabilities				
10% loan notes		4,000		3,000
Current liabilities				
Bank overdraft	3,600		nil	
Trade payables	4,200		4,500	
Taxation	3,000		5,300	
Warranty provision	1,000	11,800	300	10,100
		63,500		39,900

Note

Non-current assets

During the year the company redesigned its display areas in all of its outlets. The previous displays had cost $10 million and had been written down by $9 million. There was an unexpected cost of $500,000 for the removal and disposal of the old display areas. Also during the year the company revalued the carrying amount of its property upwards by $5 million, the accumulated depreciation on these properties of $2 million was reset to zero.

All depreciation is charged to operating expenses.

Required

(a) Prepare a statement of cash flows for Coaltown for the year ended 31 March 2009 in accordance with IAS 7 *Statement of Cash Flows* by the indirect method. **(15 marks)**

(b) The directors of Coaltown are concerned at the deterioration in its bank balance and are surprised that the amount of gross profit has not increased for the year ended 31 March 2009. At the beginning of the current accounting period (ie on 1 April 2008), the company changed to importing its purchases from a foreign supplier because the trade prices quoted by the new supplier were consistently 10% below those of its previous supplier. However, the new supplier offered a shorter period of credit than the previous supplier (all purchases are on credit). In order to encourage higher sales, Coaltown increased its credit period to its customers, and some of the cost savings (on trade purchases) were passed on to customers by reducing selling prices on both cash and credit sales by 5% across all products.

Required

(i) Calculate the gross profit margin that you would have expected Coaltown to achieve for the year ended 31 March 2009 based on the selling and purchase price changes described by the directors; **(2 marks)**

(ii) Comment on the directors' surprise at the unchanged gross profit and suggest what other factors may have affected gross profit for the year ended 31 March 2009; **(4 marks)**

(iii) Applying the trade receivables and payables credit periods for the year ended 31 March 2008 to the credit sales and purchases of the year ended 31 March 2009, calculate the effect this would have had on the company's bank balance at 31 March 2009 assuming sales and purchases would have remained unchanged. **(4 marks)**

Note: the inventory at 31 March 2008 was unchanged from that at 31 March 2007; assume 365 trading days.

(Total = 25 marks)

83 Preparation question: Changing prices

The following information has been extracted from the accounts of Norwich prepared under the historical cost convention for 20X6.

INCOME STATEMENT EXTRACTS 20X6

	$m
Revenue	200
Profit	15
Less finance costs	3
Profit for the year	12

SUMMARISED STATEMENT OF FINANCIAL POSITION AT 31 DECEMBER 20X6

Assets	$m	$m
Property, plant & equipment at cost less depreciation		60
Current assets		
Inventories	20	
Receivables	30	
Bank	2	
		52
Total assets		112
Equity and liabilities		
Equity		62
Non-current liabilities		20
Current liabilities		30
Total equity and liabilities		112

The company's accountant has prepared the following current cost data.

	$m
Current cost adjustments for 20X6	
Depreciation adjustment	3
Cost of sales adjustment	5
Replacement cost at 31 December 20X6	
Property, plant & equipment, net of depreciation	85
Inventories	21

Required

(a) Calculate the current cost operating profit of Norwich for 20X6 and the summarised current cost statement of financial position of the company at 31 December 20X6, so far as the information permits.

(b) Calculate the following ratios from both the historical cost accounts and current cost accounts:

   (i)   Interest cover
   (ii)   Rate of return on shareholders' equity
   (iii) Debt/equity ratio

(c) Discuss the significance of the ratios calculated under (b) and of the reasons for differences between them.

Note. Ignore taxation.

Approaching the question

1   To save time in this question, the current cost adjustments are given to you. You should, of course, understand how they are calculated.

2   Part (b) is straightforward. Make sure you allow yourself time to give adequate weight to the discussion in part (c).

84 Update (2.5 6/03 part)   22 mins

Most companies prepare their financial statements under the historical cost convention. In times of rising prices it has been said that without modification such financial statements can be misleading.

Required

(a) Explain the problems that can be encountered when users rely on financial statements prepared under the historical cost convention for their information needs.   **(6 marks)**

Note. Your answer should consider problems with the income statement and the statement of financial position.

(b) Update has been considering the effect of alternative methods of preparing their financial statements. As an example they picked an item of plant that they acquired from Suppliers on 1 April 20X0 at a cost of $250,000.

The following details have been obtained:

–   the company policy is to depreciate plant at 20% per annum on the reducing balance basis.

–   the movement in the retail price index has been:

1 April 20X0	180
1 April 20X1	202
1 April 20X2	206
31 March 20X3	216

–   Suppliers' price catalogue at 31 March 20X3 shows an item of similar plant at a cost of $320,000. On reading the specification it appears that the new model can produce 480 units per hour whereas the model owned by Update can only produce 420 units per hour.

Required

Calculate for Update the depreciation charge for the plant for the year to 31 March 20X3 (based on year end values) and its carrying value in the statement of financial position on that date using:

–   the historical cost basis;
–   a current purchasing power basis; and
–   a current cost basis.   **(6 marks)**

(Total = 12 marks)

85 Appraisal (pilot paper part)   9 mins

Explain in what ways your approach to performance appraisal would differ if you were asked to assess the performance of a not-for-profit organisation.
                                                                                               (5 marks)

Answers

ACCA examiner's answers

Remember that you can access the ACCA examiner's solutions to questions marked '**Pilot paper**' 12/07, 6/08 or 12/08 on the BPP website using the following link:

www.bpp.com/acca/examiner-solutions

Additional question guidance

Remember that you can find additional guidance to certain questions on the BPP website using the following link:

www.bpp.com/acca/extra-question-guidance

1 Peterlee

(a) The primary purpose of the *Framework* is to provide a frame of reference to help the IASB itself in developing new accounting standards and reviewing existing ones. Its main impact on accounting practice is therefore through its influence on the standard-setting process. It also has the following purposes:

- To assist auditors in forming an opinion as to whether financial statements conform with accounting standards.
- To help preparers of financial statements and auditors faced with new or emerging accounting issues to carry out an initial analysis of the issues involved.
- To provide a common set of principles for use by standard setters which should reduce the number of alternative treatments allowed by IFRS and therefore facilitate harmonisation of accounting practice.

The *Framework* is not an accounting standard and does not contain requirements on how financial statements should be prepared or presented. This is governed by accounting standards and the overriding requirement of fair presentation. It is also not the only influence on standard setting. Factors such as legal requirements, implementation issues and industry-specific issues also play a part.

However, it is the frame of reference within which the standard-setting takes place and it contains the definitions and recognition criteria for assets, liabilities, income and expense. Fair presentation requires that these elements are accounted for in accordance with the criteria set out in the *Framework*.

(b) *Assets* are defined as 'a resource controlled by an entity as a result of past events and from which future economic benefits are expected to flow to the entity'. The use of 'controlled' agrees with the principle of substance over form in that where an entity may not legally 'own' an asset but has control of the rights to future economic benefits accruing from it, the asset should be recognised. The most obvious example of this is an asset held under a finance lease. This is not legally owned, but is shown on the statement of financial position as a non-current asset. The emphasis on 'past transactions or events' prevents the recognition of contingent assets.

Liabilities are defined as 'a present obligation of the entity arising from past events, the settlement of which is expected to result in an outflow from the entity of resources embodying economic benefits'. This obligation may be legal or it may be constructive. For instance, a company may have no legal obligation to fulfil certain environmental requirements, but it may have created, by its previous actions, the expectation that it will do so. This will be regarded as a constructive obligation per IAS 37 and the cost of carrying it out will be provided for. Again, 'past transactions or events' prevents the use of liabilities for 'profit smoothing'. An entity cannot set up a provision for an obligation which has not yet been incurred, such as a restructuring which it intends to carry out in the following year.

The emphasis placed upon correctly defining and recognising assets and liabilities underlines the importance of the statement of financial position. The elements of financial statements identified in the *Framework*, other than assets and liabilities themselves, are measured in terms of changes in assets and liabilities. Ownership interest is the excess of assets over liabilities and gains and losses are defined as increases or decreases in ownership interest, aside from contributions from and distributions to owners. So correct identification and measurement of assets and liabilities is crucial to the preparation of financial statements which present fairly the entity's position and results.

2 Derringdo

(a) *Framework*

The *Framework* states that 'recognition of income occurs simultaneously with the recognition of increases in assets or decreases in liabilities'. This implies that all gains reported in the statement of financial position, whether realised or unrealised, should be claimed as income in the income statement. Traditionally, only realised gains have been recognised as income. IAS 18 *Revenue* follows the traditional approach, with revenue being measured as the consideration for a transaction rather than as the side effect of an asset revaluation. For example profit on the sale of property is recognised as income, whereas the revaluation of the same item would be taken directly to the revaluation surplus. Some recent standards have followed the

Framework rather than tradition; IAS 40 *Investment Property* and IAS 41 *Agriculture* require unrealised gains to be reported as income in the income statement.

Substance over form requires the commercial substance of a transaction to be reported, rather than its legal form. For example, if a manufacturer sells its factory to a Bank for $1m, and the Bank has the option to demand that the manufacturer buys it back a year later for $1.1m, then this is a secured loan, not a sale. The $1m cash received is treated as a liability, not as income.

(b)   *Sale of goods*

When selling the A grade goods, Derringdo acts as an agent for Gungho. The goods never belong to Derringdo, and so they do not appear in the statement of financial position as inventory or in the income statement as cost of sales. Instead Derringdo's revenue in the income statement will include the commissions earned on these sales.

The B grade goods are normal goods purchased for resale. The income statement will show the gross sales revenue and the related cost of sales.

			$'000
Revenues	(4,600 + 11,400)		16,000
Cost of sales			(8,550)
Gross profit			7,450

Workings

		$'000	$'000
A grade goods			
Revenues	(18,400 × 100/50)		36,800
Cost of sales	Opening inventory	2,400	
	Purchases	18,000	
	Closing inventory	(2,000)	
			18,400
Gross profit (25%)			18,400
Commission	36,800 @ 12.5%		4,600

		$'000	$'000
B grade goods			
Revenues	(8,550 × 100/75)		11,400
Cost of sales	Opening inventory	1,000	
	Purchases	8,800	
	Closing inventory	(1,250)	
			(8,550)
Gross profit (25%)			2,850

3 Porto

Text reference. Chapter 1.

Top tips. You should have had no trouble explaining the characteristics, but remember to state how they make financial information useful. Working out how the characteristics related to the scenarios took a bit more thought.

Easy marks. Part (a) was 9 easy marks.

(a) **Relevance**

The relevance of information must be considered in terms of the decision-making needs of users. It is relevant when it can influence their economic decisions or allow them to reassess past decisions and evaluations. Economic decisions often have a predictive quality – users may make financial decisions on the basis of what they expect to happen in the future. To some degree past performance gives information on expected future performance and this is enhanced by the provision of comparatives, so that users can see the direction in which the company is moving. The separate presentation of discontinued operations also shows how much profit or loss can be attributed to that part of the operation will be not be there in the future. This can also affect valuation of assets. One aspect of relevance is materiality. An item is material if its omission or misstatement could influence the economic decisions of users. Relevance would not be enhanced by the inclusion of immaterial items which may serve to obscure the important issues.

Reliability

Information can be considered to be reliable when it is free from error or bias and faithfully represents what it is expected to represent. The income statement must be a reliable statement of the results of the entity for the period in question and the statement of financial position must faithfully represent its financial position at the end of the period. Financial statements in which provision had not been made for known liabilities or in which asset values had not been correctly stated could not be considered reliable. This also brings in the issue of substance over form. Transactions should be represented in accordance with their economic substance, rather than their legal form. This principle governs the treatment of finance leases, sale and leaseback transactions and consignment inventory. If these types of transactions are not accounted for in accordance with their economic substance, then the financial statements are unreliable.

Comparability

Comparability operates in two ways. Users must be able to compare the financial statements of the entity with its own past performance and they must also be able to compare its results with those of other entities. This means that financial statements must be prepared on the same basis from one year to the next and that, where a change of accounting policy takes place, the results for the previous year must also be restated so that comparability is maintained. Comparability with other entities is made possible by use of appropriate accounting policies, disclosure of accounting policies and compliance with International Financial Reporting Standards. Revisions to standards have to a large degree eliminated alternative treatments, so this has greatly enhanced comparability.

(b) (i) The 'substance' of a finance lease is that the lessee has acquired an asset using a loan from the lessor. Porto should capitalise the asset and depreciate it over its useful life (which is the same as the lease term). A finance lease liability should be set up for the same amount. The liability will be reduced by the lease payments, less the notional finance charge on the loan, which will be charged to profit or loss. This presents the transaction in accordance with its substance, which is a key aspect of reliability.

(ii) This issue has to do with relevance. It could be said that the use of historical cost accounting does not adequately reflect the value of assets in this case. This can be remedied by revaluing the properties. If this is done, all properties in the category will have to be revalued. This will probably give rise to a higher depreciation charge, so it will not improve the operating loss in the income statement, but the excess can be credited back to retained earnings in the statement of financial position.

4 Regulatory framework

Marking scheme

		Marks
(a)	1 mark per relevant point to a maximum	10
(b)	1 mark per relevant point to a maximum	10
(c)	1 mark per relevant point to a maximum	5
	Maximum for question	25

(a) Structure and function of IASCF

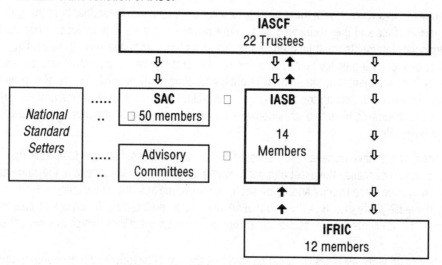

⇩   Appoints
↑   Reports to
☐   Advises
......   Membership links

IASCF International Accounting Standards Committee Foundation

The Trustees of the IASCF oversee the whole organisation. They arrange funding, appoint the IASB, IFRIC and SAC, and set the agenda for the IASB. The aims of the IASCF are:

- to develop a single set of high quality global accounting standards,
- to promote the use of these standards, and
- to bring about convergence of national and international accounting standards.

IASB International Accounting Standards Board

The IASB develops and issues International Financial Reporting Standards in its own right. It reports to the IASCF. Members of the IASB are appointed for their technical competence and independence.

IFRIC International Financial Reporting Interpretations Committee

IFRIC provides rapid guidance on accounting issues where divergent or unacceptable treatments are likely to arise. It reports to the IASB. Membership of IFRIC is drawn from a diverse range of geographical and professional backgrounds.

SAC Standards Advisory Council

The SAC provides a forum for organisations or individuals to take part in the standard setting process. It advises the IASB on agenda decisions, priorities, and its views on standard setting projects. Membership is drawn from a diverse range of geographical and professional backgrounds.

Advisory Committees

These are set up to advise the IASB on specific issues.

National Standard Setters

Although the IASCF is an independent organisation it works closely with national standard setters. The IASB, SAC and advisory committees draw heavily on personnel from national bodies. In return, many national standard setters incorporate IFRS's into their own accounting standards.

(b)   **Setting, enforcing and supplementing standards**

Setting standards

The IASCF sets the agenda for producing accounting standards, but the IASB produces and issues these standards. The process is as follows:

1   The IASCF, taking into account advice from the SAC and others, identifies an issue requiring an accounting standard.

2   The IASB sets up an Advisory Committee to investigate the issue and report back to the IASB.

3   The IASB issues a Discussion Draft for public comment. A Discussion Draft needs a simple majority to be issued. Comments must be received within ninety days.

4   The IASB issues an Exposure Draft; comments must be received within ninety days. The Exposure Draft must be approved by 8 of the 14 members of the IASB.

5   The IASB issues an International Financial Reporting Standard on the internet. An IFRS must be approved by 8 of the 14 members of the IASB.

Public discussion is encouraged. The basis of conclusions for ED's and IFRS's are published, along with dissenting opinions. Most meetings of the IASB, IFRIC and SAC are open to the public, and they are exploring ways of using technology to make public access easier globally.

Enforcing standards

The IASB has no legal power to enforce adoption or compliance with standards, but enforcement of a sort is achieved (more or less successfully) in a number of ways:

•   Quoted companies within the European Union must comply with IFRS's, but it is up to each member state to police compliance. Some countries have a formal process to review published financial statements and punish non-compliance (for example the Financial Reporting Review Panel in the UK), but this is not universal. To a certain extent the onus is on the auditors to police compliance, but auditing standards themselves are not globally consistent.

•   Companies using IFRS to obtain cross-border listings are required to have their financial statements audited in accordance with International Auditing Standards. This will help to ensure that these companies are complying with IFRS.

•   Many countries are bringing their own standards into line with IFRS's, but again policing of national standards is inconsistent.

Supplementing standards

The IFRIC issues interpretations when divergent or unacceptable accounting treatments arise, whether through misinterpreting an existing standard or on an important issue not yet covered by a standard.

Financial statements must comply with all of these interpretations if they claim to comply with International Financial Reporting Standards.

(c) Has the move towards global accounting standards been successful?

On a practical level the move towards global accounting standards has been one of the accounting successes of the last decade. The standards themselves have improved, with the elimination of contradictory alternatives and the creation of an open and independent standard setting organisation. This in turn has lead to greater acceptance of these standards, culminating in 2005 with the adoption of IFRS for consolidated accounts by all quoted companies in the European Union and in many other countries. The on-going project with the International Organisation of Securities Commissions will encourage the use of IFRS for cross-border listings, and could even lead to the acceptance of IFRS in the USA.

However, as mentioned earlier, there is no global system of enforcement, and so it is too early to say if IFRS are being adopted properly.

Some countries with their own highly developed accounting standards see the adoption of IFRS as a backward step, whereas other countries see IFRS as unnecessarily complicated.

There is also the assumption that the globalisation of accounting standards is a good thing. Recent developments in IFRS have focussed on quoted companies in the western world; they may not be suitable for all types and sizes of business organisation, or for all stages of economic development.

5 Winger

> **Text reference.** Chapter 3.
>
> **Top tips.** As with consolidated accounts questions, a question on the preparation of a single company's accounts needs a methodical approach. Lay out proformas and fill the numbers in gradually by systematically working through the question.

(a) WINGER
INCOME STATEMENT FOR THE YEAR ENDED 31 MARCH 20X1

	$'000
Sales revenues (358,450 – 27,000)	331,450
Cost of sales (W1)	(208,550)
Gross profit	122,900
Distribution expenses	(28,700)
Administration expenses	(15,000)
Profit on disposal of land and buildings (95,000 – 80,000)	15,000
Loss on abandonment of research project	(30,000)
Finance cost (W3)	(11,200)
Profit before tax	53,000
Income tax (15,000 – 2,200)	(12,800)
Profit for the year	40,200

STATEMENT OF CHANGES IN EQUITY

	Share capital $'000	Retained earnings $'000	Total $'000
Opening	150,000	101,600*	251,600
Dividends paid	–	(12,000)	(12,000)
Total comprehensive income for the year	–	40,200	40,200
Closing	150,000	129,800	279,800

* *Opening retained earnings*

$71,600 from the trial balance, plus $30,000 from the revaluation surplus.

(b) STATEMENT OF FINANCIAL POSITION AS AT 31 MARCH 20X1

	$'000	$'000
Assets		
Property, plant and equipment		
Property (200,000 – 6,000 (W2))		194,000
Plant and equipment (W4)		160,000
		354,000
Current assets		
Inventories (28,240 + 22,500 (W1))	50,740	
Trade receivables (55,000 – 27,000 (W1))	28,000	
Cash	10,660	
		89,400
Total assets		443,400
Equity and liabilities		
Equity		
Equity shares 25c each		150,000
Retained earnings (see (a))		129,800
		279,800
Non-current liabilities		
Leasing liabilities (W5)	47,200	
8% loan notes	50,000	
		97,200
Current liabilities		
Trade and other accounts payable (W6)	51,400	
Income tax	15,000	
		66,400
Total equity and liabilities		443,400

Workings

1	*Cost of sales*	$'000
	Per question	185,050
	Less sale/return goods (27,000 × 100/120)	(22,500)
	Add depreciation (W2)	46,000
		208,550

2	*Depreciation*	$'000
	Building (100,000 ÷ 50)	2,000
	Heating system (20,000 ÷ 10)	2,000
	Lifts (30,000 ÷ 15)	2,000
		6,000
	Leased plant (80,000 × 20%)	16,000
	Owned plant (154,800 – 34,800) × 20%	24,000
		46,000

3	*Finance costs*	$'000
	Loan interest (50,000 × 8%)	4,000
	Finance lease (80,000 – 20,000) × 12%	7,200
		11,200

4	*Plant and equipment*	$'000
	Cost: owned plant	154,800
	leased plant	80,000
		234,800
	Depreciation: owned plant (34,800 + 24,000 (W2))	(58,800)
	leased plant (80,000 × 20%)	(16,000)
		160,000

5	*Leasing liabilities*	$'000
	Total capital due	80,000
	Less amount paid	(20,000)
		60,000
	Add accrued interest (60,000 × 12%)	7,200
	Total creditor	67,200
	Due within one year	20,000
	Due after one year	47,200

6	*Trade and other payables*	$'000
	Trial balance	29,400
	Lease creditor (W5)	20,000
	Accrued loan interest (4,000 – 2,000)	2,000
		51,400

(c)   Companies often used to justify the non-depreciation of buildings on several grounds, including:

(i)   That the current value of the buildings was **higher than cost**.

(ii)   That the level of **maintenance** meant that no deterioration or consumption had taken place.

(iii)   That the depreciation charge would **not be material.**

However, IAS 16 requires the **depreciable amount** of an asset to be charged against profit over its useful life. Using the cost model, the depreciable amount is obtained by comparing the cost of the asset with its **estimated residual value** at the end of its useful life. By requiring the residual value to be estimated at **current prices**, the standard removes any **potential inflationary effects** which would otherwise increase the residual value and hence reduce, even to zero, the depreciable amount. This overcomes the argument that high residual values remove the need for depreciation, unless the value of a second-hand asset has greater value than the same asset new – an unlikely proposition.

The argument regarding **immateriality** of the depreciation charge because of a long economic life may have some validity. Although it is not addressed directly by IAS 16, accounting standards generally only apply to **material items,** according to the *Framework.* However, under this principle, it will be necessary to consider not only each year's potential depreciation charge, but also the **accumulated depreciation** that would need to be provided against the asset. Over time, this latter amount would inevitably become material and the 'long life' argument would cease to hold.

Thus, Winger's **previous policy** was not appropriate and the change to depreciate assets was necessary to comply with IAS 16.

The directors' treatment of the deferred development expenditure is also incorrect. It needs to be written off because its **value** has become **impaired due to adverse legislation, not a change of accounting policy**. It now has no effective value. There has therefore not been a change of accounting policy, so it cannot be treated as a prior period adjustment. It must be written off to the income statement.

6 Harrington

Text reference. Chapter 3.

Top tips. There is a lot to get through in this question. Work through the adjustments methodically, but keep an eye on the time. Make sure that you attempt all three statements.

Easy marks. If you work methodically through the information, you can easily obtain 13 marks.

Examiner's comments. Most candidates answered this question well. However many candidates ignored part (b).

			Marks
(a)	Restated income statement		
	Sales revenue		1
	Cost of sales		5
	Operating expenses		1
	Investment income		1
	Loan interest		1
	Income tax		2
		Available	11
		Maximum	9
(b)	Statement of changes in equity		
	Brought forward figures		1
	Rights issue		1
	(restated) profit for the financial year		1
	Surplus on land and buildings		2
	Transfer to realised profits		1
	Dividend paid		1
		Available	7
		Maximum	6
(c)	Statement of financial position		
	Land and buildings		1
	Plant		1
	Investments		1
	Inventory and trade receivables		1
	Bank and trade payables		1
	Accrued loan interest		1
	Current tax		1
	10% loan note		1
	Deferred tax		1
	Share capital and premium		1
	Revaluation reserve		1
	Retained earnings		1
		Available	12
		Maximum	10
		Maximum for question	25

(a) STATEMENT OF COMPREHENSIVE INCOME FOR THE YEAR ENDING 31 MARCH 20X5

	$'000
Revenue (13,700 – 300 proceeds)	13,400
Cost of sales (W1)	(8,910)
Gross profit	4,490
Investment income ($1.2m × 10%)	120
Operating expenses	(2,400)
Finance costs ($500m × 10%)	(50)
Profit before tax	2,160
Taxation (W5)	(385)
Profit for the year	1,775
Other comprehensive income:	
Revaluation gain on property (W)	1,800
Total comprehensive income for the year	3,575

(b)   STATEMENT OF CHANGES IN EQUITY FOR THE YEAR ENDING 31 MARCH 20X5

	Share Capital $'000	Share Premium $'000	Revaluation surplus $'000	Retained Earnings $'000	Total $'000
Opening (W6)	1,600	40	–	2,990	4,630
Share issue (W6)	400	560	–	–	960
Dividends paid	–	–	–	(500)	(500)
Total comprehensive income for the year			1,800	1,775	3,575
Transfer to retained earnings	–	–	(80)	80	–
Closing	2,000	600	1,720	4,345	8,665

(c)   STATEMENT OF FINANCIAL POSITION AS AT 31 MARCH 20X5

	$'000
Assets	
Non-current assets	
Property, plant and equipment (W4)	8,060
Investments ($1.2m × 110%)	1,320
	9,380
Current assets	
Inventories	1,750
Trade receivables	2,450
Bank	350
	4,550
Total assets	13,930
Equity and liabilities	
Equity	
Share Capital	2,000
Share Premium	600
Revaluation surplus	1,720
Retained earnings	4,345
	8,665
Non-current liabilities	
Loan note	500
Deferred tax ($1.4m × 25%)	350
	850
Current liabilities	
Trade payables	4,130
Accrued Loan Note interest ($50m charged – $25m paid)	25
Income Tax	260
	4,415
Total equity and liabilities	13,930

Workings

		$'000
1	Cost of sales	
	From question	9,200
	Less: profit on disposal (W2)	(30)
	Less: capitalisation (W3)	(1,000)
	Add: depreciation (W4)	740
		8,910

2 *Disposal* $'000
Proceeds (transferred from sales)   300
Carrying value (900 – 630)   (270)
Profit on disposal   30

3 *Capitalisation* $'000
Total costs incurred (150+800+65+20)   9,200
Less: rectification costs (10+25)   (35)
                                                          1,000

4 *Property, plant and equipment*

		Land $'000		Buildings $'000		Plant $'000	Total $'000
Cost	Opening	1,000		4,000		5,200	
	Additions	–	W3	1,000		–	
	Disposals	–		–	W2	(900)	
	Revaluation	200		800		–	
	Closing	1,200		5,800		4,300	
Depreciation	Opening	–		800		3,130	
	Charge	–		290		450	
	Disposals	–		–	W2	(630)	
	Revaluation	–		(800)		–	
	Closing	–		290		2,950	
Carrying value		1,200		5,510		1,350	8,060

Total revaluation   200 + 800 + 800 = $1,800,000
Total depreciation   290 + 450 = $740,000

Buildings

Revaluation of building excludes the addition during the year.

Depreciation: $5.8m/20 years = $290,000

Excess depreciation on revaluation

		$'000
Revalued depreciation	$4.8m/20 years	240
Historic cost depreciation	$3.2m/20 years	160
Excess		80

Depreciation on plant

		$'000
Cost		4,300
Cumulative depreciation	(3,130 – 630)	(2,500)
Balance		1,800
25% depreciation		450

5 *Income tax*

		$'000	$'000
Estimate for current year	(current liability)		260
Under-provision for prior year			55
Deferred tax			
Provision required ($1.4m × 25%)	(non-current liability)	350	
Opening provision		(280)	
Increase			70
			385

6 *Share issue*

The 1 for 4 rights issue means that there are five shares in issue at the year-end for every four in issue at the start. Therefore the opening capital must have been $2m × $^4/_5$ = $1.6m.

	Capital $'000	Premium $'000
Opening balance		
6.4m shares @ 25 cents each	1,600	40
1 for 4 rights issue at 60 cents		
Capital: 1.6m shares @ 25 cents	400	–
Premium: 1.6m shares @ 35 cents	–	560
	2,000	600

(The opening share premium is a balancing figure.)

7 Llama

Text references. Chapters 3, 4 and 18.

Top tips. The main part of the workings here involves property, plant and equipment. You must set this working out carefully and remember that the cost of manufacturing the plant which is now being capitalised must be credited back to cost of sales.

Easy marks. The income statement and statement of financial position were easy marks apart from the property, plant and equipment. The EPS was easy if you were clear on how to calculate it, but was only worth 3 marks.

Examiner's comments. Most candidates did well on this question. Common errors were:

- confusion over timing of the revaluation. A year's depreciation should have been deducted before the adjustment.
- reducing cost of sales by closing inventory
- basing finance costs on the loan on nominal rate of 2% rather than effective interest rate of 6%
- incorrect tax calculation

Marking scheme

		Marks
(a)	Statement of comprehensive income	
	Revenue	½
	Cost of sales	3
	Distribution costs and administrative expenses	1
	Investment income and gain on investment	1½
	Finance costs	1
	Tax	1½
	Revaluation loss	½
		9
(b)	Statement of financial position	
	Property, plant and equipment	3
	Investments	1
	Current assets	1
	Equity shares	1
	Share premium	1
	Revaluation surplus	1
	Retained earnings	1
	2% loan notes	1½
	Deferred tax	1
	Trade payables and overdraft	1
	Income tax provision	½
		13

(c) Earnings per share
Calculation of theoretical ex rights value 1
Weighted average number of shares 1
Earnings and calculation of eps 1
$$\frac{3}{}$$
Total for question $\frac{25}{}$

(a) LLAMA: STATEMENT OF COMPREHENSIVE INCOME FOR THE YEAR ENDED 30 SEPTEMBER 2007

	$'000
Revenue	180,400
Cost of sales (W1)	(81,700)
Gross profit	98,700
Investment income	2,200
Gain on fair value of investments (27,100 – 26,500)	600
Distribution costs (W1)	(12,000)
Administrative expenses (W1)	(13,500)
Finance costs (W4)	(2,400)
Profit before tax	73,600
Income tax expense (W5)	(17,100)
Profit for the year	56,500
other comprehensive income:	
Revaluation loss on building	(3,000)
Total comprehensive income for the year	53,500

(b) LLAMA: STATEMENT OF FINANCIAL POSITION AT 30 SEPTEMBER 2007

	$'000
Non-current assets	
Property, plant and equipment (W2)	228,500
Investments	27,100
	255,600
Current assets	
Inventory	37,900
Trade receivables	35,100
	73,000
Total assets	328,600
Equity and liabilities	
Equity	
Equity shares of 50c each (W3)	75,000
Share premium (30,000 × 30c (W3))	9,000
Revaluation surplus (14,000 – 3,000 (W2))	11,000
Retained earnings (25,500 + 56,500)	82,000
	177,000
	$'000
Non-current liabilities	
2% Loan note (W4)	81,600
Deferred tax	10,000
	91,600
Current liabilities	
Trade payables	34,700
Income tax payable	18,700
Overdraft	6,600
	60,000
Total equity and liabilities	328,600

Workings

1   *Expenses*

	Cost of sales $'000	Distribution costs $'000	Administrative expenses $'000
Per question	89,200	11,000	12,500
Plant capitalised	(24,000)		
Depreciation – buildings (60%/20%/20%)	3,000	1,000	1,000
Depreciation - plant (W2)	12,000		
Depreciation plant addition (W2)	1,500	–	–
	81,700	12,000	13,500

2   *Property, plant and equipment*

	Land $'000	Buildings $'000	Plant $'000	Total $'000
Cost				
1 October 2006	30,000	100,000	128,000	258,000
Additions*			24,000	24,000
Revaluation loss (95m – 92m)	–	(3,000)	–	(3,000)
	30,000	97,000	152,000	279,000
Depreciation				
1 October 2006			32,000	32,000
Current year chg (100m/20)		5,000		5,000
On plant 1.10.06 ((128m – 32m) × 12.5%)			12,000	12,000
On addition (24m × 12.5% × 6/12)	–	–	1,500	1,500
	–	5,000	45,500	50,500
Carrying value	30,000	92,000	106,500	228,500

* Note that all of the expenses originally charged to cost of sales in respect of the plant addition are now capitalised, giving a total amount of $24m.

3   *Share issue*

	Shares
50c shares at 1.10.06	120,000
1 for 4 issue	30,000
Shares at 30.9.07	150,000
Receipt from rights issue (30,000 × 80c)	$24,000
CR Share capital (30,000 × 50c)	$15,000
CR Share premium (30,000 × 30c)	$ 9,000

4   *Finance costs*

	$'000
2% loan note proceeds	80,000
Interest (6% × 6/12)	2,400
Interest paid	(800)
Balance at 30.9.07	81,600

5   *Taxation*

	$'000
Charge for year	18,700
Prior year overprovision	(400)
Movement in deferred tax ((40m × 25%) – 11,200)	(1,200)
Income statement charge	17,100

(c) EARNINGS PER SHARE FOR THE YEAR ENDED 30 SEPTEMBER 2007

Theoretical ex-rights price

		$
4	shares at $1	4.00
1	share at 80c	0.80
5	shares	4.80

Theoretical ex-rights price is therefore 4.80/5 = 96c

Weighted average number of shares

Date	Shares	Months	Bonus fraction	Weighted average
30.6.07	120,000	9/12	100/96	93,750
30.9.07	150,000	3/12		37,500
				131,250

EPS = 56,500 / 131,250 = 43c

8 Tadeon

Top tips. Start by working through (i) to (v). Read each requirement twice and then do neat workings which the marker can read. If you cannot do one of these, leave it.

Easy marks. The actual financial statements were easy once you had worked through the issues which needed to be brought in. You may have had trouble with the deferred tax but the depreciation and suspense account workings were easy. Don't spend time on any issues which you don't understand or can't do, just move on.

Examiner's comments. This style of question has been asked frequently in the past. It is a popular question which candidates tend to find time consuming, but do score well on. Common errors involved incorrect depreciation on the revaluated property and problems dealing with the lease, the loan and the deferred tax.

Marking scheme

		Marks
(a)	Statement of comprehensive income	
	Revenue	1
	cost of sales	1
	operating expenses	1
	investment income	1
	finance costs	2
	income tax expense	3
	Other comprehensive income	1
	Available	10
	Maximum	8
(b)	Statement of financial position	
	property, plant and equipment	3
	investment	1
	inventory and trade receivables	1
	share capital and premium	3
	revaluation surplus	2
	retained earnings (including 1 mark for the dividend)	2
	loan note	2
	deferred tax	1
	lease obligation (1 for current, 1 for long-term)	2
	trade payables and overdraft	1
	accrued lease finance costs	1
	income tax payable	1
	Available	20
	Maximum	17
	Maximum for question	25

(a) TADEON

STATEMENT OF COMPRREHENSIVE INVOICE FOR THE YEAR ENDED 30 SEPTEMBER 20X6

	$'000
Revenue	277,800
Cost of sales (118,000 + 26,000 (W1))	(144,000)
Gross profit	133,800
Investment income	2,000
Operating expenses (40,000 + 1,200 (W3))	(41,200)
Finance cost (2,750 (W2) + 1,500 (W3))	(4,250)
Profit before tax	90,350
Income tax expense (W5)	(36,800)
Profit for the year	53,550
Other comprehensive income:	
Revaluation gain on leasehold property	20,000
Total comprehensive income for the year	73,550

(b) TADEON

STATEMENT OF FINANCIAL POSITION AS AT 30 SEPTEMBER 20X6

	$'000	$'000
Non-current assets		
Property, plant and equipment (W1)		299,000
Investments		42,000
		341,000
Current assets		
Inventories	33,300	
Trade receivables	53,500	
		86,800
Total assets		427,800
Equity and liabilities		
Equity		
Equity shares (150,000 + 50,000 (W6))		200,000
Share premium (W6)		28,000
Revaluation surplus (20,000 (W1) – 4,000 (W5))		16,000
Retained earnings (18,600 + 53,550 – 30,000 (W6))		42,150
		286,150
Non-current liabilities		
Amount due under finance lease (W3)	10,500	
Loan note (W2)	51,750	
Deferred tax (W5)	14,800	
		77,050
Current liabilities		
Amount due under finance lease (W3)	6,000	
Trade payables	18,700	
Income tax payable	38,000	
Overdraft	1,900	
		64,600
Total equity and liabilities		427,800

Workings

1   *Property, plant and equipment*

	Property	Plant & equipment	Vehicle	Total
	$'000	$'000	$'000	$'000
Cost	225,000	181,000		406,000
Accumulated depreciation	(36,000)	(85,000)		(121,000)
Addition			20,000	20,000
Current year depreciation	(9,000)	(12,000)	(5,000)	(26,000)
Revaluation (W4)	20,000	–	–	20,000
	200,000	84,000	15,000	299,000

2   *Loan note*

	$'000
Proceeds	50,000
Interest @ 5.5%	2,750
Interest paid	(1,000)
Carrying value	51,750

3   *Finance lease*

	$'000
Fair value of asset	20,000
Deposit paid	(5,000)
	15,000
Interest to 30 September 20X6	1,500
Balance at 1 October 20X6	16,500
Amount due within one year	(6,000)
Amount due after one year	10,500

Therefore $1.2m is charged to operating lease rentals and $1.5m to finance costs on the finance lease.

4   *Revaluation*

	$'000
Carrying value of leasehold at 1 October 20X5	189,000
Depreciation to 30 September 20X6 (225,000/25)	(9,000)
	180,000
Revaluation	20,000
Carrying value at 30 September 20X6	200,000
Revaluation surplus balance (20,000 – 4,000 (W5))	16,000

5   *Income tax expense*

	$'000
Current year tax charge	38,000
Transfer from deferred tax ((54,000 × 20%) – 12,000)	(1,200)
Income statement charge	36,800
Deferred tax balance (74,000 × 20%)	14,800

Note

Deferred tax on revaluation (20,000 × 20%) charged to revaluation surplus	4,000

6   *Suspense account*

	$'000
Dividend paid (750m shares @ 80c × 5%)	(30,000)
Rights issue – shares (250m × 20c)	50,000
Rights issue – premium (250m ×12c)	30,000
Issue costs – to share premium account	(2,000)
Balance on suspense account	48,000
Net amount to share premium (30,000 – 2,000)	28,000

9 Kala

Marking scheme

			Marks
(a)	Statement of comprehensive income		
	Revenue		2
	Cost of sales		2
	operating expenses		1
	investment income		1
	finance costs		1
	Taxation		1
	Revaluation gain		2
			10
(b)	Statement of changes in equity		
	brought forward figures		1
	Total comprehensive income for the year		2
	dividends paid		1
			4
(c)	Statement of financial position		
	land and buildings		2
	plant and equipment		2
	investment property		1
	inventory and trade receivables		1
	8% loan		½
	deferred tax		½
	lease obligation : interest and capital one year		1
	capital over one year		1
	trade payables and overdraft		1
	accrued interest		½
	income tax provision		½
			11
		Total for question	25

KALA
STATEMENT OF COMPREHENSIVE INCOME FOR THE YEAR ENDED 31 MARCH 20X6

	$'000
Revenue	278,400
Cost of sales (W1)	(115,700)
Gross profit	162,700
Investment income (W2)	10,800
Operating expenses	(15,500)
Finance costs (W3)	(10,000)
Profit before tax	148,000
Income tax expense (W4)	(29,900)
Profit for the year	118,100
Other comprehensive income:	
Revaluation gain on property (W8)	45,000
Total comprehensive income for the year	163,100

KALA
STATEMENT OF CHANGES IN EQUITY FOR THE YEAR ENDED 31 MARCH 20X6

	Share capital $'000	Revaluation surplus $'000	Retained Earnings $'000	Total $'000
At 1 April 20X5	150,000		119,500	269,500
Dividends paid	–	–	(15,000)	(15,000)
Total comprehensive income for the year		45,000	118,100	163,100
Balance at 31 March 20X6	150,000	45,000	222,600	417,600

KALA
STATEMENT OF FINANCIAL POSITION AS AT 31 MARCH 20X6

	$'000	$'000
Non-current assets		
Property, plant and equipment (W5)		434,100
Investment property		96,300
		530,400
Current assets		
Inventory	43,200	
Trade receivables	53,200	
		96,400
Total assets		626,800
Equity and liabilities		
Equity		
Equity shares $1		150,000
Revaluation surplus		45,000
Retained earnings		222,600
		417,600
Non-current liabilities		
Deferred tax	14,100	
Amounts due under finance lease (W6)	55,000	
Loan note	50,000	
		119,100
Current liabilities		
Trade payables	33,400	
Loan interest payable (3,000 – 2,000)	1,000	
Amount due under finance lease (W6)	22,000	
Overdraft	5,400	
Income tax payable	28,300	
		90,100
Total equity and liabilities		626,800

Workings

1 Cost of sales

	$'000
Opening inventory	37,800
Purchases	78,200
Depreciation (W7)	42,900
Closing inventory	(43,200)
	115,700

2 Investment income

	$'000
Per trial balance	4,500
Increase in value (90,000 × 7%)	6,300
	10,800

3 Finance cost

	$'000
Loan note (50,000 × 8% × 9/12)	3,000
Finance lease interest (W6)	7,000
	10,000

4 Income tax

	$'000
Provision for year	28,300
Transfer to deferred tax (14,100 – 12,500)	1,600
	29,900

5 Property, plant and equipment

	Land $'000	Buildings $'000	Plant $'000	Leased plant $'000	Total $'000
Cost	70,000	200,000	156,000	92,000	518,000
Accumulated depreciation		(60,000)	(26,000)		(86,000)
Revaluation (W8)	10,000	35,000			45,000
Current year depreciation (W7)		(5,000)	(19,500)	(18,400)	(42,900)
Carrying value	80,000	170,000	110,500	73,600	434,100

6 Finance lease

	$'000
Purchase price	92,000
Instalment paid 1 April X5	(22,000)
Balance 1 April X5	70,000
Interest 10%	7,000
Balance 31 March X6	77,000
Due within one year	22,000
Due after one year	55,000
	77,000

[Note that the amount due within one year will be paid on 1 April X6 ie before the accrual of any further interest. Therefore we do not need to deduct any future interest from this amount.]

7 Depreciation

	$'000
Buildings Revalued amount/remaining useful life (175,000/(50-15))	5,000
Plant (156,000 – 26,000) × 15%	19,500
Leased plant (92,000/5)	18,400
	42,900

8   *Revaluation surplus*

	$'000
Land (80m-70m)	10,000
Buildings (175m (200m-60m))	35,000
	45,000

10 Wellmay

Text reference. Chapter 3.

Top tips. There is a lot to do in this question – an income statement, statement of financial position and statement of changes in equity. The complications were the maturing goods and the convertible loan. It was important to do really clear workings so that the marker could see where you had used the correct method.

Easy marks. You may have had trouble with the maturing goods and the convertible loan, but there were still easy marks to be gained on property, plant and equipment, deferred tax and the bonus issue. The statement of changes in equity was six relatively easy marks.

Examiner's comments. Most candidates attempting this question did well, picking up good marks even if they did not fully understand all the issues or were not able to complete all the parts. A number of candidates laid out very elaborate journal entries for the adjustments but failed to follow them through to the financial statements.

Marking scheme

	Marks
Income statement:	
Revenue	1
Cost of sales	2
Operating expenses	1
Rental income	1
Loss of investment property (in income statement)	1
Finance costs	2
Income tax	1
Statement of other comprehensive income	3
Changes in equity:	
Balances b/f	1
Equity option	1
Bonus issue	1
Revaluation	1
Total comprehensive income for the year	1
Dividends	1
Statement of financial position:	
Property, plant and equipment	2
Investment property	1
Current assets (re inventory)	1
Deferred tax	1
8% loan note	2
Loan from Westwood	2
Current liabilities	1
Available	28
Total for question	25

WELLMAY: STATEMENT OF COMPREHENSIVE INCOME FOR THE YEAR ENDED 31 MAY 20X7

	$'000
Revenue (4,200 – 500 (W1))	3,700
Cost of sales (W2)	(2,417)
Gross profit	1,283
Operating expenses (470 + 8 (W2))	(478)
Investment property rental income	20
Fair value loss on investment property	(25)
Finance costs (W5)	(113)
Profit before taxation	687
Income tax expense (360 + 30 (W6))	(390)
Profit for the year	297
Other comprehensive income:	
Revaluation gain on factory (W3)	190
Total comprehensive income for the year	487

WELLMAY: STATEMENT OF CHANGES IN EQUITY
FOR THE YEAR ENDED 31 MARCH 20X7

	Share capital $'000	Equity option $'000	Revaluation surplus $'000	Retained earnings $'000	Total $'000
Balance at 1 April 20X6	1,200		350	2,615	4,165
Dividend paid				(400)	(400)
Bonus issue (W7)	300			(300)	
Equity element of loan note (W4)		40			40
Total comprehensive income for the year			190	297	487
	1,500	40	540	2,212	4,292

WELLMAY: STATEMENT OF FINANCIAL POSITION AT 31 MARCH 20X7

	$'000
Assets	
Non-current assets	
Property, plant and equipment (W3)	4,390
Investment property	375
	4,765
Current assets (1,400 + 200 (W1))	1,600
Total assets	6,365
Equity and liabilities	
Equity	
Equity shares 50c (1,200 + 300 (W7))	1,500
Equity share option (W4)	40
Revaluation surplus (350 + 190 (W3))	540
Retained earnings (as above)	2,212
	4,292
Non-current liabilities	
Deferred tax (W6)	210
8% loan note (W4)	568
	778
Current liabilities	
As per draft financial statements	820
Reversal of contingency provision	(75)
Loan from Westwood	500
Interest at 10% (W5)	50
	1,295
Total equity and liabilities	6,365

Workings

1   *Maturing goods*

In substance, the goods have acted as security for a 2 year loan at 10% per annum. The sale should therefore be derecognised. The journal to correct this is:

	DR	CR
	$'000	$'000
Revenue	500	
Cost of sales		200
Loan payable		500
Interest payable (current liability)		50
Finance charge	50	
Inventory	200	–
	750	750

Note that as the loan is repayable within 12 months it will be classified under current liabilities.

2   *Cost of sales*

	$'000
Per draft financial statements	2,700
Adjustment re maturing goods (W1)	(200)
Less contingent costs	(75)
Depreciation on office accommodation (40 × 20% (note (iii))	(8)
	2,417

3   *Property, plant and equipment*

	$'000
As per draft financial statements	4,200
Revaluation gain on factory (1,350 – (1,200 – 40))	190
	4,390

4   *Convertible loan*

This needs to be split into liability and equity components. The effective interest rate is 10%.

Liability component:

Payable at end of year:

	$'000
1 (48 × 0.91)	43.6
2 (48 × 0.83)	39.8
3 (48 × 0.75)	36.0
4 ((600 + 48) × 0.68)	440.6
	560.0
Equity component	40.0
	600.0

The interest to be charged for this first year is therefore $560,000 × 10% and the carrying value of the loan will be:

	$'000
Liability component	560
Interest at 10%	56
Instalment paid	(48)
	568

$48,000 has already been charged to finance costs, so an additional $8,000 needs to be charged.

5   *Finance costs*

	$'000
Per draft income statement	55
Interest on loan from Westwood (W1)	50
Additional interest on convertible loan note (W4)	8
	113

6   *Deferred tax*

	$'000
Deferred tax balance ($600,000 × 35%)	210
Less balance per draft financial statements	(180)
Addition to tax charge	30

7   *Bonus shares*

	$'000
Share capital per draft financial statements	1,200
1 for 4 issue (1,200/4)	300

11 Dexon

Text references. Chapters 3, 7, 17.

Top tips. It is important to read a question like this carefully. You need to adjust back for the rights issue in order to work out what the dividend payments were. It is also important to notice that the land and buildings need to be adjusted for current year depreciation before the revaluation surplus can be calculated.

Easy marks. This was not an easy question and you would have been unlikely to get it all done. However, easy marks were available for the depreciation calculations and accounting for current tax.

Examiner's comments. The recalculation of profit was quite well done by those who knew how to do it. The most common errors were:

–   failing to add dividends back to the retained earnings

–   adjusting for sales revenue rather than profit on goods on SOR

–   treating the revaluation as having taken place at the beginning of the year.

–   not taking part of the deferred tax increase to the revaluation surplus.

These errors were then carried forward to the SOCIE and SFP.

Marking scheme

		Marks
(a)	Adjustments	
	Add back dividends	1
	Balance of fraud loss	1
	Goods on sale or return	1
	Depreciation charges	2
	Investment gain	1
	Taxation provision	1
	Deferred tax	1
		8
(b)	Statement of changes in equity	
	Balances b/f	1
	Restated earnings b/f	1
	Rights issue	2
	Total comprehensive income	3
	Dividends paid	1
		8
(c)	Statement of financial position	
	Property	1
	Plant	1
	Investment	1
	Inventory	1
	Trade receivables	2

Equity from (b)			1
Deferred tax			1
Current liabilities			1
			9
		Total for question	25

(a)

	$'000	$'000
Draft retained profit		96,700
Dividends paid (W6)		15,500
Draft profit for the year		112,200
Profit on goods on sale or return (2,600 × 30/130)		(600)
Depreciation:		
Buildings (165,000/15)	11,000	
Plant (180,500 × 20%)	36,100	
		(47,100)
Gain on investment (W3)		1,000
Current year fraud loss		(2,500)
Increase in deferred tax provision (W5)		(800)
Current year tax		(11,400)
		50,800

(b)   DEXON - STATEMENT OF CHANGES IN EQUITY FOR THE YEAR ENDED 31 MARCH 2008

	Share capital $'000	Share premium $'000	Revaluation surplus $'000	Retained earnings $'000	Total equity $'000
At 1 April 2007	200,000	30,000	18,000	12,300	260,300
Prior period adjustment	-	-	-	(1,500)	(1,500)
Restated balance	200,000	30,000	18,000	10,800	258,800
Share issue	50,000	10,000			60,000
Dividends paid				(15,500)	(15,500)
Total comprehensive income for the year	-	-	4,800 *	50,800	55,600
At 31 March 2008	250,000	40,000	22,800	46,100	358,900

* Revaluation surplus:		
Land and buildings at 31 March 2007		185,000
Depreciation (165,000 / 15)		(11,000)
		174,000
Valuation at 31 March 2008		180,000
Surplus		6,000
Deferred tax provision (6,000 × 20%)		(1,200)
Net surplus		4,800

(c)   DEXON – STATEMENT OF FINANCIAL POSITION AS AT 31 MARCH 2008

	$'000	$'000
Non-current assets		
Property (W1)		180,000
Plant (W1)		144,400
Investments (W3)		13,500
		337,900
Current assets		
Inventory (84,000 + 2,000 (W2))	86,000	
Trade receivables (W7)	45,600	
Bank	3,800	
		135,400
Total assets		473,300

Equity and liabilities		
Share capital		250,000
Share premium		40,000
Revaluation surplus		22,800
Retained earnings		46,100
Total equity		358,900
Non-current liabilities		
Deferred tax (19,200 + 2,000 (W5))		21,200
Current liabilities		
As per draft SFP	81,800	
Tax payable	11,400	
		93,200
Total equity and liabilities		473,300

Workings

1　*Property, plant and equipment*

	Land	Buildings	Plant	Total
	$'000	$'000	$'000	$'000
Per question	20,000	165,000	180,500	365,500
Depreciation	-	(11,000)	(36,100)	(47,100)
	20,000	154,000	144,400	318,400
Revaluation	-	6,000	-	6,000
Balance c/d	20,000	160,000	144,400	324,400

2　*Sale or return*

	$'000	$'000
Cancel sale:		
Dr Sales	2,600	
CR Receivables		2,600
Record inventories:		
DR Inventories (SOFP) 2,600 × 100/130	2,000	
CR Cost of sales (closing inventories)		2,000

3　*Investments at FV through profit or loss*

	$'000
FV at year end (12,500 × 1,296/1,200)	13,500
Per draft SOFP	(12,500)
Gain – to profit or loss	1,000

4　*Fraud*

	$'000	$'000
DR Retained earnings re prior year	1,500	
DR Current year profit	2,500	
CR Receivables		4,000

5　*Deferred tax*

	$'000	$'000
DR Revaluation surplus (6,000 × 20%)		1,200
DR Income statement (tax charge) (4,000 × 20%)		800
CR Deferred tax liability (10,000 × 20%)		2,000

6	Dividends paid	
	May 2007 (200m* × $0.04)	8,000
	November 2007 (250m × $0.03)	7,500
		15,500
	*250m × 4/5 = 200m	

7	Trade receivables	
	Per draft SFP	52,200
	Sale or return	(2,600)
	Adjustment re fraud	(4,000)
		45,600

12 Candel

Text references. Chapters 3 and 7

Top tips. There is quite a lot to do in this question, so it is important to tackle it in an organised manner. Get the formats down, put in any figures that do not require workings and then start the workings. Getting non-current assets done will enable you to fill in quite a few gaps.

Easy marks. The tricky parts of this question were the development costs and the legal provision. However, there were marks available in both the statement of comprehensive income and the SFP for property, plant and equipment and even if your final figure for comprehensive income was incorrect, you could have obtained marks for presenting it correctly in the statement of changes in equity.

Examiner's comments. Most candidates were able to produce financial statements from a trial balance but some of the adjustments caused problems. Students had difficulties with:

- timing of the revaluation
- treatment of development costs
- reversal of the provision
- the deferred tax adjustment
- treatment of preference shares

Marking scheme

			Marks
(a)	Statement of comprehensive income:		
	revenue	1	
	cost of sales	5	
	distribution costs	½	
	administrative expenses	1½	
	finance costs	1½	
	income tax	1½	
	other comprehensive income	1	
			12
(b)	Statement of changes in equity:		
	brought forward figures	1	
	dividends	1	
	comprehensive income	1	
			3

(c)   Statement of financial position:
       property, plant and equipment   2
       deferred development costs   2
       inventory   ½
       trade receivables   ½
       deferred tax   1
       preference shares   1
       trade payables   1½
       overdraft   ½
       current tax payable   1

Total for question

                                                $\frac{10}{25}$

CANDEL

STATEMENT OF COMPREHENSIVE INCOME FOR THE YEAR ENDED 30 SEPTEMBER 2008

	$'000
Revenue (300,000 – 2,500 (plant disposal))	297,500
Cost of sales (W1)	(225,400)
Gross profit	72,100
Distribution costs	(14,500)
Administrative expenses (W1)	(21,900)
Finance costs (1,200 (W5) + 200)	(1,400)
Profit before tax	34,300
Income tax expense (W6)	(11,600)
Profit for the year	22,700
Other comprehensive income:	
Loss on property revaluation (W2)	(4,500)
Total comprehensive income for the year	18,200

CANDEL

STATEMENT OF CHANGES IN EQUITY FOR THE YEAR ENDED 30 SEPTEMBER 2008

	Share capital	Retained earnings	Revaluation Surplus	Total
	$'000	$'000	$'000	$'000
Balance at 1 October 2007	50,000	24,500	10,000	84,500
Dividends paid	-	(6,000)	-	(6,000)
Total comprehensive income	-	22,700	(4,500)(W2)	18,200
Balance at 30 September 2008	50,000	41,200	5,500	96,700

CANDEL

STATEMENT OF FINANCIAL POSITION AT 30 SEPTEMBER 2008

	$'000	$'000
Assets		
Non-current assets		
Property, plant and equipment (W2)		81,400
Development expenditure (W3)		14,800
		96,200
Current assets		
Inventory	20,000	
Trade receivables	43,100	
		63,100
Total assets		159,300
Equity and liabilities		
Equity		

	$'000	$'000
Share capital		50,000
Retained earnings		41,200
Revaluation surplus		5,500
		96,700
Non-current liabilities		
Redeemable preference shares (W5)		20,400
Deferred tax (5,800 + 200 (W6))		6,000
Current liabilities		
Trade payables	23,400	
Provision (W4)	100	
Tax payable	11,400	
Overdraft	1,300	
		36,200
Total equity and liabilities		159,300

Workings

1   Expenses

	Cost of sales	Distribution	Admin
	$'000	$'000	$'000
Per question	204,000	4,500	22,200
Depreciation: Property	2,500	-	-
Plant and equipment	9,600	-	-
Loss on plant (4,000 – 2,500)	1,500	-	-
Research and development (W3)	3,800	-	-
Amortisation (W3)	4,000	-	-
Legal claim (W4)	-	-	(300)
	225,400	4,500	21,900

2   Property, plant and equipment

	Property	P & E	Total
	$'000	$'000	$'000
Cost/valuation b/d	50,000	76,600	
Acc depreciation b/d	-	(24,600)	
	50,000	52,000	102,000
Depn: Property (50,000/20)	(2,500)	-	(2,500)
P&E ((52,000 – 4,000) × 20%)	-	(9,600)	(9,600)
Disposal (8,000 – 4,000)	-	(4,000)	(4,000)
Revaluation (β)	(4,500)	-	(4,500)
	43,000	38,400	81,400

3   Development expenditure

	$'000
Cost b/d	20,000
Accumulated amortisation b/d	(6,000)
	14,000
Additional expenditure capitalised (800 × 6)	4,800
Amortisation (20,000 × 20%)	(4,000)
Balance c/d	14,800
Charged to cost of sales:	
Research	1,400
Development when criteria not met (800 × 3)	2,400
Amortisation	4,000
	7,800

4   *Legal claim*

	$'000	
Damages are not probable, therefore not accrued - Reverse in admin expenses	400	
Legal costs should be provided as results from past event (claim)	(100)	Provision
	300	Credit to Admin

5   *Preference shares*

Financial liability at amortised cost – IAS 39

	$'000
Financial liability b/d	20,000
Effective interest (× 12% × 6/12)	1,200
Coupon paid (per TB) (× 8% × 6/12)	(800)
Financial liability c/d	20,400

Adjustment required:

	$'000
Dr Finance costs	400
Cr Financial liability	400

The $800k coupon paid in the TB is increased to effective cost of $1,200k.

6   *Taxes*

		$'000
Current tax:		
Dr	Income tax expense (income statement)	11,400
Cr	Current tax payable (SOFP)	11,400
Deferred tax:		
Dr	Income tax expense (6,000 – 5,800)	200
Cr	Deferred tax liability	200

13 Pricewell

Text references. Chapters 3 and 12

Top tips. This is a relatively straightforward accounts preparation question. Complications are the leasehold property, which could be mistaken for an investment property, and the construction contract.

Easy marks. There are easy marks here on property, plant and equipment, the lease and the preference shares, which would all have been worth some marks but were not complicated.

Examiner's comments. This question was less well answered than usual. Common errors were:

- Not accounting for commission on the agency sales
- Deducting closing inventory from cost of sales
- Treating the revaluation as if it had taken place at the beginning of the year
- Confusing the leasehold property with the leased plant

Examiner's answer. The examiner's answer to this question is included at the back of this kit.

		Marks
(a)	Statement of comprehensive income	
	Revenue	2
	Cost of sales	5
	Distribution costs	½
	Administrative expenses	½
	Finance costs	2
	Income tax expense	2
		12
(b)	Statement of financial position	
	Property, plant and equipment	2½
	Inventory	½
	Due on construction contract	2
	Trade receivables	½
	Bank	½
	Equity shares	½
	Retained earnings (1 for dividend)	1½
	Deferred tax	1
	Finance lease – non-current liability	½
	Preferences shares	1
	Trade payables	½
	Finance lease – current liability	1
	Current tax payable	1
		13
		25

PRICEWELL : STATEMENT OF COMPREHENSIVE INCOME FOR THE YEAR ENDED 31 MARCH 2009

	$'000
Revenue (310,000 + 22,000 (W4) – 6,400 (W5))	325,600
Cost of sales (W1)	(255,100)
Gross profit	70,500
Distribution costs	(19,500)
Administrative expenses	(27,500)
Finance costs (1,248 (W3) + 4,160 (W6))	(5,408)
Profit before tax	18,092
Income tax expense (W7)	(2,400)
Profit for the year	15,692

PRICEWELL: STATEMENT OF FINANCIAL POSITION AS AT 31 MARCH 2009

	$'000	$'000
Assets		
Non-current assets		
Property, plant and equipment (W2)		66,400
Current assets		
Inventory	28,200	
Amount due from customer on contract (W4)	17,100	
Trade receivables	33,100	
Bank	5,500	
		83,900
Total assets		150,300
Equity and liabilities		
Equity shares of 50c each		40,000
Retained earnings (4,900 + 15,692 – 8,000)		12,592
		52,592
Non-current liabilities		
Deferred tax	5,600	
Obligation under finance lease (W3)	5,716	
Redeemable preference shares (W6)	43,360	
		54,676
Current liabilities		
Trade payables	33,400	
Obligation under finance lease (W3)	5,132	
Tax payable (W7)	4,500	
		43,032
Total equity and liabilities		150,300

Workings

1. Expenses

	Cost of sales $'000	Distribution costs $'000	Administrative Expenses $'000
Per question	234,500	19,500	27,500
Depreciation (W2)	15,300		
Reversal of impairment (W2)	(1,500)		
Construction contract (W4)	13,200		
Agency sales (W5)	(6,400)		
	255,100		

2. Property, plant and equipment

	Leasehold property $'000	Owned plant $'000	Leased plant $'000	Total $'000
B/d per question	25,200	46,800	20,000	92,000
Depreciation b/d	-	(12,800)	(5,000)	(17,800)
	25,200	34,000	15,000	74,200
Depreciation L/hold (25,200/14 years)	(1,800)			
Depreciation (34,000 × 25%)		(8,500)		
Depreciation (20,000 × 25%)			(5,000)	(15,300)
Reversal of impairment loss (β)	1,500	-	-	1,500
	24,900	25,500	10,000	60,400
Construction contract plant (8,000 – 2,000) (W4))				6,000
				66,400

3. *Finance lease*

	$'000
Balance 1.4.08 per question	15,600
Interest to 31.3.09 at 8%	1,248
Payment 31.3.09	(6,000)
Balance 31.3.09	10,848
Interest to 31.3.10 at 8%	868
Payment due 31.3.10	(6,000)
Balance due – non current liability	5,716
Current liability (10,848 – 5,716)	5,132
	10,848

4. *Construction contract*

	$'000
Contract price	50,000
Materials to date	(12,000)
Plant	(8,000)
Further costs to complete	(10,000)
Profit on contract	20,000

Profit to date = 20 × 22/50 (44%) = 8,800

Revenue	22,000
Cost of sales (30 × 44%)	(13,200)
Profit	8,800

Amount due from customer:

Costs to date (12 + plant depreciation (8 × 6m/24m)	14,000
Profit to date	8,800
Progress billings	(5,700)
	17,100

5. *Sales on commission*

	DR	CR
Revenue	6,400	
Cost of sales		6,400

This leaves commission of $m 1.6 in revenue.

6. *Preference shares*

	$'000
Balance at 31.3.08	41,600
Finance cost 10%	4,160
Dividend paid	(2,400)
Balance at 31.3.09	43,360

7. *Income tax*

	$'000
Prior year underprovision	700
Current provision	4,500
Movement on deferred tax (8.4 – 5.6)	(2,800)
Charge for current year	2,400

14 Derringdo II

Grant

(a)   *Liability*

There are two issues here:

1   Should a capital grant be treated as deferred income in the financial statements, and
2   Should a liability be recognised for the potential repayment of the grant.

Derringdo has credited the $240,000 grant to a deferred income account which is shown as a liability in the statement of financial position. It is then released to the income statement over the ten year life of the related asset. However, the *Framework* states that a liability should only be recognised if there is a probable outflow of economic benefits. This is not true for a grant; under normal circumstances the grant will not have to be repaid and so a liability does not exist.

This example is complicated by the possibility of having to repay the grant if the asset is sold. At the end of the reporting period the asset has not been sold, and so there is no past event to give rise to a liability. Derringdo intends to keep the asset for its ten year useful life. Nor can it be classified as a contingent liability. Under IAS 37 the 'uncertain future event' that creates a contingent liability must be 'not wholly within the control of the entity'. In this case Derringdo will make the decision to keep or sell the asset.

Following on from the above, the *Framework* would not permit the grant to be shown as a liability. Instead the grant would be claimed as income in the year that it was received (provided that there was no intention to sell the asset within the four year claw-back period). However, the treatment of the grant as deferred income is in accordance with IAS 20 *Accounting for Government Grants*.

(b)   *Extracts*

Company policy. This complies with one of the two alternatives in IAS 20
INCOME STATEMENT

	$
Operating expenses	
Depreciation charge (W1)	34,000
Release of grant (W2)	(12,000)
	22,000

STATEMENT OF FINANCIAL POSITION

	$'000
Non-current assets	
Property, plant and equipment (W1)	766,000
Non-current liabilities	
Deferred income (W2)	24,000
Current liabilities	
Deferred income (W2)	204,000
	228,000

Workings

1   *Property, plant, equipment*

	$'000
Cost (gross, excluding grant)	800,000
Depreciation (10 years straight line, 15% residual value for 6 months	
800,000 × 85% × 10% × $^6/_{12}$)	(34,000)
Carrying value	766,000

2   *Deferred income*

	$
Grant received ($800,000 × 30%)	240,000
Release for this year ($240,000 × 10% × ⁶/₁₂)	(12,000)
Total balance at year-end	228,000

Presentation	
Current liability ($240,000 × 10%)	24,000
Non-current liability (balance)	204,000
	228,000

Theoretical approach under the Framework

Because the 'deferred' element of the grant cannot be recognised as a liability, the grant will be claimed in full in the year that it is received. The repayment clause will not affect this policy because, at the end of the reporting period, Derringdo has not sold the asset and so no liability exists.

INCOME STATEMENT

	$
Operating expenses	
Depreciation charge (as before)	34,000
Grant received and claimed	(240,000)
	(206,000)

STATEMENT OF FINANCIAL POSITION

	$'000
Non-current assets	
Property, plant and equipment	766,000

15 Broadoak

Text reference. Chapter 4.

Top tips. The question was on IAS 16. Parts (a) and (b) were written sections covering the principles of identifying the cost of assets, the capitalisation of subsequent expenditure, and the requirements with regard to the revaluation of non-current assets including the treatment of gains and losses. Part (c) contained two small numerical examples to test the principles in (a) and (b).

Examiner's comment. Answers to this question were rather polarised. Good candidates did very well whereas weaker students gave poor answers – there did not seem too much in the middle ground. In general answers to Parts (a) and (b) were above average, particularly with regard to subsequent expenditures. Most candidates had a grasp of the basis principles. However, for the cost of non-current assets, many students gave the rules relating to determining whether an asset was impaired. Other incorrect answers discussed the fair values of assets. Most candidates scored well on Parts (c)(i) and (ii), but there were some common errors, for example incorrect capitalisation of maintenance costs.

Answer plan

It always pays to answer the discussion parts first, as these will often highlight the particular difficulties to be found in the calculations.

Part (a)

(i)   IAS 16: cost = purchase price + import duties + directly attributable costs.

Deal with each item separately. Mention costs that must be dealt with as expenses eg admin costs.

Bonus points: mention the treatment of self-constructed assets and abnormal costs.

(ii)   Subsequent expenditure – give treatment per IAS 16. For three marks, give three examples of subsequent expenditure.

Part (b)

Revaluation – measured reliably
- consistency
- whole class of asset
- regular revaluations
- up to date
- treatment of surplus
- treatment of deficit

Disposal – treatment of gains
- treatment of losses

Part (c)

(i) Use information given to calculate the initial capitalisation. Remember that you need to consider all the items in part (a)(i).

(ii) If you follow the points on revaluation in part (b), you will need the following extracts:

INCOME STATEMENT

	20X1	20X2
	$	$
Amortisation	X	X
Revaluation loss		X

STATEMENT OF FINANCIAL POSITION

	20X1	20X2
Leasehold	X	X
Revaluation surplus	X	

(a) (i) IAS 16 states that an item of property which qualifies for recognition as an asset must initially be measured at **cost.** Cost comprises the following components.

　　(1) **Purchase price**, less any trade discounts or rebates, but not settlement discounts

　　(2) **Import duties** and non-refundable purchase taxes

　　(3) **Directly attributable costs** of bringing the asset to working condition for its intended use. These include the cost of site preparation, initial delivery and handling costs, installation costs and professional fees. Also included is the estimated cost of removing the asset and restoring the site, to the extent that it is recognised as a provision under IAS 37 *Provisions, contingent liabilities and contingent assets.*

Certain costs **will not normally be part of the cost** of property, plant and equipment, and must instead be expensed. These are administration costs, start-up costs and initial operating losses.

In the case of **self-constructed assets, the principles are the same** as for acquired assets. This may include labour costs of the entity's own employees. **Abnormal costs** such as wastage and errors are **excluded.**

In addition to IAS 16 and IAS 37 we also need to consider IAS 20 on government grants which states that the **cost of an asset may be reduced by any such grants.**

(ii) There may be **subsequent expenditure** on an item of property, plant or equipment, after its purchase and recognition. Such expenditure may be **added to the carrying amount of the asset,** but only when the **original criteria** are met. **All other subsequent expenditure is recognised as an expense as it is incurred.**

The standard gives **examples** of the kind of improvements that would allow subsequent expenditure to be capitalised.

　　(1) **Modification** of an item of plant to extend its useful life

　　(2) **Upgrade** of machine parts to improve the quality of output

　　(3) Adoption of a **new production process,** leading to large reductions in operating costs

(b)   IAS 16 allows property, plant and equipment (most commonly property) to be shown at a revalued amount. Such **revaluations are permitted** under the allowed alternative treatment rules providing that the **fair value of the asset can be measured reliably.** However, revaluation, particularly of property has been open to abuse, with companies **'cherry picking'** those properties whose valuation is favourable to show at valuation. Accordingly, IAS 16 tries to bring some **consistency** to the practice of revaluation.

When an item of property, plant and equipment is revalued, **the whole class of assets to which it belongs should be revalued.** All the items within a class should be **revalued at the same time** to prevent selective revaluation of certain assets and to avoid disclosing a mixture of costs and values from different dates in the financial statements. Revaluations must be **sufficiently regular**, so that the carrying value of an asset does not differ significantly from its market value. In addition, **revaluations must be kept up to date.**

Surpluses and deficits

In the case of a **surplus**, IAS 16 requires the increase to be recognised in other comprehensive income and accumulated in equity under the heading of **revaluation surplus**. The **exception** is when the increase is **reversing a previous decrease which was recognised as an expense.** Then it is treated as **income.**

The treatment is similar for a **decrease in value** on revaluation. Any decrease should be **recognised as an expense, except where it offsets a previous increase** taken as a revaluation surplus. In this case the decrease will be recognised in other comprehensive income reducing the balance on the revaluation surplus. Any **decrease greater** than the previous upwards increase in value must be taken as an expense in the income statement section of the statement of comprehensive income.

Gains and losses on disposal

Gains or losses are the difference between the estimated net disposal proceeds and the carrying amount of the asset. They should be **recognised as income or expense in the income statement**. Any **revaluation surplus** standing to the credit of a disposed asset should be **transferred to retained earnings** as a reserve movement.

(c)   (i)   Following IAS 16, not all the components of the cost of the item of plant may be capitalised. While trade discounts may be capitalised, **settlement discounts** may not. Such discounts are a **revenue item** and will probably be deducted from administration costs in the income statement. Likewise, **maintenance** is a **revenue item**. There will be a prepayment in the statement of financial position for maintenance costs relating to subsequent years. The cost of the **error** in specifying the power loading is an **abnormal cost** and must be charged to the income statement. The costs to be capitalised may now be calculated as follows.

	$'000	$'000
Basic list price of plant		240,000
Less trade discount at 12.5% on list price		(30,000)
		210,000
Shipping and handling costs		2,750
Estimated pre-production testing		12,500
Site preparation costs		
Electrical cable installation (14,000 – 6,000)	8,000	
Concrete re-inforcement	4,500	
Own labour costs	7,500	
		20,000
Dismantling and restoration costs (15,000 + 3,000)		18,000
Initial cost of plant		263,250

(ii)   BROADOAK
INCOME STATEMENT (EXTRACT) FOR THE YEAR TO 30 SEPTEMBER

	20X1	20X2
	$	$
Amortisation	(20,000)	(21,000)
Revaluation loss		(25,000)

BROADOAK
STATEMENT OF FINANCIAL POSITION (EXTRACT) AS AT 30 SEPTEMBER

	20X1	20X2
	$	$
Leasehold	231,000	175,000
Revaluation surplus		
Balance at 1 October 20X0	50,000	
Revaluation gain (see working)	11,000	
	61,000	
Transfer to retained earnings (11,000 × 1/11)	(1,000)	
Portion of revaluation loss (W)	(10,000)	
	50,000	

Working

	$
Cost at 1 October 20X0	240,000
Amortisation for year to 30 September 20X1: $\dfrac{240,000}{12 \text{ years}}$	(20,000)
	220,000
Revaluation gain	11,000
Carrying value at 30 September 20X1	231,000
Amortisation to 30 September 20X2 $\dfrac{231,000}{11 \text{ years}}$	(21,000)
	210,000
Revaluation loss to revaluation surplus	(10,000)
Revaluation loss to income statement	(25,000)
Carrying value 30 September 20X2	175,000

16 Elite Leisure

Elite Leisure's cruise ship

Although there is only one ship, the ship is a complex asset made up from a number of smaller assets with different costs and useful lives. Each of the component assets of the ship will be accounted for separately with its own cost, depreciation and profit or loss on disposal.

At 30 September 20X4 the ship is eight years old and its cost and carrying value is as follows:

	Cost	Depreciation period	Accumulated Depreciation	Carrying value
	$m		$m	$m
Ship's fabric	300	$\dfrac{8 \text{ years}}{25 \text{ years}}$	96	204
Cabins and entertainment areas	150	$\dfrac{8 \text{ years}}{12 \text{ years}}$	100	50
Propulsion system	100	$\dfrac{30,000 \text{ hours}}{40,000 \text{ hours}}$	75	25
	550		271	279

Changes during Y/E 30 September 20X5

Replacing the propulsion system $140m

The old engines will be scrapped giving rise to a $25m loss on disposal.

The new engines will be capitalised and depreciated over their 50,000 hour working life. The charge for this year will be $140m $\times \dfrac{5,000 \text{ hours}}{50,000 \text{ hours}}$ = $14m.

Upgrading cabins and entertainment areas $60m

These costs can be capitalised because they are improvements and because they extend the useful life of the assets. The revised carrying value at 1 October 20X4 is $110m ($50m + $60m).

The depreciation charge for the year is $22m ($110 ÷ 5 years).

Repainting the ship's fabric $20m

This is a maintenance cost. It will be charged to the income statement for the year. The depreciation for the ship itself will be $12m, based on its $300m cost and 25 year life.

Summary

STATEMENT OF FINANCIAL POSITION

	Ship's Fabric	Cabins etc	Propulsion	Total
	$m	$m	$m	$m
Opening carrying value	204	50	25	279
Disposals	–	–	(25)	(25)
Additions	–	60	140	200
Depreciation	(12)	(22)	(14)	(48)
Closing carrying value	192	88	126	406

INCOME STATEMENT

	$m
Depreciation	48
Loss on disposal	25
Repainting	20
Total charge	93

17 Dearing

Top tips. This question is quite complicated. Set out really clear workings so that you don't get lost.

Marking scheme

	Marks
Initial capitalised cost	2
Upgrade improves efficiency and life therefore capitalise	1
Revised carrying amount at 1 October 2008	1
Annual depreciation (1 mark each year)	3
Maintenance costs charged at $20,000 each year	1
Discount received (in income statement)	1
Staff training (not capitalised and charged to income)	1
Total for question	10

Year ended	30 Sept 2006	30 Sept 2007	30 Sept 2008
Income statement:	$	$	$
Depreciation (W3)	180,000	270,000	119,000
Maintenance (60,000/3)	20,000	20,000	20,000
Discount received (840,000 × 5%)	(42,000)	-	-
Staff training	40,000	-	-
	198,000	290,000	139,000

As at:	30 Sept 2006	30 Sept 2007	30 Sept 2008
Statement of financial position	$	$	$
Property, plant and equipment:			
Cost/valuation (W1), (W2)	920,000	920,000	670,000
Accumulated depreciation	(180,000)	(450,000)	(119,000)
Carrying value	740,000	470,000	551,000

Workings

1   *Cost price*

	$
Base price	1,050,000
Trade discount (1,050,000 × 20%)	(210,000)
	840,000
Freight charges	30,000
Electrical installation cost	28,000
Pre-production testing	22,000
	920,000

2   *Valuation after upgrade*

	$
Original cost	920,000
Depreciation to 30 September 2007 (W3)	(450,000)
Carrying amount	470,000
Upgrade	200,000
Valuation	670,000

3   *Depreciation*

	$
30 September 2006:	
(920,000 – 20,000) × 1,200/6,000	180,000
30 September 2007:	
(920,000 – 20,000) × 1,800/6,000	270,000
	450,000
30 September 2008:	
(670,000 – 40,000) × 850/4,500	119,000

18 Flightline

Text references. Chapter 4

Top tips. This was a very time pressured question with a lot of work to do for 10 marks. It is important in a question like this to provide really clear workings so that you get the marks for all the parts you do correctly.

Easy marks. The amounts for the exterior structure and the cabin fittings were relatively easy to calculate, so you should have done those before embarking on the engines.

Marking scheme

	Marks
Income statement	
Depreciation – exterior	1
– cabin fittings	2
– engines	2
Loss on write off of engine	1
Repairs	1
Statement of financial position	
Carrying amount at 31 March 2009	3
Total for question	10

Income statement for the year ended 31 March 2009

	$'000
Depreciation:	
Exterior structure (W1)	6,000
Cabin fittings (W2)	6,500
Engines (W3)	1,300
	13,800
Loss on disposal of engine (W3)	6,000
Engine repairs	3,000
Exterior painting	2,000

Statement of financial position at 31 March 2009

	$'000
Property, plant and equipment	
Aircraft – exterior (W1)	36,000
– cabin (W2)	8,000
– engines (W3)	16,100
	60,100

Workings

1. *Exterior structure*

	$'000
Cost	120,000
Accumulated depreciation to 31.3.08 (120,000 × 13/20)	(78,000)
	42,000
Depreciation to 31.3.09 (120,000/20)	(6,000)
Carrying value	36,000

2. *Cabin fittings*

	$'000
Cost	25,000
Accumulated depreciation to 31.3.08 (25,000 × 3/5)	(15,000)
	10,000
Depreciation to 1.10.08 (25,000 /5 × 6/12)	(2,500)
Upgrade	4,500
	12,000
Depreciation to 31.3.09 (12,000 × 6/18)	(4,000)
Carrying value	8,000
Total depreciation for current year (2,500 + 4,000)	6,500

3. *Engines*

	$'000
Replaced engine:	
Cost	9,000
Depreciation to 31.3.08 (9,000 × 10.8/36)	(2,700)
Carrying value at 1.4.08	6,300
Depreciation to 1.10.08 (9,000 × 1.2/36)	(300)
Written off at 1.10.08	6,000
Replacement:	
Cost	10,800
Depreciation to 31.3.09 (10,800/36)	(300)
Carrying value	10,500
Damaged engine:	
Carrying value at 1.4.08	6,300
Depreciation to 1.10.08	(300)
Carrying value at 1.10.08	6,000
Depreciation to 31.3.09 (6,000/15)	(400)
Carrying value at 31.3.09	5,600
Total carrying value (10,500 + 5,600)	16,100
Total current year depreciation	
(300 + 300 + 300 + 400)	1,300

19 Emerald

Text reference. Chapter 5

Top tips. There were two aspects to this question – the treatment of development costs and accounting for prior period adjustments. It was important to set out a proper working for the second part of the question so that you could see what you were doing.

Examiner's comments. Answers to this question were generally quite poor. Many candidates did not apply the definition of an asset to the development expenditure. In part (b) some candidates assumed that amortisation commenced in the year of capitalisation, rather than the following year. The prior period adjustment was rarely mentioned.

		Marks
(a)	One mark per valid point to	4
(b)	Income statement amortisation	1½
	Cost in statements of financial position	1
	Accumulated amortisation	1½
	Prior year adjustment in changes in equity	2
		6
	Total for question	10

The IASB *Framework* defines an asset as a resource controlled by the entity as a result of past events and from which future economic benefits are expected to flow to the entity. The recognition criteria also require that the asset has a cost or value that can be measured reliably.

In the case of development expenditure it is not always possible to determine whether or not economic benefits will result. IAS 38 deals with this issue by laying down the criteria for recognition of an intangible asset arising from development expenditure. An entity must be able to demonstrate that it is able to complete and use or sell the asset and has the intention to do so, that the asset will generate probable future economic benefits and that the expenditure attributable to the asset can be reliably measured. If these criteria are met, the asset is recognised and will be amortised from the date when it is available for use.

EMERALD

	$'000	$'000
Income statement		
Amortisation of development expenditure (W)	335	135
Statement of financial position		
Intangible asset: development expenditure (W)	1,195	1,130
Statement of changes in equity		
Prior period adjustment		
Added to retained earnings balance at 1.10.05 (W)		465

Working

	Expenditure	Amortisation	Carrying amount
	$'000	$'000	$'000
2004	300		300
2005	240	(75)*	165
Balance 2005	540	(75)	465
2006	800	(135)**	665
Balance 2006	1,340	(210)	1,130
2007	400	(335)***	65
	1,740	(545)	1,195

* 300 × 25% ** 540 × 25% *** 1,340 × 25%

20 Dexterity

Marking scheme

			Marks
(a)		Discussion of goodwill	3
		Other intangibles – separate transactions	2
		– part of an acquisition	3
		– internally developed	3
		Available	11
		Maximum	10
(b)	(i)	One mark for each item in statement of financial position	4
	(ii)	Does it qualify as development expenditure	1
		The need for an active market	1
		Drugs are unique, not homogeneous	1
	(iii)	Neither an acquired asset nor internally generated	1
		Really recognition of goodwill	1
		Can recognise both the asset and the grant at fair value	1
		Or at cost – granted asset has zero cost	1
	(iv)	In reality a valuable asset, in accounting a pseudo-asset	1
		Cannot control workforce	1
		Does not meet recognition criteria	1
	(v)	Effective advertising really part of goodwill	1
		Cannot be recognised as a non-current asset	1
		Prepayment of $2.5 million	1
		Cannot spread over two years	1
		Available	18
		Maximum	15
		Maximum for question	25

(a)   **Recognition and amortisation**

Goodwill

Only goodwill arising from a business combination is recognised. Under IFRS 3 goodwill is the excess of the cost of a business combination over the acquirer's interest in the net fair value of the assets, liabilities and contingent liabilities of the business acquired. Once recognised goodwill is held indefinitely, without amortisation but subject to impairment reviews.

One of the key aspects of goodwill is that it cannot be separated from the business that it belongs to. Therefore goodwill cannot be purchased separately from other assets. In addition, IAS 38 states that internally generated goodwill must not be capitalised.

Other intangible assets

Other intangibles can be recognised if they can be distinguished from goodwill; typically this means that they can be separated from the rest of the business, or that they arise from a legal or contractual right.

Intangibles acquired as part of a business combination are recognised at fair value provided that they can be valued separately from goodwill. The acquirer will recognise an intangible even if the asset had not been recognised previously. If an intangible cannot be valued, then it will be subsumed into goodwill.

Internally generated intangibles can be recognised if they are acquired as part of a business combination. For example, a brand name acquired in a business combination is capitalised whereas an internally generated brand isn't. Expenditure on research can not be capitalised. Development expenditure is capitalised if it meets the IAS 38 criteria. It is then amortised over the life-cycle of the product.

Goodwill and intangibles with an indefinite useful life are not amortised but tested annually for impairment.

(b)   **Dexterity**

   (i)   *Temerity*

      The following assets will be recognised on acquisition:

	$m
Fair value of sundry net assets	15
Patent at fair value	10
Research carried out for customer	2
Goodwill (balancing figure)	8
Total consideration	35

      The patent is recognised at its fair value at the date of acquisition, even if it hadn't previously been recognised by Temerity. It will be amortised over the remaining 8 years of its useful life with an assumed nil residual value.

      The higher value of $15m can't be used because it depends on the successful outcome of the clinical trials. The extra $5m is a contingent asset, and contingent assets are not recognised in a business combination. (Only assets, liabilities and contingent liabilities are recognised.)

      Although research is not capitalised, this research has been carried out for a customer and should be recognised as work-in-progress in current assets. It will be valued at the lower of cost and net realisable value unless it meets the definition of a construction contract.

      The goodwill is capitalised at cost. It is not amortised but it will be tested for impairment annually.

   (ii)   *New drug*

      Under IAS 38 the $12m costs of *developing* this new drug are capitalised and then amortised over its commercial life. (The costs of *researching* a new drug are never capitalised.)

      Although IAS 38 permits some intangibles to be held at valuation it specifically forbids revaluing patents, therefore the $20m valuation is irrelevant.

(iii) *Government licence*

IAS 38 states that assets acquired as a result of a government grant may be capitalised at fair value, along with a corresponding credit for the value of the grant.

Therefore Dexterity may recognise an asset and grant of $10m which are then amortised/released over the five year life of the license. The net effect on profits and on shareholders funds will be nil.

(iv) *Training costs*

Although well trained staff add value to a business IAS 38 prohibits the capitalisation of training costs. This is because an entity has 'insufficient control over the expected future economic benefits' arising from staff training; in other words trained staff are free to leave and work for someone else. Training is part of the general cost of developing a business as a whole.

(v) *Advertising costs*

IAS 38 Para 69 states that advertising and promotional costs should be recognised as an expense when incurred. This is because the expected future economic benefits are uncertain and they are beyond the control of the entity.

However, because the year-end is half way through the campaign there is a $2.5m prepayment to be recognised as a current asset.

21 Advent

Advent

(a)   STATEMENT OF FINANCIAL POSITION EXTRACTS 30 SEPTEMBER 20X9

Assets	$m
Non-current assets	
Property, plant and equipment (Note 1)	316
Other intangible assets (Note 2)	100
	416

Note 1 *Property, plant and equipment*

	Land and buildings	Plant	Total
	$m	$m	$m
1 October 20X8			
Cost/ valuation	280	150	430
Accumulated depreciation	(40)	(105)	(145)
	240	45	285
30 September 20X9			
Cost/ valuation	265	200	465
Accumulated depreciation	(9)	(140)	(149)
	256	60	316
Carrying value			
1 October 20X8	240	45	285
Additions		50	50
Revaluations	(15)	–	(15)
Depreciation:			
Charge for year	(9)	(35)	(44)
On revaluation	40	–	40
	256	60	316

Buildings are depreciated over 25 years and plant over 5 years.

On 1st October 20X8 the land and buildings were valued by XYZ, Chartered Surveyors, on an open market existing use basis.

Workings

1   Plant

Installation and commissioning costs are included in the cost of the asset.

Depreciation	$m
Opening cost of $150m (full year at 20%)	30
Additions of $50m (half year at 20%)	5
	35

2   Property

	Land	Buildings: Value	Total Value	Building Dep'n	Carrying Value
	$m	$m	$m	$m	$m
Opening	80	200	280	(40)	240
Revaluation	5	(20)	(15)	40	25
	85	180	265	–	265
Depreciation (20 years)	–	–	–	(9)	(9)
Closing	85	180	265	(9)	256

Note 2 *Intangible assets: Telecommunications license*

	$m
Cost	
Opening and closing	300
Depreciation	
Opening	30
Charge	30
Impairment loss	140
Closing	200
Carrying value	
30 September 20X9	100
30 September 20X8	270

The closing carrying value must not exceed the impaired value of $100m; therefore the accumulated depreciation must be fixed at $200m. This in turn gives the impairment charge as a balancing figure of $140m.

The new carrying value of $100m will be depreciated over the remaining 8 year life of the license.

(b)   *Usefulness of the disclosures*

The disclosures give the reader more information about the nature and value of the non-current assets.

Firstly, there is the split between tangible assets (property, plant and equipment) and intangible assets. Lenders are less willing to use intangibles as security for loans than tangibles, and in the event of a winding up intangibles are often worthless without the business to support them.

Within property, plant and equipment there is the split between land and buildings and the rest. Land and buildings are often seen as the best source of security by lenders.

Land and buildings can go up in value as well as down, and so the note indicates the effect of revaluations during the year. The revaluation reserve note elsewhere in the financial statements will show the total revaluation compared with original cost. Because valuations are subjective the identity and qualifications of the valuer are disclosed.

The rates of depreciation indicate how prudent (or otherwise) the depreciation policies are, and whether the reported profits are fairly stated. The ratio between carrying value and cost gives a rough idea of the age of the assets, and of how soon they will need replacing.

The disclosure of the impairment loss flags a bad investment; the shareholders will want more information about this at their annual general meeting.

22 Wilderness

Marking scheme

				Marks
(a)	(i)	Impairment where carrying amounts higher than recoverable amounts		1
		Discussion of fair value		2
		Discussion of value in use		2
		Discussion of CGU		1
		Goodwill/ intangibles with in definite life tested annually		1
		Review for indicators of impairment		1
		Only test if there is an indication of impairment		1
			Available	9
			Maximum	6
	(ii)	Impairment loss – individual asset:		
		Impairment loss applied to carrying value of asset		1
		And changed to any previous revaluation surplus then income		2
		CGU:		
		Applied to goodwill		1
		Then pro rata to other assets		1
		Other assets not reduced below fair value/ value in use		1
			Available	6
			Maximum	5
(b)	(i)	Depreciation/ carrying value 1 April 2004		2
		Fair value less costs to sell is disposal value of $20,000, not trade-in value		2
		Recoverable is therefore $150,000		1
		Impairment loss is $50,000		1
		Depreciation six months to 30 September 2004		1
		Carrying value $112,500		1
			Available	8
			Maximum	7
	(ii)	Old brand written off, cannot recognise new brand		2
		Inventories correct at cost		2
		Improvement to plant not relevant		1
		Impairment loss is $5 million		1
		Land reduced to $9 million		1
		Plant reduced to $6 million		1
			Available	8
			Maximum	7
			Maximum for question	25

(a) (i) **Define an impairment loss**

An impairment occurs when the carrying value of an asset exceeds its recoverable amount. Recoverable amount represents the amount of cash that an asset will generate either through use (value in use) or through disposal (fair value less costs to sell).

The value in use is the present value of all future cash flows derived from an asset, including any disposal proceeds at the end of the asset's life. The present value of future cash flows will be affected by the timing, volatility and uncertainty of the cash flows. This can be reflected in the forecasted cash flows or the discount rate used.

Very few business assets generate their own cash flows, and so assets are often grouped together into cash generating units for impairment purposes. A cash generating is the smallest group of assets generating independent cash flows

Fair value less costs to sell is the amount obtainable for an asset in an arm's length transaction between knowledgeable, willing parties, less the cost of disposal. The fair value of used assets with no active market will have to be estimated. Valuations are based on willing parties, and so a 'forced sale' value would not normally be used.

Impairment reviews

- At each reporting date an entity shall assess whether there are any indications that an impairment has occurred; if there are such indications then the recoverable amount of the asset must be estimated.
- Intangible assets with indefinite lives (and those not ready for use) should be reviewed for impairment annually. The review should take place at the same time each year.
- Cash generating units that include goodwill should be reviewed for impairment annually.

(ii) **Accounting for an impairment loss**

Impairment losses should be recognised immediately. They will normally be charged to the income statement alongside depreciation, but the impairment of a revalued asset should be taken directly to the revaluation surplus (until the balance on the revaluation surplus is reduced to zero). In the statement of financial position the impairment will normally be included within accumulated depreciation, although it could be disclosed separately if material. Future depreciation charges will be based on the impaired value and the remaining useful life at the date of the impairment.

Impairments of cash generating units must be apportioned to the individual assets within that unit. The impairment is firstly allocated to goodwill, and then it is apportioned to all other assets (both tangible and intangible) on a pro rata basis. However, individual assets are not impaired below their own realisable value; any unused impairment being re-apportioned to the other assets.

(b) (i) **Wilderness**

Summary

INCOME STATEMENT

		$
Depreciation	First six months	40,000
	Second six months	37,500
Impairment		50,000
		127,500

STATEMENT OF FINANCIAL POSITION 30 SEPTEMBER 20X5

	$
Cost	640,000
Accumulated depreciation and impairment	
($400,000 + $40,000 + $50,000 + $37,500)	(527,500)
Carrying value	112,500

At 1 April 20X5 the asset should be restated at the lower of carrying value and recoverable amount. Recoverable amount is the higher of *value in use* and *fair value less costs to sell*.

Carrying value 1 April 20X5	$
Cost	640,000
Opening depreciation	(400,000)
Depreciation for 6 months ($640,000 × 12½% × 6/12)	(40,000)
Carrying value 1 April 20X5	200,000

Recoverable amount	$
Value in use and recoverable amount	150,000
Fair value less costs to sell*	20,000

* Wilderness does not intend to replace the machine and so the trade-in value of $180,000 is irrelevant.

The asset is impaired and should be written down to the recoverable amount of $150,000, giving an impairment loss of $50,000. This new valuation will then be depreciated over the remaining useful life of the asset, which is two years from the date of the accident.

Carrying value 30 September 20X5		$
Impaired value 1 April 20X5		150,000
Depreciation for 6 months	$150,000 × 6/24	(37,500)
Carrying value 1 April 20X5		112,500

(ii) **Mossel**

The question raises four issues:

- The value of the Quencher brand name,
- The $1.5m upgrade costs,
- The old bottles in inventories, and
- The overall impairment of the whole operation.

(1) *The value of the Quencher brand name*

The $7m Quencher brand name should have been written off in April as it is no longer used. The Phoenix brand name is internally generated and so it cannot be capitalised. This will reduce the carrying value of the net assets at 30 September to $25m.

(2) *The $1.5m upgrade costs*

These costs reflect the directors' intentions for the coming year. There is no obligation to incur these costs and so they cannot be recognised in the current year. However they may be disclosed in the notes.

(3) *The old bottles in inventories*

These should be stated at the lower of normal cost ($2m) and net realisable value ($2.75m), therefore they remain at their cost of $2m. The NRV is the normal sales price of $3m (normal cost of $2m plus 50%) less the $250,000 re-labelling costs.

(4) *The overall impairment of the whole operation at September 20X5*

The value in use and recoverable amount of the whole operation has been reduced to $20m. This is less than the carrying value of $25m and so an impairment has to be accounted for and apportioned to the assets within the cash generating unit. This is done as follows:

	Carrying value	Impairment	Impaired values
	$'000	$'000	$'000
Brand (already impaired)	–	–	–
Land	12,000	(3,000)	9,000
Plant	8,000	(2,000)	6,000
	20,000	(5,000)	15,000

Note. Inventory of $5m is not subject to impairment.

23 Derringdo III

Carpets

A change of accounting policy is when a new policy is used to report the same situations. In this case there is a new situation, Derringdo's terms of trade have changed, and so a new policy has been applied to report it. This is not a change of policy. The old trade will still be reported under the old method and the new trade will be reported under the new method.

INCOME STATEMENT

	$'000
Carpets fitted under the old terms of trade	1,200
(these will not have been claimed in the previous year)	
Carpets sold under the new terms of trade	23,000
Total revenue for this year	24,200

24 Telenorth

Text reference. Chapters 7 and 18.

Top tips. This was a 'typical' published financial statements type question with an earnings per share calculation. Candidates had to prepare the financial statements from a trial balance and include several adjustments which were used to cover many areas of the syllabus.

Examiner's comment. This was the one question where some less methodical candidates appeared to run out of time. On the whole this was well answered and remarkably some candidates scored full marks on Part (a). Again the 'trickier' adjustments proved to be stumbling blocks. Two of the worst errors were:

(a)   Not providing for the second half of the debenture (loan) interest and preference dividend.

(b)   Incorrect calculation of basic depreciation charges and inclusion of them in the wrong category. (The question was specific as to where depreciation should be charged.)

Answers to Part (b), the calculation of the earnings per share figure, were surprisingly disappointing. A significant proportion of candidates did not even attempt this section, of those that did very few correctly handled the rights issue and several candidates thought that the question involved a dilution calculation.

(a)   (i)   TELENORTH
                INCOME STATEMENT FOR THE YEAR ENDED 30 SEPTEMBER 20X1

	$'000
Revenue	283,460
Cost of sales (W1)	(155,170)
Gross profit	128,290
Other income	1,500
Distribution costs	(22,300)
Administrative expenses (W2)	(42,200)
Finance costs: (W11)	(1,656)
Profit before tax	63,634
Income tax expense (W10)	(24,600)
Profit for the year	39,034

(ii)   TELENORTH
         STATEMENT OF FINANCIAL POSITION AS AT 30 SEPTEMBER 20X1

	$'000	$'000
Assets		
Non-current assets		
Property, plant and equipment (W3)		83,440
Investments		34,500
		117,940
Current assets		
Inventory (W4)	16,680	
Trade accounts receivable: 35,700 + 12,000 (W5)	47,700	
		64,380
Total assets		182,320
Equity and liabilities		
Equity		
Ordinary shares of $1 each (W8)		30,000
Revaluation surplus 3,400 – 1,000		2,400
Share premium (W8)		16,000
Retained earnings (W9)		51,194
		99,594
Non-current liabilities		
8% preference shares	12,000	
6% loan notes	10,000	
Deferred tax: 5,200 + 2,200	7,400	
		29,400
Current liabilities		
Trade and other accounts payable (W6)	18,070	
Loan from factor: 9,600 + 96 (W5)	9,696	
Current tax payable	23,400	
Preference dividend payable (W7)	480	
Bank overdraft	1,680	
		53,326
Total equity and liabilities		182,320

Workings

1   *Cost of sales*

	$'000
Opening inventory	12,400
Purchases	147,200
	159,600
Closing inventory (W4)	(16,680)
	142,920
Depreciation of leasehold and plant (W3)	12,250
	155,170

2   *Administration expenses*

	$'000
Per question	34,440
Depreciation of computer system (W3)	10,160
Incorrect factoring charge (W5)	(2,400)
	42,200

3 Property, plant and equipment

	Cost	Depn	NBV
	$'000	$'000	$'000
Leasehold	56,250	20,250*	36,000
Plant and equipment	55,000	22,800*	32,200
Computer system	35,000	19,760*	15,240
			83,440

	$'000
*Depreciation charge:	
Leasehold: 56,250/25 years	2,250
Plant: (55,000 – 5,000)/5 years	10,000
Charge cost of sales	12,250
Computer equipment: charged to administration (35m – 9.6m) × 40%	10,160

4 Closing inventory

No inventory count took place at the year end. To arrive at the figure for closing inventory, the count needs to be adjusted for the movements between 30 September and 4 October, making appropriate adjustments for mark ups.

	$'000
Balance as at 4 October 20X1	16,000
Normal sales at cost: $1.4m × 100/140	1,000
Sale or return at cost: 650,000 × 100/130	500
Less goods received at cost	(820)
Adjusted inventory value	16,680

5 Accounts receivable and factoring

In the case of factoring of receivables, the **substance of a transaction** rather than its legal form needs to be considered. It may be that it is not appropriate to remove a receivable from the statement of financial position. In this case, Telenorth bears the risk of slow payment and bad debts. This means that the substance of the transaction is a loan, which in turn will incur finance charges. It was therefore incorrect to derecognise the amount receivable. Also, the difference between the amount due from the customer ($12m) and the amount received from the factor ($12m × 80% = $9.6m) should not have been charged to administration costs. Adjustments need to be made to reinstate the amount receivable, accrue one month's finance charge and add back the incorrect charge to administration expenses, as follows.

	Dr	Cr
	$'000	$'000
Accounts receivable	12,000	
Loan from factor		9,600
Administration: $12m – $9.6m		2,400
Finance costs: accrued interest $9.6m × 1%	96	
Accruals		96
	12,096	12,096

There will also be loan note interest of $600,000, $300,000 paid and $300,000 accrued.

6 Current liabilities

	$'000
Trade and other payables	
Per question	17,770
Interest on loan note	300
	18,070

7 Dividend payable

	$'000
Preference: ($12m × 8%) – 480	480

8 *Share capital and suspense account*

Elimination of suspense account:

	Dr $'000	Cr $'000
Suspense account (per trial balance)	26,000	
Directors' options: share capital (4m at $1)		4,000
share premium (4m at $1)		4,000
Rights issue: $\dfrac{20m + 4m}{4}$ share capital		6,000
Share premium 6m × (3 − 1)		12,000
	26,000	26,000

Share capital: $20m + $4m + $6m = $30m
Share premium: $4m + $12m = $16m

9 *Retained earnings*

	$'000
As at 1 October 20X0	14,160
Net profit for the year (Part (a)(i))	39,034
Dividend: ordinary	(2,000)
	51,194

10 *Income tax*

	$'000	$'000
Provision for year		23,400
Increase in deferred tax provision	2,200	
Less charged to revaluation surplus	(1,000)	
		1,200
		24,600

11 *Finance costs*

	$'000
8% Preference shares	960
6% Loan notes	600
Factoring finance cost (W5)	96
	1,656

(b) TELENORTH

EARNINGS PER SHARE FOR THE YEAR TO 30 SEPTEMBER 20X1

Date	Narrative	Shares '000	Time	Bonus fraction	Weighted average
1.10.X0	Share b/f	20,000			
1.10.X0	Options exercised	4,000			
		24,000	9/12	4/3.80 (W)	18,947
1.7.X1	Rights issue (1/4)	6,000			
		30,000	3/12		7,500
					26,447

Workings

Calculation of theoretical ex-rights price:

	$
4 shares @ $4	16
1 share @ $3	3
	19

$\therefore$ Theoretical ex-rights price $= \dfrac{19}{5} = \$3.80$

$\therefore$ Bonus fraction $= \dfrac{4.00}{3.80}$

$EPS = \dfrac{\$39,034}{26,447} = 148c$

25 Tourmalet

Text reference. Chapters 7 and 15.

Top tips. As well as examining you on the format and content of the income statement and statement of changes in equity, this question also tests your knowledge of seven specific situations.

One key point is to separate out the discontinued activities. Under IFRS 5 the profit or loss on these activities is reported after the profit after tax for continuing activities.

As always, be methodical and don't get bogged down in the detail.

Easy marks. Parts (a) and (c) are 8 easy marks. You should be able to answer these even if you get bogged down in the income statement.

Examiner's comments. Part (a) covered the sale and leaseback of plant. Most candidates realised that this should be treated as a secured loan. However, some failed to recognise the correct treatment.

In part (b), candidates had to prepare an income statement and this was generally well-answered. However some problems arose: discontinued operation, provision for slow moving inventory, and the treatment of interest on the loan from part (a).

Part (c) was generally ignored. Those who did attempt the statement of changes in equity failed to realise that the preference shares should be treated as debt and so the preference dividend should be treated as a finance cost.

Marking scheme

			Marks
(a)	Should not be treated as sales/cost of sales		1
	Normally only the profit in income (may require disclosure)		1
	The substance of the transaction is a secured loan		1
	Plant should be left on statement of financial position		1
	'Sale' proceeds of $50 million shown as loan		1
	Rentals are partly interest and partly capital repayments		1
		Available	6
		Maximum	5
(b)	Income statement		
	Discontinuing operations figures		3
	Sales		2
	Cost of sales		5
	Distribution expenses		1
	Administration expenses		2
	Finance costs (including 1 for preference dividends)		2
	Loss on investment properties		1
	Investment income		1
	Taxation		2
		Available	19
		Maximum	17

(c)

(c)   Changes in equity
       Profit for period   1
       Dividends   1
       Transfer to realised profits   1
                                                                    Maximum   3
                                                          Maximum for question   25

(a)   **Sale of plant**

The substance of this transaction is a financing arrangement, not a sale.

- Tourmalet will continue to enjoy the risks and benefits of ownership for the remainder of the asset's life because of the leaseback deal.
- The lease appears to be a finance lease, so Tourmalet will continue to recognise the asset.
- Over the period of the lease Tourmalet will repay the sale proceeds in full, plus interest at 12%, indicating that this is a loan and not a sale.

Tourmalet should continue to recognise the asset at its original cost, and depreciate it as before. The sale proceeds will be treated as a loan, and the lease payments will be split between repayment of this loan and a finance charge.

Even if the sale was a genuine sale, it should not have been included with the normal trading revenues and cost of sales.

(b)   TOURMALET
       INCOME STATEMENT FOR THE YEAR ENDED 30 SEPTEMBER 20X4

	$'000
Continuing operations	
Sales revenues (W1)	247,800
Cost of sales (W2)	(128,800)
Gross profit	119,000
Other income (W3)	1,200
Distribution costs (W4)	(26,400)
Administrative expenses (W5)	(20,000)
Other expenses (W6)	(200)
Finance costs (W7)	(3,800)
Profit before tax	69,800
Income tax expense (W8)	(7,100)
Profit for the year from continuing activities	62,700
Discontinued operations	
Loss for the year from discontinued operations (W9)	(5,500)
Profit for the year	57,200

Workings

Continuing operations	$'000	$'000
1 *Sales revenues*		
From TB		313,000
Disposal of plant		(50,000)
Discontinued activities		(15,200)
		247,800
2 *Cost of sales*		
Opening inventory		26,550
Purchases		158,450
Disposal of plant		(40,000)
Closing inventory: Cost	28,500	
NRV allowance (4,500 – 2,000)	(2,500)	
		(26,000)

Depreciation		
Leased item $40m/5 years		8,000
Others ($98.6m − $24.6m) × 20%		14,800
Buildings ($120m/40 years)		3,000
Discontinued activities		(16,000)
		128,800

3 **Other income**

From the TB ... 1,200

4 **Distribution costs**

From the TB ... 26,400

5 **Administrative expenses**

From the TB	23,200
Discontinued activities	(3,200)
	20,000

6 **Other expenses**

Fall in value of investment property (10m − 9.8m) ... 200

7 **Finance costs**

Interim preference dividend from the TB	900
Accrued final preference dividend ($30m × 6% × 6/12)	900
Finance cost of lease back ($50m × 12% × 4/12)	2,000
	3,800

8 **Income tax expense**

Over-provision from the trial balance	(2,100)
Charge for the year	9,200
	7,100

9 **Discontinued operations**

Revenue	15,200
Operating expenses (16,000 + 3,200 + 1,500 termination penalty)	(20,700)
Loss	(5,500)

(c)   TOURMALET
STATEMENT OF CHANGES IN EQUITY FOR THE YEAR TO 30 SEPTEMBER 20X4

	Share Capital $'000	Revaluation Surplus $'000	Retained Earnings $'000	Total $'000
Opening	50,000	18,500	47,800	116,300
Transfer of depreciation on revaluation	–	(500)	500	–
Dividends	–	–	(2,500)	(2,500)
Total comprehensive income for the year	–	–	57,200	57,200
Closing	50,000	18,000	103,000	171,000

26 Partway

Text reference. Chapter 7.

Top tips. This question covers discontinued operations and changes of accounting policy. Not to be attempted unless you knew something about both of these. There are 5 separate parts to this question. Do something on each of them, do not get carried away with the income statement.

Easy marks. (a) (i) and (ii) and (b) (i) were quite easy and you should have been able to do well on them. (a) (iii) was not difficult but you may have ended up spending too long on it and (b) (ii) was a bit tricky. However you were asked to comment, so a sensible comment supported by the evidence would have secured you a mark or two.

Marking scheme

				Marks
(a)	(i)	Definitions		2
		Usefulness of information		2
			Maximum	4
	(ii)	Discussion of whether a discontinued operation		3
		Conclusion		1
			Maximum	4
	(iii)	Figures for revenue from continuing operations (20X5 and 20X6)		1
		Figures for revenue from discontinued operations (20X5 and 20X6)		1
		Figures for cost of sales from continuing operations (20X5 and 20X6)		1
		Figures for cost of sales from discontinued operations (20X5 and 20X6)		1
		Figures for profit from continuing operations (20X5 and 20X6)		1
		Figures for profit from discontinued operations (20X5 and 20X6)		1
			Maximum	6
(b)	(i)	1 mark per relevant point	Maximum	5
	(ii)	1 mark per relevant point	Maximum	6
			Maximum for question	25

(a) (i) IFRS 5 defines 'non-current assets held for sale' to be those non-current assets whose carrying amount will be recovered principally through a sale transaction rather than through continuing use.

A discontinued operation is described in IFRS 5 as:

'a component of an entity that either has been disposed of, or is classified as held for sale, and:

(a) represents a separate major line of business or geographical area of operations

(b) is part of a single co-ordinated plan to dispose of a separate major line of business or geographical area of operations or

(c) is a subsidiary acquired exclusively with a view to resale.'

IFRS 5 states that *a component of an entity* comprises operations and cash flows that can be clearly distinguished, operationally and for financial reporting purposes, from the rest of the entity.

This very precise definition is needed to ensure that only operations which can properly be regarded as discontinued are classified as such. Users of accounts, particularly financial analysts, will be more interested in the results of continuing operations as a guide to the company's future profitability and it is not unacceptable for discontinued operations to show a loss. Companies could therefore be tempted to hide loss-making activities under the umbrella of discontinued operations, hence the requirement for the operations and cash flows of the discontinued operation to be clearly distinguishable from those of continuing operations. It is also conceivable that a company could seek to include the results of a profitable operation which has been sold under continuing operations.

IFRS 5 requires an entity to disclose a single amount on the face of the income statement comprising the total of:

(i) the post tax profit or loss of discontinued operations and

(ii) the post-tax gain or loss recognised on the measurement to fair value less costs to sell or on the disposal of the assets constituting the discontinued operation

The separation of the results of continuing and discontinued operations on the face of the income statement makes possible more meaningful year on year comparison. The inclusion of prior year information for discontinued operations means that it can be seen exactly how the continuing operations have performed, and it is possible to forecast more accurately how they can be expected to perform in the future.

(ii)   This can be correctly classified as a discontinued operation. The termination was completed before the end of the financial year. The interested parties were notified at that time and an announcement was made in the press, making the decision official. Although the company will continue to sell holidays over the internet, the travel agency business represents a separate major line of business. The internet business will have quite different property and staffing requirements and a different customer base. The results of the travel agency business are clearly distinguished.

(iii)   PARTWAY
        INCOME STATEMENT FOR THE YEAR ENDED

	31 October 20X6	31 October 20X5
Continuing operations	$'000	$'000
Revenue	25,000	22,000
Cost of sales	(19,500)	(17,000)
Gross profit	5,500	5,000
Operating expenses	(1,100)	(500)
Profit from continuing operations	4,400	4,500
Profit(loss) from discontinued operations	(4,000)	1,500
Profit for the year	400	6,000
Discontinued operations		
Revenue	14,000	18,000
Cost of sales	(16,500)	(15,000)
Gross profit (loss)	(2,500)	3,000
Operating expenses	(1,500)	(1,500)
Profit(loss) from discontinued operations	(4,000)	1,500

(b) (i)   Accounting policies can be described as the principles, conventions, rules and practices applied by an entity that prescribe how transactions and other events are to be reflected in its financial statements. This includes the recognition, presentation and measurement basis to be applied to assets, liabilities, gains, losses and changes to shareholders funds. Once these policies have been adopted, they are not expected to change frequently and comparability requires that ideally they do not change from year to year. However, IAS 8 does envisage situations where a change of accounting policy is required in the interests of fair presentation.

An entity may have to change an accounting policy in response to changes in a Standard or in applicable legislation. Or it may be an internal decision which can be justified on the basis of presenting a more reliable picture. An accounting policy adopted to deal with transactions or events which did not arise previously is not treated as a change of accounting policy.

Where a change of accounting policy has taken place it must be accounted for by retrospective restatement. This means that the comparative financial statements must be restated in the light of the new accounting policy. This makes it possible to compare results for these years as if the new accounting policy had always been in place. The financial statements must disclose the reason for the change of accounting policy and the effects of the change on the results for the previous year.

(ii)   The directors' proposal here is that revenue recognition can be accelerated based on the imposition of compulsory holiday insurance. This is based on the presumption that the risk of not receiving the balance of the payment has now been covered. However, at the point when the deposit is received, Partway has not yet done anything to earn the revenue. Under IAS 18 *Revenue,* revenue from a service contract should be recognised by reference to the stage of completion of the transaction. Under this method, revenue is recognised in the accounting periods in which the services are rendered. In this case the service is rendered at the time when the holiday is taken. The existing policy is therefore correct and should not be changed.

27 Preparation question: Simple consolidation

BOO GROUP
CONSOLIDATED INCOME STATEMENT
FOR THE YEAR ENDED 31 DECEMBER 20X8

	$'000
Revenue (5,000 + 1,000 – 100)	5,900
Cost of sales (2,900 + 600 – 80)	(3,420)
Gross profit	2,480
Other expenses (1,700 + 320)	(2,020)
Profit before tax	460
Tax (130 + 25)	(155)
Profit for the year	305
Profit attributable to	
Owners of the parent	294
Non-controlling interest (20% × 55)	11
	305

CONSOLIDATED STATEMENT OF CHANGES IN EQUITY (retained earnings only)

	$'000
Opening retained earnings (230 + (185 × 80%))	378
Total comprehensive income for the year	294
Closing retained earnings	672

CONSOLIDATED STATEMENT OF FINANCIAL POSITION AS AT 31 DECEMBER 20X8

	$'000	$'000
Assets		
Non-current assets (2,000 + 200 – 80)		2,120
Current assets		
Inventory (500 + 120 + 80)	700	
Trade receivables (650 – 100 + 40)	590	
Bank and cash (390 + 35)	425	
		1,715
Total assets		3,835
Equity and liabilities		
Equity attributable to owners of the parent		
Share capital (Boo only)		2,000
Retained earnings (W3)		672
		2,672
Non-controlling interest (W4)		68
Total equity		2,740
Current liabilities		
Trade payables (910 + 30)	940	
Tax (130 + 25)	155	
		1,095
Total equity and liabilities		3,835

Workings

1 *Group structure*

Boo

↓ 80% since incorporation

Goose

2 Retained earnings

	Boo $'000	Goose $'000
Per question	500	240
Unrealised profit (W1)	(20)	
	480	
Less pre acquisition		–
		240
Goose: 80% × 240	192	
Total, as per Statement of Changes in Equity	672	

3 Non-controlling interest

	$'000
NCI at acquisition (SC 100 × 20%)	20
NCI share of post acquisition retained earnings (240 × 20%)	48
	68

4 Inter company issues

Step 1: Record Goose's purchase

DEBIT Purchases	$100,000	
CREDIT Payables		$100,000
DEBIT Closing inventory (B/S)	$100,000	
CREDIT Closing inventory I/S (COS)		$100,000

Step 2: Cancel unrealised profit

DEBIT COS (and retained earnings) in BOO	$20,000	
CREDIT Inventory (B/S)		$20,000

Step 3: Cancel intragroup transaction

DEBIT Revenue	$100,000	
CREDIT Cost of sales		$100,000

Step 4: Cancel intragroup balances

DEBIT Receivables	$100,000	
CREDIT Payables		$100,000

28 Hideaway

IAS 24 Related Parties

(a) *Importance of related party disclosures*

Investors invest in a business on the assumption that it aims to maximise its own profits for the benefit of its own shareholders. This means that all transactions have been negotiated at arm's length between willing and informed parties. The existence of related parties may encourage directors to make decisions for the benefit of another entity at the expense of their own shareholders. This can be done actively by selling goods and services cheaply to related parties, or by buying in goods and services at an above market price. It can also happen when directors chose not to compete with a related party, or offer guarantees or collateral for other party's loans.

Disclosure is particularly important when a business is being sold. It may receive a lot of custom, supplies, services or general help and advice from family or group companies. When the company is sold these benefits may be withdrawn.

Related party transactions are not illegal, nor are they necessarily a bad thing. However shareholders and potential investors need to be informed of material related party transactions in order to make informed investment and stewardship decisions.

(b) *Hideaway, Benedict and Depret*

The directors and shareholders of Hideaway, the parent, will maximise their wealth by diverting profitable trade into wholly owned subsidiaries. They have done this by instructing Depret (a 55% subsidiary) to sell goods to Benedict (a 100% subsidiary) at $5m below fair value. As a result the non-controlling shareholders of Depret have been deprived of their 45% interest in those lost profits, amounting to $2.25m. The non-group directors of Depret will also lose out if their pay is linked to Depret's profits.

Because Depret's profits have been reduced, the non-controlling shareholders might be persuaded to sell their shares to Hideaway for less than their true value. Certainly potential shareholders will not be willing to pay as much for Depret's shares as they would have if Depret's profits had been maximised.

The opposite possibility is that the Directors of Hideaway are boosting Benedict's reported performance with the intention of selling it off for an inflated price.

Depret's non-controlling shareholders might be able to get legal redress because the majority shareholders appear to be using their power to oppress the non-controlling shareholders. This, however, will depend on local law. The tax authorities might also suspect Depret of trying to avoid tax, especially if Benedict is in a different tax jurisdiction.

29 Highveldt

Text reference. Chapter 9.

Top tips. Don't forget **Part (b)**. There are five marks here for explaining the purpose of consolidated financial statements. Do it first, before getting tied up with Part (a).

Part (a) Make sure that you read the question before doing anything. You are not asked to prepare a statement of financial position; just the goodwill and reserves. This makes the question easier to manage as effectively you are just doing the workings without having to tie it all together in a set of financial statements.

There are quite a few complications to consider. For each calculation go through each of the six additional pieces of information and make appropriate adjustments when relevant.

Easy marks. Part (b) is 5 easy marks.

Examiner's comments. Part (a) was unusual in asking for extracts from the statement of financial position. Many candidates were confused by this and wasted time preparing a full statement of financial position. Other common errors were: fair value adjustments; consolidated reserves; revaluation and share premium reserves; and the cost of the investment.

Part (b) was disappointing as many candidates did not answer the question set, ie **why** consolidated accounts are prepared.

Marking scheme

				Marks
(a)	(i)	*Goodwill*		
		– Consideration transferred		2
		– Share capital and premium		1
		– Pre-acquisition profit		2
		– Fair value adjustments		2
		– Goodwill impairment		1
			Maximum	8
	(ii)	*Non-controlling interest*		
		– Share capital and premium		1
		– Retained earnings		2
		– Fair value adjustment		1
			Maximum	4

(iii)	Consolidated reserves			
		– Share premium		1
		– Revaluation surplus		2
	Retained earnings			
		– Post acquisition profit		2
		– Interest receivable		1
		– Finance cost		1
		– Goodwill impairment		1
			Maximum	8
(b)	1 mark per relevant point to		Maximum	5
			Maximum for question	25

(a) *Group Structure as at 31 March 20X5*

Highveldt	
parent	
75%	Since 1.4.X4
Samson	
subsidiary	

(i) *Goodwill in Samson*

	$m	$m
Consideration transferred		
80m shares × 75% × $3.50		210
Deferred consideration; $108m × $^1/_{1.08}$		100
		310
Non-controlling interests (296 × 25%)		74
Fair value of net assets at acquisition:		
Carrying value of net assets at 1.4.20X4:		
Ordinary shares	80	
Share premium	40	
Retained earnings	134	
Fair value adjustments (W)	42	
		(296)
		88
Impairment charge given in question		(22)
Carrying value at 31 March 20X5		66

Goodwill: alternative working

	$m	$m
Consideration transferred		
80m shares × 75% × $3.50		210
Deferred consideration; $108m × $^1/_{1.08}$		100
		310
Share of the net assets acquired at fair value		
Carrying value of net assets at 1.4.20X4:		
Ordinary shares	80	
Share premium	40	
Retained earnings	134	
	254	
Fair value adjustments (W)	42	
Fair value of the net assets at acquisition	296	
75% Group share		(222)
Cost of Goodwill		88
Impairment charge given in question		(22)
Carrying value at 31 March 20X5		66

Notes (not required in the exam)

Goodwill is based on the present value of the deferred consideration. During the year the $8m discount will be charged to Highveldt's income statement as a finance cost. (In (a)(iii) retained earnings will be adjusted for this accrued interest.)

Only the $20m fair valuation is relevant at the date of acquisition. The $4m arising post acquisition will be treated as a normal revaluation and credited to the revaluation surplus. (See (a)(iii) below.)

Samson was right not to capitalise an internally developed brand name because, without an active market, its value cannot be measured reliably. However the fair value of a brand name can be measured as part of a business combination. Therefore the $40m fair value will be recognised at acquisition and an additional $4m amortisation will be charged in the consolidated income statement.

At acquisition Samson had capitalised $18m of development expenditure. Highveldt does not recognise this as an asset, so the net assets at acquisition are reduced by $18m. A further $32m is capitalised by Samson post acquisition; this will be written off in the consolidated income statement (net of the $10m amortisation already charged).

(ii)   *Non-controlling interest in Samson's net assets*

	$m
NCI at acquisition (W(i))	74
NCI share of post acquisition retained earnings ((W(iii)) 48 × 25%)	12
NCI share of post-acquisition revaluation surplus ((W(iii)) 4 × 25%)	1
	87

Alternative working:

	$m
Samson's net assets from the question	330
Fair value adjustment (W)	42
Post-acquisition revaluation of land	4
Amortisation of brand	(4)
Capitalised development expenditure – carrying value (32-10)	(22)
Unrealised profit ($6m/3)	(2)
	348
Non-controlling interest 25%	87

(iii)   *Consolidated Reserves*

Share premium

The share premium of a group, like the share capital, is the share premium of the parent only ($80m)

Revaluation surplus

	$m
Parent's own revaluation surplus	45
Group share of Samson's post acquisition revaluation; $4m × 75%	3
	48

Retained earnings

Retained earnings attributable to owners of the parent

	Highveldt $m	Samson $m
Per question	350	76
Accrued interest from Samson ($60m × 10%)	6	–
Unwinding of discount on deferred consideration	(8)	–
Amortisation of brand ($40m/10 years)	–	(4)
Write off development expenditure as incurred ($50m – $18m)	–	(32)
Write back amortisation of development expenditure	–	10
Unrealised profit	–	(2)
	348	48
Group share (75%)	36	
Impairment of goodwill in Samson	(22)	
	362	

Working	$m
Fair value adjustment:	
Revaluation of land	20
Recognition of fair value of brands	40
Derecognition of capitalised development expenditure	(18)
	42

(b) *Usefulness of consolidated financial statements*

The main reason for preparing consolidated accounts is that groups operate as a single economic unit, and it is not possible to understand the affairs of the parent company without taking into account the financial position and performance of all the companies that it controls. The directors of the parent company should be held fully accountable for all the money they have invested on their shareholders behalf, whether that has been done directly by the parent or via a subsidiary.

There are also practical reasons why parent company accounts cannot show the full picture. The parent company's own financial statements only show the original cost of the investment and the dividends received from the subsidiary. As explained below, this hides the true value and nature of the investment in the subsidiary, and, without consolidation, could be used to manipulate the reported results of the parent.

- The cost of the investment will include a premium for goodwill, but this is only quantified and reported if consolidated accounts are prepared.
- A controlling interest in a subsidiary can be achieved with a 51% interest. The full value of the assets controlled by the group is only shown through consolidation when the non-controlling interest is taken into account.
- Without consolidation, the assets and liabilities of the subsidiary are disguised.
    - A subsidiary could be very highly geared, making its liquidity and profitability volatile.
    - A subsidiary's assets might consist of intangible assets, or other assets with highly subjective values.
- The parent company controls the dividend policy of the subsidiary, enabling it to smooth out profit fluctuations with a steady dividend. Consolidation reveals the underlying profits of the group.
- Over time the net assets of the subsidiary should increase, but the cost of the investment will stay fixed and will soon bear no relation to the true value of the subsidiary.

30 Parentis

Marking scheme

	Marks
Non-current assets	2
Goodwill (1 for impairment)	7
Inventory	1
Trade receivables	1
Receivable re intellectual property	1
Bank	1½
Equity shares	1
Share premium	1
Retained earnings	4
Non-controlling interest	3
10% loan notes	1
Trade payables	1
Deferred consideration	1
Overdraft	1
Tax liability	½
Available	26
Maximum for question	25

PARENTIS GROUP: CONSOLIDATED STATEMENT OF FINANCIAL POSITION AS AT 31 MARCH 20X7

	$m
Assets	
Non-current assets	
Property, plant and equipment (640 + 340 + 38 (W8))	1,018
Goodwill (W3)	108
	1,126
Current assets	
Inventory (76 + 22 – 2 (W6))	96
Trade receivables (84 + 44 – 4 (W7) – 7 intragroup)	117
Government compensation receivable	10
Cash (4 + 4)	8
	231
Total assets	1,357

	$m
Equity and liabilities	
Equity attributable to owners of the parent	
Equity shares 25c (300 + 75 (W2))	375
Share premium	150
Retained earnings (W4)	264
	789
Non-controlling interest (W5)	89
	878
Non-current liabilities	
10% loan notes (120 + 20)	140
Current liabilities	
Trade payables (130 + 57 – 7 intragroup)	180
Deferred consideration (discount unwound)	66
Tax payable (45 + 23)	68
Overdraft	25
	339
Total equity and liabilities	1,357

Workings

1   *Group structure*

Parentis

| 75%

Offspring

2   *Investment in Offspring*

	$m
Parentis shares (600/2 × 0.75) (sc 75/premium 150)	225
Loan note	120
Deferred consideration	66
Discount on deferred consideration (66/1.1 × 0.1)	(6)
	405

3   *Goodwill*

	$m	$m
Consideration transferred (W2)		405
Non-controlling interests at acquisition (360 × 25%)		90
FV net assets at acquisition:		
Share capital	200	
Retained earnings	120	
Fair value adjustment (W8)	40	
		(360)
Goodwill on acquisition		135
Impairment loss		(27)
		108

Alternative working

	$m	$m
Consideration transferred (W2)		405
Acquired:		
Share capital	200	
Retained earnings	120	
Fair value adjustment (W8)	40	
	360	
× 75%		(270)
Goodwill on acquisition		135
Impairment		(27)
		108

4 *Retained earnings*

	Parentis	Offspring
	$m	$m
Opening balance	300	20
Loss on intellectual property (30 – 10)		(20)
Unrealised profit		(2)
Additional depreciation (W8)		(2)
		(4)
Group share 75%	(3)	
Goodwill impairment	(27)	
Unwinding of discount (as per W2)	(6)	
	264	

5 *Non-controlling interest*

	$m
NCI at acquisition (W3)	90
NCI share of post acquisition retained earnings ((W4) (4) × 10%)	(1)
	89

Alternative working

	$m
Offspring net assets	340
Unrealised profit (W6)	(2)
Loss on intellectual property (30 – 10)	(20)
Fair value adjustment (W8)	38
	356
Non-controlling share 25%	89

6 *Unrealised profit*

$6m × 5/15 = $2m

DR retained earnings/CR Group inventories

7 *Cash in transit*

DR Cash $4m/CR Receivables $4m

8 *Fair value adjustment*

	Acquisition 1.4.X6	Movement (1 year)	Year end 31.3.X7
Properties	40	(2)	38

31 Pedantic

Marking scheme

		Marks
(a)	Income statement:	
	revenue	1½
	cost of sales	3
	distribution costs	½
	administrative expenses	1
	finance costs	½
	income tax	½
	non-controlling interest	2
		9
(b)	Statement of financial position:	
	property, plant and equipment	2
	goodwill	5
	current assets	1½
	equity shares	1
	share premium	1
	retained earnings	2
	non-controlling interest	2
	10% loan notes	½
	current liabilities	1
		16
	Total for question	25

PEDANTIC

CONSOLIDATED INCOME STATEMENT FOR THE YEAR ENDED 30 SEPTEMBER 2008

	$'000
Revenue (85,000 + (42,000 × 6/12) – 8,000 (W7))	98,000
Cost of sales (W8)	(72,000)
Gross profit	26,000
Distribution costs (2,000 + (2,000 × 6/12))	(3,000)
Administrative expenses (6,000 + (3,200 × 6/12))	(7,600)
Finance costs (300 + (400 × 6/12))	(500)
Profit before tax	14,900
Income tax expense (4,700 + (1,400 × 6/12)	(5,400)
Profit for the year	9,500
Profit attributable to:	
Owners of the parent	9,300
Non-controlling interests (W4)	200
	9,500

PEDANTIC

STATEMENT OF FINANCIAL POSITION AT 30 SEPTEMBER 2008

	$'000
Non-current assets	
Property, plant and equipment (40,600 + 12,600 + 1,800 (W6))	55,000
Goodwill (3,000 + 1,500 (W2))	4,500
	59,500
Current assets (W9)	21,400
Total assets	80,900
Equity attributable to owners of the parent	
Share capital (10,000 +1,600 (W5))	11,600
Share premium (W5)	8,000
Retained earnings (W3)	35,700
	55,300
Non-controlling interests (W4)	6,100
	61,400
Non-current liabilities	
10% loan notes (3,000 + 4,000)	7,000
Current liabilities (8,200 + 4,700 – 400 (W10))	12,500
	80,900

Workings

1   *Group structure*

Pedantic

1.4.08   ↓   60%   Mid-year acquisition, 6 months before year end.

Sophistic

2   *Goodwill*

	$'000	$'000
Consideration transferred (W5)		9,600
Non-controlling interests (at 'full' FV) ((11,000 × 40%) + 1,500 NCI in goodwill)		5,900
Less: Fair value of net assets at acquisition:		
Share capital	4,000	
Retained earnings (6,500 – (3,000 × 6/12))	5,000	
Fair value adjustment (W6)	2,000	
		(11,000)
Goodwill		4,500

Alternative working

	$'000	Group $'000	NCI $'000
Consideration transferred (W5)		9,600	
Less: Net assets acquired			
Share capital	4,000		
Retained earnings (6,500 – (3,000 × 6/12))	5,000		
Fair value adjustment (W6)	2,000		
	11,000		
Group share 60%		(6,600)	
Goodwill		3,000	1,500

3 Retained earnings

	Pedantic $'000	Sophistic $'000
Per question	35,400	6,500
Movement on FV adjustment (W6)		(200)
PUP (W7)		(800)
Pre- acquisition (W2)		(5,000)
		500
Group share (500 × 60%)	300	
	35,700	

4 Non-controlling interests

INCOME STATEMENT

	$'000
Post acquisition profit of Sophistic (3,000 × 6/12)	1,500
PUP (W7)	(800)
Movement on FVA (W6)	(200)
	500
× 40%	200

STATEMENT OF FINANCIAL POSITION

	$'000
NCI at acquisition (W2)	5,900
NCI share of post acquisition retained earnings ((W3) 500 × 40%)	200
	6,100

Alternative working

	$'000	$'000
Net assets at year end of Sophistic per question	10,500	
FV adjustments (W6)	1,800	
PUP (W7)	(800)	
	11,500	
NCI share 40%		4,600
Goodwill in NCI (W2)		1,500
		6,100

5 Share exchange

	DR $'000	CR $'000
Consideration transferred (4,000 × 60% × 2/3 = 1,600 × $6)	9,600	
Share capital of Pedantic (1,600 × $1)		1,600
Share premium of Pedantic (1,600 × $5)		8,000

6   Fair value adjustments

	$,000 Acq'n 1.4.08	$'000 Mov't 6/12	$'000 Year end 30.9.08
Plant (*$2m/5 × 6/12)	2,000	(200)*	1,800

7   Intragroup trading

	DR	CR
Cancel intragroup sales/purchases:		
Sales	8,000	
Purchases		8,000
Eliminate unrealised profit:		
Cost of sales/retained earnings ((8,000 – 5,200) × 40/140)	800	
Inventories (SOFP)		800

8   Cost of sales

	$,000
Pedantic	63,000
Sophistic (32,000 × 6/12)	16,000
Movement on FV adjustment (W6)	200
Intragroup purchases (W7)	(8,000)
Unrealised profit (W7)	800
	72,000

9   Current assets

	$'000
Pedantic	16,000
Sophistic	6,600
Unrealised profit in inventory (W7)	(800)
Intercompany receivables (per question)	(600)
Cash in transit (W10)	200
	21,400

10   Cash in transit

	DR	CR
Receivables		600
Payables	400	
Group cash	200	

32 Preparation question: Acquisition during the year

(a)   PORT GROUP: CONSOLIDATED INCOME STATEMENT FOR THE YEAR ENDING 31 DECEMBER 20X4

	Port	Alfred 2/12	Adjustment	Group
	$'000	$'000		$'000
Revenue	100	166		266
Cost of sales	(36)	(43)		(79)
Gross profit				187
Interest on loan to Alfred	276	–	(46)	230
Other investment income	158	–		158
Operating expenses	(56)	(55)		(111)
Finance costs	–	(46)	46	–
Profit before tax				464
Taxation	(112)	(6)		(118)
Profit for the year				346
Profit attributable to:				
Owners of the parent				342
Non-controlling interest (W5)				4
				346

PORT GROUP STATEMENT OF FINANCIAL POSITION AS AT 31 DECEMBER 20X4

		Adjustments	Group $'000
Assets			
Non-current assets			
Goodwill		(W2)	275
Property, plant and equipment	100 + 3,000		3,100
Investments			
Loan to Alfred	2,300 + 0	(2,300)	–
Other investments	600 + 0		600
			3,975
Current assets	800 + 139		939
Total assets			4,914
Equity and liabilities			
Equity attributable to owners of the parent			
$1 equity shares		(W3)	235
Share premium		(W3)	1,115
Retained earnings		(W4)	2,912
			4,262
Non-controlling interest		(W5)	129
Total equity			4,391
Non-current liabilities			
Loan from Port	0 + 2,300	(2,300)	–
Current liabilities			
Sundry	200 + 323		523
Total equity and liabilities			4,914

Workings

1   *Group structure*

Port	
	75% Subsidiary Two months only
Alfred	

2   *Calculation of the cost of investment and goodwill*

	$'000	$'000	$'000
Consideration transferred (shares)			650
Non-controlling interests at acquisition (500 × 25%)			125
Net assets at date of acquisition (Note)			
Share capital		100	
Share premium		85	
Retained earnings:			
Opening	235		
Add: accrued profit for the year: $96,000 × 10/12	80		
Pre-acquisition retained earnings		315	
			(500)
Goodwill			275

Alternative working

	$'000	$'000	$'000
Consideration transferred (shares)			650
Net assets at date of acquisition (Note)			
Shares		100	
Share Premium		85	
Retained earnings			
Opening	235		
Add: accrued profit for the year: $96,000 × 10/12	80		
Pre-acquisition retained earnings		315	
Net assets		500	
Group share: 75%			(375)
Goodwill			275

Note. The net assets at the date of acquisition are also calculated by time-apportioning profits. The share capital and retained earnings brought forward obviously all arose before acquisition. The profit for the year is assumed to have arisen evenly over time.

3   *Issue of shares*

	Draft	New issue	Revised
	$'000	$'000	$'000
Share Capital	200	35	235
Share Premium	500	615	1,115
Fair value of proceeds		650	

4   *Group retained earnings*

	Port	Alfred
	$'000	$'000
Per question	2,900	331
Less pre acquisition (W2)		(315)
		16
Share of Alfred: (16 × 75%)	12	
	2,912	

5   *Non-controlling interests*

Income statement

The rule here is to time apportion the non-controlling interest in the subsidiary acquired during the year. After all, you can only take out in respect of the non-controlling interest what was put in the first place. So, if two months were consolidated then two months of non-controlling interest will be deducted.

$96,000 × 2/12 × 25% = $4,000.

Statement of financial position

	$'000
NCI at acquisition (W2)	125
NCI share of post acquisition retained earnings ((W4) 16 × 25%)	4
	129

Alternative working

Alfred's equity is $516,000. The non-controlling interest is 25% of that = $129,000.

33 Hillusion

Marking scheme

		Marks
(a)	*Income statement*	2
	Sales revenue	3
	Cost of sales	2
	Operating expenses including goodwill	1
	Loan interest	1
	Tax	1
	Non-controlling interest	1
	Retained earnings b/f	1
	Statement of financial position:	
	Goodwill	3
	Property, plant and equipment	2
	Current assets	2
	Retained earnings	1
	Non-controlling interest	2
	10% loan notes	1
	Current liabilities	1
	Available	24
	Maximum	20
(b)	1 mark per relevant point to Maximum	5
	Maximum for question	25

(a) THE HILLUSION GROUP
CONSOLIDATED INCOME STATEMENT FOR THE YEAR ENDED 31 MARCH 20X3

	$'000
Sales revenues (60,000 + ($^9/_{12}$ 24,000) – 12,000 (W5))	66,000
Cost of sales (42,000 + ($^9/_{12}$ 20,000) – 12,000 + 500 (W5) + 600 (W4))	(46,100)
Gross profit	19,900
Operating expenses (6,000 + (200 × $^9/_{12}$) + 300 (W3))	(6,450)
Finance costs (200 × $^9/_{12}$ less 75 income)	(75)
Profit before tax	13,375
Income tax expense (3,000 + (600 × $^9/_{12}$))	(3,450)
Profit for the year	9,925
Profit attributable to:	
Owners of the parent	9,655
Non-controlling interest ((3,000 × $^9/_{12}$) – 600 (W6)) × 20% - 60(W3))	270
	9,925

CONSOLIDATED STATEMENT OF FINANCIAL POSITION AS AT 31 MARCH 20X3

	$'000
Assets	
Non-current assets	
Property, plant and equipment (19,320 + 8,000 + 2,600 fair valuation (W6))	29,920
Goodwill (W5)	1,130
Investments (11,280 – 10,280 (W5) – 1,000 loan notes)	–
	31,050
Current assets (15,000 + 8,000 – 500 unrealised profit (W5) – 750 inter-company)	21,750
Total assets	52,800
Equity and liabilities	
Equity attributable to owners of the parent	
Share capital (Parent only)	10,000
Retained earnings (W4)	26,180
	36,180
Non-controlling interest (W7))	2,770
Non-current liabilities (0 + 2,000 – 1,000 loan notes)	1,000
Current liabilities (10,000 + 3,600 – 750 inter-company)	12,850
	52,800

Workings

1 *Group Structure as at 31 March 20X3*

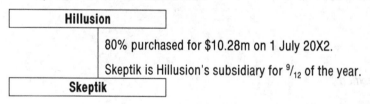

80% purchased for $10.28m on 1 July 20X2.

Skeptik is Hillusion's subsidiary for $^9/_{12}$ of the year.

2 *Timeline*

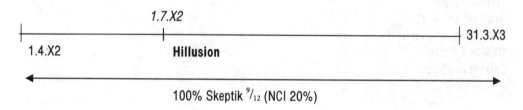

3   Goodwill in Skeptik

	$'000	$'000
Consideration transferred		10,280
Non-controlling interests (at 'full' fair value)		2,500
Fair value of net assets at acquisition:		
Share capital	2,000	
Opening retained earnings	5,400	
Time apportioned profits for the year; $3m \times \frac{3}{12}$	750	
Fair value increase for the plant	3,200	
		(11,350)
		1,430
Impairment losses		(300)
		1,130

Alternative working

	Group	Group	NCI
	$'000	$'000	$'000
Consideration transferred/Fair value of NCI		10,280	2500
Net assets at acquisition			
Share capital	2,000		
Opening retained earnings	5,400		
Time apportioned profits for the year; $3m \times \frac{3}{12}$	750		
Fair value increase for the plant	3,200		
Fair value of the net assets at acquisition	11,350		
× Group /NCI %		(9,080)	(2,270)
Cost of goodwill		1,200	230
Impairment (300 × 80% / 20%)		(240)	(60)
		960	170
		1,130	

4   Retained earnings attributable to owners of the parent

	Hillusion	Skeptik
	$'000	$'000
Per question	25,600	8,400
Pre-acquisition reserves	–	(6,150)
Provision for unrealised profit (W5)	(500)	–
Depreciation on fair valuation (W6)	–	(600)
	25,100	1,650
Group share (80%)	1,320	
Group share of impairment losses (300 × 80%)	(240)	
	26,180	

5   Intra group trade and the provision for unrealised profit

Group revenues and cost of sales are reduced by the $12m of intra-group sales at invoiced value. This adjustment does not affect profits.

An adjustment is made for the unrealised profit on goods sold by Hillusion to Skeptik but still unsold at the year-end. This increases the cost of sales in the income statement and reduces the value of the inventories in the statement of financial position. The gross profit margin was 25% ($3m/$12m).

		$'000
Goods unsold at the year-end; $12m - $10m		2,000
Unrealised profit: $2m × 25%		500

6   Fair valued plant

		$'000
Fair value at acquisition		3,200
Depreciation over four years for nine months; $3.2m \times \frac{1}{4} \times \frac{9}{12}$	I/S	(600)
Carrying value of licence 31 March 20X3		2,600

The extra $600,000 depreciation is taken into account when apportioning the profit for the year between the parent and the non-controlling interest. It also affects the group's retained earnings in the statement of financial position.

7   *Non-controlling interests*

	$'000
NCI at acquisition (W3)	2,500
NCI share of post acquisition retained earnings ((W4) 1,650 × 20%)	330
NCI share of impairment losses (300 × 20%)	(60)
	2,770

(b)   **Unrealised profits**

Unrealised profits arise when group companies trade with each other. In their own individual company accounts profits and losses will be claimed on these transactions, and goods bought from a fellow group company will be recorded at their invoiced cost by the purchaser.

However, consolidated accounts are drawn up on the principle that a group is a single economic entity. From a group point of view, no transaction occurs when goods are traded between group companies, and no profits or losses arise. Revenue and profits will only be claimed when the goods are sold onto a third party from outside of the group.

In this example, Hillusion sold $12m of goods to Skeptik making a profit of $3m. The sale by Hillusion and the purchase by Skeptik must be eliminated from the group income statement. This adjustment will not affect profits because both the sales and the purchases have been reduced by the same amount.

By the year-end Skeptik had sold $10m of these items making a profit of $5m. From a group point of view, the profit on these items, including their share of the profit claimed by Hillusion, has now been realised. However, Skeptik still has $2m of goods bought from Hillusion. This valuation includes an element of profit ($500,000) that has not yet been realised and needs to be eliminated. This will reduce the carrying value of the inventory to the amount originally paid for them by Hillusion. If unrealised profits were not eliminated, then groups could boost their profits and asset values by selling goods to each other at inflated prices.

A future purchaser of Skeptik would obviously review Skeptik's own financial statements. These show a $3.6m profit before tax, which gives a very healthy 15% net profit on revenues. However, over 60% of Skeptik's revenue comes from selling goods supplied by Hillusion. The gross profit earned on these items is $5m, which is more than the $4m gross profit for the company as a whole. A new owner might not get such favourable terms from Hillusion, leaving them with the loss making products. Nobody would be interested in buying such a business, but this information cannot be gleaned from the entity's own financial statements.

34 Hydan

Text reference. Chapters 9 and 10.

Top Tips. Note that Systan made a loss in the post-acquisition period – therefore the retained earnings at acquisition were higher than the retained earnings at the year end. This means that, in the income statement, the non-controlling will be allocated their share of a loss. This is unusual – do not be put off by it.

Easy marks. In this question you had to deal with NCI at fair value and post-acquisition loss in Systan. There were no other major complications. You were told what the additional depreciation was on the fair value adjustment, and the unrealised profit calculation was simple. The rest was straightforward consolidation procedure, with easy marks for issues such as cancelling out the intercompany loan.

The information in the question and your answer will have told you all you needed to know to answer (b), and there were five easy marks available there

Marking scheme

		Marks
(a)	**Income statement**	
	Revenue	2
	Cost of sales	3
	Operating expenses including 1 mark for goodwill	2
	Interest receivable/payable	1
	Income tax	1
	Non-controlling interest	2
	Statement of financial position	
	Goodwill	3
	Property, plant and equipment	2
	Investments	1
	Current assets/current liabilities	2
	7% bank loan	1
	Elimination of 10% intra-group loan	1
	Non-controlling interest	2
	Share capital and share premium	1
	Retained earnings	1
	Available	25
	Maximum	20
(b)	1 mark per relevant point to Maximum	5
	Maximum for question	25

(a) HYDAN CONSOLIDATED INCOME STATEMENT YEAR ENDED 31 MARCH 20X6

	$'000
Revenue (98,000 + 35,200 – 30,000 intra-group)	103,200
Cost of sales (76,000 + 31,000 – 30,000 intra-group + 200 (W6) + 300 (W7))	(77,500)
Gross profit	25,700
Operating expenses (11,800 + 8,000 + 375 (W2))	(20,175)
Interest receivable (350 – 200 intra-group (4,000 × 10% × $^6/_{12}$))	150
Finance costs	(420)
Profit before tax	5,255
Income tax expense (4,200 – 1,000)	(3,200)
Profit for the year	2,055

Profit attributable to:	
Owners of the parent	3,605
Non-controlling interest (W4)	(1,550)
	2,055

HYDAN CONSOLIDATED STATEMENT OF FINANCIAL POSITION AT 31 MARCH 20X6

	$'000
Non-current assets	
Property, plant and equipment (18,400 + 9,500 + 1,200 – 300 (W7))	28,800
Goodwill (W2)	3,025
Investments (16,000 – 10,800 (W2) – 4,000)	1,200
Current assets (18,000 + 7,200 – 200 (W6) – 1,000 intra-group)	24,000
Total assets	57,025
Equity and liabilities	
Equity attributable to owners of the parent	
Ordinary shares of $1 each	10,000
Share premium	5,000
Retained earnings (W3)	17,675
	32,675
Non-controlling interest (W5)	4,050
	36,725
Non-current liabilities	
7% bank loan	6,000
Current liabilities (11,400 + 3,900 – 1,000 intra-group)	14,300
Total equity and liabilities	57,025

Workings

1   *Group structure*

Hydan

| 60% 1.10.X5

Systan

2   *Goodwill in Systan*

	$'000	$'000
Consideration transferred (1,200 × $9)		10,800
Non-controlling interests (at 'full' fair value) (800 × $7)		5,600
Fair value of net assets at acquisition:		
Ordinary shares	2,000	
Share premium	500	
Pre-acquisition reserves (6,300 + 3,000)	9,300	
Fair value adjustment	1,200	
		(13,000)
Goodwill		3,400
Impairment losses		(375)
Carrying value		3,025

Alternative working

	Group	Group	NCI
	$'000	$'000	$'000
Consideration transferred (1,200 × $9)/Fair value of NCI (800 × $7)		10,800	5,600
Net assets at acquisition			
Ordinary shares	2,000		
Share premium	500		
Pre-acquisition reserves (6,300 + 3,000)	9,300		
Fair value adjustment	1,200		
	13,000		
× Group/NCI %		(7,800)	(5,200)
Goodwill		3,000	400
Impairment (375 × 60%/40%)		(225)	(150)
Carrying value		2,775	250
			3,025

3 *Group retained earnings*

	Hydan	Systan
	$'000	$'000
Per question	20,000	6,300
Pre-acquisition		(9,300)
Unrealised profit in inventory (W6)		(200)
Additional depreciation (W7)		(300)
	20,000	(3,500)
Group share of Systan ((3,500) × 60%)	(2,100)	
Goodwill impairment (375 × 60%)	(225)	
	17,675	

4 *Non controlling interest: income statement*

	$'000
Post-acquisition loss	(3,000)
Unrealised profit in inventory (W6)	(200)
Additional depreciation (W7)	(300)
Adjusted loss	(3,500)
Non-controlling share 40%	(1,400)
Goodwill impairment (W2)	(150)
	(1,550)

5 *Non-controlling interest: statement of financial position*

	$'000
NCI at acquisition (W2)	5,600
NCI share of post acquisition retained earnings ((W3) (3,500) × 40%)	(1,400)
NCI share of impairment losses (375 × 40%)	(150)
	4,050

Alternative working

	$'000
Ordinary shares	2,000
Share premium	500
Retained earnings	6,300
Unrealised profit in inventory	(200)
Fair value adjustment (W7)	900
	9,500
Non-controlling share 40%	3,800
Goodwill attributable to non-controlling interest (W2)	250
	4,050

6 *Unrealised profit*

	$'000
Goods sold by Systan to Hydan and still in inventory	4,000
Unrealised profit – 5% of selling price to Hydan	200
Dr Retained earnings (Systan)	200
Cr Group inventory	200

7 *Fair value adjustment*

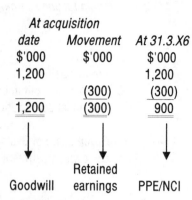

	At acquisition date $'000	Movement $'000	At 31.3.X6 $'000
Property, plant and equipment (Note (i))	1,200		1,200
Additional depreciation		(300)	(300)
	1,200	(300)	900
	↓	↓	↓
	Goodwill	Retained earnings	PPE/NCI

(b) If we look at Systan's pre-acquisition operating performance, we can see a gross profit margin of 25% and a net profit margin of 15%. During the post-acquisition 6-month period revenue is up by 46% but the gross profit margin is only 12% and the company has made a net loss of 8.5%. Clearly this requires some explanation.

Hydan obtained a controlling interest in Systan in order to secure its supplies of components. In the post-acquisition period $30m of Systan's $35m sales were to Hydan and realised 5% gross profit. In order to compensate for this, Systan has substantially increased the price charged to its other customers to give a 50% gross profit margin on those sales. The eventual result of this may be that it will no longer have any other customers.

Systan's results for the second half-year have also suffered from a large rise in operating expenses – from $1.2m in the pre-acquisition half year to $8m in the post-acquisition half year. It looks as though Systan has been charged a large share of group operating expenses. Hydan itself has operating expenses for the year of $11.8m on a revenue of $98m, while Systan has expenses of $8m on 6 months revenue of $35m. As there are no current account balances outstanding, Systan has obviously had to pay the intra-group portion of this $8m, facilitated by a loan from Hydan at 10%. At the same time, Hydan owes Systan $1m on which no interest is being paid.

The overall conclusion must be that Systan's position has been adversely affected by the acquisition and by the resulting related party transactions. Hydan has used transfer pricing and inter-company charges to transfer profits from the subsidiary to the parent company, thus benefiting its own shareholders at the expense of the non-controlling shareholders.

35 Hydrate

Text reference. Chapters 9 and 10.

Top tips. Start with **Parts (b)** and **(c).** There are seven easy marks here.

Part (a) Although there are quite a few parts to this question, each part is in itself quite straightforward. If you take a methodical approach then you should earn high marks.

(1) Sketch out the group structure, noting percentage holdings and the date of acquisition.

(2) Prepare a pro-forma income statement and statement of financial position for your answer, including the assets and liabilities of the parent and its subsidiary.

(3) Adjust for the fair valuation.

(4) Calculate the carrying value of the goodwill in the subsidiary.

(5) Calculate the balance on the consolidated retained earnings.

(6) Draft the statement of changes in equity.

Easy marks. A straightforward question and you should easily gain 13 marks just by being methodical.

Examiner's comments. This was a fairly straightforward question and was generally well answered. In the statement of financial position, the calculations of goodwill, share capital and reserves caused problems. Some poorly prepared candidates calculated non-controlling interest when the question stated that the parent had acquired 100% of the subsidiary.

(a) THE HYDRATE GROUP
CONSOLIDATED INCOME STATEMENT FOR THE YEAR ENDED 30 SEPTEMBER 20X2

	$'000
Sales revenue (24,000 + 6/12 × 20,000)	34,000
Cost of sales (16,600 + 6/12 × 11,800)	(22,500)
Gross profit	11,500
Operating expenses (1,600 + (6/12 × 1,000) + 3,000 impairment)	(5,100)
Profit before tax	6,400
Income tax expense (2,000 + 2,000 + (6/12 × 3,000))	(3,500)
Profit for the year	2,900

CONSOLIDATED STATEMENT OF FINANCIAL POSITION AS AT 30 SEPTEMBER 20X2

	$'000	$'000
Assets		
Non-current assets		
Property, plant and equipment (64,000 + 35,000)		99,000
Goodwill (W2)		27,000
Available for sale investments (0 + 12,800 + 5,000 fair valuation)		17,800
		143,800
Current assets		
Inventory (22,800 + 23,600)	46,400	
Trade receivables(16,400 + 24,200)	40,600	
Bank and cash (500 + 200)	700	
		87,700
Total assets		231,500

EQUITY AND LIABILITIES	$'000
Equity attributable to owners of the parent	
Share capital (Parent only) SOCIE	35,000
Share premium (Parent only) SOCIE	79,000
Retained earnings (W3)	56,300
	170,300
Non-current liabilities	
8% Loan Notes (5,000 + 18,000)	23,000
Current liabilities	
Trade payables (15,300 + 17,700)	33,000
Income tax (2,200 + 3,000)	5,200
	38,200
Total equity and liabilities	231,500

CONSOLIDATED STATEMENT OF CHANGES IN EQUITY FOR THE YEAR

	Share Capital	Share premium	Retained Earnings	Total
	$'000	$'000	$'000	$'000
Opening	20,000	4,000	53,400	77,400
Share issue (W2)	15,000	75,000	–	90,000
Total comprehensive income for the year	–	–	2,900	2,900
	35,000	79,000	56,300	170,300

Workings

1   *Group Structure as at 30 September 20X2*

```
        ┌─────────────────┐
        │     Hydrate     │
        │   The Parent    │
        └─────────────────┘
                │
 100%           │
 1 April 20X2   │
        ┌─────────────────┐
        │    Sulphate     │
        │ The Subsidiary  │
        └─────────────────┘
```

Consolidate in full for six months

2   *Consideration transferred and goodwill in Sulphate*

Number of shares issued: 12m × 5/4 = 15 million

		$'000
Nominal value	$1	15,000
Share premium (balancing figure)	$5	75,000
Fair value of shares and cost of the business combination	$6	90,000

Fair value of the net assets acquired		
Share Capital		12,000
Share premium		2,400
Retained earnings at 30 September 2002	42,700	
Less post acquisition profits (6/12 × $4.2m)	(2,100)	
		40,600
Fair value increase in the value of the investments		5,000
Fair value of the net assets at acquisition		60,000

	$'000
Goodwill at cost	30,000
Impairment	(3,000)
Carrying value	27,000

3   *Group retained earnings*

	$'000	$'000
Parent's retained earnings		57,200
100% share of subsidiary's post acquisition profits (($4.2m × 6/12)		2,100
Impairment of goodwill		(3,000)
		56,300

36 Preparation question: Laurel

Laurel Group - Consolidated statement of financial position as at 31 December 20X9

	$'000
Non-current assets	
Property, plant and equipment (220 + 160 + (W7) 3)	383
Goodwill (W2)	9
Investment in associate (W3)	96.8
	488.8
Current assets	
Inventories (384 + 234 − (W6) 10)	608
Trade receivables (275 + 166)	441
Cash (42 + 10)	52
	1,101
	1,589.8

	$'000
Equity attributable to owners of the parent	
Share capital – $1 ordinary shares	400
Share premium	16
Retained earnings (W4)	326.8
	742.8
Non-controlling interests (W5)	47
	789.8
Current liabilities	
Trade payables (457 + 343)	800.0
	1,589.8

Workings

1   Group structure

Laurel

80%   40%
1.1.X7   1.1.X7

Hardy   Comic (associate)
$64,000 $24,000 Pre acq'n retained earnings

2   Goodwill

	$'000	$'000
Consideration transferred		160
Non-controlling interests (at 'full' fair value)		39
Fair value of net assets at acq'n:		
Share capital	96	
Share premium	3	
Retained earnings	64	
Fair value adjustment (W7)	12	
		(175)
		24
Impairment losses		(15)
		9

Alternative working

		Group	NCI
	$'000	$'000	$'000
Consideration transferred / FV of NCI		160	39
Share of net assets acquired:			
Share capital	96		
Share premium	3		
Retained earnings	64		
Fair value adjustment (W7)	12		
	175		
Group/NCI share (80%/20%)		(140)	(35)
		20	4
Impairment losses (15 × 80%/20%)		(12)	(3)
		8	1
		9	

3   Investment in associate

	$'000
Cost of associate	70
Share of post acquisition retained reserves (W4)	29.2
Unrealised profit (W6)	(2.4)
Impairment losses	(0)
	96.8

4   *Consolidated retained earnings*

	Laurel	Hardy	Comic
	$'000	$'000	$'000
Ret'd earnings per question	278	128	97
Less: PUP re Hardy (W6)	(10)		
PUP re Comic (W6)	(2.4)		
Fair value adjustment movement (W7)		(9)	
	265.6	119	97
Less: pre-acquisition retained earnings		(64)	(24)
		55	73

Group share of post acquisition retained earnings:

Hardy (55 × 80%)	44
Comic (73 × 40%)	29.2
Less: group share of impairment losses (15 × 80%)	(12.0)
	326.8

5   *Non-controlling interests*

	$'000
Non-controlling interests at acquisition (W2)	39
NCI share of post acquisition retained earnings:	
Hardy (55 × 20%)	11
Less: NCI share of impairment losses (15 × 20%)	(3)
	47

Alternative working

	$'000	$'000
Net assets per question	227	
Fair value adjustment (W7)	3	
	230 × 20%	46
Non-controlling interest in goodwill (W2)		1
		47

6   *Unrealised profit*

Laurel's sales to Hardy: $32,000 – $22,000 = $10,000

DR Retained earnings (Laurel)	$10,000
CR Group inventories	$10,000

Laurel's sales to Comic (associate) ($22,000 – $10,000) × ½ × 40% share = $2,400.

DR Retained earnings (Laurel)	$2,400
CR Investment in associate	$2,400

7   *Fair value adjustments*

	At acquisition date	Movement	At year end
	$'000	$'000	$'000
PPE (57 – 45)	+12	(9)*	+3

*Extra depreciation $12,000 × ¾

At acquisition date → Goodwill

Movement → Ret'd earnings

At year end → PPE/NCI

37 Preparation question: Tyson

STATEMENT OF COMPREHENSIVE INCOME

Tyson Group – Consolidated statement of comprehensive income for the year ended 31 December 20X9

	$'000
Revenue (500 + 150 – 66)	584
Cost of sales (270 + 80 – 66 + (W3) 18)	(302)
Gross profit	282
Other expenses (150 + 20 + (W2) 15))	(185)
Finance income (15 + 10)	25
Finance costs	(20)
Share of profit of associate [(10 × 40%) – 2.4*]	1.6
Profit before tax	103.6
Income tax expense (25 + 15)	(40)
PROFIT FOR THE YEAR	63.6
Other comprehensive income:	
Gains on property revaluation, net of tax (20 + 10)	30
Share of other comprehensive income of associate (5 × 40%)	2
Other comprehensive income for the year, net of tax	32.0
TOTAL COMPREHENSIVE INCOME FOR THE YEAR	95.6
Profit attributable to:	
Owners of the parent (63.6 – 2.4)	61.2
Non-controlling interests [(45 – (W3) 18) × 20% – (W2) 3]	2.4
	63.6
Total comprehensive income attributable to:	
Owners of the parent (95.6 – 4.4)	91.2
Non-controlling interests [(55 – (W3) 18) × 20% – (W2) 3]	4.4
	95.6

*   Impairment losses could either be included in expenses or deducted from the share of profit of associates figure. IAS 28 is not prescriptive.

Workings

1   *Group structure*

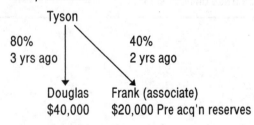

Tyson

80%
3 yrs ago

40%
2 yrs ago

Douglas
$40,000

Frank (associate)
$20,000 Pre acq'n reserves

2   *Goodwill*

	$'000	$'000
Consideration transferred		188
Non-controlling interests (at 'full' fair value)		40
Net assets at acquisition:		
Share capital	100	
Reserves	40	
		(140)
		88
Impairment loss		(15)
		73

Alternative working

	Group $'000	Group $'000	NCI $'000
Consideration transferred / FV of NCI		188	40
Net assets acquired:-			
Share capital	100		
Reserves	40		
	140		
Group/NCI share (80%/20%)		(112)	(28)
		76	12
Impairment loss (15 × 80%/20%)		(12)	(3)
		64	9
		73	

3   *Unrealised profit*

	$'000
Selling price	66
Cost	(48)
PUP	18

38 Plateau

Text references. Chapters 10 and 11.

Top tips. This is a standard consolidation question, similar to the pilot paper question. Note the treatment of goodwill relating to the non-controlling interest.

Easy marks. Apart from the fair value adjustment and the NCI at fair value there were no other particular complications and easy marks were available on investments, current assets and liabilities. Do not neglect part (b) which is 5 easy marks.

Examiner's comments. The consolidated statement of financial position was well answered but few candidates got to grips with the written section and many did not attempt it at all. The main areas where candidates went wrong were:

- deducting fall in fair value of land from PPE, when it had already been written down
- failing to adjust for additional depreciation
- not using equity accounting for the associate
- failing to adjust share capital and premium for the share issue on acquisition.

		Marks
(a)	Statement of financial position	
	Property, plant and equipment	2
	Goodwill	4
	Investments – associate	2
	– other	1
	Current assets	2
	Equity shares	1
	Share premium	1
	Retained earnings	4
	Non-controlling interest	1
	7% loan notes	1
	Current liabilities	1
		20
(b)	One mark per relevant point	5
	Total for question	25

(a)   PLATEAU
CONSOLIDATED STATEMENT OF FINANCIAL POSITION AS AT 30 SEPTEMBER 2007

	$'000
Non-current assets	
Property, plant and equipment	
(18,400 + 10,400 – (W7) 400)	28,400
Goodwill (W3)	5,000
Intangible asset - customer contract	1,000
Investment in associate (W4)	10,500
Available-for-sale investment (note v to question)	9,000
	53,900
Current assets	
Inventories (6,900 + 6,200 – (W7) 300)	12,800
Trade receivables (3,200 + 1,500)	4,700
	17,500
Total assets	71,400
Equity and liabilities	
Equity attributable to owners of the parent	
Share capital (10,000 + (W2) 1,500)	11,500
Share premium (W2)	7,500
Retained earnings (W5)	30,300
	49,300
Non-controlling interest (W6)	3,900
	53,200
Non-current liabilities	
7% loan notes (5,000 + 1,000)	6,000
Current liabilities (8,000 + 4,200)	12,200
Total equity and liabilities	71,400

Workings

1   *Group structure*

Plateau

1.10.06   1.10.06

75%   30%

Savannah   Axle

2   *Purchase of Savannah*

DEBIT Cost of Savannah (3m/2 × $6) + (3m × $1.25)	12.75m
CREDIT Share capital (3m/2 × $1)	1.5m
CREDIT Share premium (3m/2 × $5)	7.5m
CREDIT Cash	3.75m

3   *Goodwill– Savannah*

	$'000	$'000
Consideration transferred		12,750
Non-controlling interests at acquisition (1,000 shares @ $3,25)		3,250
Less: Net fair value of assets and liabilities at acquisition:		
Share capital	4,000	
Retained earnings	6,000	
Fair value adjustment (W8)	1,000	
		(11,000)
		5,000

Alternative working

	Group		NCI
	$'000	$'000	$'000
Consideration transferred (W2) / FV of NCI		12,750	3,250
Less: net fair value of assets and liabilities acquired:			
Share capital	4,000		
Retained earnings	6,000		
Customer based contract	1,000		
	11,000		
Group share 75%		(8,250)	(2,750)
		4,500	500
		5,000	

4   *Investment in Axle*

	$'000
Cost : (4,000 × 30% × $7.50)	9,000
Share of post-acquisition retained earnings (W5)	1,500
	10,500

5   *Group retained earnings*

	Plateau	Savannah	Axle
	$'000	$'000	$'000
Per statement of financial position	25,250	2,900	5,000
Unrealised profit (W7)	(400)	(300)	–
	24,850	2,600	5,000
Group share: 2,600 × 75%	1,950		
5,000 × 30%	1,500		
Gain on available-for-sale investment			
(9,000 – 6,500)	2,500		
Professional costs of acquisition	(500)		
Group retained earnings	30,300		

6   *Non-controlling interests – Savannah*

	$'000
NCI at acquisition (W3)	3,250
NCI share of post acquisition retained earnings ((W5) 2,600 × 25%)	650
	3,900

Alternative working

	$'000
Net assets per question	12,900
Intangible asset – customer contract	1,000
Unrealised profit (W7)	(300)
	13,600
Non-controlling share 25%	3,400
Goodwill (W3)	500
	3,900

7   *Intragroup trading*

Unrealised profit on sale of inventories:

$2.7m × 50/150 × 1/3 $0.3m

DR Cost of sales/CR Inventories in books of Savannah (affects NCI)

Unrealised profit on transfer of plant:

	$
Unrealised profit ($2.5m – $2m)	0.5m
Less realised by use (depreciation) 1/5	(0.1m)
	0.4m

DEBIT Retained earnings/CREDIT Property, plant and equipment in books of Plateau

8   *Fair value adjustment – customer contract*

Acquisition date		*End of reporting period*
1.10.06	Movement	30.9.07
1,000	–	1,000

9   *Available-for-sale investments*

	$'000
Fair value at 1 October 2006	6,500
Fair value at 30 September 2007	9,000
Increase in fair value	2,500

DEBIT Available-for-sale investments/CREDIT Retained earnings

(b)   IFRS 3 requires the consideration for a business combination to be allocated to the fair values of the assets, liabilities and contingent liabilities acquired.

Although this is usually not the same as the original cost of the asset when acquired by the subsidiary, it is taken to be the cost of the asset to the group. If assets are not valued at fair value, this leads to an incorrect goodwill valuation and incorrect depreciation and goodwill impairment charges in subsequent years.

The financial assistant is confusing two different issues. The assets of the subsidiary are assumed to be acquired at their fair value at the date of acquisition by the parent. After acquisition they will be carried at depreciated amount, rather than subjected to regular revaluations. So they will be treated in the same way as other assets owned by the parent. The parent may decide to revalue all the assets of a class, including those acquired as part of a business combination, in which case they would all be carried at revalued amount.

39 Holdrite

Marking scheme

			Marks
(a)	*Goodwill of Staybrite:*		
	Value of shares exchanged		1
	8% loan notes issued		1
	Equity shares and share premium		1
	Pre-acquisition reserves		1
	Fair value adjustments		1
	Carrying value of Allbrite:		
	Value of shares exchanged		1
	Cash paid		1
	Equity shares and share premium		1
	Share of post-acquisition profit		1
		Available	9
		Maximum	8
(b)	*Income statement:*		
	Revenue		4
	Cost of sales		2
	Operating expenses		1
	Interest expense		2
	Income from associate		2
	Income tax		2
	Non-controlling interest		3
		Available	16
		Maximum	15
(c)	Dividends		1
	Retained profits b/f and c/f		1
		Maximum	2
		Maximum for question	25

(a)   *Goodwill*

Goodwill in Staybrite

	$'000	$'000
Consideration transferred		
Share exchange: (2/3 × 75% × 10m shares) × $6		30,000
Loan Note: (100/250 × 75% × 10m shares) × $1		3,000
		33,000
NCI at acquisition (34,000 × 25%)		8,500
Share of the net assets acquired at fair value		
Share Capital	10,000	
Share premium	4,000	
Opening retained earnings	7,500	
Time apportioned profits for the year; $9m × $^6/_{12}$	4,500	
Fair value adjustment (W5)	8,000	
		(34,000)
Goodwill		7,500

The fair value of the share exchange is the market price of the shares issued by the acquirer.

The fair value of the loan note is its nominal value.

Carrying value of Allbrite

	$'000
Cost of investment:	
Share exchange: (3/4 × 40% × 5m shares) × $6	9,000
Cash: ($1 × 40% × 5m shares)	2,000
	11,000

(b)   THE HOLDRITE GROUP
CONSOLIDATED INCOME STATEMENT FOR THE YEAR ENDED 30 SEPTEMBER 20X4

	$'000
Sales revenue (75,000 + (40,700 × 6/12) – 10,000 (W3))	85,350
Cost of sales (47,400 + (19,700 × 6/12) – 10,000 + 1,000	
(W4) + 500 (W5))	(48,750)
Gross profit	36,600
Operating expenses (10,480 + (9,000 × 6/12) + 750	
goodwill impairment)	(15,730)
Finance costs	(170)
Share of profit of associate (4,000 × 6/12 × 40%)	800
Profit before tax	21,500
Income tax expense (4,800 + ($^6/_{12}$ × 3,000))	(6,300)
Profit for the year	15,200
Profit attributable to:	
Owners of the parent	14,200
Non-controlling interest ((9,000 × 6/12) – 500) × 25%)	1,000
	15,200

Workings

1   *Group Structure as at 30 September 20X4*

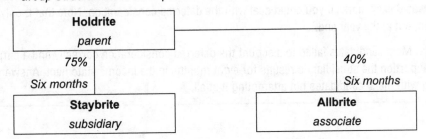

2   *Timeline*

1.10.X3	1.4.X4	30.9.X4

Holdrite
Staybrite 100% × 6/12 with MI 25%

Allbrite 40% × PFP × 6/12

3   *Intragroup trading*

Dr	Revenue	10,000
Cr	Cost of sales	10,000

4   *Unrealised profit*

Dr	Cost of sales ($4,000 \times \frac{1}{4}$)	1,000
Cr	Inventories	1,000

5   *Fair value adjustments*

	At consolidation 1.4.X4	Movement	At 30.9.X4
Land (23,000 – 20,000)	3,000	–	3,000
Plant (30,000 – 25,000)	5,000	(500)	4,500
	8,000	(500)	7,500
	↓	↓	↓
	Goodwill	I/S and non-controlling interest (I/S)	Non-controlling interest

(c)   *Movement on consolidated retained earnings*

	$'000
Opening (Parent only, as there were no subsidiaries or associates.)	18,000
Profit for the year attributable to parent company shareholders	14,200
Equity dividends paid	(5,000)
	27,200

40 Patronic

Text reference. Chapters 10 and 11

Top tips. The most important thing to notice here is that Patronic acquired its interest in Sardonic eight months before the year end. Always pay attention to dates. This also affects the intragroup sales which need to be cancelled.

Easy marks. Part (a) was 6 easy marks if you could deal with the deferred consideration. Note that it only required goodwill on acquisition, not at the year end.

Examiner's comments. Most candidates failed to discount the deferred consideration correctly and a surprising number did not time apportion the subsidiary's results for eight months in the income statement. Answers to part (c) were disappointing with many candidates not attempting it at all.

(a) Goodwill

	$'000	$'000
Consideration transferred:		
Shares (12m × $5.75)		69,000
Deferred consideration (18m × $2.42 × 1/1.21(10% over 2 years))		36,000
		105,000
NCI at acquisition (104,000 × 25%)		26,000
Fair value of identifiable net assets acquired:		
Share capital	24,000	
Reserves b/f	69,000	
Current year to date (13,500 × 4/12)	4,500	
Fair value adjustments (W2)	6,500	
		(104,000)
Goodwill		27,000

(b) PATRONIC GROUP – CONSOLIDATED INCOME STATEMENT FOR THE YEAR ENDED 31 MARCH 2008

	$'000
Revenue (W3)	192,000
Cost of sales (W4)	(119,100)
Gross profit	72,900
Distribution costs (7,400 + (3,000 × 8/12))	(9,400)
Administrative expenses (12,500 + (6,000 × 8/12))	(16,500)
Finance costs (W5)	(5,000)
Impairment of goodwill	(2,000)
Share of profit of associate (6,000 × 30%)	1,800
Profit before tax	41,800
Income tax expense (10,400 + (3,600 × 8/12)	(12,800)
Profit for the year	29,000
Profit attributable to :	
Owners of the parent	26,900
Non-controlling interest (W6)	2,100
	29,000

Workings

1   *Group structure*

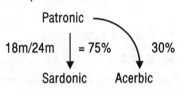

Patronic
18m/24m = 75%   30%
Sardonic   Acerbic

2   Non-controlling interest

Profit after tax (13,500 × 8/12)	9,000
Additional depreciation (W2)	(600)
	8,400
Non-controlling share 25%	2,100

3   *Fair value adjustments*

	Acquisition 1.8.07 $'000	Movement 8/12 $'000	Year end 31.3.08 $'000
Property	4,100	(200)*	3,900
Plant	2,400	(400)**	2,000
	6,500	(600)	5,900

* given in the question
** 2,400/4 × 8/12

	$'000
4 *Revenue*	
Patronic	150,000
Sardonic (78,000 × 8/12)	52,000
Intra-group (1,250 × 8)	(10,000)
	192,000
5 *Cost of sales*	
Patronic	94,000
Sardonic (51,000 × 8/12)	34,000
Intragroup (W3)	(10,000)
URP in inventory (3,000 × 20/120)	500
Additional depreciation on FVA:	
Property	200
Plant (2.4m/4 × 8/12)	400
	119,100
6 *Finance costs*	
Patronic	2,000
Sardonic (900 × 8/12)	600
Unwinding of discount (36,000 × 10% × 8/12)	2,400
	5,000

(c) At 31 March 2008 Patronic could be presumed to have 'significant influence' over Acerbic arising from its 30% shareholding. Acerbic was therefore treated as an associate and its results were brought into Patronic's financial statements using the equity method.

Spekulate's purchase of 60% changes Patronic's position. Spekulate now has control, so Patronic can no longer be regarded as having significant influence. This is illustrated by the fact that Patronic has lost its seat on the board.

Patronic's investment in Acerbic should be treated in 2009 under IAS 39, carried at fair value, with any gains and losses shown in the statement of comprehensive income.

41 Hedra

Text reference. Chapters 9 and 11.

Top tips. This is a big question, but as always a methodical approach will ensure a good score.

Note that you are given the goodwill attributable to the non-controlling interest.

Look out for the fair value adjustments to Salvador, and remember that increases in fair value *after* acquisition are treated as normal revaluations. The contingent consideration is recognised at the acquisition date per IFRS 3 (revised). Finally the goodwill in Salvador has been impaired.

Aragon's net assets at acquisition and fair value of consideration must be calculated.

Easy marks. There are no particular easy marks here. Read the question carefully and make your workings very clear.

Examiners comments. A majority of candidates show a good knowledge of the basic principles of consolidation. The main errors were:

- Use of proportional consolidation for the subsidiary. This demonstrates that a candidate has not studied the most important topic in the syllabus and has not attempted past questions.
- Use of full consolidation or proportional consolidation (rather than equity accounting) for the associate.
- Incorrectly calculating cost of the investment in the subsidiary.
- Not including fair value adjustments in the non-controlling interest.

	Marks
Goodwill	4
Goodwill impairment	1
Property, plant and equipment	2
Investment in associate	2
Other investments	1
Inventories and trade receivables	1
Cash and bank	1
Share capital and premium	1
Revaluation surplus	2
Retained earnings	2
Non-controlling interest	3
Deferred consolidation	1
Deferred tax	1
Elimination of 8% loan note	1
Trade payables and tax	1
Overdraft	1
	25

HEDRA
CONSOLIDATED STATEMENT OF FINANCIAL POSITION AS AT 30 SEPTEMBER 20X5

	$m	$m
Assets		
Non-current assets		
Property, plant and equipment (W8)		650
Investment in associate (W4)		220
Investment in Salvador:Equity (195 taken to cost of control)		–
Loan Notes (50 inter-company)		–
Investments		45
Goodwill (W2)		90
		1,005
Current assets		
Inventories (130 + 80)	210	
Trade receivables (142 + 97)	239	
Cash at bank	4	
		453
Total assets		1,458
Equity and liabilities		
Equity attributable to owners of parent		
Share capital (Parent only; 400 + 80 (W4))		480
Share premium (Parent only; 40 + 120 (W4))		160
Revaluation surplus (15 + (5 × 60%) + 12)		30
Retained earnings (W5)		269
		939
Non-controlling interest (W6)		114
Total equity		1,053

	$m	$m
Non-current liabilities		
8% Loan Notes (50 inter-company)	–	
Deferred tax (45 – 10 (tax losses))	35	
		35
Current liabilities		
Trade payables (118 + 141)	259	
Bank overdraft	12	
Current tax payable	50	
Deferred consideration (W2)	49	
		370
Total equity and liabilities		1,458

Workings

1   *Group structure*

    Group Structure as at 30 September 20X5

Hedra *Parent*		40% 1.4.X5		Aragon *Associate*

60% | 1-10-X4

Salvador *Subsidiary*

2   *Goodwill in Salvador*

	$m	$m
Consideration transferred		
Cash		195
Deferred consideration		49
		244
NCI ((240 × 40%) + 10 (NCI in goodwill per question))		106
Fair value of net assets at acquisition:		
Ordinary shares	120	
Share premium	50	
Retained earnings	20	
Fair value adjustments (W7)	50	
		(240)
		110
Impairment loss (given in question)		(20)
Carrying value at 30 September 20X5		90

Alternative working

	$m	$m
Consideration transferred		
Cash		195
Deferred consideration		49
		244
Share of the net assets acquired at fair value		
Carrying value of net assets at 1.10. X4:		
Ordinary shares	120	
Share premium	50	
Retained earnings	20	
Fair value adjustments (W7)	50	
Fair value of the net assets at acquisition	240	
60% Group share		(144)
Cost of Goodwill		100
Impairment loss given in question (20 × 60%)		(12)
Carrying value at 30 September 20X5		88
Goodwill attributable to NCI (W3)		2
		90

The revised IFRS 3 requires the deferred consideration to be recognised at the acquisition date. It will be accrued for as a current liability.

The $5m increase in the fair value of Salvador's land post acquisition is treated as a revaluation. This will be shared between the parent (60% = $3m) and the non-controlling interest (40% = $2m).

3   *Goodwill attributable to NCI*

	$m
Goodwill per question	10
Impairment (20m × 40%)	(8)
	2

4   *40% Investment in associate*

	$m
Cost of acquisition	
2 shares in Hedra issued for each of 40m shares acquired in Aragon	
Fair value = 80m shares × $2.50	200
Hedra's share of post acquisition profits (W5)	20
Carrying value of associate	220

Nominal value and premium on shares issued

	$m
Nominal value of shares issued ($1)	80
Share premium (balancing figure)	120
Fair value ($2.50)	200

5   *Retained earnings attributable to the owners of the parent*

	Hedra	Salvador	Aragon
	$m	$m	$m
Per question	240	60	300
Additional depreciation (25% × $20m)	–	(5)	–
Pre-acquisition profits – Salvador	–	(20)	–
– Aragon (200 + ½ (300 – 200))	–	–	(250)
	240	35	50
Group share of subsidiary (60%)	21		
Group share of associate (40%)	20		
Impairment of goodwill in Salvador (20 × 60%)	(12)		
	269		

6   *Non-controlling interest in Salvador's net assets*

	$m
NCI at acquisition (W2)	106
NCI share of post acquisition retained earnings ((W5) 35 × 40%)	14
NCI share of post acquisition revaluation of land (5 × 40%)	2
NCI share of impairment losses (20 × 40%)	(8)
	114

Alternative working

	$m
Salvador's net assets from the question	230
Fair value adjustments (W7)	45
Revaluation of land post acquisition	5
Consolidated value of Salvador's net assets	280
Non-controlling 40% interest	112
Goodwill attributable to NCI (W3)	2
	114

7   *Fair value adjustments*

	Acquisition 1.10.X4	Movement	Reporting date 30.9.X5
Land	20	–	20
Plant	20	(5)	15
Deferred tax asset ($40m × 25%)	10		10
	50	(5)	45
	(W3)	(W5)	(W6)

8   *Non-current assets*

	$m	$m
Hedra		358
Revaluation		12
		370
Salvador	240	
Fair valuation increase of land	20	
Revaluation of land	5	
Fair valuation increase of plant	20	
25% Depreciation on fair valuation	(5)	
		280
		650

42 Hosterling

Text reference. Chapters 10 and 11.

Top tips. This is a consolidated income statement including an associate, less common than a consolidated statement of financial position but with no serious problems. Start by noting down the shareholdings and the number of months during which the investment in the associate has been held, then do (a) and (b) and get the proforma down for (c).

Easy marks. The only complex part of this question was dealing with the associate. Accounting for the subsidiary was very straightforward and you should have had no trouble with the unrealised profit or the fair value adjustment. So make sure you get these simple parts of the question correct.

Examiner's comments. This required preliminary calculations of consolidated goodwill and the carrying amount of an associate followed by the preparation of a consolidated income statement. There were less candidates achieving very high marks compared to recent diets and a significant issue was the number of candidates who used proportional consolidation for either the subsidiary, the associate or both. There were also problems eliminating intra-group trading and calculating the non-controlling interest.

Marking scheme

			Marks
(a)	Goodwill of Sunlee:		
	consideration		1
	equity shares		1
	pre acquisition reserves		1
	fair value adjustments		2
		Maximum	5
(b)	Carrying amount and impairment of Amber:		
	cash paid		1
	6% loan note		1
	post acquisition		2
		Maximum	4

(c) Income statement:

revenue	2
cost of sales	4
distribution costs and administrative expenses	1
finance costs	1
impairment of goodwill in subsidiary	1
impairment of associate	1
share of associate's loss	2
income tax	1
non-controlling interests	2
eliminate dividend from Sunlee	1
Maximum	16
Maximum for question	25

(a) **Goodwill in Sunlee**

	$'000	$'000
Consideration transferred (16,000 × 5 × 3/5)		48,000
Non-controlling interests (50m × 20%)		10,000
Fair value of net assets at acquisition:		
Shares	20,000	
Pre-acquisition reserves	18,000	
Fair value adjustment (W)	12,000	
		(50,000)
		(40,000)
Goodwill		8,000

Working

Total fair value adjustment = 4,000 + 3,000 + 5,000 = $12m.

(b) **Investment in Amber**

	$'000
Cost of investment (6m × $4) ($3 cash + $1 loan note)	24,000
Share of post-acquisition loss (20m × 3/12 × 40%)	(2,000)
Carrying value prior to impairment	22,000

Per note (v) the investment was valued at $21.5m at 30 Sept 20X6. The impairment loss was therefore $500,000.

(c) HOSTERLING GROUP
CONSOLIDATED INCOME STATEMENT FOR THE YEAR ENDED 30 SEPTEMBER 20X6

	$'000
Revenue (105,000 + 62,000 – 18,000)	149,000
Cost of sales (W4)	(89,000)
Gross profit	60,000
Distribution costs (4,000 + 2,000)	(6,000)
Administrative expenses (7,500 + 7,000 + 1,600 (note (v))	(16,100)
	37,900
Share of loss of associate (W5)	(2,500)
Finance costs (1,200 + 900)	(2,100)
Profit before tax	33,300
Income tax expense (8,700 + 2,600)	(11,300)
Profit for the year	22,000
Profit attributable to:	
Owners of the parent	19,600
Non-controlling interest ((13,000 – 1,000 (W4)) × 20%)	2,400
	22,000

Workings

1   *Group structure*

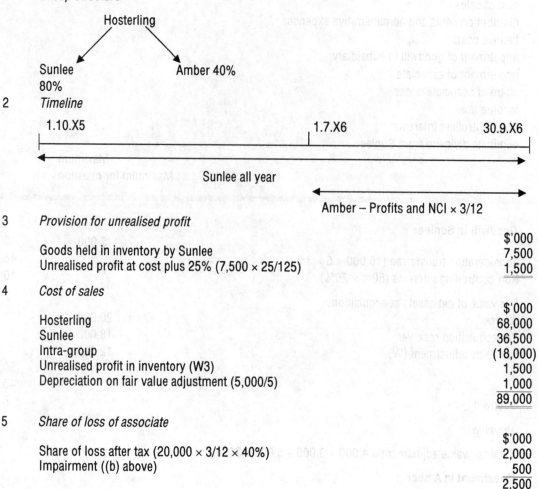

Hosterling

Sunlee   Amber 40%
80%

2   *Timeline*

1.10.X5   1.7.X6   30.9.X6

Sunlee all year

Amber – Profits and NCI × 3/12

3   *Provision for unrealised profit*

	$'000
Goods held in inventory by Sunlee	7,500
Unrealised profit at cost plus 25% (7,500 × 25/125)	1,500

4   *Cost of sales*

	$'000
Hosterling	68,000
Sunlee	36,500
Intra-group	(18,000)
Unrealised profit in inventory (W3)	1,500
Depreciation on fair value adjustment (5,000/5)	1,000
	89,000

5   *Share of loss of associate*

	$'000
Share of loss after tax (20,000 × 3/12 × 40%)	2,000
Impairment ((b) above)	500
	2,500

43 Pacemaker

Text references. Chapters 9 and 11.

Top tips. This is a relatively straightforward consolidated statement of financial position including an associate. Complications are NCI at fair value, and sorting out the investments. Pay attention to which items are already included in the individual financial statements and which are not.

Easy marks. There are easy marks here on property, plant and equipment and inventory – both required just one adjustment. The investment in associate was also straightforward and would have been worth a few marks.

Examiner's comments. This was the best answered question. Areas where candidates went wrong were:

- Failing to account for the loan note and the non-controlling element in the goodwill calculation
- Treating the post-acquisition period as one year, rather than two
- URP in inventory ignored or incorrectly calculated
- Non-controlling interest not calculated as per revised standard

Examiner's answer. The examiner's answer to this question is included at the back of this kit.

	Marks
Property, plant and equipment	2
Brand	1
Goodwill	4½
Investment in associate	2
Other investments	1
Inventories	2
Trade receivables, cash and bank	1
Equity shares	1
Share premium	1
Retained earnings	6½
Non-controlling interest	2
Loan notes	½
Current liabilities	½
Total for question	**25**

PACEMAKER – CONSOLIDATED STATEMENT OF FINANCIAL POSITION AS AT 31.3.2009

	$m
Non-current assets	
Property, plant and equipment (520 + 280 + 18 (W7))	818
Goodwill (W2)	23
Other intangible assets (W7)	20
Investment in associate (W3)	144
Available-for-sale financial assets (W9)	119
	1,124
Current assets	
Inventories (142 + 160 – 16 (W8)	286
Trade receivables (95 + 88)	183
Cash and cash equivalents (8 + 22)	30
	499
	1,623
Equity attributable to owners of the parent	
Share capital (500 + 75 (W6))	575
Share premium (100 + 45 (W6))	145
Retained earnings (W4)	247
	967
Non-controlling interest (W5)	91
	1,058
Non-current liabilities	
10% loan notes (180 + 20)	200
Current liabilities (200 + 165)	365
	1,623

Workings

1. **Group structure**

Pacemaker

1.4.07		1.10.08
116/145 = 80%		30/100 = 30%
Pre-acq reserves		Pre-acq =
= 120m		240-100+20=160m

Syclop   Vardine

2. **Goodwill**

	$m	$m
Consideration transferred (W6)		268
NCI at fair value		65
Fair value of net assets at acquisition		
Share capital	145	
Retained earnings	120	
Fair value adjustments (W7)	45	
		(310)
Goodwill		23

Alternative working

	Group	NCI
Consideration/FV of NCI	268	65
Net assets 80%/20%	(248)	(62)
Goodwill	20	3

3. **Investment in associate**

	$m
Cost (W6)	120
Share of post-acquisition retained earnings (W4)	24
	144

4. **Retained earnings**

	Pacemaker $m	Syclop $m	Vardine $m
Per question	130	260	240
Fair value movement (W7)		(7)	
PUP (W8)	(16)		
Gain on financial assets (82-(345-268))	5		
Loss on financial assets (37-40)		(3)	
Pre-acquisition earnings (W1)		(120)	(160)
		130	80
Group share of Syclop 80%	104		
Group share of Vardine 30%	24		
	247		

5. **Non-controlling interest**

	$m
At acquisition per question	65
Share of post-acquisition retained earnings	
(130 (W4) × 20%)	26
	91

Alternative working

	$m
Share of net assets (405 + 45(W2)-7-3(W4)) x 20%	88
Goodwill (W2)	3
	91

6. Investments

	$m	$m	
DR Cost of investment in Syclop	268		
CR Cash		210	Already
CR Loan notes		58	recorded
DR Cost of investment in Vardine (75 × 1.60)	120		
CR Share capital (75 × 1)		75	Not
CR Share premium (75 × 0.60)		45	recorded

7. Fair value adjustments

	Acquisition 1.4.2007	Movement (2 years)	Year end 31.3.2009
	$m	$m	$m
Property (82-62)	20	(2)	18
Brand	25	(5)	20
	45	(7)	38

8. Intragroup trading
Unrealised profit: PUP = 56 × 40/140 = 16

	$m	$m
DR Cost of sales (retained earnings)	16	
CR Inventories		16

9. Available-for-sale financial assets

	$m	$m
Pacemaker (345-268)	77	
Gain (W4)	5	
		82
Syclop	40	
Loss (W4)	(3)	
		37
		119

44 Preparation question: Contract

	Contract 1 $	Contract 2 $	Contract 3 $	Contract 4 $
Income statement				
	(W1)	(W2)	(W3)	(W4)
Revenue	54,000	8,000	84,000	125,000
Expenses	(43,200)	(8,000)	(92,400)	(105,000)
Expected loss	–	–	(15,600)	–
Recognised profit/(loss)	10,800	–	(24,000)	20,000
Gross amounts due from/to customers				
Contract costs incurred	48,000	8,000	103,200	299,600
Recognised profits less recognised losses	10,800	–	(24,000)	56,000
	58,800	8,000	79,200	355,600
Less: progress billings to date	(50,400)	–	(76,800)	(345,200)
	8,400	8,000	2,400	10,400
Trade receivables				
Progress billings to date	50,400	–	76,800	345,200
Less: cash received	(50,400)	–	(76,800)	(345,200)
	–	–	–	–

Workings

1   *Contract 1*

Revenue   45% ×120,000 =   54,000
Expenses   45% × (48,000 + 48,000) =   43,200

2   *Contract 2*

Expenses All costs to date charged as expense ∴ 8,000
Revenue   Probable that all costs incurred will be recovered ∴ 8,000

3   *Contract 3*

Revenue   35% × 240,000 =   84,000
Expenses   35% × (103,200 + 160,800) =   (92,400)
Loss   (8,400)
∴ Expected loss   (15,600)
Total loss 240,000 − (103,200 + 160,800) =   (24,000)

4   *Contract 4*

Revenue   (70% × 500,000) − 225,000 =   125,000
Expenses   (70% × 420,000) − 189,000 =   105,000

45 Concepts

			Marks
(a)	explanations 1 mark each		5
(b)	examples 2 marks each		10
		Total for question	15

(a)   **Matching/accruals**

This dictates that the effects of transactions and other events are recognised in the financial statements in the period in which they occur, rather than in the period when cash is received or paid.

Substance over form

This is the principle that transactions and other events are accounted for and presented in accordance with their substance and economic reality and not merely their legal form. This is important in considering whether or not a sale has taken place.

Prudence

Prudence requires accountants to exercise a degree of caution in making estimates under conditions of uncertainty, in order to ensure that assets are not overstated, not liabilities understated.

Comparability

This requires consistent application of accounting policies and adequate disclosure in order that a) the financial statements of an entity can be compared with its financial statements for previous accounting periods and b) the financial statements of an entity can be compared with the financial statements of other entities.

Materiality

The *Framework* describes this as a 'threshold' quality and it requires the application of judgement. An item of information is material if its omission or misstatement could influence the economic decisions of users taken on the basis of the financial statements. An item can be material on account of its size or on account of its nature.

(b)   **Application to inventory**

Matching/accruals

Inventory is charged to profit or loss in the period in which it is used, not the period in which it is received or paid for. This is done by adjusting cost of sales for opening and closing inventory.

Substance over form

Goods may be purchased for resale on a consignment basis, which means that they can be returned if unsold. This means that while the legal form is that a sale has taken place, the substance is that the risks and rewards attached to the goods have not been transferred to the purchaser. In this situation the goods are not treated as inventory until, for instance, the period within which they can be returned has expired.

Prudence

Prudence must be applied in the valuation of inventory. IAS2 requires it to be carried at the lower of cost and NRV. For instance, if the net realisable value of an item of inventory falls below original cost, then the item is valued at NRV. This is important because if closing inventory is overvalued profit will be overstated.

Comparability

Inventory should be valued in financial statements using FIFO or weighted average and this should be consistently applied from one period to the next. If a change is made to the method of valuation, it must be disclosed, so that the current and prior periods can still be compared.

Materiality

Inventory is counted at the end of each reporting period and the valuation is based on this physical count, because inventory is generally regarded as a material item. However, it could be decided that a small discrepancy in the count would not be investigated because the amounts involved were too small to affect the decisions of users and so were not material.

46 Linnet

(a)   *Two methods of accounting for contracts*

When the outcome of a contract can be estimated reliably, then revenue is recognised by reference to the stage of completion of contract activity. As a result revenue reflects the value of work done and profit is claimed in proportion to the work done. This is an application of the accruals principle.

If the outcome of a contract cannot be estimated reliably (for example if the contract has only just begun) then the amount of revenue claimed will not exceed the costs incurred. This means that revenue reflects the cost of work done rather than its value and no profit is claimed. The conforms with the prudence concept. As soon as the outcome of the contract is known revenue should be based on the stage of completion. This means that profits might be artificially low in the early stages of a contract and then unrealistically high in the period when the change to the stage of completion method occurs.

Losses are always provided for in full as soon as they are foreseen, regardless of how revenues are being calculated.

(b)   *Football stadium*

Income Statement (extracts)

	$m
Revenue	70
Cost of sales	(81)
Gross loss	(11)

Statement of financial position (extracts)

	$m
Current assets	
Amounts recoverable on construction contracts	59

Workings

This year's revenues, cost of sales and profit is the difference between the cumulative amounts at the beginning and end of the year. The rectification costs will be charged in full as they are incurred. As they cannot be recovered from the customer they will be excluded from the calculation of attributable revenue and profit.

Income Statement

	(i) Revenue	(ii) Cost of sales	(iii) Profit/(loss)
Cumulative to 31 March 20X4	220	176	44
Cumulative to 31 March 20X3 (from q)	(150)	(112)	(38)
Recognised this year	70	64	6
Rectification costs		17	(17)
		81	(11)

(i) **Revenue**

$180m of progress payments received for work done to 29 February = 90% of value of work done.

100% value of work done to 29 February	200
Value of further work done to 31 March	20
Total work done to 31 March 20X4	220

(ii) **Cost of sales**

$$(195 + 45) \times \frac{220}{300} \qquad 176$$

(iii) **Profit**

Contract price	300
Costs to date	(195)
Costs to complete	(45)
Expected contract profit	60

Recognised to date:

$$\text{Value of work done to date: } \frac{220}{300} \times 60 = 44$$

Statement of financial position

	$m
Costs to date	212
Profit recognised to date	44
Less rectification costs	(17)
Less progress billings	(180)
Gross amount due from customers	59

47 Torrent

Alfa

INCOME STATEMENT

	$m
Revenue ((12.6 – 5.4) × 100/90)	8
Cost of sales (W1)	(7)
Profit (W2)	1

STATEMENT OF FINANCIAL POSITION

Gross amount due from customers (W3)	1.0

Workings

1   *Cost of sales*

	$m
Recognised to date (15 × 14/20)	10:5
Less recognised at 31 March 20X5 (15 × 6/20)	(4:5)
Plus rectification costs	1
	7

2   *Profit*

	$m	$m
At 31 March 20X5		
Total expected profit	5	
Invoiced to date (5.4 × 100/90)	6	
Profit recognised (5 × 6/20)		1.5
At 31 March 20X6		
Total expected profit	5	
Invoiced to date (12.6 × 100/90)	14	
Profit recognised (5 × 14/20)		3.5
Less recognised in 20X5		(1.5)
Less rectification costs		(1.0)
Profit 20X6		1.0

3   *Gross amount due from customers*

	$m
Costs to date	12.5
Recognised profit (1.5 + 1)	2.5
Progress billings (12.6 × 100/90)	(14.0)
Due from customers	1.0

Beta

INCOME STATEMENT

	$m
Revenue (1.8 × 100/90)	2.0
Cost of sales (7.5 × 2/6)	(2.5)
Provision for loss	(1.0)
Loss for the year (total loss now recognised)	(1.5)

STATEMENT OF FINANCIAL POSITION

	$m
Gross amount due to customers (W)	(1.5)

Working

	$m
Costs to date	2.0
Recognised loss	(1.5)
Progress billings (1.8 × 100/90)	(2.0)
Gross amount due to customers	(1.5)

Ceta

INCOME STATEMENT

	$m
Revenue (12 × 4/10)	4.8
Cost of sales (10 × 4/10)	(4.0)
Profit (2 × 4/10)	0.8

STATEMENT OF FINANCIAL POSITION

	$m
Gross amount due from customers (W)	4.8

Working

Costs to date	4.0
Recognised profit	0.8
Gross amount due from customers	4.8

Total

INCOME STATEMENT

	$m
Revenue (8 + 2 + 4.8)	14.8
Cost of sales (7 + 3.5 + 4)	(14.5)
Profit/(Loss) (1 + (1.5) + 0.8)	0.3

STATEMENT OF FINANCIAL POSITION

Amounts due from customers (1.0 + 4.8)	5.8
Amount due to customers	(1.5)
Receivables ((14 + 2) × 10%)	1.6

48 Beetie

Text references. Chapters 12 and 15.

Top tips. Construction contracts appeared regularly under the old syllabus and will probably feature regularly in F7. Make sure you know how to calculate the amounts for the statement of financial position.

Easy marks. Part (a) was 4 easy marks and you could get another 2 easy marks for getting the income statement amounts correct.

(a) Revenue recognition is an important issue in financial reporting and it is generally accepted that revenue is earned when goods have been accepted by the customer or services have been delivered. At that stage revenue is said to have been realised. However, if this were applied to construction contracts, the effect would not necessarily be to give faithful representation.

As a construction contract can span several accounting periods, if no revenue were recognised until the end of the contract, this would certainly be prudent but would not be in accordance with the accruals concept. The financial statements would show all of the profit in the final period, when in fact some of it had been earned in prior periods. This is remedied by recognising attributable profit as the contract progresses, as long as ultimate profitability is expected. Any foreseeable loss is recognised immediately.

(b) INCOME STATEMENT

	Contract 1	Contract 2	Total
	$'000	$'000	$'000
Contract revenue	3,300	840	4,140
Contract expenses: (Contract 1: 4,000 × 60%)	(2,400)	(720)	(3,120)
Expected loss recognised (Contract 2)	–	(170)	(170)
Attributable profit/(loss)	900	(50)	850

STATEMENT OF FINANCIAL POSITION

	$'000
Current assets	
Gross amount due from customers	1,800
Current liabilities	
Gross amounts due to customers	210

Workings

Contract 1

	$'000
Contract price	5,500
Costs to date	(3,900)
Costs to complete (4,000 – 3,900)	(100)
Estimated total profit	1,500
Profit to date: 1,500 × 3,300/5,500 =	900

Gross amount due from customers

Costs to date	3,900
Profit to date	900
Less progress billings	(3,000)
	1,800

Contract 2

	$'000
Contract price	1,200
Costs to date	(720)
Costs to complete (1,250 – 720)	(530)
Expected total loss	(50)

Gross amount due to customers

Costs to date	720
Loss to date	(50)
Less progress billings	(880)
	(210)

49 Bodyline

Text reference. Chapter 13.

Top tips. Parts (a) and (b) require you to rehearse the standard discussion about the nature of provisions and the need for IAS 37. The well-prepared candidate should score highly.

The calculations in Part (c) can be tricky, but if you lay out your workings in a methodical manner then you should score good marks even if you don't get the answer perfectly right.

Part (d) requires you to criticise the directors' proposed treatment and then to outline and explain the correct accounting treatment.

Easy marks. The discussion parts (a) and (b) represent 12 easy marks.

Examiner's comments. This question dealt with the nature and treatment of provisions. Parts (a) and (b) were discursive; while (c) and (d) were practical examples of the application.

Generally candidates answered parts (a) and (b) well, but failed to deal with the practical applications in part (c) and (d).

		Marks
(a)	One mark per valid point to max	6
(b)	The need for the Standard and examples to a max of 2 each	6
(c)	28 day refund policy – constructive obligation	1
	Calculation of provision for unrealised profits where goods resold at full price	1
	Calculation of provision for loss on goods sold at half normal price	1
	The product warranties are treated collectively	1
	Warranty cost can be estimated reliably therefore a liability, not a contingency	1
	Faulty goods other than from Header – not a loss, but	1
	Must remove profit made on them – quantified	1
	Return of faulty goods manufactured by Header creates a loss	1
	Quantification of loss	1
	Available	9
	Maximum	8
(d)	Director's treatment is incorrect	1
	This is an example of a complex asset	1
	Depreciation is $1.65m per annum plus $1,500 per machine hour	2
	Replacement does not meet the definition of a liability	
	Maximum	5
	Maximum for question	25

(a) **Provisions and IAS 37**

Provisions are liabilities of uncertain timing or amount. Because they are liabilities they must meet the recognition criteria for liabilities - that is there must be:

- A *present* obligation arising from *past* transactions or events
- The *transfer* of economic benefits to settle the obligation must be *probable*
- A *reliable estimate* can be made of the amount of the obligation

The obligation giving rise to a provision can be legal or constructive. A constructive obligation can arise when the actions or statements made by an entity create an expectation that they will meet certain obligations, even if there is no legal requirement for them to do so; for example they may have a well- known policy of replacing goods beyond the normal warranty period.

Provisions are recognised in full as soon as an entity is aware of them, but long term provisions are recognised at present value. As time goes by the discount unwinds, increasing the provision. The increase in the provision is charged to the income statement as a finance cost.

If an obligation depends upon a future event, then it is a contingent liability, not a provision. Also, if the amount of an obligation cannot be measured reliably, then it is a contingent liability. Contingent liabilities are not recognised in the financial statements, although they need to be disclosed unless the possibility of an outflow of economic benefits is remote.

(In the past the term provision has been used to describe the reduction in the carrying value of an asset; for example the provision for depreciation. This use of the word provision does not meet the criteria of IAS 37, and so the term allowance is used instead; for example the allowance for receivables.)

(b) **The need for a standard**

Although provisions have been a key area of financial reporting for many years, IAS 37 was the first standard to address this issue. Before IAS 37 there were no rules governing the

- Definition
- Recognition
- Measurement
- Use, and
- Presentation

of provisions.

IAS 37 definition of a provision as a liability of uncertain timing or amount means that provisions must meet the recognition for liabilities. This means that provisions cannot be created to suit management needs. In the past provisions were often created and released in order to smooth profits, rather than to provide for a specific liability. These were sometimes called 'big bath provisions' because they could be used for any and every purpose.

A specific example of this was the creation of provisions for reorganisation or restructuring. The charge to set these provisions up could be explained away by management to their investors as one-off exceptional items, but the release of the provision in the future would boost profits. Under IAS 37 provisions for restructuring can only be recognised if the restructuring has begun or if the restructuring has been announced publicly.

The measurement rules have standardised practice in an area where there were genuine differences of opinion. For example there are at least three ways in which the cost of cleaning up an industrial site after it is closed down (restoration costs) can be accounted for:

- ignore the costs until the site is abandoned,
- accrue the costs evenly over the productive life of the site, or
- provide for the costs in full immediately.

IAS 37 states that these costs should be provided for in full immediately, but at their present value.

Under IAS 37 provisions can only be used for the purpose that they were created for; if a provision is no longer needed it must be released. In the past provisions were sometimes created for one purpose and then used to cover the costs of another.

IAS 37 includes detailed disclosure requirements, including the movement on provisions during the year and an explanation of what each provision has been created for. This ensures that the rules set out above have been complied with.

(c) **Bodyline**

This provision can be reliably measured on the basis of past experience. Although Bodyline does not know which items will be returned or develop faults, it can make an estimate of the total value of returns and faults that there will probably be.

The question does not make it clear whether the 28 day refund is part of the sales contract (in which case it is a legal obligation) or whether it is just a well-known and established part of Bodyline's trading practices (in which case it is a constructive obligation). Either way, an obligation exists that needs to be provided for.

The provision itself can be reliably measured on the basis of past experience. Although Bodyline does not know which items will be returned or develop faults, it can make an estimate of the total value of returns and faults that there will probably be.

The returns provision is $52,850, calculated as follows:

- Of the 10% of sales that are returned under this policy, 70% are resold at the full price. Therefore only the profit element is provided against on these items.

- A further 30% are sold at half the normal sales price, so the provision required will be half of the sale proceeds.

		$
70% resold at full price		
Goods from Header	$1.75m × 20% × 10% × 70% × 40/140	7,000
Other goods	$1.75m × 80% × 10% × 70% × 25/125	19,600
		26,600
30% resold at half price	$1.75m × 10% × 30% × ½	26,250
		52,850

The faulty goods provision is $57,600, calculated as follows:

- 20% of the goods returned will have been supplied by Header; Bodyline will suffer the loss in full on these items.
- Bodyline reclaims the cost of the other 80% returned. Only the profit element is provided for.

		$
Goods from Header	$160,000 × 20%	32,000
Other goods	$160,000 × 80% × 25/125	25,600
		57,600

(d) **Rockbuster**

No obligation exists to replace the engine and so it is wrong to create a provision for its replacement. Rockbuster may decide to trade in the earthmover rather than replace the engine. Also, the $2.4m depreciation charge includes an element in respect of the engine, so to make a provision as well is double-counting.

Instead IAS 16 states that the earth-mover should be treated as an asset with two separate components (the engine and the rest) with different useful lives. The engine (cost $7.5m) will be depreciated on a machine hours basis over 5,000 hours, while the rest of the machine (cost $16.5m) will be depreciated over ten years.

	Cost	Depreciation charge
	$'000	
Engine	7,500	Depreciated on a machine hours basis over 5,000 hours. The charge is $1,500 per hour
The rest	16,500	Depreciated on a straight line basis over its ten year useful life. The charge is $1,650,000 per annum.
Total	24,000	

When the engine is replaced the cost and accumulated depreciation on the existing engine will be retired and the cost of the new engine will be capitalised and depreciated over its working life.

50 Tentacle

(i) This is an adjusting event after the reporting period within the terms of IAS 10. $23,000 should be written off to irrecoverable debts at the year end and the trade receivables balance correspondingly reduced.

(ii) In this case sales after the reporting period have demonstrated that the NRV of inventory item W32 is below cost. In accordance with IAS 2, inventories of W32 should now be written down to NRV as follows:

	$
Cost (12,000 × 6)	72,000
NRV (12,000 × (5.4 × 85%))	(55,080)
Write off to income statement	16,920

(iii) As it is not yet known whether the employee's legal action will be successful, Tentacle is correct to show it as a contingent liability. However, on the basis of the settlement in the other case, the contingent liability should be increased to $750,000. If the case is settled before the financial statements are authorised for issue, this will be an adjusting event requiring a provision for damages if Tentacle is found liable.

(iv) IAS 11 requires that the profit on the contract be recalculated to take into account these additional costs. Profit is based on costs to date as a percentage of total costs. As costs to date are $3m and total costs $6m, the percentage is currently 50%. This will change when the additional costs are included as follows:

	Costs to date	Total expected costs	%	Total expected profit	Profit to date
	$m	$m		$m	$m
Original	3	6	50%	2.4	1.20
Additional costs	–	1.5		(1.5)	–
Amended	3	7.5	40%	0.9	0.36

Recognised profit for the year to 31 March 20X7 should therefore be restated as $360,000. $840,000 (1.2m – 0.36m) will be written off in the income statement and adjusted in the statement of financial position against amounts due to/from customers.

51 Promoil

			Marks
(a)		1 mark per relevant point	5
(b)	(i)	Explanation of treatment	2
		Depreciation	1
		Finance cost	1
		Non-current asset	2
		Provision	1
			7
	(ii)	Figures for asset and depreciation if not a constructive obligation	1
		What may cause a constructive obligation	1
		Subsequent treatment if it is a constructive obligation	1
			3
			15

(a)   The *Framework* defines a liability as a present obligation of an entity arising from past events, the settlement of which is expected to result in an outflow from the entity of resources embodying economic benefits. The obligation can be legal or constructive.

A provision is a liability of uncertain timing or amount. It can be recognised when the outflow of resources is probable and when the amount concerned can be reliably estimated. Because it is regarded as a liability, a provision must meet the definition of a liability. This regulates when a provision should, or should not, be made. For instance, entities are not allowed to provide for future operating losses, which used to be a means of 'profit smoothing', because the losses are in the future, rather than arising from past events. At the same time, an entity which has a future environmental liability because of past polluting activities, is required to make a provision as soon as the liability becomes apparent.

(b)   (i)   Promoil must provide for dismantling and restoration costs at 30 September 2008, as the liability came into existence with the granting of the licence and the cost has been reliably estimated.

The provision at 30 September 2008 will be for the future cost discounted over 10 years. This will be added to the carrying amount of the oil platform and depreciated over 10 years. The discount will be 'unwound' each year and charged to finance costs. The credit entry will increase the provision until at the end of 10 years it will stand at $15m.

At 30 September 2008:

INCOME STATEMENT

	$'000
Depreciation (see SFP)	3,690
Finance costs (6,900 (see SFP) × 8%)	552

STATEMENT OF FINANCIAL POSITION

		$'000
Non-current assets:		
Oil platform	30,000	
Dismantling (15m × .46)	6,900	
		36,900
Depreciation (36,900/10)		(3,690)
Carrying value		33,210
Non-current liabilities:		
Environmental provision at 1 October 2007		6,900
Discount unwound (6,900 × 8%)		552
		7,452

(ii)   If the government licence did not require an environmental clean up, Promoil would have no legal obligation. It would then be necessary to determine whether or not Promoil had a constructive obligation. This would apply if on past performance it had established a practice of carrying out an environmental clean up where required, which would give rise to the expectation that it would do so in this case. If a constructive obligation existed, the accounting would be as per the above.

If no obligation were established, there would be no liability. No provision would be made for the clean-up. The platform would be capitalised at $30m and depreciated over 10 years. There would be no finance costs.

52 Peterlee II

(a)   The goodwill in Trantor is purchased goodwill and can be capitalised and shown as an asset in the consolidated statement of financial position at the value calculated. However, the goodwill in Peterlee itself is internally generated goodwill, and per IAS 38 it cannot be capitalised because it cannot be reliably measured. So the directors will be allowed to include the goodwill in Trantor of $2.5 million in the financial statements, but the goodwill estimated to exist in Peterlee cannot be recognised.

(b)   Per IAS 37 this treatment is not correct. The $2 million present value of the landscaping cost should be recognised as a provision at 31 March 20X6. The debit will be to the asset account, giving an asset value for the mine of $8 million. This total value will be depreciated over 10 years. In this way the landscaping cost will be charged to the income statement over the life of the mine. At the same time, the discount to present value will 'unwind' over the 10 year period. This will be credited to the provision and charged as a finance cost. At the end of 10 years, the amount in the provision account should equal the amount due to be paid.

(c)   As this is a convertible loan, it must be apportioned between debt and equity. Per IAS 32 and IAS 39 this is calculated as follows:

	$'000
Present value of the principal to be repaid: $5 million × 0.75	3,750
Present value of interest: $0.4 million × 2.49 (0.91 + 0.83 + 0.75)	996
Debt element	4,746
Equity element	254
Proceeds of issue	5,000

The income statement and statement of financial position amounts will be as follows:

	$'000	$'000
Debt element of loan		4,746
Interest at 10% (income statement)	475	
Interest paid	(400)	
Balance due		75
Balance of loan at 31 March 20X6 (statement of financial position)		4,821

53 Jedders

(a) (i) IAS 16 *Property, plant and equipment* does not allow **selective revaluations** of non-current tangible assets: if one asset is revalued, all in that class must be revalued, thus avoiding 'cherry picking' of asset gains where others in the class may have fallen in value. In addition, non-recording of a fall in value of an asset cannot be justified on the basis that a recovery in market prices is expected in the future.

(ii) INCOME STATEMENT (EXTRACTS)

	$'000
Depreciation charge	
North (($1.2m × 80%)/20 years)	48
Central (($4.8m × 140%)/40 years)	168
South ($2.25m/30 years)	75
	291
Loss on revaluation	
(20% × $1.2m)	240

STATEMENT OF FINANCIAL POSITION (EXTRACTS)

	Cost/revaluation	Depreciation	NBV
	$'000	$'000	$'000
North	960	48	912
Central	6,720	168	6,552
South	2,250	75	2,175
	9,930	291	9,639

At 1 January 20X0 the accumulated depreciation of the Central property is $1.2m, which represents 10 years' worth of depreciation, leaving 40 years remaining life. For the South and North properties, the respective lives on these calculations are 30 and 20 years. If there is no previous revaluation surplus on the North property, then the loss in the current year is classed as an impairment and must be taken to the income statement.

(b) A statement of how the trade receivables should be treated:

Group A. These are normal non-factor receivables and the allowance should be calculated as usual.

Group B. Although these receivables have been factored, the risks of late collection and irrecoverable debts remain with Jedders. Thus, the outstanding balance less the receivables allowance should still appear in Jedders' statement of financial position, with a liability recorded for the amount received from Fab Factors. In addition, an interest charge would be made for the 1% charge for the monies advanced.

Group C. In a non-recourse situation such as this, Jedders has effectively sold its receivables for 95% of their value. The receivables would therefore be taken off Jedders' statement of financial position, leaving cash and a residual finance charge.

Applying these treatments to the figures given:

INCOME STATEMENT

	$
Receivables allowance	
Group A (20% × (1,250 × 20%))	50,000
Group B (20% × (1,500 × 10%))	30,000
Group C	nil
	80,000
Finance charge	
Group A	nil
Group B (1% × 1,500) + (1% × 900) + (1% × 450)	28,500
Group C (5% × 2,000)	160,000
	128,500

STATEMENT OF FINANCIAL POSITION (EXTRACTS)

Trade receivables		Less allowance	Net balance
			$
Group A	(1,250 × 20%)	20%	200,000
Group B	(1,500 × 10%)	20%	120,000
Group C		nil	nil
			320,000

(c) IAS 32 *Financial instruments: presentation* requires the issuer of a **hybrid or compound instrument** of this nature – containing elements that are characteristic of both debt and equity – to separate out the components of the instrument and classify them separately. Fab Factors are thus wrong in their advice that such instruments should be recorded and shown as debt.

The proceeds of issue should be split between the amounts attributable to the conversion rights, which are classed as **equity**, and the remainder which must be classed as a **liability**. Although there are several methods that might be used, the question only gives sufficient information to allow the amounts of debt liability to be calculated, leaving the equity element as the residual.

Year	Cash flows	Factor at 10%	Present value
	$'000		$'000
1 Interest ($15m × 7%)	1,050	0.91	955.5
2	1,050	0.83	871.5
3	1,050	0.75	787.5
4	1,050	0.68	714.0
5 Interest + capital	16,050	0.62	9,951.0
Total debt component			13,279.5
Proceeds of issue			15,000.0
Equity component (residual)			1,720.5

INCOME STATEMENT (EXTRACTS)

	$'000
Interest paid ((7% × $15m) + 278 (W1))	1,328

Working

((10% × $13.2795m) – $1.05m) (rounded)	278

STATEMENT OF FINANCIAL POSITION (EXTRACTS)

	$'000
Non-current liabilities	
7% convertible loan notes (13,279.5 + 278)	13,557.5
Equity	
Option to convert to equity	1,720.5

54 Pingway

Top tips. This question was easy if you knew what to do. If you had recognised that it was a compound instrument and made some sensible comments there would have been marks for that even if the calculations were incorrect.

Examiner's comments. The majority of answers to this question were poor. The proceeds of the loan had to be split between debt and equity by discounting the future cash flows at 8% to give the debt element, with the balance being the equity element. Common mistakes were to project the cash flows with an interest rate of 8% (rather than 3%), to discount them at 3% (rather than 8%) and to calculate the interest charge as 3% of $10m (rather than 8% of the debt element).

	Marks
1 mark per valid comment up to	4
use of 8%	1
initial carrying amount of debt and equity	2
finance cost	2
carrying amount of debt at 31 March 2008	1
Total for question	10

This convertible loan note is a compound financial instrument. It contains both a liability and an equity component and IAS 32 *Financial Instruments: Presentation* requires these components to be separately recognised. Interest costs on the liability element will be based on the non-convertible rate of 8%, so the charge to the income statement will not be significantly lower than if a non-convertible instrument were issued. The liability element will also add to gearing. So the financial assistant's observations are incorrect.

Financial statement extracts

$

Income statement

Finance costs (8,674,000 × 8%)	693,920

Statement of financial position

Equity – option to convert (W1)	1,326,000

Non-current liabilities

3% convertible loan note (W2)	9,067,920

Workings

1   *Equity and liability elements*

	$
Proceeds of loan note	10,000,000
3 years interest (10,000 × 3% × (0.93 + 0.86 + 0.79))	(774,000)
Redemption (10,000 × 0.79)	(7,900,000)
Equity element of loan note	1,326,000
Liability element (10,000 – 1,326)	8,674,000

2   *Loan note balance*

	$
Liability element	8,674,000
Interest at 8%	693,920
Less interest paid	(300,000)
Carrying value at 31 March 2008	9,067,920

55 Triangle

Text reference. Chapters 13 and 15.

Top tips. This question had four short sections dealing with various matters: environmental costs, events after the reporting period, contingent assets and substance over form.

The way to deal with such questions is to identify the issue and so the accounting standard needed. After that, it is simply a matter of applying the provision of the relevant standard.

Easy marks. If you know how to apply the standards, this is 25 very easy marks.

Marking scheme

			Marks
(i)	Explanation of treatment of provision		2
	Cost of plant at $20 million		1
	Revised depreciation		1
	Provision initially at $5 million		1
	Increase by finance cost		1
	Income statement charges 1 each		2
		Maximum	8
(ii)	An example of an adjusting event		1
	No overall effect on profit, but presentation incorrect		1
	Remove from cost of sales and show as an expense		1
	$30,000 is a non-adjusting event if material		1
	Disclose as a note to the financial statements		1
		Maximum	5
(iii)	Due to the dispute this is an example of a contingent asset		1
	Describe the treatment of contingent assets		1
	Not probable therefore ignore, financial statements unchanged		2
		Maximum	4
(iv)	Identify it as a sale and repurchase agreement (or financing arrangement)		1
	Substance is not likely to be a sale		1
	Will repurchase if value is more than $7,320,500 plus storage costs		2
	Business of Factorall is financing therefore terms likely to favour repurchase		1
	Adjustments to – sales/loan; cost of sales/inventory;		2
	– trade receivables/inventory (re storage costs); accrued finance costs/loan		2
		Available	9
		Maximum	8
		Maximum for question	25

(i)   *Contamination*

There are two errors in the current accounting treatment.

Firstly, the obligation to clean up the contamination existed in full from the day that the plant was brought into use. Therefore the provision should be recognised in full immediately at present value; it should not be accrued incrementally over the life of the plant. Over the next ten years the present value will increase as the discount unwinds. This will be reported by increasing the provision and charging the increase to the income statement as a finance cost.

Secondly, on initial recognition, the cost of the plant should include the present value of the decontamination.

The plant and the provision should be reported as follows:

	$'000
Plant (a non-current asset)	
1 April 20X4: cost ($15m + $5m)	20,000
Depreciation ($20m/10 years)	(2,000)
31 March 20X5: carrying value	18,000
Provision (a non-current liability)	
1 April 20X4	5,000
Finance cost @ 8%	400
31 March 20X5	5,400

(ii) *Fraud*

The fraud means that the draft financial statements for the year-ended 31 March 2005 are incorrect. This probably won't affect the net profit for the year, but it will affect the amounts shown for cost of sales and gross profit.

The discovery of this fraud provides new evidence about conditions existing at the end of the reporting period, and so it is classified as an adjusting event. The $210,000 fraud that occurred during the year will be charged to the income statement as an operating expense and disclosed.

The $30,000 fraud occurring after the year-end does not affect conditions existing at the end of the reporting period and so it will not be adjusted for. However it will be disclosed if it is considered to be material in its own right.

(iii) *Insurance claim*

The insurance claim gives rise to a contingent asset for $240,000. However, under IAS 37 contingent assets are not recognised unless the realisation of income is virtually certain, and this is not the case here because the insurers are disputing the claim.

A contingent asset is disclosed when an inflow of economic benefits is probable, but without legal opinion it is not possible to regard the success of the claim as probable.

Following on from the above, the insurance claim should be ignored altogether in the financial statements for the year-ending 31 March 20X5.

(iv) *Factorall*

The $5m proceeds from Factorall cannot be claimed as income because the substance of the transaction appears to be a $5m loan secured on the maturing inventory.

This is because Triangle still retains the cost and benefits of ownership through its option to repurchase the inventory before 31 March 20X8. Although legally Triangle could refuse to repurchase the inventory, there is evidence of a constructive obligation to do so as noted below:

- The initial sale was below market price, and so there is an opportunity cost arising from not repurchasing.
- The repurchase price is based on the sales price plus interest rather than on its true market value at the date of repurchase. The market price will probably be higher, suggesting an additional opportunity cost from not repurchasing.
- Factorall, as a finance house, will not have the expertise to bring the product to market, and so it will be expecting Triangle to repurchase. If Triangle refuses to repurchase then it is unlikely that Factorall (or any similar company) will be willing to enter into such an agreement with Triangle again.

Because there is a constructive obligation to repurchase the inventory Triangle should recognise this as a liability (at present value) and continue to recognise the inventory at cost (including the storage costs).

For Factorall the benefit of this arrangement is the 10% compound interest receivable, not the purchase of the product.

The correct accounting treatment for this transaction in Triangle's books is as follows:

INCOME STATEMENT

Finance costs ($5m @ 10%) $500,000

STATEMENT OF FINANCIAL POSITION
Current assets
Inventory ($3m + $300,000 holding costs) $3,300,000
Non-current liabilities
Secured loan ($5m + 10%) $5,500,000

The journal to correct the old treatment is as follows:

			Debit $'000	Credit $'000
DEBIT	I/S	Sales (Proceeds)	5,000	
CREDIT	F/P	Secured loan (Proceeds)		5,000
DEBIT	F/P	Inventory (Cost of inventory)	3,000	
CREDIT	I/S	Cost of sales (Cost of inventory)		3,000
DEBIT	F/P	Inventory (Holding costs)	300	
CREDIT	F/P	Receivables (Holding costs)		300
DEBIT	I/S	Finance costs (10% interest)	500	
CREDIT	F/P	Secured loan (10% interest)		500

(F/P = Statement of financial position)

56 Atkins

(i)   This problem arises whenever goods are delivered on a consignment stock basis, with deferred payment and the option to return unsold goods. The question is, who should recognise the goods as an asset between the date of delivery and the date of payment?

The party that bears the risks and benefits of the cars recognises them as assets in their statement of financial position. Even though the cars are held at one of Atkins' showrooms does not mean that Atkins recognises them as assets. If the benefits are shared between the two parties, then the party that bears most of the risks will recognise the asset.

If the manufacturer still bears the risks and benefits then the manufacturer recognises the cars in its own statement of financial position as inventory at production cost. No revenue or profit is claimed by the manufacturer, and no purchase or inventory item is recognised by Atkins.

If Atkins bears the risks and benefits of the cars then Atkins will recognise them as assets at their purchase price, along with the related liability to pay for them. The manufacturer will no longer recognise the cars; instead it will claim a sale and recognise a trade receivable.

In this situation the risks and benefits are borne as follows:

•   The price paid by Atkins is fixed at the date of delivery. This means that Atkins bears any risk (or benefit) of price changes arising after that date. (If the retail price falls, then Atkins will lose out because its own purchase price is based on 80% of the retail price on delivery. Likewise if the retail price rises Atkins gets extra profit because its own purchase price is fixed.)

•   The 1.5% per month 'display charge' represents interest on the money owed by Atkins to the manufacturer from the date of delivery. This means that Atkins bears the risk of slow moving cars, because Atkins will be charged interest for as long as a car remains unsold (or until six months has passed and Atkins pays for the car in full).

•   Atkins right to return unsold cars could, in theory, offset the risk of price cuts and slow moving items. However, in practice Atkins has never taken advantage of this right and so it suggests that for commercial reasons it cannot be exercised (for example the manufacturer may stop supplying cars to Atkins if the right is exercised frequently).

•   The one area where the manufacturer still appears to have some rights of ownership is in its right to recall or transfer cars held at Atkins' showrooms.

It is clear from this that Atkins bears all the risks attached to these assets from the date of delivery. Therefore Atkins will recognise them as assets from the date of delivery, along with the related trade payable. The 'display charge' will be accrued as it is incurred over time.

The manufacturer will recognise a sale as soon as the cars are delivered, and claim the display charge over time. The manufacturer's experience of trading with Atkins will decide the level of provision needed in respect of returns.

(ii)   The legal form of this transaction is that Atkins has sold three plots of land costing $1.2m for $2.4m making a profit of $1.2m. However, there are a number of points that suggest that this is a financing arrangement rather than a true sale:

The sale is for below the market price. Why would Atkins make a genuine sale for $800,000 less than its open market value?

On 30 September 20X5 Atkins has the option to repurchase at $3.2m. On that day the open market value may be higher, in which case Atkins can repurchase and resell again. Atkins will then benefit from any price rises occurring after the original sale in 20X2.

If on 30 September 20X5 the price has fallen below $3.2m, and Atkins does not want to exercise its right to repurchase, then Atkins can be forced to repurchase the following day. Atkins will therefore bear any fall in value arising after 20X2.

The difference between the $2.4m sales price in 20X2 and the $3.2m repurchase price in 20X5 represents interest at the market rate of 10% per annum.

The probability that Atkins will benefit from any future price rises and suffer from any price falls, along with the finance charge implicit in the sale and repurchase prices, suggests that this is a secured loan rather than a true sale.

Extracts from the financial statements for the year to 30 September 20X3

(1)   Legal form (the land is considered to be sold by Atkins)

INCOME STATEMENT	$'000
Revenue	2,400
Cost of sales	(1,200)
Gross profit	1,200

STATEMENT OF FINANCIAL POSITION	$'000
Non-current assets	
Land at cost ($2m - $1.2m)	800

(2)   Commercial substance (the transaction is a $2.4m loan secured on the land)

INCOME STATEMENT	$'000
Gross profit	–
Finance cost ($2.4m @ 10%)	(240)

STATEMENT OF FINANCIAL POSITION	$'000
Non-current assets	
Land at cost	2,000
Non-current liabilities	
Secured loan due 20X5 (2,400 + 240)	2,640

57 Angelino

Marking scheme

				Marks
(a)		1 mark per relevant point to a	Maximum	9
(b)	(i)	1 mark per relevant point to a	Maximum	5
	(ii)	sale price not at fair value raises substance issues		1
		leaseback is not a finance lease		1
		treat building as sold (derecognise) at a profit of $2.5m		1
		rental treated as: $800,000 rental cost		1
		$200,000 finance cost		1
		$300,000 loan repayment		1
			Maximum	6
	(iii)	general discussion of risks and rewards re consignment goods		2
		Issues and accounting treatment relating to supplies from Monza		2
		Issues and accounting treatment relating to supplies from Capri		2
			Available	6
			Maximum	5
			Maximum for question	25

(a) Off balance sheet finance is a form of creative accounting which seeks to obscure financial transactions. It has been described as 'the funding or refinancing of a company's operations in such a way that, under legal requirements and existing accounting conventions, some or all of the finance may not be shown on its balance sheet.' (Note that the IASB now refers to the 'balance sheet' as the 'statement of financial position'. However, the term 'off-balance sheet finance' is still in use.)

In practice, most off-balance sheet finance transactions are intended to keep debt off the statement of financial position. In order to achieve this, the related asset is also kept off the statement of financial position. An example of this is where an asset is actually acquired under a finance lease. Rather than show the asset and the related loan, the acquirer may decide that the asset is not to be capitalised and the lease is accounted for as an operating lease. Or inventory may be purchased on consignment, under a legal agreement which allows the purchaser to not record the current asset or the related trade payable. Potential suppliers doing a credit reference check on the company will not discover the true value of its existing trade payables or be able to accurately assess its payment record. Another example can be where an asset is 'sold' and 'repurchased' under an arrangement which is in substance a loan secured on the asset. The asset disappears from the statement of financial position and the loan is represented as sale proceeds.

Obviously, this conflicts with the requirement for 'fair presentation' in financial statements and the IASB has sought to deal with the off balance sheet problem by means of the definitions and recognition criteria for assets and liabilities in the *Framework*. The *Framework* specifically addresses the issue of **substance over form** and refers to a situation such as that above where 'the reporting of a sale would not represent faithfully the transaction entered into'.

Why do companies want to keep debt out of the statement of financial position? Mainly to improve the appearance of the statement of financial position and avoid any impact on gearing. They want to satisfy the expectations of analysts. An increase in borrowing brings an increase in interest payments, which reduces the amount left to distribute to shareholders. An increase in borrowing above a certain limit can therefore be negatively perceived by investors, leading to a possible fall in the share price. A fall in the share price can leave the company vulnerable to takeover.

A company which is short of funds and needs to raise further loans also needs to convince lenders that it is a good risk. If it already has large loans outstanding, lenders will be less willing to make further loans, or will require a higher rate of interest to compensate for the increased risk of default. The company may therefore seek to move some of its borrowing off balance sheet (perhaps by paying off one loan with another disguised as a sale and repurchase) and thereby reduce its gearing to a more acceptable level.

Off balance sheet finance is to some degree a dynamic issue; new forms of it will continue to arise and it will continue to be a problem for standard setters, auditors, lenders and investors. A number of the high-profile collapses of recent years have revealed substantial amounts of borrowing off balance sheet.

(b)   (i)   In this situation the trade receivables have been factored 'with recourse'. Angelino still bears the risks of slow payment (they receive a residual amount depending upon how quickly customers pay) and non-payment (they refund to Omar any balances uncollected after six months). The substance of the transaction is therefore that Omar is providing a loan to Angelino on the security of the trade receivables.

The receivables have therefore not been sold and should not be derecognised. The payment from Omar should be accounted for as a loan. When a customer pays, the amount lent in respect of his balance should be debited to the loan and credited to his account and the amount needed to clear his balance should be charged to loan interest/ debt collection expenses.

(ii)   This is a sale and leaseback transaction in which the sale price has been inflated to include a loan and the lease payments have been inflated to include interest and loan repayments.

Taking the transaction at its face value, Angelino could record the sale at $12m, showing a profit on disposal of $4.5m. The lease payments of $1.3m per annum would be charged to the income statement as rent.

However, representing the substance of the transaction, the sale should be recorded at market value of $10m, giving a profit on disposal of $2.5m and the additional $2m should be recorded as a loan. The $0.5m per annum above market value in the lease payments should be treated as loan repayments.

The loan will be accounted for as follows:

	$'000
Initial balance	2,000
Finance cost 10%	200
Instalment paid	(500)
Balance 30.9.X6	1,700
Finance cost 10%	170
Instalment paid	(500)
Balance 30.9.X7	1,370
Current liability (1,700 – 1,370)	330
Non-current liability	1,370

(iii)   Angelino's contract with Monza is a typical consignment agreement. The cars remain the property of Monza and Angelino bears none of the risks of ownership. When Angelino sells a car or decides to keep it at the end of three months, it purchases it at that point from Monza, at the list price in force at that date. This is therefore the point at which the risks and rewards pass to Angelino. Up to that point there is no sale and the cars should not appear in inventory.

The agreement with Capri is of the nature of purchase under a credit agreement. Angelino pays a 10% deposit and obtains ownership of the vehicles at that point. If it fails to pay the balance, it forfeits its deposit and has to return the cars at its own expense, so it has taken on the risks of ownership, principally the risk of not being able to sell the vehicle. In this case Angelino should show the cars in inventory and set up a trade payable for the list price, less the deposit paid. The 1% display charge should be accounted for as interest.

58 Preparation question: Branch

INCOME STATEMENT (EXTRACT)

	$
Depreciation (W1)	5,000
Finance costs (W2)	2,074

STATEMENT OF FINANCIAL POSITION (EXTRACT)

Property, plant and equipment includes assets held under finance lease with a net book value of $15,000.

	$
Non-current liabilities	
Finance lease liabilities (W2)	14,786

	$
Current liabilities	
Finance lease liabilities (W2) (16,924 – 14,786)	2,138

Workings

1   Depreciation

$$\frac{20,000}{4} = \$5,000 \text{ pa}$$

2   Finance leases liabilities

		$
Year ended 31 December 20X1		
1.1.X1	Liability b/d	20,000
1.1.X1	Deposit	(1,150)
		18,850
1.1.X1 – 31.12.X1	Interest at 11%	2,074
31.12.X1	Instalment	(4,000)
31.12.X1	Liability c/d	16,924
Year ended 31 December 20X2		
1.1.X2 – 31.12.X2	Interest at 11%	1,862
31.12.X2	Instalment	(4,000)
31.12.X2	Liability c/d	14,786

59 Evans

INCOME STATEMENT (extract)

	$
Depreciation ($61,570/10)*	6,157
Operating lease rentals (2 × 5,000)	10,000
Finance costs (W)	1,171

STATEMENT OF FINANCIAL POSITION (extract)

Non-current assets
Property, plant and equipment ($61,570 – $6,157)   55,413
Non-current liabilities
Finance lease liabilities (W)   51,033
Current liabilities
Finance lease liabilities (59,741 – 51,033 (W))   8,708

Working

Interest on finance lease

	$
Cash price	61,570
Instalment 1 October 20X3	(3,000)
	58,570
Interest October - December 20X3 (2%)	1,171
Balance 31 December 20X3	59,741
Instalment 1 January 20X4	(3,000)
	56,741
Interest January - March 20X4 (2%)	1,135
Balance 31 March 20X4	57,876
Instalment 1 April 20X4	(3,000)
	54,876
Interest April - June 20X4 (2%)	1,098
Balance 30 June 20X4	55,974
Instalment 1 July 20X4	(3,000)
	52,974
Interest July - September 20X4 (2%)	1,059
Balance 30 September 20X4	54,033
Instalment 1 October 20X4	(3,000)
	51,033

*As there is a secondary lease period for which only a nominal rental is payable we can assume that Evans will keep the rocket booster for the full 10 years of its useful life. If this were not the case it would be depreciated over the 6.5 years of the lease term.

60 Bowtock

Leased asset

The first task is to decide what sort of lease the asset is held under. This is a finance lease because it transfers substantially all the risks and rewards of ownership to the lessee, as shown by the length of the lease and its cost:

- The asset's useful life is five years (as shown by the 20% straight line depreciation policy) and the lease is also for five years. Therefore the asset is being held for the whole of its useful life.

- The minimum lease payments are $60,000, spread over four years as payments are made in advance. The present value of these payments at an 8% discount rate is $51,745, which is almost the same as the asset's fair value.

The asset is capitalised and depreciated over its five year useful life, and the obligation to make lease payments is recognised as a liability.

EXTRACTS FROM BOWTOCK'S FINANCIAL STATEMENTS
FOR THE YEAR-ENDING 30 SEPTEMBER 20X3

Income statement

		$
Depreciation charge ($52,000 × 20%)		10,400
Finance costs (800 + 1,872(W3))		2,672

Statement of financial position
Non-current assets

Assets held under finance leases (W1)	33,800

Non-current liabilities

Finance lease obligations (W2)	21,696

Current liabilities

Finance lease obligations (W2)	11,376

Workings

1   *Carrying value of asset*

	$	$
1 January 20X2: Fair value of lease and asset		52,000
Depreciation to 30 September 20X2 ($52,000 × 20% × 9/12)	7,800	
Depreciation to 30 September 20X3 ($52,000 × 20%)	10,400	
		(18,200)
Carrying value 30 September 20X3		33,800

2   *Presentation of the lease liability*

	$
Total balance 30 September 20X3 (W3)	33,072
Capital amount due within 12 months (33,072 – 21,696)	11,376
Capital amount due after 12 months	21,696

3   *Movement on the lease liability*

	$
1 January 20X2: Fair value of lease and asset	52,000
First payment 1.1.X2	(12,000)
Balance 1.1 X2	40,000
Interest on $40,000 at 8% for 9 months	2,400
Balance 30 September 20X2	42,400
Interest on $40,000 at 8% for 3 months	800
Second payment 1.1.X3	(12,000)
Balance 1.1.X3	31,200
Interest on $31,200 at 8% for 9 months	1,872
Balance 30 September 20X3	33,072
Interest due to 1.1.X4 ($31,200 × 8% for 3 months)	624
Third payment 1.1X4	(12,000)
	21,696

61 Fino

Text references: Chapter 16.

Top tips: Only 5 marks were available for calculations here. Intelligent comment on faithful representation and its application to leasing would have earned the greater part of the marks.

Marking scheme

							Marks
(a)	one mark per valid point to					Maximum	5
(b)	(i)	1 mark per valid point to				Maximum	4
	(ii)	(1)	operating lease	–	income statement charge		1
				–	prepayment		1
						Maximum	2
		(2)	finance lease	–	income statement: depreciation and finance costs		1
				–	statement of financial position:		
					• non-current asset		1
					• non-current liabilities		1
					• current liabilities interest and capital		1
						Maximum	4
						Total for question	15

(a) The concept of faithful representation requires that the financial statements give a true picture of the nature and effect of financial transactions. If users can be confident that this is the case, then the financial statements can be considered to be reliable.

This means that assets and liabilities as shown in the statement of financial position exist, are assets or liabilities of the entity and are shown at the correct amount, in accordance with the stated accounting policies of the entity. For instance, it may seem that a property shown at original cost when its market value is twice that amount is not faithfully represented, but if the disclosed accounting policy of the entity is not to revalue its properties, users will know what they are looking at and can adjust accordingly.

The most obvious examples of faithful representation not being adhered to involve off-balance-sheet finance transactions, such as sale and leaseback, where secured loans are disguised as the sale of assets. This keeps borrowing out of the statement of financial position and avoids any consequent impact on gearing. The accounting scandals of the past decade revealed numerous off-balance-sheet schemes and underlined the importance of faithful representation.

(b) (i) The finance director is correct in that, if the plant is regarded as being held under an operating lease, it will not be capitalised. In this case the cost of the plant will not be included in capital employed and so will not have an adverse effect on ROCE.

However, the finance director's comments betray an ignorance of IAS 17. Under IAS 17 leases are classified according to the *substance* of the transaction, on the basis of whether or not the risks and rewards of ownership have been transferred. The standard gives examples of situations where a lease would normally be classified as a finance lease, including:

- where the lease transfers ownership to the lessee at the end of the lease term
- where an option to purchase exists on terms which make it reasonably certain that the option will be exercised
- where the lease term is for the major part of the asset's economic life
- where the present value of the minimum lease payments amounts to at least substantially all of the fair value of the asset

In this case the lease term is for the whole of the asset's economic life and the present value of the minimum lease payments (four payments of $100,000 over three years) amounts to substantially all of the fair value of the plant. This must therefore be regarded as a finance lease and consequently will impact the ROCE.

(ii) 1 Operating lease

	$
Income statement	
Payment under operating lease (100,000 × 6/12)	50,000
Statement of financial position	
Current assets	
Prepayment (100,000 × 6/12)	50,000

2 Finance lease

	$
Income statement	
Depreciation (350,000/4 × 6/12)	43,750
Finance costs (W)	12,500
Statement of financial position	
Non-current assets	
Leased plant (350,000 – 43,750)	306,250
Non-current liabilities	
Amount due under finance lease (W)	175,000
Current liabilities	
Amount due under finance lease	
(262,500 – 175,000)	87,500

Working	
	$
Cost 1.4.07	350,000
1.4.07 deposit	(100,000)
Balance 1.4.07	250,000
Interest to 30.9.07 (250,000 × 10% × 6/12)	12,500
Balance 30.9.07	262,500
Interest to 1.4.08 (250,000 × 10% × 6/12)	12,500
1.4.08 payment	(100,000)
Capital balance due 30.9.08	175,000

62 Preparation question: Julian

(a)

	Carrying Value	Tax base	Temporary difference
	$'000	$'000	$'000
Property, plant and equipment	460	270	190
Development expenditure	60		60
Interest receivable (55 – 45)	10		10
Provision	(40)		(40)
			220

(b)   **Notes to the statement of financial position**

Deferred tax liability

	$'000
Accelerated depreciation for tax purposes [(190 – 90) × 30%]	30
Product development costs deducted from taxable profit (60 × 30%)	18
Interest income taxable when received (10 × 30%)	3
Provision for environmental costs deductible when paid (40 × 30%)	(12)
Revaluations (90 × 30%)	27
	66

	$'000
At 1 January 20X4 [(310 – 230) × 30%]	24
Amount charged to income statement (balancing figure)	15
Amount charged to equity (90 × 30%)	27
At 31 December 20X4 (220 × 30%)	66

Note to the income statement

Income tax expense

	$'000
Current tax	45
Deferred tax	15
	60

63 Deferred taxation

Top tips. The explanations and calculations required here are very straightforward.

Answer plan

(a) • Introduction – IAS 12
     • Examples – Interest revenue
              – Depreciation
              – Development costs
              – Retirement benefit costs
              – Research costs
              – Fair value/revaluation

(b)

	$'000
Timing difference b/f	100
In year (100-90)	10
	110

Deferred tax = 110,000 × 30%
            = 33,000

(a) IAS 12 *Income taxes* prescribes the accounting treatment for income taxes including the recognition of deferred tax assets and liabilities. These assets and liabilities arise due to **temporary differences** between the tax base of an asset or liability and its carrying amount in the statement of financial position. The tax base of an asset or liability is the amount attributed to that asset or liability for tax purposes. Temporary differences may be either taxable or deductible.

Taxable temporary differences will result in taxable amounts in determining taxable profit (loss) of future periods when the carrying amount of the asset or liability is recovered or settled.

Deductible temporary differences will result in amounts that are deductible in determining taxable profit (tax loss) of future periods when the carrying amount of the asset is recovered or settled.   (IAS12)

IAS 12 identifies the main categories in which temporary differences can occur, which include the following:

(i) **Interest revenue** is included in accounting profit on a time proportion basis but may, in some jurisdictions, be included in taxable profit when cash is collected. The tax base of any receivable recognised in the statement of financial position with respect to such revenues is nil because the revenues do not affect taxable profit until cash is collected;

(ii) **Depreciation** used in determining taxable profit (tax loss) may differ from that used in determining accounting profit. The temporary difference is the difference between the carrying amount of the asset and its tax base which is the original cost of the asset less all deductions in respect of that asset permitted by the taxation authorities in determining taxable profit of the current and prior periods. A taxable temporary difference arises, and results in a deferred tax liability, when tax depreciation is accelerated (if tax depreciation is less rapid than accounting depreciation, a deductible temporary difference arises, and results in a deferred tax asset);

(iii) **Development costs** may be capitalised and amortised over future periods in determining accounting profit but deducted in determining taxable profit in the period in which they are incurred. Such development costs have a tax base of nil as they have already been deducted from taxable profit. The temporary difference is the difference between the carrying amount of the development costs and their tax base of nil.

(iv) **Retirement benefit costs** may be deducted in determining accounting profit as service is provided by the employees, but deducted in determining taxable profit either when contributions are paid to a fund by the entity or when retirement benefits are paid by the entity. A temporary difference exists between the carrying amount of the liability and its tax base; the tax base of the liability is usually nil. Such a deductible temporary difference results in a deferred tax asset as economic benefits will flow to the entity in the form of a deduction from taxable profits when contributions or retirement benefits are paid.

(v) **Research costs** are recognised as an expense in determining accounting profit in the period in which they are incurred but may not be permitted as a deduction in determining taxable profit (tax loss) until a later period. The difference between the tax base of the research costs, being the amount the taxation authorities will permit as a deduction in future periods, and the carrying amount of nil is a deductible temporary difference that results in a deferred tax asset;

(vi) Certain assets may be carried at **fair value**, or may be revalued, without an equivalent adjustment being made for tax purposes. A deductible temporary difference arises if the tax base of the asset exceeds its carrying amount.

(b) **G Co**

Timing difference at 31 March 20X3:

	$
Timing differences b/f at 1 April 20X2	100
Arising in year (100 – 90)	10
	110

Deferred tax liability will be 110 × 30% = $33,000

This figure will be included in the statement of financial position.

The decrease in the provision of ($35,000 – $33,000) = $2,000 will reduce the tax charge for the year.

64 Bowtock II

(a) **Principles of deferred tax**

In many countries different rules are used for calculating accounting profit (as used by investors) and taxable profit. This can give rise to **temporary differences**.

Temporary differences arise when income or expenditure is recognised in the financial statements in one year, but is charged or allowed for tax in another. Deferred tax needs to be provided for on these items.

The most important temporary difference is that between depreciation charged in the financial statements and capital allowances in the tax computation. In practice capital allowances tend to be higher than depreciation charges, resulting in accounting profits being higher than taxable profits. This means that the actual tax charge (known as *current tax*) is too low in comparison with accounting profits. However, these differences even out over the life of an asset, and so at some point in the future the accounting profits will be lower than the taxable profits, resulting in a relatively high current tax charge.

These differences are misleading for investors who value companies on the basis of their post tax profits (by using EPS for example). Deferred tax adjusts the reported tax expense for these differences. As a result the reported tax expense (the current tax for the period plus the deferred tax) will be comparable to the reported profits, and in the statement of financial position a provision is built up for the expected increase in the tax charge in the future.

There are many ways that deferred tax could be calculated. IAS 12 states that the *liability method* should be used. This provides for the tax on the difference between the carrying value of an asset (or liability) and its tax base. The tax base is the value given to an asset (or liability) for tax purposes. The deferred tax charge (or credit) in the income statement is the increase (or decrease) in the provision reported in the statement of financial position.

(b) *Bowtock*

The provision for deferred tax in Bowtock's statement of financial position at 30 September 20X3 will be the potential tax on the difference between the accounting carrying value of $1,400,000 and the tax base of $768,000. The difference is $632,000 and the tax on the difference is $158,000.

The charge (or credit) for deferred tax in profit or loss is the increase (or decrease) in the provision during the year. The closing provision of $158,000 is less than the opening provision of $160,000, so there is a credit for $2,000 in respect of this year.

Movement in the provision for deferred tax for the year-ending 30 September 20X3

	$
Opening provision	160,000
Credit released to the income statement	(2,000)
Closing provision	158,000

Workings

		Accounting Carrying value		Tax base	Difference	Tax @ 25%
Y/E 09/X1		$		$	$	$
Purchase		2,000,000		2,000,000	–	–
Depreciation	W1	(200,000)	W2	(800,000)		
Balance		1,800,000		1,200,000	600,000	150,000
Y/E 09/X2						
Depreciation		(200,000)	W3	(240,000)		
Balance		1,600,000		960,000	640,000	160,000
Y/E 09/X3						
Depreciation		(200,000)	W4	(192,000)		
Balance		1,400,000		768,000	632,000	158,000

(W1) $2,000,000 cost - $400,000 residual value over 8 years.
(W2) $2,000,000 × 40%
(W3) $1,200,000 × 20%
(W3) $960,000 × 20%

65 Preparation question: Fenton

(a)

Date	Narrative	Shares	Time	Bonus fraction	Weighted average
1.1.X1	b/d	5,000,000	$\times \,^{1}/_{12}$	$\times \,^{2.00}/_{1.95} \times \,^{11}/_{10}$	470,085
31.1.X1	Rights issue	+ 1,250,000			
		6,250,000	$\times \,^{5}/_{12}$	$\times \,^{11}/_{10}$	2,864,583
30.6.X1	FMP	+ 125,000			
		6,375,000	$\times \,^{5}/_{12}$	$\times \,^{11}/_{10}$	2,921,875
30.11.X1	Bonus issue	+ 637,500			
		7,012,500	$\times \,^{1}/_{12}$		584,375
					6,840,918

TERP

$$
\begin{array}{lll}
4 @ 2 & = & 8.00 \\
1 @ 1.75 & = & 1.75 \\
\overline{5} & & \overline{9.75}
\end{array}
$$

$\therefore$ 1.95

EPS for y/e 31.12.X1 = $\dfrac{\$2,900,000}{6,840,918}$ = 42.4c

Restated EPS for y/e 31.12.X0 = 46.4c $\times \dfrac{1.95}{2.00} \times \,^{10}/_{11}$ = 41.1c

(b) **Sinbad**

Basic EPS = $\dfrac{\$644,000}{10,000,000}$ = 6.44

Earnings

Profit for the year	644,000
Interest saving (1,200,000 @ 5% × 70%)	42,000
	686,000

Number of shares

Basic	10,000,000
On conversion	4,800,000
	14,800,000

Diluted EPS = $\dfrac{\$686,000}{14,800,000}$ = 4.64c

(c) **Talbot**

Basic EPS = $\dfrac{540,000}{5,000,000}$ = 10.8c

Diluted EPS:

Consideration on exercise
400,000 × $1.10 = $440,000

Shares acquired at FV
$440,000/$1.60 = 275,000

$\therefore$ shares issued for no consideration
(400,000 – 275,000) = 125,000

EPS = $\dfrac{540,000}{5,000,000 + 125,000}$ = 10.5c

66 Savoir

(a) *Year ended 31 March 20X4*

Date	Narrative	Shares	Time	Bonus fraction	Weighted average
1.4.X3	Opening	40,000,000	$\times\,^3/_{12}$	$\times\,^5/_4$	12,500,000
1.7.X3	Full market price	8,000,000			
		48,000,000	$^6/_{12}$	$\times\,^5/_4$	30,000,000
1.1.X4	Bonus issue ($^1/_4$)	12,000,000			
		60,000,000	$^3/_{12}$		15,000,000
					57,500,000

Earnings $13.8m, therefore EPS = 13.8/57.5 = 24c

Comparative

The EPS for 20X3 would be restated to allow for the dilutive effect of the bonus issue as follows:

25c × 48/60* = 20c

*   Existing shares + new issue = 48
      Existing shares + new issue + bonus issue = 60

Note that the 8m shares issued at full price are non-dilutive and are therefore added to both sides of the fraction.

Year ended 31 March 20X5

'2 for 5' rights issue takes place halfway through the year and results in 24m additional shares.

Weighted average number of shares calculated as follows:

Date	Narrative	Shares	Time	Bonus fraction	Weighted average
1.4.X4	Opening	60,000,000	$^6/_{12}$	$^{2.4}/_2$ (W)	36,000,000
30.9.X4	Rights issue ($^2/_5$)	24,000,000			
		84,000,000	$^6/_{12}$		42,000,000
					78,000,000

Earnings $19.5m, therefore EPS = 19.5/78 = 25c

Comparative

The EPS for 20X4 is now restated following the rights issue in October 20X4 as follows:

24c × Theoretical ex-rights price (W)/Market price = 24c × 2/2.40 = 20c

Working

		$
Theoretical ex-rights price		
5 shares at market price (5 × 2.4)	5 @ $2.4	12
2 shares at $1	2 @ 1	2
	7	14

∴ Theoretical ex-rights price = $14/7 = $2

(b) Basic EPS = $25.2m/84m = 30c

Diluted EPS:

	Shares m	Earnings $m
Existing	84.0	25.2
Loan stock	10.0	1.2 (W1)
Share options	4.8 (W2)	–
	98.8	26.4

EPS = 26.4/98.8 = 26.7c

Workings

1   *Loan stock*

                                                        $m

When conversion takes place there will be a saving of:

	$m
Interest (20m × 8%)	1.6
Less tax (1.6 × 25%)	(0.4)
	1.2

2   *Share options*

Shares issued will be 12m @ $1.50 = $18m.

At market price of $2.50 the value would be $30m.

The shortfall is $12m, which is equivalent to 4.8m shares at market price

67 Niagara

(a)   *Dividend cover*

Dividend cover describes how many times the equity dividend is covered by the profits attributable to the owners. A high ratio (say above three) means that the company could maintain its present level of dividend even if profits were to fall in future years; this makes the company attractive to some investors because there is a lower risk of a reduction in investment income. If this ratio is low (say less than 2) then any reduction in profits could easily lead to a forced reduction in the level of equity dividend. This increases the risks of investing in the company, and makes the company less attractive to investors. A ratio below 1 means that the company is using previous year's profits to pay this year's dividend. This is unsustainable in the long run.

Niagara's dividend cover is 2.02. This is not in the danger zone, but it is unspectacular. Although Niagara may not have to reduce its dividend unless profits halve, there is no room for increasing the dividend unless profits rise.

Workings

Niagara's draft accounts show a $2,585,000 profit attributable to the equity holders, but this is before accounting for the preference dividends. The revised profit attributable to the equity shareholders is as follows:

	$
Draft equity shareholders profit	2,585,000
$1m 8% preference shares (full year)	(80,000)
$1m 6% preference shares (half year)	(30,000)
Revised profits attributable to the equity shareholders	2,475,000

Niagara has declared two equity dividends for the year. The interim dividend was paid to its original shareholders, but the final dividend will also be paid to the new shares arising from the one-for-five rights issue:

	Share capital	Nominal Value	Number of shares	Dividend per share	Total dividend $
Interim	$3m	25 cents	12,000,000	3 cents	360,000
Final	$3.6m	25 cents	14,400,000	6 cents	864,000
					1,224,000

Dividend cover = $2,475,000/$1,224,000 = 2.02

(b)   *Basic earnings per share*

This is the profits attributable to the owners of the parent divided by the weighted average number of ordinary shares outstanding during the period. This year's calculation takes into account the rights issue half way through the year. Last year's reported EPS of 24c will have to be adjusted for the bonus element of the rights issue.

Basic EPS

20X3	17.7 cents
20X2 (restated)	22.5 cents

20X3 Basic EPS

$$\frac{\text{Profit attributable to the ordinary equity holders of the parent}}{\text{Weighted average number of ordinary shares outstanding during the period}}$$

$$\frac{\$2,475,000\text{ (see above)}}{14,000,000\text{ shares (see below)}} = 17.7\text{ cents}$$

Weighted average number of ordinary shares

Date	Narrative	Shares	Time	Bonus fraction	Weighted average
1.4.X2		12,000,000	$^{3}/_{12}$	$^{2.4}/_{2.25}$	3,200,000
1.7.X2	Rights issue ($^{1}/_{5}$)	2,400,000			
		14,400,000	$^{9}/_{12}$		10,800,000
					14,000,000

Theoretical ex-rights price

	$
5 @ $2.4	12.0
1 @ $1.5	1.5
6	13.5

Theoretical ex-rights price = $13.5/6 = $2.25

20X2 Restated EPS

Original EPS scaled down for 'bonus' issue

24 cents as originally reported $\times \dfrac{\$2.25}{\$2.40} = 22.5$ cents

(c) *Diluted earnings per share*

Investors need to be aware of circumstances that might reduce earnings per share in the future. Diluted EPS measures the effect that existing commitments might have on future EPS. The two examples in this question are typical:

- When the convertible loan stock is converted into ordinary shares there will be an increase in the number of shares that the earning must be shared between. However, there will also be an increase in available earnings because the loan interest will no longer be paid.

- When the directors receive their free shares in 20X5 there will also be an increase in the number of equity shares, but this time with no compensating increase in profits.'

The net effect of increases in profits and shares can increase or reduce EPS. If the diluted EPS is less than the basic EPS then it must be reported in the financial statements.

Niagara's fully diluted EPS is 16.5 cents, about 7% less than the basic EPS of 17.7 cents. This is not a prediction of what Niagara's EPS will be in 20X5, merely an illustration of how this year's profits would have been shared had these events already taken place. It serves to warn investors of the effects of existing obligations to issue shares.

Workings

$$\frac{\text{Revised earnings for the year (W1 below)}}{\text{Revised number of shares in issue (W2 below)}} \qquad \frac{\$2,573,000}{15,550,000} = 16.5\text{ cents}$$

1   *Revised earnings*

	$'000
Basic earnings	2,475
Add: Interest saved ($2m × 7%)	140
Less: Tax charge ($140,000 @ 30%)	(42)
Diluted earnings	2,573

2   *Revised number of shares*

Weighted average number of shares in issue this year	14,000,000
Maximum conversion of loan stock: $2m × 40 shares/$100	800,000
Directors' warrants	750,000
Diluted number of shares in issue	15,550,000

68 Rytetrend

Text reference. Chapters 19 and 21.

Top tips. Part (a) Cash flow questions are a good choice in an exam. The format and content are straight forward and easy to learn. All the information needed for your answer must be given to you in the question. A methodical approach will generate good marks.

Part (b) This question refers to operating performance and financial position, and so the income statement and statement of financial position need to be discussed along with the statement of cash flows. Note that more marks are available for this analysis than for the cash flow itself, so make sure that you leave yourself enough time for Part (b). Also, with only about 20 to 25 minutes available, you must be economical with the number of ratios you calculate and concentrate on making comments.

Easy marks. Part (a) is 12 easy marks.

Examiner's comments. This question consisted of a statement of cash flows and an interpretation of it.

Part (a), the statement of cash flows, was relatively straightforward but candidates are still not adjusting for non-cash elements. Also many candidates described inflows as outflows and vice versa.

Part (b), the report analysing performance, was poorly answered. As has happened in the past, candidates calculated ratios but then failed to explain why the ratio had moved. Other candidates calculated too many ratios: the marking scheme gave five marks to calculation and 9 marks to 'appropriate comments'.

Marking scheme

			Marks
(a)	Profit before tax		1
	Depreciation adjustment		1
	Loss on sale of plant		1
	Warranty provision		1
	Working capital changes		2
	Interest paid		1
	Tax paid		1
	Purchase of non-current assets		2
	Share issue; issue/redemption of loan		2
	Ordinary dividends		1
	Decrease in cash		1
		Available	14
		Maximum	12
(b)	Relevant ratios	Available	5
	Appropriate comments	Available	9
			14
		Maximum	13
		Total for question	25

(a)   RYTETREND
       STATEMENT OF CASH FLOWS FOR THE YEAR ENDED 31 MARCH 20X3

	$'000	$'000
Cash flows from operating activities		
Profit before taxation (W1)		3,640
Adjustments for:		
Depreciation (W2)		7,410
Loss on disposal of PPE (W2)		700
Warranty charge		580
Warranty costs paid (150 + 580 – 500)		(230)
Interest expense		460
		12,560
(Increase) decrease in trade & other receivables (1,100 – 1,950)		850
(Increase) decrease in inventories (2,650 – 3,270)		620
Increase (decrease) in trade payables (2,850 – 1,980)		870
Cash generated from operations		14,900
Interest paid		(460)
Income taxes paid (630 + 1,000 – 720)		(910)
Net cash from operating activities		13,530
Cash flows from investing activities		
Purchase of property, plant and equipment (W2)	(15,550)	
Net cash used in investing activities		(15,550)
Cash flows from financing activities		
Proceeds from issue of share capital (13,000 – 10,000)	3,000	
Proceeds of 6% Loan Notes	2,000	
Repayment of 10% Loan Notes	(4,000)	
Dividends paid: Ordinary	(430)	
Net cash from financing activities		570
Net decrease in cash and cash equivalents		(1,450)
Opening cash and cash equivalents (Note)		400
Closing cash and cash equivalents (Note)		(1,050)

Note. Cash and cash equivalents

	31.3.X3	31.3.X2
	$'000	$'000
Cash at bank and in hand	–	400
Overdrafts	(1,050)	–
	(1,050)	400

Workings

1   *Construction costs and profit before tax*

The statement of cash flows will take into account the changes to assets and profits caused by capitalising $300,000 of construction costs.

	$'000
Profit before tax in the draft income statement	3,400
Add back capitalised installation costs	300
Less 20% depreciation on these costs	(60)
	3,640

2   Property, plant and equipment

Movement for the year

	Cost $'000	Depreciation $'000
Opening balance	27,500	10,200
Disposal: Cost	(6,000)	–
Depreciation ($6m × 20% × 4 years)	–	(4,800)
Additions (balancing figure)	15,750	–
Depreciation (balancing figure)	–	7,350
Closing balance (In draft accounts)	37,250	12,750
Capitalised installation costs	300	60
Revised closing balance	37,550	12,810

Depreciation charge

	$'000
Draft (from above)	7,350
Installation costs (from above)	60
Charge for the year	7,410

Loss on disposal

	$'000
Proceeds (trade in allowance)	500
Carrying value of disposals (6,000 – 4,800)	(1,200)
Loss	700

Payments for additions

	$'000
Draft (from above)	15,750
Installation costs (from above)	300
Less trade in allowance	(500)
Loss	15,550

(b)   **Commentary**

Operating performance

Rytetrend has posted a 35% increase in revenues, which is exceptionally good (assuming that inflation is negligible). One way to boost revenues is to cut the selling price in the hope of attracting more customers on the basis of price. This would lead to a steep fall in the gross profit margin. In this case Rytetrend's gross profit margin has fallen from 31.9% to 29.2%, which is only a modest fall. Maybe Rytetrend has attracted new customers owing to the quality of its products as well as because of its prices.

Although operating expenses have increased, they now only account for 17% of revenues rather than 20%. This suggests that Rytetrend has benefited from economies of scale as their business has increased.

Rytetrend's return on capital employed has improved from 14.4% to 18%. This is good, especially considering the $16m of capital expenditure during the year. Next year should be even better as a full year's profits will be earned from these new assets.

Financial position

Although the statement of cash flows shows a net decrease in cash of $1.45m, Rytetrend is in a much better financial position now than at the start of the year.

- Rytetrend has generated $14.9m from its operations, which covers its finance costs ($460,000) and dividends ($430,000) sixteen times over.

- The only reason why net cash has decreased is because $15.55m has been invested in new equipment, which should boost profits and cash flows even more next year.

- The burden of Rytetrend's loan finance has been reduced in two ways. Firstly the total amount of debt has been reduced from $4m to $2m. Secondly, the cost of debt has been reduced from 10% to 6%. In the future Rytetrend's finance costs should only be $120,000 instead of $400,000. This reduction was made possible by an extra $3m of share capital raised during the year.

Controls over working capital have also been tightened.

- Inventory days have been reduced from 75 to 43 days. This is good for cash flow and it also reduces the likelihood of obsolescence.
- The cash collection period from trade receivables has been reduced from 30 to 13 days. As well as boosting cash flows this also reduces the chances of debts going bad. This reduction could have been caused by better credit control, or by fewer sales being made on credit.
- The supplier payment period has remained at about 45 days. This is acceptable to most suppliers and also helps Rytetrend's cash flow.

The net effect of these changes is that the working capital cycle has been reduced from 60 days to 10 days, which is good. It also means that the current ratio has reduced from 2.04 to 0.73. In the past this would have been considered worrying, but today's thinking is that this reflects an efficient use of resources, especially by a retail business with strong cash generation.

Overall this business is generating a lot of cash. It will only take 25 working days to pay off the overdraft, and the modest level of dividends compared to profits or investment suggests that the management take a prudent view of their stewardship of the company.

Summary of ratios (based on revised figures)

	20X3	20X2
Increase in revenues	+35%	
Gross profit margin	29.2%	31.9%
Operating expense % $\dfrac{\text{Operating expenses}}{\text{Revenues}}$	17%	20%
Interest cover $\dfrac{\text{Profit before finance costs}}{\text{Finance costs}}$	8.9	5.8
Net profit margin $\dfrac{\text{Profit before tax}}{\text{Revenues}}$	11.4%	10.2%
Return on capital employed $\dfrac{\text{Profit before finance costs}}{\text{Assets - current liabilities}}$	18%	14.6%
Inventory days $\dfrac{\text{Inventory days} \times 365}{\text{Cost of sales}}$	43 days	75 days
Receivables days $\dfrac{\text{Trade receivables} \times 365}{\text{Revenues}}$	13 days	30 days
Payables days $\dfrac{\text{Trade payables} \times 365}{\text{Cost of sales}}$	46 days	45 days
Working capital cycle	10 days	60 days
Current ratio $\dfrac{\text{Current assets}}{\text{Current liabilities}}$	0.73	2.04
Finance cover $\dfrac{\text{Cash generated from operations}}{\text{Finance costs and dividends}}$	16.7	

69 Reactive

Marking scheme

		Marks
(a)	One mark per ratio	10
(b)	1 mark per valid point	10
	Maximum	10
	Total for questions	20

(a)   ROCE = 220/680 × 100 = 32.3%

Net asset turnover = 4,000/680 = 5.9 times

Gross profit margin = 550/4,000 × 100 = 13.8%

Net profit margin = 200/4,000 × 100 = 5%

Current ratio = 610/480 = 1.3:1

Closing inventory holding period = 250/3,450 × 365 = 26 days

Trade receivables collection period = 360/3,000* ×365 = 44 days

* credit sales

Trade payables payment period = 430/3450 × 365 = 45 days

Dividend yield = 22.5/375* × 100 = 6%

* Dividend per share(90/400)/market price of share

Dividend cover = 150/90 = 1.67 times

(b)   **Analysis of the comparative financial performance and position of Reactive for the year ended 31 March 20X6**

The first thing to notice about Reactive's results is that the ROCE has increased by 4.2 percentage points, from 28.1 to 32.3. On the face of it, this is impressive. However, we have to take into account the fact that the capital employed has been reduced by the plant disposal and the net profit has been increased by the profit on disposal. So the ROCE has been inflated by this transaction and we should look at what the ROCE would have been without the disposal. Taking out the effects of the disposal gives us the following ratios:

ROCE = 180/ (680 + 80) × 100 = 23.7%

Net asset turnover = 4,000/760 = 5.3 times

Net profit margin = 160/4,000 × 100 = 4%

Comparing these ratios to those for the period ended 31 March 20X5 we can see that ROCE has fallen. This fall has been occasioned by a fall in the net profit margin. The asset turnover has improved on the previous year even after adding back the disposal.

The net profit margin can be analysed into two factors – the gross profit margin and the level of expenses. The **gross profit percentage is 3.2% down** on the previous year. This is probably due to the rebates offered to wholesale customers, which will have increased sales at the expense of profitability. The replacement of some production lines by bought in products will probably also have reduced profit margins. Sales may have been increased by the advertising campaign, but this has been additional expense charged against net profit. It looks as if management have sought to boost revenue by any available means. The plant disposal has served to mask the effect on profits.

Reactive's **liquidity has also declined** over the current year. The current ratio has gone down from 1.6 to 1.3. However, there has also been a sharp decline in the inventory holding period, probably due to holding less raw material for production. It could be that the finished goods can be delivered direct to the wholesalers from the supplier. This will have served to reduce the current ratio. The receivables collection period has remained fairly constant but the payables payment period has gone down by 10 days. It looks as if, in return for prompt delivery, the finished goods supplier demands prompt payment. This fall in the payables period will have served to improve the current ratio. We do not have details of cash balances last year, but Reactive currently has no cash in the bank and a $10m overdraft. Without the $120m from the sale of plant the liquidity situation would obviously have been much worse.

The **dividend yield has increased** from 3.75% to 6%, which looks good as far as potential investors are concerned. But we are told that the dividend amount is the same as last year. As there have been no share issues, this means that the dividend per share is the same as last year. Therefore the increase in dividend yield can only have come about through a fall in the share price. The market is not that impressed by Reactive's results. At the same time the dividend cover has declined. So the same dividend has been paid on less profit (last year's dividend cover was 2.0, so profit must have been $180m). Management decided it was important to maintain the dividend, but this was not sufficient to hold the share price up.

To conclude, we can say that **Reactive's position and performance is down** on the previous year and any apparent improvement is due to the disposal of plant.

70 Greenwood

Marking scheme

	Marks
Up to 10 marks for relevant ratios	10
Up to 5 marks for effect of discontinued operation	5
Up to 1 mark per relevant interpretive comment	10
Maximum	
Total for question	25

The application of IFRS 5 *Non-current assets held for sale and discontinued operations* makes it possible to separate out the results of continuing and discontinued operations. This is important for analysts as discontinued operations will not be contributing to future performance and non-current assets held for sale will be disposed of in the near future.

In the case of Greenwood we have excluded the results of discontinued operations and the value of non-current assets held for sale from ratios where applicable.

Greenwood's ROCE based on continuing operations has declined from 33.5% to 29.7% between 20X6 and 20X7. Separating this ratio into its component parts, we can see that there has been a slight improvement in the profit before interest and tax ratio, from 17.7% to 17.8%. The problem therefore lies with the asset turnover, which has declined from 1.89 to 1.67. This means that Greenwood made less effective use of its assets in 20X7 than in 20X6. An additional $3m of loan notes were issued during the year, but this capital has not yet generated a commensurate return.

There has been a healthy increase in revenue in 20X7 and gross profit % has almost kept pace, but the margin has been eroded by an increase in operating expenses and finance costs which have increased by 140%. These are due to the additional $3m loan notes and the overdraft, on which Greenwood appears to be paying about 17% per annum.

The analysis of discontinued operations demonstrates why this activity has been terminated. A gross profit of $1m in 20X6 represented a return of 11%, compared with the 29% gross profit percentage on the continuing operations. In 20X6 the discontinued operation made a pre-tax profit of $450,000 which represents a ROCE of about 7% on its $6.3m assets. In 20X7 the ROCE was of course negative.

At first sight Greenwood's current ratio of 2.11 for 20X7 looks healthy, but this has been distorted by the assets of the discontinued operation. Adjusted for this, we get a current ratio of 0.77. This is alarming in itself and is a decline from 0.97 in 20X6. The quick ratio, similarly adjusted, stands at 0.62 in 20X6 and 0.44 in 20X7. During 20X7 Greenwood's cash balances have declined by $1.2m, despite the further $3m loan, and it has a tax bill of $950,000, which will presumably accrue interest if it is not paid by the due date.

Greenwood's working capital ratios also reflect the pressure exerted by shortage of cash. The company has reduced its inventory holding period by 5 days over the course of the year and receivables are now paying in 26.5 days, down from 40 days in 20X6. This is less than normal terms of trade and may have been achieved by means of settlement discounts, further reducing cash receipts. Part of the pressure to collect cash has no doubt come from suppliers and Greenwood has reduced its payables days outstanding from 68 to 50, which is still high. Greenwood's liquidity problems will be eased when it disposes of the assets of the discontinued operation, assuming this can be done relatively quickly, at or close to fair value and for cash.

Gearing gives less immediate cause for concern. The $3m loan has increased gearing from 28.6% to 35.5% and Greenwood's finance costs have risen from $250,000 to $600,000, but without the extra loan the company would have been running a $4m overdraft, at much greater expense.

Overall, Greenwood's results do not inspire confidence. Discontinuing the unprofitable activity was no doubt the correct action and management now needs to dispose of the assets and do whatever else can be done to handle the liquidity situation.

Appendix

Ratios	20X7	20X6
ROCE – continuing operations		
(4,500 + 400*)/(14,500 + 8,000 - 6,000)	29.7%	
(3,750/(12,500 + 5,000 – 6,300))		33.5%

*Note that of the finance costs shown for 20X7 only $400,000 is loan note interest

Gross profit % - continuing operations		
(8,000/27,500)	29.1%	
(6,200/21,200)		29.2%
Net profit before tax %		
(4,500/27,500)	16.36%	
(3,500/21,200)		16.5%

Net profit before interest and tax %
(4,900/27,500)   17.8%
(3,750/21,200)   17.7%

Asset turnover
(27,500/(14,500 + 8,000 – 6,000))   1.67
(21,200/(12,500 + 5,000 – 6,300))   1.89

Current ratio
Including held for sale (9,500/4,500)   2.11
Excluding held for sale (3,500/4,500)   0.77
(3,700/3,800)   0.97

Quick ratio (acid test)
Including held for sale (8,000/4,500)   1.77
Excluding held for sale (2,000/4,500)   0.44
(2,350/3,800)   0.62

Inventory days held
(1,500/19,500) × 365   28
(1,350/15,000) × 365   33

Receivables days outstanding
(2,000/27,500) × 365   26.5
(2,300/21,200) × 365   39.6

Payables days
(2,400/19,500) × 365   50
(2,800/15,000) × 365   68

Gearing
(8,000/(8,000 + 14,500))   35.5%
(5,000/(5,000 + 12,500))   28.6%

71 Victular

Text references. Chapters 19 and 20

Top tips. Note that only 8 marks are available for calculating the ratios. If you had trouble remembering how to calculate any of them, you could work back the ratios given for Grappa. The major part of the answer is the analysis and it's best to organise this under headings.

Easy marks. The ratios were easy marks and so was part (c). The analysis was slightly challenging because it was not a clear-cut picture, but you should have found enough useful points to make.

Examiner's comments. Many candidates were able to calculate the ratios but analysing and interpreting them was a different matter. Much of the information in the scenario was ignored and many candidates failed to attempt part (c), thereby throwing away 5 marks.

Marking scheme

		Marks
(a)	Merlot's ratios	8
(b)	1 mark per valid comment up to	12
(c)	1 mark per relevant point	5
	Total for question	25

(a)

ROCE	(2,500 – 500 – 10) / (2,800 + 3,200 + 3,000 + 500) %	= 20.9%
Pre-tax ROE	(1,400/2,800)%	= 50%
Net asset turnover	20,500/(14,800 – 5,700)	= 2.3 times
Gross profit margin	(2,500/20,500)%	= 12.2%
Operating profit margin	(2,000/20,500)%	= 9.8%
Current ratio	7,300/5,700	= 1.3 : 1
Closing inventory holding period	(3,600/18,000) × 365	= 73 days
Trade receivables collection period	(3,700 / 20,500) × 365	= 66 days
Trade payables payment period	(3,800 / 18,000) × 365	= 77 days
Gearing	(3,200 + 500 + 3,000) / 9,500%	= 71%
Interest cover	2,000 / 600	= 3.3 times
Dividend cover	1,000 / 700	= 1.4 times

(b) **Assessment of relative position and performance of Grappa and Merlot**

Profitability

At first sight it appears that Victular would see a much greater return on its investment if it acquired Merlot rather than Grappa. A closer analysis of the figures suggests that this may not be the case.

Merlot has an ROCE over 40% higher than Grappa's and an ROE more than double Grappa's ROE. However, the difference is due more to the lower level of equity in Merlot than to the superiority of its profit. Merlot's equity (2,800) is only half that of Grappa (5,500). This reduces the denominator for ROCE and doubles the ROE. A closer look at the profits of both companies shows that the operating profit margin of Grappa is 10.5% and that of Merlot is 9.75%.

The net asset turnover of Merlot (2.3 times) suggests that it is running the more efficient operation. Merlot has certainly achieved a much greater turnover than Grappa and with a lower level of net assets. The problem is that, on a much higher level of turnover, its net profit is not much higher than Grappa's.

Further analysis of net assets shows that Grappa owns its factory, while Merlot's factory must be rented, partly accounting for the higher level of operating expenses. Grappa's factory is carried at current value, as shown by the property revaluation reserve, which increases the negative impact on Grappa's ROCE.

Gearing

Merlot has double the gearing of Grappa, due to its finance lease obligations. At 7.5% Merlot is paying less on the finance lease than on its loan notes, but this still amounts to a doubling of its interest payments. Its interest cover is 3.4 times compared to 6 times for Grappa, making its level of risk higher. In a bad year Merlot could have trouble servicing its debts and have nothing left to pay to shareholders. However, the fact that Merlot has chosen to operate with a higher level of gearing rather than raise funds from a share issue also increases the potential return to shareholders.

Liquidity

Grappa and Merlot have broadly similar current ratios, but showing a slightly higher level of risk in the case of Merlot. Merlot is also running an overdraft while Grappa has $1.2m in the bank. Grappa is pursuing its receivables slightly less aggressively than Merlot, but taking significantly longer to pay its suppliers. As this does not appear to be due to shortage of cash, it must be due to Grappa being able to negotiate more favourable terms than Merlot.

Summary

Merlot has a higher turnover than Grappa and a policy of paying out most of its earnings to shareholders. This makes it an attractive proposition from a shareholder viewpoint. However, if its turnover were to fall, there would be little left to distribute. This is the risk and return of a highly geared company. Merlot is already running an overdraft and so has no cash to invest in any more plant and equipment. In the light of this, its dividend policy is not particularly wise. Grappa has a lower turnover and a much more conservative dividend policy but may be a better long-term investment. Victular's decision will probably depend upon its attitude to risk and the share prices of Grappa and Merlot

(c)   While ratio analysis is a useful tool, it has a number of limitations, particularly when comparing ratios for different companies.

Some ratios can be calculated in different ways. For instance, gearing can be expressed using debt as a proportion of debt and equity or simply debt as a proportion of equity. Ratios can be distorted by inflation, especially where non-current assets are carried at original cost.

Ratios are based upon financial statements which may themselves not be comparable due to the adoption of different accounting policies and different estimation techniques. For instance, whether non-current assets are carried at original cost or current value will affect ROCE, as will the use of different depreciation rates. In addition, financial statements are often prepared with the key ratios in mind, so may have been subject to creative accounting. The year end values also may not be representative of values during the year, due to seasonal trading.

Victular will find further information useful in making a decision regarding this acquisition. The relative share prices have already been mentioned. It will also be instructive to compare the P/E ratios. A higher P/E ratio will reflect a higher level of confidence in the market regarding the company. Victular should look at the composition of the Board of each company and the expertise it may be acquiring. It will also want to see the audited final accounts and any available management information, such as management accounts, budgets and cash flow forecasts.

72 Harbin

Text references. Chapters 19 and 20.

Top tips. It is really important in these interpretation questions not to get bogged down in the ratios. You can see from the mark allocation that twice as many marks are available for the analysis. The examiner frequently points out that to compare two ratios and say something went up or down is not analysis. You must look behind the numbers and make some suggestion why this has happened.

Easy marks. The ratios were easy and should not have taken long. If you had trouble remembering how to do any of them, you could work them out from last year's. However, you were told that the purchase of Fatima was significant, so you must allow for this in calculating the ratios. If you did this, the ratios gave you plenty to analyse.

Examiner's comments. In general candidates did well in calculating ratios, although ROCE and gearing gave problems. Unfortunately, the performance assessment that followed was quite poor. Some candidates did not even point out obvious issues arising from the purchase of Fatima.

Marking scheme

		Marks
(a)	one mark per required ratio	8
(b)	for consideration of Chief Executive's report	3
	impact for purchase	6
	remaining issues 1 mark per valid point	8
		17
	Total for question	25

(a)   *Ratios*

		Including Fatima	Excluding Fatima
ROCE	$\dfrac{16,000 + 8,000}{114,000 + 100,000}$ %	11.2%	
	$\dfrac{24,000 - 22,000}{114,000 - (22,000 - 5,500)}$ %		2.05%
Net asset turnover	$\dfrac{250,000}{114,000 + 100,000}$	1.17	
	$\dfrac{250,000 - 70,000}{114,000 - (22,000 - 5,500)}$		1.85
Net profit margin	$\dfrac{16,000}{250,000}$ %	6.4%	
	$\dfrac{24,000 - 22,000}{250,000 - 70,000}$ %		1.1%
Current ratio	38,000:44,000	0.86:1	
Closing inventory holding period	$\dfrac{25,000}{200,000} \times 365$	46 days	
Trade receivables collection period	$\dfrac{13,000}{250,000} \times 365$	19 days	
Payables payment period	$\dfrac{23,000}{200,000} \times 365$	42 days	
Gearing	$\dfrac{100,000}{100,000 + 114,000}$	46.7%	

(b)   It is clear that the acquisition of Fatima has had a very positive impact on Harbin's results for the year ended 30 September 2007. For this reason it is instructive to look at the 2007 ratios which have been affected by the acquisition and see what they would have been without the addition of Fatima's results.

Profitability

It is immediately apparent that without the purchase of Fatima the Chief Executive's report would have looked very different. The increase in sales revenue of 39% would have disappeared. The sales revenue of Harbin is static. The increase in gross profit margin from 16.7% to 20% would have been a fall to 11.1%. The profit for the period would not have doubled. It would have gone from an $8m profit before tax in 2006 to a $2m profit before tax in 2007, assuming that the loan note interest would not have arisen. This would have given an ROCE of 2.05% for 2007 rather than the 11.2% when Fatima is included. If we break ROCE down into net profit% and asset turnover, we can see that Fatima's results have increased the net profit% by almost six times, while having an adverse effect on the asset turnover due to the $100m funding through loan notes. There is some distortion in the 2007 figures arising from interest charges which are not deducted in calculating ROCE but have been deducted in arriving at net profit.

Liquidity

While it has greatly enhanced Harbin's profitability, the purchase of Fatima has done little for liquidity, an aspect not touched on in the extract from the Chief Executive's report. Harbin borrowed $100m to pay for Fatima, so the purchase was not funded from working capital. However, it has paid $8m loan note interest, increased its inventory holding by $10m, invested in additional property, plant and equipment and paid a $10m dividend. In this way it has, despite the increased profit, converted a positive cash balance of $14m to an overdraft of $17m. The ratios show this very clearly. Harbin's current ratio has declined from 2.5:1 to 0.86:1 and its quick ratio (not shown above) has declined from 1.47:1 to 0.30:1, casting some doubt upon whether it will be able to continue to meet its commitments as they fall due.

The increase in the inventory holding period is worrying, as it suggests that Harbin may have inventory which is slow-moving, and the increase in the payables period by 10 days suggests problems paying suppliers. Harbin has a $4m tax bill outstanding. If this is not paid on time it will incur interest, which will further weaken the cash position.

Gearing

The cost of acquiring Fatima is directly reflected in the gearing ratio, which has gone from nil in 2006 to 46.7% in 2007, with the issue of the loan notes. This will reduce profits available for distribution to shareholders in the future and if Harbin's cash position does not improve it may be forced to seek further loans. In the light of this, the increase of 25% in the dividend is hard to justify.

73 Breadline

Text reference. Chapter 20.

Top tips. Part (a) The question gives the game away by asking you to consider related party issues. If you mentally go through the normal consolidation adjustments you should be able to think of five ways in which they could affect the perceived performance of a subsidiary.

Part (b) Financial analysis is a key part of the syllabus and a key skill throughout your professional career. The first thing you must do is to identify who you are performing the analysis for and why. In this case you are reporting to your own Chief Executive. The purpose of the report is not so clear. The body of the question refers to the possibility of acquiring Breadline and the recoverability of the money owed to Judicious, but the requirement itself asks you to analyse the overall financial performance of Breadline. The question also reminds you to refer to areas that cause concern or require further investigation. The second thing you should do is to review the financial statements to pick out obvious changes from one year to the next. When you have identified these, then you can switch on your calculator and calculate the ratios. Finally, remember that the marks are for your comments, not for the calculations.

Easy marks. Part (a) should be 5 easy marks.

Examiner's comments. Part (a) was a discussion of issues that may arise in part (b), although several candidates failed to realise this. Part (b) was generally well answered, although far too many answers gave the movements without discussing reasons for those movements. The notes given to the financial statements contained vital information that was ignored by too many candidates.

Marking scheme

		Marks
(a)	1 mark per relevant point to a maximum of	5
(b)	Format and presentation of report	1
	Calculation of relevant ratios – up to	6
	Appropriate comments on above ratios	10
	References to areas of concern	5
	Available	22
	Maximum	20
	Maximum for question	25

(a) **Assessing a subsidiary's performance**

The trade of a subsidiary is carried out for the benefit of the group as a whole, not for the benefit of the subsidiary itself. Therefore there will be transactions, assets and liabilities that only exist because of the subsidiary's position within the group. The value of these transactions (and the transaction itself) will not have been agreed on an 'arm's length' basis. Some typical examples are noted below:

Revenues and cost of sales

Group companies often trade between themselves at an agreed price. This price is normally above or below the market price. Either way it means that one group company will be reporting a higher gross profit at the expense of another.

Also, these transactions might not take place at all if the companies were independent. For example, a baker might buy its flour from a subsidiary, but would choose a completely different supplier if the companies were independent.

Group companies normally don't compete against each other. This means that a subsidiary might refrain from making sales that it would otherwise have made. Also, it might be protected against competition from other group companies.

Shared costs and benefits

Group companies often pool resources in order to get economies of scale. For example office buildings and administration costs can be shared, reducing the cost to each company. Marketing, distribution, research and development will also be better and cheaper if they are shared across a group.

Finance is often raised at competitive rates for the group as a whole, with the funds then being passed on to the subsidiaries. Sometimes the finance for a subsidiary will be deliberately subsidised via an inter-company loan account.

All of the above practices are legitimate and make sound business sense. However, they all distort the reported performance of an individual subsidiary company. If the subsidiary were independent its trade and its profitability would be very different.

(b) **Report to the Chief Executive of Judicious on the financial position of Breadline**

From: Assistant Financial Controller

Introduction

This report investigates the overall financial position of Breadline with particular reference to the possibility of acquiring Breadline and the recoverability of the amounts owed to Judicious.

This report is based on the published financial statements of Breadline for the year ending 31 December 20X1. Breadline is a wholly owned subsidiary of Wheatmaster.

There are a number of areas that cause concern, or where further investigation is necessary. These are highlighted in the report.

Revenues and profitability

Breadline has **increased revenues** by 31% and increased its reported gross profit margin from 26% to 30%. On the face of it this looks like good sustainable growth.

However, the notes to the accounts report that the **profit on disposal** of the freehold premises was credited to cost of sales. This will have reduced the cost of sales and **inflated gross profit**. It is a one off profit that cannot be repeated in the future. The financial effect of this sale is not known but it can be estimated. The company's business address and trading premises have not changed; this suggests that the company is still occupying the same buildings. In 20X0 Breadline had freehold buildings valued at $1,250,000 and no leasehold buildings. In 20X1 Breadline had no freeholds but owned a leasehold costing $2,500,000. This suggests a sale and lease back arrangement. Because the proceeds of the freehold must have been greater than the cost of the leasehold this puts a minimum value on the sale proceeds of $2.5m and a minimum profit of $1.25m. If 20X1's cost of sales are adjusted for this then the gross profit in 20X1 would be $1.3m and the gross profit margin only 15%. This suggests that Breadline has boosted sales by cutting its selling price. This has reduced operating profits in the current year and is unsustainable in the long run.

Interest cover

Although the reported interest cover has dropped from 206 to 100 it is still at an **extremely safe level** (interest cover of 6 would be adequate). However, excluding the profit on disposal of the freehold reduces profit before interest in 20X1 to $740,000. Also, Breadline has taken out a $500,000 loan note at a 2% interest rate. This is below the market rate of 8%. In one way or another Breadline will have to pay the market rate of interest, either by offering a premium on redemption or conversion rights, and so the true interest charge on the loan notes will be $40,000, not $10,000. This makes the total interest charge for the year $50,000 and reduces the interest cover to 15.

Interest cover of fifteen is still good, but with the overdraft increasing and profitability declining the chances are that this is going to deteriorate further over the coming years.

Working capital management

Inventory levels have remained **steady** at about 18 days. **Receivables have increased** from 34 days to 41 days. This may have been because the credit control department has been unable to cope with the 31% increase in sales. However, 41 days is acceptable. Likewise payables have edged up from 45 days to 52 days. Overall, the working capital cycle has remained steady at 7.8 days this year compared with 7.1 days last year.

What is worrying for Judicious is that Breadline has **not been paying us as quickly** as other suppliers. Last year the balance owed to Judicious was 45.6 days old which was close to the average of 44.8 days. This year the balance is 103.4 days, which is twice the average. This difference could have been caused by increased sales by Judicious in the last two months of the year, or more likely by Breadline favouring other suppliers over Judicious. Maybe Breadline is paying amounts owing to group companies before it is paying its third party suppliers.

Financing

Breadline has received $600,000 from issuing new shares ($400,000 capital + $200,000 premium) and $500,000 from issuing a loan note. The shares were issued to Wheatmaster, its parent, and the loan note was also probably issued to a related party. (That would account for the below market rate of interest.) In total $1,100,000 has been raised, but then $900,000 has been paid out by way of dividend. It would have been much more efficient to have forgone the shares and loans and not paid a dividend either. The only explanation for this **money-go-round** is that it has transferred $900,000 of distributable profits up to the parent.

The **dividend is particularly worrying** because Breadline could only pay it by distributing the profit made on disposal of the freehold property. This is reducing Breadline's capital base.

Breadline has also received a substantial (but unknown) amount from the disposal of property. The only obvious investment during the year is the purchase of another $870,000 of plant.

Despite all this cash coming in, during the year the bank balance has fallen from $250,000 in hand to an overdraft of $220,000, a cash outflow of $470,000.

Conclusion

Breadline's apparent progress and prosperity does not survive detailed examination. Its profits and cash flows appear to have been **manipulated** for the benefit of its parent, and to inflate the reported profits before selling the business. The dividends and sale and leaseback transactions also suggest that Wheatmaster is trying to extract as much value from the business as possible before selling it. Therefore I would **not recommend that Judicious should acquire Breadline**.

Also, Judicious should seek to recover the amount owed to it for supplies, and to enforce stricter credit control in the future.

Summary of ratios

	20X1	20X0
Increase in revenues: ($8,500 – $6,500)/$6,500	31%	
Gross profit margins: $2,550/$8,500 ($1,690/$6,500)	30%	26%
Revised gross profit in 20X1: $2,550,000 – $1,250,000	$1.3m	
Revised gross profit margin in 20X1: $1.3m/$8.5m	15%	
Reported interest cover: 20X1 ($2,550 – $560)/$20	100	
20X0 ($1,690 – $660)/$5		206
Revised profit before interest 20X1: ($2,550 – $1,250 – $560)	$740K	

Revised interest 20X1: ($500,000 × 8%) + $10,000	$50K	
Revised interest cover 20X1: $740,000/$50,000	15	
Working capital management		
Inventory days		
Based on a revised cost of sales in 20X1 of $7,200 ($5,950 + $1,250)		
20X1: (370/7,200) × 365 days 20X0: (240/4,810) × 365 days	18.8	18.2
Receivable days		
20X1: (960/8,500) × 365 days 20X0: (600/6,500) × 365 days	41.2	33.7
Payable days		
Based on a revised cost of sales in 20X1 of $7,200		
20X1: (1,030/7,200) × 365 days 20X0: (590/4,810) × 365 days	52.2	44.8
Working capital cycle:	7.8	7.1
Ageing of the amounts owed to Judicious		
20X1: (340/1,200) × 365 days 20X0: (100/800) × 365 days	103.4	45.6

74 Toogood

Text reference. Chapter 7

Top tips. To answer this successfully you needed to read the question carefully and give it some thought. It is easy in a discussion question to just put down whatever you know, but it does not tend to bring in many marks. A few notes of the main points scribbled down first would have helped to get your thoughts in order.

Easy marks. Part (a) was easy as long as you were clear about what was required. Part (b) was a simple question on the purpose of depreciation and for part (c) you should at least have been able to get the point for saying that a subsidiary cannot be excluded from consolidation simply on the grounds that it is making losses.

Examiner's comments. This question was very poorly answered, although it was a reasonably popular choice. For large elements of the question, candidates completely missed the point. Part (a) required candidates to discuss provisional calculations for changes in accounting policies, errors and the effect of share issues. Instead most answers discussed irrelevant items such as bad debts and inventory loss adjustments and some thought it was a question on events after the reporting period.

Marking scheme

			Marks
(a)	Up to 4 marks for each example	Maximum	12
(b)	1 mark per point to a	Maximum	7
(c)	1 mark per point to a	Maximum	6
		Maximum for question	25

(a) (i) **Changes of accounting policy**

IAS 8 *Accounting policies, changes in accounting estimates and errors* requires retrospective restatement in the case of changes of accounting policy and errors. Each financial statement line affected by a change of accounting policy must be restated, to present the comparative financial statements as if the new policy had always been applied.

Errors

IAS 8 requires the same treatment as above for the correction of errors. For instance, if it is found that revenue for the previous year was overstated, the correction will affect the income statement, the assets in the statement of financial position and the retained earnings for the comparative period.

(iii) **EPS**

Any retrospective changes under IAS 8 which affect profit will also affect EPS. Because the change is to the earnings rather than to the number of shares, it cannot be explained by adjusting the average weighted number of shares.

(b) This suggestion contravenes the accruals concept and the purpose of depreciation, which is the allocation of the cost of a non-current asset over its useful life. If this is done, it will lead to profits being overstated up to the final ten years and understated thereafter. It will also mean that the financial statements from one year to the next will not be comparable.

Contrary to what the trainee accountant is suggesting, this proposal would have no effect on cash flows.

(c) Toogood would not be allowed under IAS 27 *Consolidated and separate financial statements* to exclude a subsidiary from consolidation on the grounds that it was making losses. However, if the intention was to dispose of the subsidiary, it could be excluded from consolidation and treated as a disposal group under IFRS 5 *Non-current assets held for sale and discontinued operations*. As the subsidiary is making losses, it seems likely that Toogood intends to dispose of it. IFRS 5 requires a disposal group held for sale to be shown under current assets. To take advantage of this exemption, the subsidiary must be being actively marketed for sale and the intention must be to complete the sale within one year.

75 Waxwork

Text references. Chapter 20

Top tips. Note that part (a) carries 5 marks. This means that the examiner is expecting more than two sentences. If you really think about this and answer it properly it will help you with part (b).

Easy marks. This was quite an easy question as long as you were clear about the period dealt with by IAS 10 and the distinction between adjusting and non-adjusting events. You may have been uncertain whether or not the commission earned should have been deducted to arrive at NRV in (b) (ii), but this would only have lost you a mark.

Examiner's comments. Performance was particularly disappointing on this question. There was confusion over the period covered by the Standard and over the definition of an adjusting event, and candidates who were unable to correctly answer part (a) did not gain many marks in part (b).

Examiner's answer. The examiner's answer to this question is included at the back of this kit.

Marking scheme

		Marks
(a)	Definition	1
	Discussion of adjusting events	2
	Reference to going concern	1
	Discussion of non-adjusting events	1
		5
(b)	(i) to (iii) 1 mark per valid point as indicated	10
		15

Answers 249

(a) IAS 10 relates to events taking place between the last day of the reporting period (the year end date) and the date on which the financial statements are approved and signed by the directors. This period is usually several months.

Adjusting events are events taking place after the reporting period which provide further evidence of conditions existing at the end of the reporting period or which call into question the going concern status of the entity. For this reason, adjusting events require adjustment to be made to the financial statements. If going concern is no longer applicable, the financial statements must be prepared on a break-up basis.

Non-adjusting events provide evidence of conditions arising **after** the end of the reporting period. If material, these should be disclosed by note, but they do not require that the financial statements be adjusted.

(b) (i) This is a non-adjusting event as it does not affect the valuation of property or inventory at the year end. However, it would be treated as adjusting if the scale of losses were judged to threaten the going concern status of Waxwork. It will certainly need to be disclosed in the notes to the financial statements, disclosing separately the $16m loss and the expected insurance recovery of $9m.

(ii) The sale in April 2009 gives further evidence regarding the realisable value of inventory at the year end and so an adjustment will be required. If 70% of the inventory was sold for $280,000 less commission of $42,000, it had a net realisable value of $238,000. On this basis, the total cost of $460,000 should be restated at NRV of $340,000. So inventory at the end of the reporting period should be written down by $120,000.

(iii) This change has occurred outside the period specified by IAS 10, so it is not treated as an event after the reporting period. Had it occurred prior to 6 May 2009, it would have been treated as a non-adjusting event requiring disclosure in the notes. The increase in the deferred tax liability will be accounted for in the 2010 financial statements.

76 Preparation question: Dickson

DICKSON
STATEMENT OF CASH FLOWS FOR YEAR ENDED 31 MARCH 20X8

Cash flows from operating activities	$'000	$'000
Profit before taxation	342	
Adjustments for:		
Depreciation	57	
Amortisation (W2)	60	
Interest expense	15	
Profit on disposal of assets	(7)	
	467	
Decrease in trade receivables (274 – 324)	50	
Increase in inventories (360 – 227)	(133)	
Decrease in trade payables (274 – 352)	(78)	
Cash generated from operations	306	
Interest paid (W5)	(10)	
Income taxes paid (W4)	(256)	
Net cash from operating activities		40
Cash flows from investing activities		
Development expenditure	(190)	
Purchase of property, plant & equipment (W1)	(192)	
Proceeds from sale of property, plant & equipment	110	
Net cash used in investing activities		(272)

	$'000	$'000
Cash flows from financing activities		
Proceeds from issue of shares [850 – 500 – (400 ×1/8)]	300	
Proceeds from issue of debentures	50	
Payment of finance lease liabilities (W3)	(31)	
Dividends paid	(156)	
Net cash from financing activities		163
Net decrease in cash and cash equivalents		(69)
Cash and cash equivalents at beginning of period		109
Cash and cash equivalent at end of period		40

Notes to the statement of cash flows

Note 1: Property, plant and equipment

During the period, the company acquired property, plant and equipment with an aggregate cost of $248,000 of which $56,000 was purchased by means of finance leases. Cash payments of $192,000 were made to acquire property, plant and equipment.

Workings

1   *Additions to property, plant and equipment*

PROPERTY, PLANT AND EQUIPMENT

	$'000		$'000
Bal b/d	637	Depreciation	57
Revaluations (152 – 60 + 8)	100	Disposals	103
Finance leases	56		
∴ Additions	192		
		Bal c/d	825
	985		985

2   *Development expenditure amortisation*

DEVELOPMENT EXPENDITURE

	$'000		$'000
Bal b/d	160		
Expenditure	190	∴ Amortisation	60
		Bal c/d	290
	350		350

3   *Finance lease payments*

FINANCE LEASE LIABILITY

	$'000		$'000
		Bal b/d – > 1 year	80
		– < 1 year	12
∴ Paid	31		
		New finance leases	56
Bal c/d – > 1 year	100		
– > 1 year	17		
	148		148

4   Income taxes paid

INCOME TAX PAYABLE

	$'000			$'000
		Bal b/d – current		45
		– deferred		153
∴ Paid	256			
		Income statement		162
Bal c/d – current	56			
– deferred	48			
	360			360

5   Interest paid

INTEREST PAYABLE

	$'000			$'000
		Bal b/d		
∴ Paid	10	I/S		15
Bal c/d				
	15			15

(b)   CASH FLOWS FROM OPERATING ACTIVITIES (Direct method)

	$'000
Cash received from customers (W1)	1,526
Cash paid to suppliers and employees (W2)	(1,220)
Cash generated from operations	306
Interest paid	(10)
Income taxes paid	(256)
Net cash from operating activities	40

Workings

1

RECEIVABLES

	$'000		$'000
Bal b/d	324	Cash received (bal)	1,526
Sales revenue	1,476	Bal c/d	274
	1,800		1,800

2

PAYABLES

	$'000		$'000
Payments (bal)	1,220	Bal b/d	352
		Purchases (W3)	1,095
Bal c/d	274	Other expenses (W4)	47
	1,494		1,494

3

INVENTORY

	$'000		$'000
Bal b/d	227	To cost of sales	962
Purchases (bal)	1,095	Bal c/d	360
	1,322		1,322

4	*Other expenses*	$'000
	Balance per income statement	157
	Depreciation	(57)
	Amortisation	(60)
	Profit on disposal	7
		47

77 Bigwood

Marking scheme

		Marks
(a)	Net profit before tax	1
	Depreciation	1
	Loss on disposal	1
	Working capital items	3
	Interest paid	1
	Income tax paid	1
	Capital expenditure	1
	Disposal proceeds	1
	Equity dividends	1
	Financing – equity shares	1
	– loans	1
	Decrease in cash	1
	Available	14
	Maximum	12
(b)	Up to 3 marks for additional ratios	3
	1 mark per relevant point including 1 mark for format	10
	Maximum	13
	Maximum for question	25

BIGWOOD
STATEMENT OF CASH FLOWS FOR THE YEAR ENDED 30 SEPTEMBER 20X4

	$'000	$'000
Cash flows from operating activities		
Profit before taxation (I/S)		700
Adjustments for:		
Depreciation (W2)		3,800
Loss on disposal of plant		1,250
Interest expense		300
		6,050
(Increase) decrease in trade receivables (100 – 50)		(50)
(Increase) decrease in inventories (2,900 – 1,500)		(1,400)
Increase (decrease) in trade payables (3,100 – 2,150)		950
Cash generated from operations		5,550
Interest paid		(300)
Income taxes paid (450 + 250 – 220)		(480)
Net cash from operating activities		4,770
Cash flows from investing activities		
Cost of disposal of plant	(50)	
Purchase of property, plant and equipment (W1)	(10,500)	
Net cash used in investing activities		(10,550)
Cash flows from financing activities		
Proceeds from issue of share capital (5,000 + 1,000 – 3,000)	3,000	
Receipt of loan (3,000 – 1,000)	2,000	
Dividends paid (SCE)	(600)	
Net cash from financing activities		4,400
Net decrease in cash and cash equivalents		(1,380)
Opening cash and cash equivalents		450
Closing cash and cash equivalents		(930)

Workings

1   PROPERTY, PLANT AND EQUIPMENT – COST

	$'000		$'000
Balance b/d	9,500	Equipment scrapped	3,000
Additions (balancing figure)	10,500	Balance c/d	17,000
	20,000		20,000

2   PROPERTY, PLANT AND EQUIPMENT – ACCUMULATED DEPRECIATION

	$'000		$'000
On equipment scrapped		Balance b/d	3,000
(3,000 – 1,200)	1,800	Charge for year	
Balance c/d	5,000	(balancing figure)	3,800
	6,800		6,800

BIGWOOD
Financial Position and Performance
Two years ending 30 September 20X4

Performance

During the year sales area increased by 35% (from 40,000m² to 54,000m²), helping to increase sales by 17% (from $19.6m to $23m). The low increase in sales compared with floor space may be explained by the timing of the increase and the disruptions caused during refurbishment. The full benefit of the expansion may only be felt next year.

The relative performance of the two lines of trade suggests that the expansion has been misdirected towards clothing at the expense of food. Food floor space has increased by only 20%, but this has yielded a 75% increase in turnover accompanied by an increase in the gross profit margin from 25% to 32.1%. Clothing floor space increased by 37% but sales only rose by 2.5% and the gross profit margin halved from 18.6% to 9.4%.

The food lines are obviously popular, as sales and margins have grown. This demand for food has probably helped to decrease the inventory holding period from 17 days to 15 days, which is always a good thing for perishable products like food.

The situation with clothing is the reverse; the fall in margins and barely static sales suggests that prices have had to be slashed to shift inventory. This is not sustainable in the long run. Even with discounted prices, the level of unsold clothes has mounted from 39 days to 68 days. This is worrying in a seasonal and fashionable business like clothing, and may suggest that further price cuts will be needed to shift clothing before it becomes out of date.

One puzzling statistic is that the margin on food is higher than that on clothing. Normally food sells at a very low margin compensated for by high turnover. This suggests that Bigwood has specialised in high value-added foods rather than basic groceries.

The information given states that depreciation has been apportioned between the products on the basis of floor space. This apportionment results in a profit of $1,500,000 for clothing, substantially less than food which has a much higher gross profit margin. This is unusual for the food sector which is normally low margin but high volume. These figures must be treated with caution because the refrigeration equipment needed to sell food will have a higher depreciation charge than the coat hangers needed to sell clothes.

Operating expenses have grown faster than sales, rising from 9.7% of revenues to 12%. Normally expenses are expected to decrease as a percentage of sales as economies of scale kick in. This increase suggests either poor cost control (which is worrying) or some one-off costs associated with the expansion and refurbishment.

The high level of investment and poor profitability is reflected by the decline in the ROCE from 33.9% to 9.3%. Hopefully next year will see a full year of profits from the enlarged and refurbished business and a reduction in costs.

Liquidity

The current ratio has deteriorated slightly from 0.77 to 0.71; however this low ratio is not unusual for retailers and is often seen as a sign of efficient working capital management. The increase in the accounts payable payment period from 50 to 59 days is not a problem as long as it does not rise further next year; a longer payment period might create bad will amongst Bigwood's suppliers.

At first glance it appears that the long-term liquidity of Bigwood gives cause for concern, with a net outflow of cash of $1.38m, an increase in gearing from 17% to 28% and a fall in interest cover from 25 times to 3.3 times. However, the situation is healthier than it looks as is explained below.

Bigwood has lost $1.38m of cash despite $3m of new share capital and $2m of new loans. But this new finance only covered half of the $10.5m of capital expenditure. This means that $4m of the expenditure came from cash generated during the year. If Bigwood takes a rest from expansion next year then it should generate another $4m of free cash which is enough to payoff the $930,000 overdraft and the $3m of loans.

Although the income statement reports a fall in interest cover from 25 to 3.3, the statement of cash flows shows that cash generated from operations is 18.5 times the interest paid, which is quite comfortable.

Investor ratios

The fall in the share price from $6 to $3 shows that investors are pessimistic about Bigwood's future, although some of the fall will have been caused by the dilution from the share issue. The dividend per share will have decreased from 20 cents to 12 cents because of this issue, which will depress the share price.

The total dividend has been maintained at the cost of reducing the dividend cover from 2.33 to 0.75. Paying out dividends bigger than profits is unsustainable, but it may be intended to advertise the management's confidence in Bigwood's future. Net cash inflows from operating activities of $4.77m are about 8 times the dividend paid, and so the relatively high dividend will not be an immediate problem.

Summary

The results for 20X4 are disappointing considering the amount of investment put into the business. However, the future should be better for the following reasons:

- The business generates $4m of free cash each year. This will reduce Bigwood's debts and finance costs, and provide funds for further expansion.
- Next year should see a full year of increased profits from this year's capital expenditure, without the disruption caused by the redevelopment.

Management could help Bigwood's recovery by allocating more resources to the profitable food lines and by purchasing more popular clothing.

Additional ratios

	20X4	20X3	
Floor space			
Clothes	48,000	35,000	+ 37%
Food	6,000	5,000	+ 20%
Total	54,000	40,000	+ 35%
Sales			
Clothes	16,000	15,600	+ 2.5%
Food	7,000	4,000	+ 75%
Total	23,000	19,600	+ 17.3%

Profitability 20X4

	Clothes	Food	Total
Sales	16,000	7,000	23,000
Cost of sales	(14,500)	(4,750)	(19,250)
Gross profit	1,500	2,250	3,750

Operating expense %

20X4			
	Expenses	2,750	= 12%
	Revenues	23,000	
20X3		1,900	
		19,600	= 9.7%

Interest cover in cash

Cash from operations	$5,550,000	= 18.5 times
Interest paid	$300,000	

Dividend cover

20X4	450/600	= 0.75
20X3	1,400/600	= 2.33

78 Casino

Text reference. Chapter 21.

Top tips. As always, the five easy marks in Part (b) should be won first.

The cash flow itself is reasonably straight forward, although there are small complications involving property and finance costs.

Easy marks. Part (b) is 5 easy marks.

Examiner's comments. This question was well answered. One common error was failure to deal with the recalculation of depreciation after the revaluation in part (a). Part (b) was reasonably well answered. However some candidates did not keep to the point and became repetitious. There are no marks awarded for repetition.

Marks

(a) Cash flows from operating activities

Operating loss	1
Depreciation and loss on sale adjustments	4
Working capital terms	3
Interest paid	1
Income tax	2
Investing activities	7
Financing 1 mark per item	4
Cash and cash equivalents b/f and c/f	1
Available	23
Maximum	20

(b) 1 mark per relevant point to

Maximum	5
Maximum for question	25

(a) CASINO
STATEMENT OF CASH FLOWS FOR THE YEAR ENDED 31 MARCH 20X5

	$m	$m
Cash flows from operating activities		
Loss before taxation		(44)
Adjustments for:		
Depreciation (W2)		93
Amortisation (510 – 400)		110
Loss on disposal of PPE (from question)		12
Interest expense		24
Investment income		(12)
		183
(Increase) decrease in trade & other receivables (350 – 420)		70
(Increase) decrease in inventories (808 – 372)		(436)
Increase (decrease) in trade payables (530 – 515)		15
Cash used in operations		(168)
Investment income (3 + 12 – 5)		10
Interest paid		(16)
Income taxes paid (W4)		(81)
Net cash outflow from operating activities		(255)
Cash flows from investing activities		
Proceeds of disposal of plant (from question)	15	
Purchase of property, plant and equipment (W1)	(170)	
Net cash used in investing activities		(155)
	$m	$m
Cash flows from financing activities		
Proceeds from issue of share capital [(300 + 60) – 200]	160	
Proceeds of loan (160 – 2 issue costs)	158	
Repayment of loan (150 + 6 penalty)	(156)	
Dividends paid (from question)	(25)	
Net cash from financing activities		137
Net decrease in cash and cash equivalents		(273)
Opening cash and cash equivalents		195
Closing cash and cash equivalents		(78)

[**Note**: Short term deposits are included in cash equivalents.]

Workings

1

PROPERTY, PLANT AND EQUIPMENT – COST

	$m		$m
Bal b/d: (490* + 445)	935	Plant disposal (W3)	65
Plant additions (from question)	60		
Property additions			
(balancing figure)	110	Bal c/d:	1,040
	1,105		1,105

* 500 – 80 (accumulated depreciation) + 70 (revaluation)

2

PROPERTY, PLANT AND EQUIPMENT – DEPRECIATION

	$m		$m
Revaluation	80	Bal b/f (80 + 105)	185
Depreciation on plant disposal			
(65(W3) – (15 + 12))	38		
		Charge for year	
Bal c/f (12 + 148)	160	(balancing figure)	93
	278		278

3

PLANT AND EQUIPMENT – COST

	$m		$m
Bal b/f	445	Disposal (balancing figure)	65
Additions	60	Bal c/f	440
	505		505

4   *Tax*

TAX

		$m			$m
C/f	Current	15	B/f	Current	110
	Deferred	90		Deferred	75
			Charge		1
Cash paid	balance	81			–
		186			186

(b)   **Usefulness and reliability**

It is often said that statements of cash flows are more useful and reliable than income statements. This claim is made because cash is the life blood of a business. Without cash the business cannot grow, repay its borrowings, service its finance, or pay a dividend. Without cash a business will wither and eventually fail. Therefore cash generation is more important than profitability.

Statements of cash flows are also seen as being more reliable than income statements. Profit is based on the accruals concept which requires asset lives, provisions, fair values, contract profitability, impairment and so on to be estimated. Because this is subjective it is possible to have two different, but equally valid, profit figures. Cash is not subjective; cash inflows and outflows are all a question of fact.

However, the income statement is useful and statements of cash flows are not as objective as they first seem. Cash inflow can be boosted by cutting back on investment and delaying paying creditors. This will give the illusion of success in the short run, but is bottling up investment expense and supplier bad will for the future. Even honest managers would be reluctant to make long-term investments if they thought that they would be judged solely on short-term cash generation. By matching income and expenditure, the income statement gives the reader a better understanding of the long term profitability of the company.

Statements of cash flows and income statements are meant to complement each other. The quality of the profits claimed in the income statement can be assessed by comparing them with the cash generated from operations in the statement of cash flows. The sustainability of dividends can also be assessed with reference to the statement of cash flows.

79 Tabba

Text reference. Chapter 21.

Top tips. Don't forget the eight marks for interpretation in Part (b). If you are running out of time break off from the main statement to make some sensible comments about the cash flows that you have already calculated; there are good marks available for some obvious (and not so obvious) comments.

The cash flow itself is reasonably straight forward, although there are some complications involving finance leases and grants.

Easy marks. None of this question is particularly difficult. Part (b) is a possible 8 easy marks, so make sure you leave time to get them.

Examiner's comments. This was a popular question and on the whole well answered. There were some examples of non-cash movements appearing as cash flows and possibly some candidates had not prepared for a cash flow question as it came up in the previous paper. Question spotting is a dangerous activity. The main errors involved depreciation calculations, the government grant, the tax calculation and the sale and leaseback transaction.

Marking scheme

		Marks
(a)	Profit before tax	½
	Depreciation	1
	Amortisation of government grant	1
	Profit on sale of factory	1
	Increase in insurance claim	1
	Working capital items 1 mark each	
	Adjustment for interest receivable/payable	½
	Interest paid	1
	Income tax paid	2
	Sale of factory	1
	Purchase of non-current assets	1
	Receipt of government grant	1
	Interest received	1
	Redemption of 10% loan	1
	Issue of 6% loan	1
	Repayment of finance lease	2
	Cash b/f and c/f	1
	Maximum	17
(b)	1 mark per relevant point to a Maximum	8
	Maximum for question	25

(a) TABBA
STATEMENT OF CASH FLOWS FOR THE YEAR ENDED 30 SEPTEMBER 20X5

	$'000	$'000
Cash flows from operating activities		
Profit before taxation		50
Adjustments for:		
Depreciation (W2)		2,200
Profit on disposal of PPE (12,000 – 7,400)		(4,600)
Release of grant (W3)		(250)
Increase in insurance claim receivable (1,500 – 1,200)		(300)
Interest expense		260
Investment income		(40)
		(2,680)
(Increase) decrease in inventories (2,550 – 1,850)		(700)
(Increase) decrease in trade & other receivables (3,100 – 2,600)		(500)
Increase (decrease) in trade payables (4,050 – 2,950)		1,100
Cash used in operations		(2,780)
Interest paid		(260)
Income taxes paid (W4)		(1,350)
Net cash outflow from operating activities		(4,390)
Cash flows from investing activities		
Interest received	40	
Proceeds of grants (From question)	950	
Proceeds of disposal of property (From question)	12,000	
Purchase of property, plant and equipment (W1)	(2,900)	
Net cash from investing activities		10,090
Cash flows from financing activities		
Proceeds of loan (6% loan received)	800	
Repayment of loan (10% loan repaid)	(4,000)	
Payments under finance leases (W5)	(1,100)	
Net cash used in financing activities		(4,300)
Net increase in cash and cash equivalents		1,400
Opening cash and cash equivalents		(550)
Closing cash and cash equivalents		850

Workings

1

PROPERTY, PLANT AND EQUIPMENT – COST

	$'000		$'000
Bal b/d	20,200	Factory disposal	8,600
Plant acquired under finance			
Leases	1,500		
Other acquisitions			
(balancing figure)	2,900	Bal c/d:	16,000
	24,600		24,600

2

PROPERTY, PLANT AND EQUIPMENT – DEPRECIATION

	$'000		$'000
Depreciation on			
factory disposal	1,200	Bal b/f	4,400
		Charge for	
Bal c/f	5,400	year (balancing figure)	2,200
	6,600		6,600

3

GOVERNMENT GRANT

	$'000		$'000
Grant released (balancing figure)	250	Bal b/f (400 + 900)	1,300
Bal c/f (1,400 + 600)	2,000	Received	950
	2,250		2,250

4

TAX

		$'000			$'000
C/f	Current	100	B/f	Current	1,200
	Deferred	200		Deferred	500
Credit in I/S		50			
Cash paid	balance	1,350			–
		1,700			1,700

5

MOVEMENT ON FINANCE LEASE

		$'000			$'000
C/f	Current	2,000	B/f	Current	1,700
	Non-current	900		Non-current	800
			New		1,500
Cash paid	balance	1,100			–
		4,000			4,000

(b)   **Changes in Tabba's financial position**

The last section of the statement of cash flows reveals a healthy increase in cash of $1.4m. However, Tabba is losing cash and its going concern status must be in doubt.

To survive and thrive businesses must generate cash from their operations; but Tabba has absorbed $2.68m. Whereas most companies report higher operating cash inflows than profits, Tabba has reported the reverse. The only reason Tabba was able to report a profit was because of the one-off $4.6m surplus on disposal. There were two other items that inflated profits without generating cash; a $300,000 increase in the insurance claim receivable and a $250,000 release of a government grant. Without these three items Tabba would have reported a $5.1m loss before tax.

Were it not for the disposal proceeds Tabba would be reporting a $10.6m net decrease in cash. Tabba has no other major assets to sell and so the coming year will see a large outflow of cash unless Tabba's trading position improves. When the current operating lease expires in four years time there will probably be a rent hike, further damaging Tabba's profitability and cash flows.

The high tax bill for the previous year suggests that Tabba's fall from profitability has been swift and steep. Despite this downturn in trade Tabba's inventories and receivables have increased, suggesting poor financial management. This in turn damages cash flow, which is indicated by the increase in the level of payables.

There are some good signs though. Investment in non-current assets has continued, although $1.5m of this was on finance leases which are often a sign of cash shortages. Some of the disposal proceeds have been used to redeem the expensive $4m 10% loan and replace it with a smaller and cheaper $800,000 6% loan. This will save $352,000 per annum.

Tabba's recovery may depend on whether the circumstances causing the slump in profits and cash flow will either disappear of their own accord or whether Tabba can learn to live with them. The statement of cash flows has however highlighted some serious issues for the shareholders to discuss with the directors at the annual general meeting.

80 Minster

Text reference. Chapters 19 and 21.

Top tips. In this question 40% of the marks were for commenting on the financial position and performance of the company. This was not that simple, and it was important not to spend too long on the statement of cash flows and leave insufficient time for (b).

Easy marks. The easy marks here were the statement of cash flows. There were a few complexities such as the unwinding of the discount, on which you should not have wasted much time, but it was otherwise straightforward and you should have scored good marks on it. Part (b) was not that easy because there were no obvious issues to report on. The company was not failing or overtrading or doing tremendously well either. So it was important to look at the information in the question and the statement of cash flows and see what you could learn from them, rather than computing a raft of ratios.

(a) MINSTER
STATEMENT OF CASH FLOWS FOR THE YEAR ENDED 30 SEPTEMBER 20X6

	$'000	$'000
Cash flows from operating activities		
Profit before tax		142
Depreciation		255
Software amortisation (180 – 135)		45
Investment income		(20)
Finance costs		40
		462
Decrease in inventories		30
Decrease in receivables		110
Decrease in payables		(205)
Increase in amounts due from construction contracts		(25)
Cash generated from operations		372
Interest paid (40 – 12 (unwinding of discount))		(28)
Income taxes paid (W2)		(54)
Net cash from operating activities		290
Cash flows from investing activities		
Property, plant and equipment (W1)	(410)	
Software	(180)	
Investments	(10)	
Investment income received (20 – 15 (investment gain))	5	
Net cash used in investing activities		(595)
Cash flows from financing activities		
Dividends paid (500 × 4 × 5c)	(100)	
9% loan note	120	
Equity share issue (125 share cap + 140 premium))	265	
Net cash from financing activities		285
Decrease in cash		(20)

Workings

1

PROPERTY, PLANT AND EQUIPMENT – CARRYING VALUE

	$'000		$'000
Bal b/f	940	Depreciation charge	255
Environmental provision	150		
Land revaluation	35		
Acquisitions (balancing figure)	410	Bal c/f	1,280
	1,535		1,535

2

INCOME TAXES DUE

	$'000		$'000
Paid (balancing figure)	54	Bal b/f	50
		Charge for year	57
		Reduction in deferred tax	
Bal c/f	60	provision	7
	114		114

(b)   Re: financial performance and position of Minster

Minster's net assets have increased by $285,000 over the year. The company shows a gross profit percentage of 20% and a net profit percentage of 10% - both quite healthy - and its cash generated from operating activities is $372,000. However, retained earnings have decreased by $15,000 due to the payment of a dividend in excess of the net profit after tax. There has also been a bonus issue during the year, so Minster's shareholders have been well rewarded.

There are some significant changes in working capital levels over the year. Inventories and trade payables have both decreased. This could be due to more efficient purchasing and inventory control, perhaps the introduction of a JIT system. The level of trade receivables has also declined, perhaps due to more efficient credit collection. Conversely, these changes could be due to a reduction in the level of activity, rather than any increase in efficiency but, looking at the large investment in non-current assets, it appears unlikely that the business is 'winding down' to any degree. This is borne out by the increase in construction contract WIP.

The most noticeable feature in the statement of cash flows is the heavy investment in non-current assets. As there are no disposals and no non-current assets were scrapped, this suggests expansion into new business activities or processes, rather than replacement of worn out or obsolete machinery. In addition to $410,000 on property, plant and equipment $180,000 has been spent on software licences, which suggests that the new non-current assets comprise equipment which will computerise some of Minster's processes. This reflects positive expectations about the future trading environment.

This investment has been funded by a 9% loan note and a share issue, presumably a rights issue. The rights issue yielded $265,000, reflecting the confidence of shareholders. The loan note issue, offset by the share issue, takes Minster's gearing to just over 7%. This is still low and the interest, while fairly high, is at least tax-deductible. There would have to be a very significant downturn in the business for it to be unable to afford the interest payments and, if the extra investment pays off and profits rise, the returns to shareholders will be greater than if more funds had been raised from another equity issue, which would have diluted shareholdings.

81 Pinto

Text references. Chapters 19,20,21

Top tips. There are only 15 marks for the statement of cash flows here and the other 10 are for comment, so it is important to make time for both. Don't get bogged down in the statement of cash flows – get the format down and push on with the workings.

Easy marks. The statement of cash flows was easy apart from the tax working. Even if you got that wrong, there were plenty of marks available for the rest of the cash flow and for useful comment.

Examiner's comments. Cash flows are generally popular and many candidates scored well on this one. A number had trouble with the tax cash flow being a refund and there were mistakes in calculating the dividend by those who had not realised that the shares were 20c. The interpretative part of the question often lacked depth and some candidates calculated ratios despite specific instructions not to do so. Some candidates discussed issues such as ROCE and profit margins which are not part of cash management while not mentioning issues such as the investment in non-current assets and the tax cash flow.

Marking scheme

		Marks
(a)	Operating activities	
	Profit before tax	½
	Depreciation/loss on sale	1
	Warranty adjustment	½
	Adjustments for investment income/finance costs	½
	Adjustment for redemption penalty	1
	Working capital items	1½

Finance costs	1
Income tax received	2
Investing activities (including 1 for investment income)	3
Financing activities	1
Issue of equity shares	1
Redemption of 6% loan note	1
Dividend paid	1
Cash and cash equivalents b/f and c/f	15

(b)   1 mark per relevant point   10

Total for question   25

PINTO - STATEMENT OF CASH FLOWS FOR THE YEAR TO 31 MARCH 2008

	$'000	$'000
Cash flows from operating activities		
Profit before tax		440
Loss on sale of plant		90
Depreciation		280
Early redemption penalty		20
Finance costs		50
Investment income		(60)
Increase in warranty provision (200 – 100)		100
		920
Increase in inventory (1,210 – 810)		(400)
Decrease in receivables (480 − 540)		60
Increase in trade payables (1,410 – 1,050)		360
Cash generated from operations		940
Interest paid		(50)
Tax refund received (W1)		60
Net cash from operating activities		950
Cash flows from investing activities		
Proceeds of sale of plant (240 – 90)	150	
Purchase of plant (W2)	(1,440)	
Income from investment property (60 – 20)	40	
Net cash used in investing activities		(1,250)
Cash flows from financing activities		
Share issue ((1,000 – 600) + 600)	1,000	
Loan notes repaid	(400)	
Early redemption penalty	(20)	
Dividend paid (1,000 × 5 × 0.03)	(150)	
Net cash from financing activities		430
Net increase in cash and cash equivalents		130
Cash and cash equivalents at beginning of period		(120)
Cash and cash equivalents at end of period		10

Workings

1

INCOME TAX PAYABLE

	$'000		$'000
Bal b/d (current tax)	50	Bal b/d (deferred tax)	30
Bal c/d (current tax)	150	Income statement charge	160
Bal c/d (current tax)	50	Cash received (balancing figure)	60
	250		250

PROPERTY, PLANT AND EQUIPMENT

	$'000		$'000
Bal b/d	1,860	Disposal	240
Revaluation (150 – 50)	100	Depreciation	280
Additions (balancing figure)	1,440	Bal c/d	2,880
	3,400		3,4000

Comments on cash flow management

Pinto provides a good illustration of why a statement of cash flows often provides more insight than an income statement. The most noticeable feature of the income statement is that $5.7m revenue has produced only $280,000 net profit and it can be seen from the statement of financial position that only $130,000 has been added to retained earnings at the end of the year. However, it is apparent from the statement of cash flows that Pinto's financial position is quite healthy.

Pinto has invested heavily in property, plant and equipment during the year, which has led to a high depreciation charge. Adjusting for this and for the increase in warranty costs and loss on sale of plant gives cash generated from operations of $940,000. The doubling of the warranty provision together with the fact that Pinto has $150,000 tax to pay this year, against a refund of $50,000 for the previous year, means that both turnover and profit must have increased substantially this year. Inventory and payables have both increased, inventory by 50%. This suggests an increased level of production, which ties in with the investment in new plant. At the same time, receivables have fallen, suggesting tighter credit control.

Pinto made a share issue during the year which contributed towards the increased investment in non-current assets and the repayment of the $400,000 loan notes. This has reduced its gearing to nil, but it should be noted that these additional shares increased the cost of the dividend by $60,000 – substantially more than the finance cost on the loan notes.

Overall, the cash management of Pinto presents a positive picture. During the year substantial investment has been made in productive capacity, gearing has been reduced to nil and an overdraft of $120,000 has been converted to a cash balance of $10,000.

82 Coaltown

Text references. Chapters 19 and 21

Top tips. Note that the statement of cash flows here is only worth 15 marks, so move quickly through it. You cannot afford to neglect (b).

Read all the information carefully. Do not miss the adjustment needed for loss on disposal in (a) or the note regarding opening inventory in (b).

Easy marks. The statement of cash flows is straightforward and you should have been able to score most of the marks. Part (iii) of (b) was quite easy as long as you did not miss the note at the end. Parts (i) and (ii) took a bit of thought.

Examiner's comments. Few candidates earned full marks on the statement of cash flows. Some had trouble distinguishing between cash and non-cash items (reserve movements, warranty provision, loss on disposal). Some had trouble dealing with the revaluation and the effect on depreciation. In part (b) some candidates adjusted the 2008 figures rather than the 2009 figures. Part (ii) was very badly answered. Most candidates were unable to identify factors which could have affected the gross profit margin. Very few were unable to compute the effect on the bank balance in Part (iii)

Examiner's answer. The examiner's answer to this question is included at the back of this kit.

				Marks
(a)	Operating activities			
	Profit before tax			½
	Add back interest			½
	Depreciation charge			2
	Loss on disposal			1
	Warranty adjustment			½
	Working capital items			1½
	Finance costs			1
	Income tax paid			1
	Purchase of non-current assets			2
	Disposal cost of non-current assets			1
	Issue of equity shares			1
	Issue of 10% loan notes			1
	Dividend paid			1
	Cash and cash equivalents b/f and c/f			1
				15
(b)	(i)	Calculation of expected gross profit margin for 2009		2
	(ii)	Comments on directors' surprise and other factors		4
	(iii)	Calculate credit periods (receivables and payables) in 2008		2
		Apply to 2009 credit sales/purchases		1
		Calculate 'savings' and effect on closing bank balance		1
				4
				25

(a) COALTOWN
STATEMENT OF CASH FLOWS FOR THE YEAR ENDED 31 MARCH 2009

	$'000	$'000
Cash flows from operating activities		
Profit before tax	10,200	
Depreciation (W2)	6,000	
Loss on disposal of displays (W3)	1,500	
Interest expense	600	
	18,300	
Increase in warranty provision (1,000 – 300)	700	
Increase in inventories (5,200 – 4,400)	(800)	
Increase in receivables (7,800 – 2,800)	(5,000)	
Decrease in trade payables (4,500 – 4,200)	(300)	
Cash generated from operations	12,900	
Interest paid	(600)	
Income tax paid (W4)	(5,500)	
Net cash from operating activities		6,800
Cash flows from investing activities		
Purchase of property, plant and equipment (W1)	(20,500)	
Cost of disposal of property, plant and equipment	(500)	
Net cash used in investing activities		(21,000)

	$'000	$'000

Cash flows from financing activities

	$'000	$'000
Share issue ((16,600 + 4,800) – (8,000 + 500))	12,900	
Loan note issue	1,000	
Equity dividends paid	(4,000)	
Net cash from financing activities		9,900
Net decrease in cash and cash equivalents		(4,300)
Cash and cash equivalents at beginning of period		700
Cash and cash equivalents at end of period		(3,600)

Workings

1.

NON-CURRENT ASSETS – COST

	$'000		$'000
Balance b/f	80,000	W/off old displays	10,000
Revaluation (5,000 – 2,000)	3,000		
Purchases (bal)	20,500	Balance c/f	93,500
	103,500		103,500

2.

NON-CURRENT ASSETS – DEPRECIATION

	$'000		$'000
W/off on disposal	9,000	Balance b/f	48,000
Revaluation adjustment	2,000		
Balance c/f	43,000	Charge in year (bal)	6,000
	54,000		54,000

3.

NON-CURRENT ASSETS – DISPOSAL

	$'000		$'000
Cost	10,000	Acc depreciation	9,000
Cost of disposal	500	Loss on disposal	1,500
	10,500		10,500

4.

INCOME TAX PAYABLE

	$'000		$'000
Tax paid (bal)	5,500	Balance b/f	5,300
Balance c/f	3,000	Charge for year	3,200
	8,500		8,500

(b) (i) Taking the figures for the year ended 31 March 2008 and applying the 10% reduction in purchase costs and the 5% discount to customers, the directors would have expected the gross profit to be as follows:

	$'000
Revenue (55,000 × 95%)	52,250
Cost of sales (33,000 × 90%)	29,700
Gross profit	22,550
Gross profit % (22,550 / 52,250 × 100)	43.2%

The actual gross profit for the year ended 31 March 2009 is:

(22,000/65,800 × 100)   33.4%

(ii) The directors should not be surprised at the unchanged gross profit as cost of sales has increased by the same amount as revenue, wiping out any possible increase in gross profit. In fact the actual gross profit margin has fallen from 40% in 2008 to 33.4% in 2009, so despite the 10% reduction in the cost of purchases the company was trading less profitably.

Possible reasons for this could be:

Shipping costs involved in importing goods having to be borne by the recipient.

Import duties.

Currency exchange losses, perhaps exacerbated by having to pay within a shorter period.

Inventory losses – uninsured damage, obsolescence etc.

Selling a larger proportion of goods on which the gross profit % is lower than the average.

Perhaps sales or special offers to customers, which will have lowered the average mark-up.

The foreign supplier may have increased his prices at some point during the year.

Also there may have been changes in accounting policy during the year – perhaps depreciation or distribution costs which were treated as expenses in 2008 and have been charged to cost of sales in 2009. If this has happened it will require retrospective restatement so that 2008 and 2009 can be correctly compared.

(iii)   Credit periods year ended 31 March 2008:

Receivables (2,800 / 28,500 × 365)	35.9 days
Payables (4,500 / 33,000 × 365)	49.8 days

In 2009 there is a movement in inventory, so we calculate purchases as follows:

43,800 – 4,400 + 5,200 = 44,600

Applying the periods above we get:

Receivables: 53,000/365 × 35.9	5,213
Payables: 44,600/365 × 49.8	6,085

Cash increase:

	$'000
Receivables (7,800 – 5,213)	2,587
Payables (6,085 – 4,200)	1,885
	4,472

83 Preparation question: Changing prices

(a)   CURRENT COST OPERATING PROFIT FOR 20X6

	$m	$m
Historical cost profit		15
Current cost adjustments:		
Depreciation adjustment	3	
Cost of sales adjustment	5	
		(8)
Current cost profit		7

SUMMARISED CURRENT COST STATEMENT OF FINANCIAL POSITION
AS AT 31 DECEMBER 20X6

	$m	$m
Property, plant & equipment		85
Current assets		
Inventories	21	
Receivables	30	
Bank	2	
		53
		138
Equity		88
Non-current liability		20
Current liabilities		30
		138

(b) (i) **Interest cover**

HC accounts: 15 ÷ 3 = 5 times
CC accounts: 7 ÷ 3 = 2.3 times

(ii) **Return on shareholders' equity**

HC accounts: 12 ÷ 62 = 19.4%
CC accounts: 4 ÷ 88 = 4.5%

(iii) **Debt/equity ratio**

HC accounts: 20 ÷ 62 = 32.3%
CC accounts: 20 ÷ 88 = 22.7%

(c) (i) **Interest cover**

Companies must maintain their capital base if they wish to stay in business. The significance of the interest cover calculation is that it indicates the extent to which profits after tax are being eaten into by payments to finance external capital. The figures calculated above indicate that only one-fifth of historical cost profit is being absorbed in this way, while four-fifths are being retained to finance future growth. On the face of it, this might seem satisfactory; however, the current cost interest cover is only 2.3 times indicating that, after allowing for the impact of rising prices, interest payments absorb nearly half of profits after tax.

(ii) **Return on shareholders' equity**

This is the ratio of profits earned for shareholders (ie profits after interest) to shareholders' equity. Once again, the position disclosed by the historical cost accounts is more favourable than appears from the current cost ratio. The historical cost profit is higher than the current cost profit because no allowance is made for the adverse impact of rising prices, and, at the same time, the denominator in the historical cost fraction is lower because, shareholders' capital is stated at historical values rather than their higher current values.

The significance of the ratio is that it enables shareholders to assess the rate of return on their investment and to compare it with alternative investments that might be available to them.

(iii) **Debt/equity ratio**

The significance of this ratio is as a measure of the extent to which the company's net assets are financed by external borrowing and shareholders' funds respectively.

In times of rising prices it can be beneficial to finance assets from loan capital. While the assets appreciate in value over time (and the gain accrues to shareholders), the liability is fixed in monetary amount. The effect of this is that current cost accounts tend to give a more favourable picture of the debt/equity ratio than historical cost accounts. In the ratios calculated above, the amount of debt is $20m in both statements of financial position. This represents nearly one-third of the historical cost value of shareholders' funds, but only one-fifth of the equity calculated on a current cost basis.

84 Update

(a) *Problems with historical cost*

Although retail price inflation has eased throughout the developed world, it is still a big issue for many businesses.

The carrying values of property and other assets with long useful lives soon become unrealistic if based on historical cost, leading to the following problems:

- Even with modest inflation, the depreciation charge on these assets will be too low in comparison with the revenues that the assets are generating, inflating operating profits.
- The return on capital employed is doubly distorted; not only are operating profits overstated, but the related net assets will be understated, resulting in a flattering and unrealistic return. This makes it difficult to compare two companies with similar assets if those assets were bought at different times.

- Low asset values reduce the net assets of a business. This exaggerates the gearing ratio, which might dissuade banks from advancing loans to the business. It might also cause the stock market to undervalue a business.

The traditional solution to these problems is to revalue certain items. However, this creates a hybrid set of financial statements, with some assets at historical cost others at valuation.

(b)   Alternative methods

	Historical Cost $		CPP $		Current cost $
Cost/Valuation	250,000	(a)	300,000	(b)	280,000
Carrying value based on 2 years depreciation (c)	160,000		192,000		179,200
Carrying value based on 3 years depreciation (d)	128,000		153,600		143,360
Depreciation charge for this year (c − d = e)	32,000		38,400		35,840

(1)   The original cost of $250,000 will be indexed up for the change in the retail price index between the date of purchase and the end of the reporting period.

$250,000 \times 216/180 = $300,000$

(2)   The current cost will be reduced to reflect the lower productivity of the old asset.

$320,000 \times 420/480 = $280,000$

(3)   The carrying value after two years depreciation at 20% reducing balance will be 64% of the gross amount (0.8 × 0.8).

(4)   The carrying value after three years depreciation at 20% reducing balance will be 51.2% of the gross amount (0.8 × 0.8 × 0.8).

(5)   This years charge will be the difference between (c) and (d).

85 Appraisal

A **not-for-profit organisation** needs funds to operate, just as a profit-making organisation does. It is also required to make good and sensible use of its assets and spend within its budget. To this degree, calculation of certain financial ratios and their comparison to the previous year is valid and would yield information about how well the organisation is run, and how well it manages its funds.

However, there are a number of differences between a profit-making and a not-for-profit organisation. A not-for-profit organisation does not have the basic purpose of increasing the wealth of its shareholders or of achieving a return on capital. Its success or failure is judged by the degree to which it achieves its objectives. These are laid down in a whole different set of parameters. A hospital has many different targets to meet – some of them apparently not that useful. One of its major targets will be to cut the length of its waiting lists for operations. Local government bodies may be judged on the basis of whether they have secured VFM (value for money) in spending local taxes. Schools are judged on their examination passes and their budgets may be affected by issues such as how many of their children are considered to have 'special needs'.

A charity will judge its success by the amount of work it has achieved in line with its mission statement, and by the level of funding and donations it has secured – without which nothing can be achieved.
It is worth pointing out that, just as a profit-making organisation may seek to enhance the picture given by its financial statements, not-for-profit organisations may also be driven in the same direction. It has been found in the UK that some hospitals have brought forward minor operations and delayed major ones in order to secure maximum impact on the waiting list and meet government targets. Some schools have a policy of only entering pupils for exams which they have a good chance of passing. This keeps up their pass rate and their position in the school league tables.

Mock Exams

ACCA

Fundamentals

Paper F7

Financial Reporting (Int)

Mock Examination 1

Question Paper	
Time allowed	
Reading and Planning Writing	**15 minutes** **3 hours**
Answer all FIVE questions	

DO NOT OPEN THIS PAPER UNTIL YOU ARE READY TO START UNDER EXAMINATION CONDITIONS

ACCA

Fundamentals

Paper F7

Financial Reporting (Int)

Mock Examination 1

Question Paper		
Time allowed		
Reading and Planning		15 minutes
Writing		3 hours
Answer ALL questions		

DO NOT OPEN THIS PAPER UNTIL YOU ARE READY TO START UNDER EXAMINATION CONDITIONS

Question 1 Pumice

On 1 October 20X5 Pumice acquired the following non-current investments:

- 80% of the equity share capital of Silverton at a cost of $13.6 million
- 50% of Silverton's 10% loan notes at par
- 1.6 million equity shares in Amok at a cost of $6.25 each.

The summarised draft statements of financial position of the three companies at 31 March 20X6 are:

	Pumice $'000	Silverton $'000	Amok $'000
Non-current assets			
Property, plant and equipment	20,000	8,500	16,500
Investments	26,000	nil	1,500
	46,000	8,500	18,000
Current assets	15,000	8,000	11,000
Total assets	61,000	16,500	29,000
Equity and liabilities			
Equity			
Equity shares of $1 each	10,000	3,000	4,000
Retained earnings	37,000	8,000	20,000
	47,000	11,000	24,000
Non-current liabilities			
8% loan note	4,000	nil	nil
10% loan note	nil	2,000	nil
Current liabilities	10,000	3,500	5,000
Total equity and liabilities	61,000	16,500	29,000

The following information is relevant:

(i) The fair values of Silverton's assets were equal to their carrying amounts with the exception of land and plant. Silverton's land had a fair value of $400,000 in excess of its carrying amount and plant had a fair value of $1.6 million in excess of its carrying amount. The plant had a remaining life of four years (straight-line depreciation) at the date of acquisition.

(ii) In the post acquisition period Pumice sold goods to Silverton at a price of $6 million. These goods had cost Pumice $4 million. Half of these goods were still in the inventory of Silverton at 31 March 20X6. Silverton had a balance of $1.5 million owing to Pumice at 31 March 20X6 which agreed with Pumice's records.

(iii) The net profit after tax for the year ended 31 March 20X6 was $2 million for Silverton and $8 million for Amok. Assume profits accrued evenly throughout the year.

(iv) An impairment test at 31 March 20X6 concluded that consolidated goodwill was impaired by $400,000 and the investment in Amok was impaired by $200,000.

(v) No dividends were paid during the year by any of the companies.

(vi) It is group policy to value non-controlling interest at acquisition at full (or fair) value. The directors valued the non-controlling interest at acquisition at $3m.

Required

(a) Discuss how the investments purchased by Pumice on 1 October 20X5 should be treated in its consolidated financial statements. **(5 marks)**

(b) Prepare the consolidated statement of financial position for Pumice as at 31 March 20X6. **(20 marks)**

(Total = 25 marks)

Question 2 Tintagel

Reproduced below is the draft statement of financial position of Tintagel, a public listed company, as at 31 March 20X4.

	$'000	$'000
Non-current assets (note (i))		
Freehold property		126,000
Plant		110,000
Investment property at 1 April 20X3 (note (ii))		15,000
		251,000
Current Assets		
Inventory (note (iii))	60,400	
Trade receivables and prepayments	31,200	
Bank	13,800	105,400
Total assets		356,400
Equity and liabilities		
Equity		
Ordinary shares of 25c each		150,000
Reserves		
Share premium	10,000	
Retained earnings – 1 April 20X3	52,500	
– Year to 31 March 20X4	47,500	110,000
		260,000
Non-current liabilities		
Deferred tax – at 1 April 20X3 (note (v))		18,700
Current liabilities		
Trade payables (note (iii))	47,400	
Provision for plant overhaul (note (iv))	12,000	
Taxation	4,200	
		63,600
Suspense account (note (vi))		14,100
Total equity and liabilities		356,400

(i)   The income statement has been charged with $3·2 million being the first of four equal annual rental payments for an item of plant. This first payment was made on 1 April 20X3. Tintagel has been advised that this is a finance lease with an implicit interest rate of 10% per annum. The plant had a fair value of $11·2 million at the inception of the lease. This is equivalent to the present value of the minimum lease payments. Rentals are paid in advance.

None of the non-current assets have been depreciated for the current year. The freehold property should be depreciated at 2% on its cost of $130 million, the leased plant is depreciated at 25% per annum on a straight line basis and the sundry plant is depreciated at 20% on the reducing balance basis. The heavy excavating plant is being depreciated over 6 years on a straight line basis.

Plant is split as follows:

	$'000
Heavy excavating plant	40,000
Sundry plant	70,000
	110,000

(ii)   Tintagel adopts the fair value model for its investment property. Its value at 31 March 20X4 has been assessed by a qualified surveyor at $12·4 million.

(iii)   During an inventory count on 31 March 20X4 items that had cost $6 million were identified as being either damaged or slow moving. It is estimated that they will only realise $4 million in total, on which sales commission of 10% will be payable. An invoice for materials delivered on 12 March 20X4 for $500,000 has been discovered. It has not been recorded in Tintagel's bookkeeping system, although the materials were included in the inventory count.

(iv)   Tintagel operates some heavy excavating plant which requires a major overhaul every three years. The overhaul is estimated to cost $18 million and is due to be carried out in April 20X5. The provision of $12 million represents two annual amounts of $6 million made in the years to 31 March 20X3 and 20X4.

This plant was purchased for $60m on 1 April 20X2 and is being depreciated over 6 years on the straight line basis.

(v)   The deferred tax liability required at 31 March 20X4 has been calculated at $22·5 million.

(vi)   The suspense account contains the credit entry relating to the issue on 1 October 20X3 of a $15 million 8% loan note. It was issued at a discount of 5% and incurred direct issue costs of $150,000. It is redeemable after four years at a premium of 10%. Interest is payable six months in arrears. The first payment of interest has not been accrued and is due on 1 April 20X4. The effective rate of interest is 12.1%.

Required

(a)   Commencing with the retained earnings figures in the above statement of financial position ($52·5 million and $47·5 million), prepare a schedule of adjustments required to these figures taking into account any adjustments required by notes (i) to (vi) above.   **(11 marks)**

(b)   Redraft the statement of financial position of Tintagel as at 31 March 20X4 taking into account the adjustments required in notes (i) to (vi) above.   **(14 marks)**

(Total = 25 marks)

Question 3 Nedburg

The financial statements of Nedberg for the year to 30 September 20X2, together with the comparative statement of financial position for the year to 30 September 20X1 are shown below:

INCOME STATEMENT – YEAR TO 30 SEPTEMBER 20X2

	$m
Sales revenue	3,820
Cost of sales (note (1))	(2,620)
Gross Profit for the period	1,200
Operating expenses (note (1))	(300)
Interest – Loan note	(30)
Profit before tax	870
Taxation	(270)
Profit for the year	600

STATEMENTS OF FINANCIAL POSITION AS AT 30 SEPTEMBER

	20X2		20X1	
Non-current assets	$m	$m	$m	$m
Property, plant and equipment		1,890		1,830
Intangible assets (note (2))		650		300
		2,540		2,130
Current assets				
Inventory	1,420		940	
Trade receivables	990		680	
Cash	70	2,480	nil	1,620
Total assets		5,020		3,750
Equity and liabilities				
Ordinary Shares of $1 each		750		500
Reserves:				
Share premium		350		100
Revaluation surplus		140		nil
Retained earnings		1,890		1,600
Total equity		3,130		2,200
Non-current liabilities (note(3))		870		540
Current liabilities (note(4))		1,020		1,010
Total equity and liabilities		5,020		3,750

Notes to the financial statements

(1) Cost of sales includes depreciation of property, plant and equipment of $320 million and a loss on the sale of plant of $50 million. It also includes a credit for the amortisation of government grants. Operating expenses include a charge of $20 million for the impairment of goodwill.

(2) Intangible non-current assets

	20X2 $m	20X1 $m
Deferred development expenditure	470	100
Goodwill	180	200
	650	300

(3) Non-current liabilities

	20X2 $m	20X1 $m
10% loan note	300	100
Government grants	260	300
Deferred tax	310	140
	870	540

(4) Current liabilities

	20X2 $m	20X1 $m
Trade payables	875	730
Bank overdraft	nil	115
Accrued loan interest	15	5
Taxation	130	160
	1,020	1,010

The following additional information is relevant:

(i) Intangible non-current assets

The company successfully completed the development of a new product during the current year, capitalising a further $500 million before amortisation charges for the period.

(ii) Property, plant and equipment/revaluation reserve

– The company revalued its buildings by $200 million on 1 October 20X1. The surplus was credited to revaluation surplus.

– New plant was acquired during the year at a cost of $250 million and a government grant of $50 million was received for this plant.

– On 1 October 20X1 a bonus issue of 1 new share for every 10 held was made from the revaluation surplus.

– $10 million has been transferred from the revaluation surplus to realised profits as a year-end adjustment in respect of the additional depreciation created by the revaluation.

– The remaining movement on property, plant and equipment was due to the disposal of obsolete plant.

(iii) Share issues

In addition to the bonus issue referred to above Nedberg made a further issue of ordinary shares for cash.

(iv) Dividends

Dividends paid during the year amounted to $320,000.

Required

(a) A statement of cash flows for Nedberg for the year to 30 September 20X2 prepared in accordance with IAS 7 *Statement of cash flows.* **(20 marks)**

(b) Comment briefly on the financial position of Nedberg as portrayed by the information in your statement of cash flows. **(5 marks)**

(Total = 25 marks)

Question 4 Shiplake (2.5 part)

Shiplake is preparing its financial statements to 31 March 20X2. The following situations have been identified by an impairment review team.

(a) On 1 April 20X1 Shiplake acquired two subsidiary companies, Halyard and Mainstay, in separate acquisitions. Consolidated goodwill was calculated as:

	Halyard $'000	Mainstay $'000
Purchase consideration	12,000	4,500
Estimated fair value of net assets	(8,000)	(3,000)
Consolidated goodwill	4,000	1,500

A review of the fair value of each subsidiary's net assets was undertaken in March 20X2. Unfortunately both companies' net assets had declined in value. The estimated value of Halyard's net assets as at 1 April 20X1 was now only $7 million. This was due to more detailed information becoming available about the market value of its specialised properties. Mainstay's net assets were estimated to have a fair value of $500,000 less than their carrying value. This fall was due to some physical damage occurring to its plant and machinery.

(3 marks)

(b) Shiplake has an item of earth-moving plant, which is hired out to companies on short-term contracts. Its carrying value, based on depreciated historical cost, is $400,000. The estimated selling price of this asset is only $250,000, with associated selling expenses of $5,000. A recent review of its value in use based on its forecast future cash flows was estimated at $500,000. Since this review was undertaken there has been a dramatic increase in interest rates that has significantly increased the cost of capital used by Shiplake to discount the future cash flows of the plant.

(4 marks)

(c) Shiplake is engaged in a research and development project to produce a new product. In the year to 31 March 20X1 the company spent $120,000 on research that concluded that there were sufficient grounds to carry the project on to its development stage and a further $75,000 had been spent on development. At that date management had decided that they were not sufficiently confident in the ultimate profitability of the project and wrote off all the expenditure to date to the income statement. In the current year further direct development costs have been incurred of $80,000 and the development work is now almost complete with only an estimated $10,000 of costs to be incurred in the future. Production is expected to commence within the next few months. Unfortunately the total trading profit from sales of the new product is not expected to be as good as market research data originally forecast and is estimated at only $150,000. As the future benefits are greater than the remaining future costs, the project will be completed, but due to the overall deficit expected, the directors have again decided to write off all the development expenditure.   **(4 marks)**

(d) Shiplake owns a company called Klassic Kars. Extracts from Shiplake's consolidated statement of financial position relating to Klassic Kars are:

	$'000
Goodwill	80,000
Franchise costs	50,000
Restored vehicles (at cost)	90,000
Plant	100,000
Other net assets	50,000
	370,000

The restored vehicles have an estimated fair value less costs to sell of $115 million. The franchise agreement contains a 'sell back' clause, which allows Klassic Kars to relinquish the franchise and gain a repayment of $30 million from the franchisor. An impairment review at 31 March 20X2 has estimated that the value of Klassic Kars as a going concern is only $240 million.   **(4 marks)**

Required

Explain, with numerical illustrations where possible, how the information in (i) to (iv) above would affect the preparation of Shiplake's consolidated financial statements to 31 March 20X2.   **(15 marks as indicated)**

Question 5 Creative accounting

(a)   Explain, with relevant examples, what is generally meant by the term 'creative accounting';   **(5 marks)**

(b)   Explain why it is important to record the substance rather than the legal form of transactions and describe the features that may indicate that the substance of a transaction is different from its legal form.   **(5 marks)**

(Total = 10 marks)

Answers

**DO NOT TURN THIS PAGE UNTIL YOU HAVE
COMPLETED THE MOCK EXAM**

A plan of attack

If this were the real Financial Reporting exam and you had been told to turn over and begin, what would be going through your mind?

Perhaps you're having a panic. You've spent most of your study time on groups and interpretation of accounts (because that's what your tutor/BPP study Text told you to do), plus a selection of other topics, and you're really not sure that you know enough. The good news is that you can always get a solid start by tackling the first question, which is **always on group accounts**. So calm down. Spend the first few moments or so **looking at the paper,** and develop a **plan of attack.**

Looking through the paper

As it will be in the real exam, Question 1 is on group accounts. Here you have a consolidated statement of financial position with one subsidiary and one associate, together with a discussion of associate status. In **Section B** you have **four questions on a variety of topics:**

- Question 2 requires adjustments to draft accounts and preparing a restated statement of financial position.

- Question 3 is a statement of cash flows and comment on financial position.

- Question 4 is a scenario question on impairment of assets.

- Question 5 is a discussion question on creative accounting.

All of these questions are compulsory

Question 1 is straightforward as long as you are able to deal with an associate.

Question 2 looks nasty but in fact the numbers are not difficult and you should get marks for detailed workings

Question 3 is a statement of cash flows. Always a good one to go for. Remember to set up your pro-forma and work logically through the points.

Question 4 requires good knowledge of IAS 36.

Question 5 requires some thought. All the points you make must be relevant.

Allocating your time

BPP's advice is always allocate your time **according to the marks for the question** in total and for the parts of the question. But **use common sense.** If you're doing Question 4 but haven't a clue how to do Part (b), you might be advised to re-allocate you time and pick up more marks on, say, Question 5, where you can always add something to your discussion.

After the exam...Forget about it!

And don't worry if you found the paper difficult. More than likely other candidates will too. If this were the real thing you would need to **forget** the exam the minute you left the exam hall and **think about the next one**. Or, if it's the last one, **celebrate!**

Question 1 Pumice

Text references. Chapters 9 and 11.

Top tips. Part (a) provides you with important information for part (b) so make sure you do that first and get clear what the shareholdings are and how you will treat them. Note also that the investments have been held for **six months**, so take care working out the pre-acquisition profits. The other complication here is NCI at fair value.

Easy marks. Most of the work in this question concerns the goodwill, the associate and non-current assets. You should be able to score easy marks on the non-current assets and the group retained earnings.

Marking scheme

		Marks
(a)	1 mark per relevant point	5
(b)	Statement of financial position	
	property, plant and equipment	2½
	goodwill	3½
	investments – associate	3
	– other	1
	current assets	2
	equity shares	1
	retained earnings	3
	non-controlling interest	1½
	8% loan notes	½
	10% loan notes	1
	current liabilities	1
		───
		20
	Total for question	**25**

(a) The acquisition of an 80% holding in Silverton can be assumed to give Pumice control. Silverton should therefore be treated as a subsidiary from the date of acquisition and its results consolidated from that date.

As Silverton is being treated as a subsidiary, the investment in loan notes is effectively an intra-group loan. This should be cancelled on consolidation, leaving the remaining $1m of Silverton's loan notes as a non-current liability in the consolidated statement of financial position.

The shares in Amok represent a 40% holding, which can be presumed to give Pumice 'significant influence', but not control. Amok should therefore be treated as an associate and its results brought into the consolidated financial statements using the equity method.

(b) PUMICE GROUP
CONSOLIDATED STATEMENT OF FINANCIAL POSITION AT 31 MARCH 20X6

	$'000
Non-current assets	
Property, plant and equipment (20,000 + 8,500 + 1,800 (W7))	30,300
Goodwill (W2)	4,200
Investment in associate (W3)	11,400
Investments – other (W8)	1,400
	47,300
Current assets (15,000 + 8,000 – 1,000 (W6) – 1,500 (intragroup))	20,500
Total assets	67,800

Equity and liabilities
Equity attributable to owners of the parent

Share capital (parent)	10,000
Retained earnings (W4)	37,720
	47,720
Non-controlling interest (W5)	3,080
	50,800

Non-current liabilities

8% loan note	4,000
10% loan note (2,000 – 1,000 (W8))	1,000
Current liabilities (10,000 + 3,500 – 1,500 (intragroup))	12,000
Total equity and liabilities	67,800

Workings

1   *Group structure*

Pumice

80%   40%

Silverton   Amok

2   *Goodwill*

	$'000	$'000
Consideration transferred		13,600
NCI (at 'full' fair value per question)		3,000
Fair value of net assets at acquisition:		
Share capital	3,000	
Pre-acquisition retained earnings (8,000 – 1,000)	7,000	
Fair value adjustments: land	400	
plant	1,600	
		(12,000)
Goodwill		4,600
Impairment losses to date		(400)
Carrying value		4,200

Alternative working

		Group	NCI
	$'000	$'000	$'000
Consideration transferred		13,600	
Fair value of NCI (per question)			3,000
Net assets at acquisition:			
Share capital	3,000		
Pre-acquisition retained earnings (8,000 – 1,000)	7,000		
Fair value adjustments: land	400		
plant	1,600		
	12,000		
Group / NCI/ share (80% / 20%)		(9,600)	(2,400)
Goodwill		4,000	600
Impairment to date (400 × 80% / 20%)		(320)	(80)
Carrying value		3,680	520
		4,200	

3   *Associate*

	$'000
Cost of investment ($6.25 × 1.6m)	10,000
Share of post-acquisition profit (W4)	1,600
	11,600
Less impairment loss	(200)
Carrying value	11,400

4   *Group retained earnings*

	Pumice	Silverton	Amok
	$'000	$'000	$'000
Per statement of financial position	37,000	8,000	20,000
Additional depreciation (W7)		(200)	
Unrealised profit ((6,000 – 4,000) /2)	(1,000)		
Pre-acquisition retained earnings (W2)	–	(7,000)	(16,000)*
	36,000	800	4,000
Group share: Silverton 800 × 80%	640		
Amok 4,000 × 40%	1,600		
	38,240		
Impairment: Silverton	(320)		
Amok	(200)		
	37,720		

* (20,000 – (8,000 × 6/12))

5   *Non-controlling interests*

	$'000
NCI at acquisition (W2)	3,000
NCI share of post acquisition retained earnings ((W4) 800 × 20%)	160
NCI share of impairment losses (400 × 20%)	(80)
	3,080

Alternative working

	$'000
Silverton – net assets	11,000
Fair value adjustments (W7)	2,000
Depreciation adjustment ($1.6m/4 × 6/12) (W7)	(200)
	12,800
Non-controlling share 20%	2,560
Goodwill (W2)	520
	3,080

6   *Unrealised profit*

	$'000
Sale of goods to Silverton	6,000
Cost to Pumice	(4,000)
Profit	2,000
50% still in inventory	1,000

DR Retained earnings/CR Inventories

7   Fair value adjustments

	Acquisition date $'000	Movement $'000	Reporting date $'000
Land	400	–	400
Plant	1,600	(200)	1,400
	2,000	(200)	1,800

8   Investments

	$'000
Pumice – per statement of financial position	26,000
Investment in Silverton	(13,600)
Investment in Amok	(10,000)
Intra-group loan note	(1,000)
Other investments	1,400

Question 2 Tintagel

Text reference. Chapters 3, 13 and 16.

Top tips. The statement of financial position in Part (b) should be straightforward after calculating the adjustments required in Part (a), but don't underestimate the time that it will take to draft it.

The adjustments are quite straightforward; work through them methodically and keep an eye on the time. Extend your workings to show the corrected balance at the year-end.

Easy marks. There are no easy marks for this question! However, if you are very happy with double entry, you may find part (a) straightforward. If so, this is 11 easy marks.

Examiner's comments. Some candidates find it very hard to redraft financial statements instead of preparing them from scratch. However most candidates did well. Common errors included: treatment of the lease as if it were payments in arrears; treatment of the deficit on the investment property; and treatment of the loan note.

Marking scheme

		Marks
(a)	Retained earnings	2
	Reversal of cyclic repair provision	2
	Depreciation charges	1
	Add back lease rental	1
	Lease interest	1
	Loan interest	1
	Loss on investment property	1
	Inventory write down	1
	Unrecorded creditor	1
	Deferred tax	1
	Available	12
	Maximum	11

(b) *Statement of financial position*
Freehold 1
Plant 2
Investment property 1
Inventory 2
Receivables and payables and bank 1
Trade receivables 1
Accrued lease interest 1
Accrued loan interest 1
Lease obligation (current liability) 1
Taxation 1
Lease obligation (non-current liability) 1
8% loan note 2
Deferred tax 1
Ordinary shares and share premium 1

Available	17
Maximum	14
Maximum for question	25

(a) **Schedule of Adjustments**

		Opening retained earnings $'000	Profit for year $'000	Closing retained earnings $'000
	From question	52,500	47,500	100,000
(i)	Lease restated as a finance lease (W1)			
	Remove existing rental		3,200	3,200
	Interest (11.2 – 3.2) × 10%		(800)	(800)
	Depreciation (11.2 × 25%)		(2,800)	(2,800)
	Depreciation			
	Freehold property ($130m × 2%)		(2,600)	(2,600)
	Sundry plant ($70m × 20%)		(14,000)	(14,000)
	Heavy excavating plant (See (iv) below)			
(ii)	Investment property			
	Fall in value ($15m – $12.4m)		(2,600)	(2,600)
(iii)	Inventory			
	NRV ($6m – ($4m × 90%))		(2,400)	(2,400)
	GRNI accrual		(500)	(500)
(iv)	Heavy excavating plant overhaul (W2)			
	Reverse overhaul provision	6,000	6,000	12,000
	Reverse old depreciation	10,000	10,000	20,000
	Charge new depreciation	(13,000)	(13,000)	(26,000)
(v)	Deferred tax			
	Increase ($22.5m – $18.7m)		(3,800)	(3,800)
(vi)	Loan Note (W3)			
	Interest expense		(853)	(853)
	Revised balances	55,500	23,347	78,847

Workings

1   *Lease restated as a finance lease*

	$'000
Fair value of asset	11,200
Rental paid 1 April 20X3	(3,200)
	8,000
Interest at 10%	800
Balance at 31 March 20X4	8,800
Rental due 1 April 20X4 (current liability)	(3,200)
Non-current liability	5,600

2   *Overhaul costs*

The $12m provision for plant overhaul does not meet the criteria for a liability because there is no obligation to overhaul the asset (it could be sold or abandoned instead). The provision of $12m (and this year's charge of $6m) should be reversed.

The need for a periodic overhaul will be reflected in the depreciation charge. The total cost of $60m will be apportioned between $18m which will be consumed over three years (the overhaul costs) and the balance which will last for six years.

		Total cost	Overhaul 3 years	Balance 6 years
		$'000	$'000	$'000
1/4/X2	Cost	60,000	18,000	42,000
	Depreciation	(13,000)	(6,000)	(7,000)
31/3/X3	Carrying value	47,000	12,000	35,000
	Depreciation	(13,000)	(6,000)	(7,000)
31/3/X4	Carrying value	34,000	6,000	28,000

3   *Loan Note*

The interest expense will reflect the full cost of this loan note (discount, interest, premium etc) rather than just the interest paid. The cost is then charged using the effective interest rate.

	$'000
Received	
Nominal Value	15,000
Discount (5%)	(750)
Issue costs	(150)
Net cash received	14,100

Balance outstanding on loan notes at 31 March 20X4

	$'000
Net amount received	14,100
Interest at 12.1% (14,100 × 12.1% × 6/12)	853
Interest payable 1 April 20X4 (accrual)	(600)
Balance at 31 March 20X4	14,353

Notes

The amount repayable at the end of four years is $16,500,000 ($15m + 10% premium).

The effective interest rate allocates the cost as follows:

	$'000
Net amount received 1.10.X3	14,100
Interest at 12.1%	1,706
Interest paid (15m × 8%)	(1,200)
Balance due 30.9.X4	14,606
Interest charge	1,767
Interest paid	(1,200)
Balance 30.9.X5	15,173
Interest charge	1,836
Interest paid	(1,200)
Balance at 30.9.X6	15,809
Interest charge (balancing figure)	1,891
Interest paid	(1,200)
Balance to be repaid 30.9.X7	16,500

You do not need to do this whole calculation in order to answer the question, and will probably not need to do it in an exam, but this is how it works. As we are dealing in $'000, the numbers are rounded, so the final interest charge is a balancing figure.

(b)   TINTAGEL
        STATEMENT OF FINANCIAL POSITION AS AT 31 MARCH 20X4

	$'000
Assets	
Non-current assets	
Freehold property (126,000 – 2,600)	123,400
Heavy excavating plant (W2)	34,000
Sundry plant (70,000 – 14,000)	56,000
Leased plant (11,200 – 2,800)	8,400
Investment property	12,400
	234,200
Current assets	
Inventories (60,400 – 2,400)	58,000
Trade receivables and prepayments	31,200
Bank	13,800
	103,000
Total assets	337,200
Equity and liabilities	
Equity	
Share Capital	150,000
Share Premium	10,000
Retained earnings (Part (a))	78,847
	238,847
Non-current liabilities	
Finance lease obligations (W1)	5,600
Loan note (W3)	14,353
Deferred tax	22,500
	42,453

		$'000
Current liabilities		
Trade payables (47,400 + 500)		47,900
Finance lease obligations (W1)		2,400
Accrued finance lease interest (W1)		800
Accrued Loan Note interest (W3)		600
Income Tax		4,200
		55,900
Total equity and liabilities		337,200

Question 3 Nedburg

Text reference. Chapter 21.

Top tips. Start by putting down the proforma. Then go methodically through the net cash flow from operating activities calculation. You will have to do the workings for property, plant and equipment and deferred development expenditure in order to complete it.

Easy marks. The statement of cash flows is straightforward and represents 20 easy marks.

Examiner's comments. This question was generally well answered and part (a) in particular was extremely well answered. However candidates still made mistakes in including non-cash items. Part (b) was poorly answered, some candidates making no effort to answer it at all. Most answers were superficial, giving general trends without commenting on them.

Marking scheme

			Marks
(a)	Net cash flows from operating activities		
	1 mark per item		8
	Except – loan interest		2
	– taxation		2
	Capital expenditure – proceeds from the sale of the plant		2
	– other items, 1 mark per component		3
	Financing – equity shares		2
	– loan note		2
	Equity dividends		1
	Movement in cash and cash equivalents		1
		Available	23
		Maximum	20
(b)	1 mark per relevant point to a	Maximum	5
		Maximum for question	25

(a) NEDBERG

STATEMENT OF CASH FLOWS FOR THE YEAR ENDED 30 SEPTEMBER 20X2

	$'000	$'000
Cash flows from operating activities		
Net profit before taxation		870
Adjustments for:		
Depreciation		320
Loss on disposal of plant		50
Amortisation of development expenditure (W3)		130
Impairment of goodwill		20
Release of government grants (W4)		(90)
Interest expense		30
		1,330
(Increase) decrease in trade and other receivables (990 – 680)		(310)
(Increase) decrease in inventories (1,420 – 940)		(480)
Increase (decrease) in trade payables (875 – 730)		145
Cash generated from operations		685
Interest paid (30 + 5 – 15)		(20)
Income taxes paid (W5)		(130)
Net cash from operating activities		535
Cash flows from investing activities		
Proceeds from sale of property, plant and equipment (W2)	20	
Purchase of property, plant and equipment	(250)	
Receipt of government grant	50	
Development expenditure capitalised	(500)	
Net cash used in investing activities		(680)
Cash flows from financing activities		
Proceeds from issue of share capital (200 + 250)(W6), (W7)	450	
Proceeds of long term borrowings (300 – 100)	200	
Dividends paid	(320)	
Net cash from financing activities		330
Net increase in cash and cash equivalents		185
Opening cash and cash equivalents		(115)
Closing cash and cash equivalents		70

Workings

1

PROPERTY, PLANT AND EQUIPMENT – CARRYING VALUE

	$m		$m
Bal b/f	1,830	Depreciation	320
		Plant disposal	
Revaluation	200	(balancing figure)	70
Plant acquisition	250	Bal c/f	1,890
	2,280		2,280

2

PROPERTY, PLANT AND EQUIPMENT – DISPOSAL

	$m		$m
Plant disposal (W1)	70	Loss on disposal (from question)	50
		Disposal proceeds (balancing figure)	20
	70		70

3 *Development expenditure*

DEFERRED DEVELOPMENT EXPENDITURE

	$m		$m
Opening	100	Closing	470
Expenditure	500	Amortised	130
	600		600

4 *Government Grants*

GOVERNMENT GRANTS

	$m		$m
Closing	260	Opening	300
Released during year	90	Cash received	50
	350		350

5 *Tax Paid*

TAX

		$m			$m
Closing liability	Current	130	Opening liability	Current	160
	Deferred	310		Deferred	140
Cash paid		130	Charge for the year		270
		570			570

6

SHARE CAPITAL

	$m		$m
		Bal b/f	500
		Bonus issue (1/10)	50
Bal c/f	750	Issue for cash	200
	750		750

7

SHARE PREMIUM

	$m		$m
		Bal b/f	100
Bal c/f	350	Premium on cash issue	250
	350		350

(b) Nedberg has positive cash flow, generating $685m from operations which is sufficient to cover interest ($20m), tax ($130m) and dividends ($320m).

Unusually, the cash flow from operations is less than the operating profit of $900m. The cause of this appears to be the increase in current assets; inventories have increased by 51% and receivables by 46%. Without the comparative income statement it is impossible to say whether these increases are in line with increased activity or whether it is the result of poor working capital management.

Nedberg has paid out $250m on property plant and equipment and capitalised $500m of development costs. In theory this is a good thing, as these investments will generate profits and cash flows in the future. However, Nedberg has had to raise $650m externally in order to pay for these investments, and this cannot be repeated year after year. Nedberg would be advised to reduce its capital investment for a year or two to enable it to get its finances back in order.

The financing section reveals that Nedberg has paid out in dividends half of the money it has received by issuing loans and shares. This seems pointless; the shareholders are getting back money that they have just invested (and they might have to pay tax on the dividends that they have received). The dividend for the year is also high compared with the profits after tax; Nedberg should reduce its dividends to a more modest and sustainable amount.

Overall, Nedberg has a healthy cash flow from operating activities. However, management need to:

- monitor working capital,
- scale back capital expenditure, and
- practise dividend restraint.

4 Shiplake

(a)   **Halyard and Mainstay**

This relates to the rules in IFRS 3 for fair valuing assets and calculating goodwill on the acquisition of a subsidiary. Fair values are initially established at the date of acquisition. However, these values must be revised if new evidence becomes available about the values **as at the date of acquisition**. These revisions should be made up until twelve months after the date of acquisition. Changes in the fair value of the assets and liabilities acquired will change the value of any goodwill arising on consolidation.

Fair values and goodwill must not be adjusted for changes that have occurred **since** the date of acquisition.
Halyard

In this example the revision downwards of the market value of Halyard's specialised properties would be treated as a revision of the fair values at acquisition. This will increase the initial cost of goodwill by $1m to $5m ($12m consideration less $7m fair valuation). At the year-end the goodwill is reviewed for impairment, particularly in light of the fall in value of the assets. If the recoverable amount of Halyard as a whole is still greater than the $12m purchase consideration then there is no impairment.

Mainstay

The $500,000 reduction in the value of Mainstay's net assets has been caused by damage. This cannot be treated as an adjustment to the initial fair values. The $500,000 must be charged through the income statement as an impairment.

(b)   **Earth moving plant**

At present the earth moving plant is not impaired. The recoverable amount is $500,000 (which is the higher of the fair value less costs to sell of $245,000 and the value in use of $500,000). This is greater than the carrying amount of $400,000.

However, an increase in interest rates will decrease the present value of future cash inflows, which in turn decreases the value in use. The affect on Shiplake will depend on the actual changes in the value in use.

If the value in use is reduced down to $400,000 or higher, then no impairment will have occurred.

If the value in use is now between $245,000 and $400,000, then the recoverable amount will be less than the carrying value and the plant will be impaired down to its value in use.

If the value in use is now less than $245,000, then the recoverable amount will be the fair value less costs to sell of $245,000. The plant will be impaired down to its fair value less costs to sell of $245,000.

(c) **Research and development**

A key point here is that at 31 March 20X1 the costs to date of $195,000 were written off. $120,000 related to research; these costs cannot be capitalised and must be expensed as incurred. The $75,000 of development costs may be capitalised, but the directors decided to write them off because of uncertainties. That was the correct decision at the time, and these costs cannot be reinstated in 20X2 when the project approached completion. Therefore, the only costs to consider at 31 March 20X2 are the $80,000 incurred during the current year and the $10,000 costs to complete.

The $80,000 consists of direct development costs and they must be capitalised. This is because the expected profits of $150,000 are greater than the $80,000 cost to date plus the $10,000 cost to complete. These costs will then be amortised over the market life of the product.

(d) **Klassic Kars**

The carrying value of Klassic Kars is $370m, whereas the value in use of the cash generating unit as a whole is only $240m. An impairment loss of $130m has occurred, and this loss needs to be apportioned between the individual assets of the unit.

The impairment loss will be allocated to the goodwill first, and then to the other assets (tangible and intangible) on a pro-rata basis. However, no asset will be reduced below:

(1)   It own fair value less costs to sell
(2)   Its own value in use
(3)   Zero

	Carrying Value $'000	Impairment $'000		Revised Value $'000
Goodwill	80,000	(80,000)		nil
Franchise costs	50,000	(16,667)	(2) (3)	33,333
Restored vehicles	90,000	nil	(1)	90,000
Plant	100,000	(33,333)	(2)	66,667
Other net assets	50,000	–	(2)	50,000
	370,000	(130,000)		240,000

Notes

(1)   The restored vehicles have a fair value less costs to sell of $115m. As this is greater than cost no impairment will be recognised against these items.

(2)   The $50m balance of the impairment (after charging $80m against goodwill) will be allocated against the franchise costs and plant on a pro-rata basis as follows:

	Carrying value $'000		Impairment $'000
Franchise costs	50,000	$50,000 × 50/150	16,667
Plant	100,000	$50,000 × 100/150	33,333
	150,000		50,000

(3)   The franchise has a fair value less costs to sell of $30m. The franchise must not be reduced below this value. As the impaired value of $33.3m is greater than the fair value less costs to sell no further adjustments are needed.

5 Creative accounting

(a) Creative accounting is the selection of accounting policies that will portray an entity's financial position and performance in the best possible light. The policies chosen will comply with all existing professional and legal standards. In itself creative accounting is not illegal, although when taken to extremes the financial statements may no longer reflect fairly the underlying financial position and performance of the business.

Creative accounting policies are normally chosen in order to boost liquidity ratios in the statement of financial position, or to increase or smooth out profits in the income statement.

Modern accounting standards have reduced the number of allowed alternatives, and so the opportunities for creative accounting are being reduced. However there are still a few areas where standards offer a choice of policies and so there is some scope for creative accounting. A few examples are noted below:

- Capitalising interest or development costs in order to boost profits in the short term.
- Revaluing or not revaluing a class of assets. (Revaluing tends to improve gearing, but it reduces the return on capital employed.)
- Accounting for a joint venture using the equity method, thereby hiding the impact that the joint venture has on the entity's gross profit, finance costs, capital employed and borrowings.

There are also occasions where management deliberately overestimate the useful lives of assets, or underestimate provisions, or fail to apply appropriate policies. These practices are probably closer to fraud than to creative accounting.

(b) IAS 1 requires financial statements to reflect the substance of transactions rather than just their legal form. This improves the reliability of the financial statements.

Most of the time there is no difference between the substance of a transaction and its legal form. For example the contract date for most sales is when the exchange of goods takes place, at which point all the rights of ownership pass from the seller to the buyer. The buyer recognises the asset, and also recognises the liability to pay for it. The seller ceases to recognise the old asset, but recognises a trade receivable instead. However there are occasions when the seller retains some of the rights of ownership. This raises the question of what assets and liabilities should be recognised, and when profits can be claimed. The legal form of these transactions often tends to overstate profits and hide liabilities.

Typical features of transactions where the substance may be different from the legal form are as follows:

- The seller continues to enjoy the risks and benefits of ownership by using the asset.
- The seller has a constructive obligation to repurchase the asset sold.
- The agreed selling price is markedly different from the market price.

The substance of these transactions are often secured loans, even though the legal form is a sale. If the legal form was reported then the 'seller' would claim a profit and ignore the obligation to repurchase the asset. This is obviously misleading to the user of the accounts.

ACCA

Fundamentals

Paper F7

Financial Reporting (Int)

Mock Examination 2

Question Paper	
Time allowed	
Reading and Planning Writing	**15 minutes** **3 hours**
Answer all FIVE questions	

DO NOT OPEN THIS PAPER UNTIL YOU ARE READY TO START UNDER EXAMINATION CONDITIONS

Question 1 Hample

Hample is a small publicly listed company. On 1 April 20X8 it acquired 90% of the equity shares in Sopel, a private limited company. On the same day Hample accepted a 10% loan note from Sopel for $200,000 which was repayable at $40,000 per annum (on 31 March each year) over the next five years. Sopel's retained earnings at the date of acquisition were $2,200,000.

STATEMENTS OF FINANCIAL POSITION AS AT 31 MARCH 20X9

	Hample		Sopel	
	$'000	$'000	$'000	$'000
Assets				
Non-current assets				
Property, plant and equipment		2,120		1,990
Intangible: Software		–		1,800
Investments: equity in Sopel		4,110		–
10% loan note Sopel		200		–
others		65		210
		6,495		4,000
Current assets				
Inventories	719		560	
Trade receivables	524		328	
Sopel current account	75		–	
Cash	20		–	
		1,338		888
Total assets		7,833		4,888
Equity and liabilities				
Equity				
Equity shares of $1 each	2,000		1,500	
Share premium	2,000		500	
Retained earnings	2,900		1,955	
		6,900		3,955
Non-current liabilities				
10% loan from Hample	–		160	
Government grant	230		40	
		230		200
Current liabilities				
Trade payables	475		472	
Hample current account	–		60	
Income taxes payable	228		174	
Operating overdraft	–		27	
		703		733
Total equity and liabilities		7,833		4,888

The following information is relevant.

(a) Included in Sopel's property at the date of acquisition was a leasehold property recorded at its depreciated historical cost of $400,000. On 1 April 20X8 the leasehold was sublet for its remaining life of four years at an annual rental of $80,000 *payable in advance* on 1 April each year. The directors of Hample are of the opinion that the fair value of this leasehold is best reflected by the present value of its future cash flows. An appropriate cost of capital for the group is 10% per annum.

The present value of a $1 annuity received at the end of each year where interest rates are 10% can be taken as:

	$
3 year annuity	2.50
4 year annuity	3.50

(b) The software of Sopel represents the depreciation cost of the development of an integrated business accounting package. It was completed at a capitalised cost of $2,400,000 and went on sale on 1 April 20X7. Sopel's directors are depreciating the software on a straight-line basis over an eight-year life (ie $300,000 per annum). However, the directors of Hample are of the opinion that a five-year life would be more appropriate as sales of business software rarely exceed this period.

(c)   The inventory of Hample on 31 March 20X9 contains goods at a transfer price of $25,000 that were supplied by Sopel who had marked them up with a profit of 25% on cost. Unrealised profits are adjusted for against the profit of the company that made them.

(d)   On 31 March 20X9 Sopel remitted to Hample a cash payment of $55,000. This was not received by Hample until early April. It was made up of an annual repayment of the 10% loan note of $40,000 (the interest had already been paid) and $15,000 off the current account balance.

(e)   Goodwill is reviewed for impairment annually. At 31 March 20X9 there had been an impairment loss of $120,000 in the value of goodwill since acquisition.

(f)   It is the group policy to value the non-controlling interest at acquisition at its proportionate share of the fair value of the subsidiary's identifiable net assets.

Required

Prepare the consolidated statement of financial position of Hample as at 31 March 20X9.   **(20 marks)**

Question 2 Chamberlain

The following trial balance relates to Chamberlain, a publicly listed company, at 30 September 20X4:

	$'000	$'000
Ordinary share capital		200,000
Retained profits at 1 October 20X3		162,000
6% Loan note (issued in 20X2)		50,000
Deferred tax (note (v))		17,500
Land and buildings at cost (land element $163 million (note (i))	403,000	
Plant and equipment at cost (note (i))	124,000	
Accumulated depreciation 1 October 20X3 – buildings		60,000
– plant and equipment		44,000
Trade receivables	48,000	
Inventory – 1 October 20X3	35,500	
Bank	52,500	
Trade payables		45,000
Revenue		246,500
Purchases	78,500	
Construction contract balance (note (iii))	5,000	
Operating expenses	29,000	
Loan interest paid	1,500	
Interim dividend	8,000	
Research and development expenditure (note (iv))	40,000	
	825,000	825,000

The following notes are relevant:

(i)   The building had an estimated life of 40 years when it was acquired and is being depreciated on a straight-line basis. Plant and equipment, other than the leased plant, is depreciated at 12·5% per annum using the reducing balance basis. Depreciation of buildings and plant and equipment is charged to cost of sales.

(ii)   The construction contract balance represents costs incurred to date of $35 million less progress billings of $30 million on a two year construction contract that commenced on 1 October 20X3. All progress billings to date have been settled by the customer. The total contract price has been agreed at $125 million and Chamberlain expects the total contract cost to be $75 million. The company policy is to accrue for profit on uncompleted contracts by applying the percentage of completion to the total estimated profit. The percentage of completion is determined by the proportion of the contract costs to date compared to the total estimated contract costs. At 30 September 20X4, $5 million of the $35 million costs incurred to date related to unused inventory of materials on site.

Other inventory at 30 September 20X4 amounted to $38·5 million at cost.

(iii) The research and development expenditure is made up of $25 million of research, the remainder being development expenditure. The directors are confident of the success of this project which is likely to be completed in March 20X5.

(iv) The directors have estimated the provision for income tax for the year to 30 September 20X4 at $22 million. The deferred tax provision at 30 September 20X4 is to be adjusted to a credit balance of $14 million.

Required

Prepare for Chamberlain:

(a) An income statement for the year to 30 September 20X4; and   **(11 marks)**

(b) A statement of financial position as at 30 September 20X4 in accordance with International Financial Reporting Standards as far as the information permits.   **(14 marks)**

Note. A Statement of Changes in equity is NOT required.

                                                                                    (Total = 25 marks)

Question 3 Boston

Shown below are the summarised financial statement for Boston, a publicly listed company, for the years ended 31 March 20X5 and 31 March 20X6, together with some segment information analysed by class of business for the year ended 31 March 20X6 only:

Income statements	Carpeting	Hotels	House building	Total 20X6	Total 20X5
	$m	$m	$m	$m	$m
Revenue	90	130	280	500	450
Cost of sales (note (i))	(30)	(95)	(168)	(293)	(260)
Gross profit	60	35	112	207	190
Operating expenses	(25)	(15)	(32)	(72)	(60)
Segment result	35	20	80	135	130
Unallocated corporate expenses				(60)	(50)
Profit from operations				75	80
Finance costs				(10)	(5)
Profit before tax				65	75
Income tax expenses				(25)	(30)
Profit for the year				40	45

Statements of financial position

	Carpeting	Hotels	House building	Total 31 March 20X6	Total 31 March 20X5
	$m	$m	$m	$m	$m
Tangible non-current assets	40	140	200	380	332
Current assets	40	40	75	155	130
Segment assets	80	180	275	535	462
Unallocated bank balance				15	Nil
Consolidated total assets				550	462
Ordinary share capital				100	80
Share premium				20	Nil
Retained earnings				232	192
				352	272
Segment current liabilities – tax	4	9	12	25	30
– other	4	51	53	108	115
Unallocated loans				65	40
Unallocated bank overdraft				Nil	5
Consolidated equity and total liabilities				550	462

The following notes are relevant

(i)   Depreciation for the year to 31 March 20X6 was $35 million. During the year a hotel with a carrying amount of $40 million was sold at a loss of $12 million. Depreciation and the loss on the sale of non-current assets are charged to cost of sales. There were no other non-current asset disposals. As part of the company's overall acquisition of new non-current assets, the hotel segment acquired $104 million of new hotels during the year.

(ii)   The above figures are based on historical cost values. The fair values of the segment net assets are:

	Carpeting $m	Hotels $m	House building $m
At 31 March 20X5	80	150	250
At 31 March 20X6	97	240	265

(iii)   The following ratios (which can be taken to be correct) have been calculated based on the overall group results:

Year ended	31 March 20X6	31 March 20X5
Return on capital employed	18.0%	25.6%
Gross profit margin	41.4%	42.2%
Operating profit margin	15%	17.8%
Net asset turnover	1.2 times	1.4 times
Current ratio	1.3:1	0.9:1
Gearing	15.6%	12.8%

(iv)   The following segment ratios (which can be taken to be correct) have been calculated for the year ended 31 March 20X6 only:

	Carpeting	Hotels	House building
Segment return on net assets	48.6%	16.7%	38.1%
Segment asset turnover (times)	1.3	1.1	1.3
Gross profit margin	66.7%	26.9%	40%
Net profit margin	38.9%	15.4%	28.6%
Current ratio (excluding bank)	5:1	0.7:1	1.2:1

Required

(a)   Prepare a statement of cash flows for Boston for the year ended 31 March 20X6.   **(10 marks)**

Note. You are not required to show separate segmental cash flows or any disclosure notes.

(b)   Using the ratios provided, write a report to the Board of Boston analysing the company's financial performance and position for the year ended 31 March 20X6.   **(15 marks)**

Your answer should make reference to your statement of cash flows and the segmental information and consider the implication of the fair value information.

Note: Segmental reporting is not in your syllabus. The segment information is provided simply to give you information about the different areas of the business for use in your answer to (b).   **(Total = 25 marks)**

Question 4 Atomic Power

You are preparing a technical note to all your clients regarding the effects of IAS 37 *Provisions, contingent liabilities and contingent assets*.

One of your clients, Atomic Power, has asked for further help in applying IAS 37 because the company is concerned that it may not be applying the standard correctly.

Atomic Power operates nuclear power stations that supply power to international, national and regional electricity companies. Environmental clear-up costs can be a substantial item of expenditure for nuclear power plant operators; in some countries Atomic Power's licences have, by law, environmental clean-up commitment written in as part of the agreement, whereas in other countries there is no legal requirement to provide for them.

Atomic Power has brought into commission, on 1 July 20X0, a new nuclear power station, built at a cost of $600m. The plant has a licence to supply electricity for 12 years, which is the estimated life of the power station. At the end of 12 years, the station must be demolished and all the waste product (ie spent fuel) buried over 100m underground in an area sealed for contamination purposes. During the station's life the company will have to pay for the clean up of any contamination leaks from the plant's water cooling system.

The company has estimated the cost of demolition and waste disposal in 12 years' time at $540m, the discounted value of which, at an appropriate rate, is $360m. Past experience suggests that there is a 30% chance of a contamination leak occurring in any 12 month period, and the cost of cleaning up will be between $60m and $120m a time, depending on its extent. The company has a legal obligation to clean-up all contamination caused by leaks.

The company has sent you extracts from its draft financial statements to 30 June 20X1 in relation to the power plant, showing the following:

INCOME STATEMENT (EXTRACTS)

	$m
Non-current asset depreciation: power station (1/12 × $600m)	50
Provision for demolition and waste disposal (1/12 × $540m)	45
Provision for contamination leak clean-up (30% × $90m (average))	27
	122

STATEMENT OF FINANCIAL POSITION (EXTRACTS)

	$m
Property, plant and equipment	
Power station at cost	600
Depreciation	(50)
	550
Non-current liabilities	
Environmental costs (45 + 27)	72

No contamination leaks occurred in the year ended 30 June 20X1.

Required

(a) Draft a technical note for your clients that explains why there is a need for an accounting standard in respect of provisions. **(2 marks)**

(b) Advise Atomic Power on the acceptability of its current accounting policy and redraft the extracts of the financial statements for the company in line with IAS 37. **(8 marks)**

(c) Explain the effect it would have on your answer to (b) if Atomic Power was operating this nuclear power station in a country that does not legislate in respect of the above types of environmental costs. **(5 marks)**

(Total = 15 marks)

Question 5 Errsea

The following is an extract of Errsea's balances of property, plant and equipment and related government grants at 1 April 20X6.

	Cost	Accumulated depreciation	Carrying amount
	$'000	$'000	$'000
Property, plant and equipment	240	180	60
Non-current liabilities			
Government grants			30
Current liabilities			
Government grants			10

Details including purchases and disposals of plant and related government grants during the year are:

(i) Included in the above figures is an item of plant that was disposed of on 1 April 20X6 for $12,000 which had cost $90,000 on 1 April 20X3. The plant was being depreciated on a straight-line basis over four years assuming a residual value of $10,000. A government grant was received on its purchase and was being recognised in the income statement in equal amounts over four years. In accordance with the terms of the grant, Errsea repaid $3,000 of the grant on the disposal of the related plant.

(ii) An item of plant was acquired on 1 July 20X6 with the following costs:

	$
Base cost	192,000
Modifications specified by Errsea	12,000
Transport and installation	6,000

The plant qualified for a government grant of 25% of the base cost of the plant, but it had not been received by 31 March 20X7. The plant is to be depreciated on a straight-line basis over three years with a nil estimated residual value.

(iii) All other plant is depreciated by 15% per annum on cost

(iv) $11,000 of the $30,000 non-current liability for government grants at 1 April 20X6 should be reclassified as a current liability as at 31 March 20X7.

(v) Depreciation is calculated on a time apportioned basis.

Required

Prepare extracts of Errsea's income statement and statement of financial position in respect of the property, plant and equipment and government grants for the year ended 31 March 20X7.

Note. Disclosure notes are not required. **(10 marks)**

Answers

DO NOT TURN THIS PAGE UNTIL YOU HAVE
COMPLETED THE MOCK EXAM

Answers

A plan of attack

Managing your nerves

As you turn the pages to start this mock exam a number of thoughts are likely to cross your mind. At best, examinations cause anxiety so it is important to stay focused on your task for the next three hours! Developing an awareness of what is going on emotionally within you may help you manage your nerves. Remember, you are unlikely to banish the flow of adrenaline, but the key is to harness it to help you work steadily and quickly through your answers.

Working through this mock exam will help you develop the exam stamina you will need to keep going for three hours.

Managing your time

Planning and time management are two of the key skills which complement the technical knowledge you need to succeed. To keep yourself on time, do not be afraid to jot down your target completion times for each question, perhaps next to the title of the question on the paper. As all the questions are **compulsory**, you do not have to spend time wondering which question to answer!

Focusing on scoring marks

When completing written answers, remember to communicate the critical points, which represent marks, and avoid padding and waffle. Sometimes it is possible to analyse a long sentence into more than one point. Always try to maximise the mark potential of what you write.

As you read through the questions, jot down on the question paper, any points you think you might forget. There is nothing more upsetting than coming out of an exam having forgotten to write a point you knew!

Structure and signpost your answers

As you read through the paper, highlight the key words and phrases in the examiner's requirements. This will help you focus precisely on what the examiner wants.

Also, where possible try to use headings and subheadings, to give a logical and easy-to-follow structure to your response. A well structured and sign-posted answer is more likely to convince the examiner that you know your subject.

Doing the exam

Actually doing the exam is a personal experience. There is not a single *right way*. As long as you submit complete answers to five questions after the three hours are up, then your approach obviously works.

Looking through the paper

Question 1, as always, is on **group accounts**. This time it requires a statement of financial position for a parent company and subsidiary. Do not neglect part (b).

- Question 2 is on **preparing financial statements for an individual company**.
- Question 3 is a statement of cash flows and interpretation of accounts
- Question 4 requires good understanding of provisions
- Question 5 is a question on non-current assets and government grants

Allocating your time

BPP's advice is to always allocate your time **according to the marks for the question.** However, **use common sense.** If you're doing a question but haven't a clue how to do part (c), you might be better off re-allocating your time and getting more marks on another question, where you can add something you didn't have time for earlier on.

Question 1 Hample

Top tips. The main difficulties in this question relate to the fair value adjustments on the non-current assets. There are lots of easy marks to be gained for straightforward adjustments, such as those for intragroup transactions.

CONSOLIDATED STATEMENT OF FINANCIAL POSITION AS AT 31 MARCH 20X9

	$'000	$'000
Assets		
Non-current assets		
Property, plant and equipment (W7)	4,020	
Goodwill (W2)	480	
Software (W8)	1,440	
Investments (65 + 210)	275	
		6,215
Current assets		
Inventory (719 + 560 – 5 (W5))	1,274	
Trade receivables (524 + 328)	852	
Cash and bank (20 + 55 cash in transit)	75	
		2,201
Total assets		8,416
Equity and liabilities		
Equity attributable to owners of the parent		
Share capital	2,000	
Share premium	2,000	
Retained earnings (W3)	2,420	
		6,420
Non-controlling interest (W4)		350
Non-current liabilities		
Government grants (230 + 40)		270
Current liabilities		
Trade payables (475 + 472)	947	
Overdraft	27	
Provisions for tax (228 + 174)	402	
		1,376
Total equity and liabilities		8,416

Workings

1   *Group structure*

Hample

90% 1.4.X8

Sopel

2   Goodwill

	$'000	$'000
Consideration transferred		4,110
Non-controlling interests at acquisition (3,900 x 10%)		390
Less net assets acquired:		
Equity shares	1,500	
Share premium	500	
Retained earnings at 1 April X8 (2,200 – 300 (W6))	1,900	
		(3,900)
		600
Impairment losses		(120)
Carrying value		480

Alternative working

	$'000	$'000
Consideration transferred		4,110
Less share of net assets acquired		
Equity shares	1,500	
Share premium	500	
Retained earnings at 1 April X8 (2,200 – 300 (W6))	1,900	
	3,900 × 90%	(3,510)
		600
Impairment		(120)
Carrying value		480

3   Retained earnings

	Hample $'000	Sopel $'000
Per question	2,900	1,955
Fair value adj (W6)		(150)
Unrealised profit (W5)		(5)
Pre-acquisition		(2,200)
		(400)
Share of post acquisition		
Sopel: (400) × 90%	(360)	
Less goodwill impairment (W2)	(120)	
	2,420	

4   Non-controlling interest

	$'000
NCI at acquisition (W2)	390
NCI share of post acquisition retained earnings ((W3) (400) × 10%)	(40)
	350

Alternative working

	$'000
Net assets per question	3,955
Less unrealised profit (W5)	(5)
Fair value adj (W6)	(450)
	3,500
	× 10%
	350

Non-controlling interest: $3,500,000 × 10% = $350,000

5   *Unrealised profit*

Sopel's sales to Hample: $25,000

Marked up at 25%, so unrealised profit is $25,000 × $\dfrac{25}{125}$ = $5,000

Dr   Retained earnings (Sopel) $5,000
Cr   Group inventories $5,000

6   *Fair value adjustments*

	1.4.X8 $'000	In year $'000	31.3.X9 $'000
Leasehold (4 yr life)	(120)	30	(90)
Software (W8)	(180)	(180)	(360)
	(300)	(150)	(450)

7   *Property, plant and equipment*

	$'000
Hample	2,120
Sopel	1,990
Fair value adjustment (Note (i))	(120)
Reduced depreciation arising from fair value adjustment (Note (ii))	30
	4,020

Notes

(i)   The leasehold carrying value would be based upon present value of future rentals (receivable in advance):

	$'000
80 + (80 × 2.5*)	280
Book value	400
Reduction	120

*2.5 is the annuity factor for years 1-3 at 10%.

(ii)   Depreciation is based upon $\dfrac{280}{4}$ = 70

Depreciation in Sopel books = 100
Reduction: 100 − 70 = 30

8   *Software*

	Sopel accounts $'000	Consolidated $'000
Capitalised	2,400	2,400
Depreciation to 31 March 20X8 (8 yrs/5 yrs)	(300)	(480)
NBV at acquisition	2,100	1,920
Depreciation to 31 March 20X9	(300)	(480)
NBV 31 March 20X9	1,800	1,440

Note. There is a fair value adjustment of 180 plus extra depreciation of 180.

9   *Elimination of current account*

	$'000
Sopel in Hample accounts	75
Less cash in transit	(15)
Hample in Sopel accounts	60

10   *Intragroup loan*

	$'000
Investment in Hample accounts	200
Repayment in transit	(40)
Liability in Sopel accounts	160

Question 2 Chamberlain

Top tips. As well as examining you on the format and content of the income statement and statement of financial position, this question also tests your knowledge of four specific situations. Work through these first, noting their effect on the income statement and statement of financial position.

As always, be methodical and don't get bogged down in the detail.

Easy marks. There are no easy marks with this question. However, a methodical approach should see you through.

Examiner's comments. This was the most popular and best answered of the optional questions. Problems occurred with: construction contracts, R & D and deferred tax.

Marking scheme

			Marks
(a)	*Income statement*		
	Revenue		2
	Cost of sales		6
	Operating costs		1
	Interest expense		2
	Taxation		2
		Available	13
		Maximum	11
(b)	*Statement of financial position*		
	Development costs		1
	Property, plant and equipment		2
	Amounts due from construction contract customers		2
	Inventory and accounts receivable		1
	Accrued finance income		1
	Bank and trade creditors		1
	Accrued finance costs		1
	Income tax provision		1
	Non-current liabilities		2
	Share capital and reserves (including 1 mark for dividend paid)		2
		Maximum	14
		Maximum for question	25

CHAMBERLAIN
INCOME STATEMENT FOR THE YEAR ENDED 30 SEPTEMBER 20X4

	$'000
Revenue (246,500 + 50,000 (W3))	296,500
Cost of sales (W1)	(146,500)
Gross profit	150,000
Operating expenses	(29,000)
Finance costs ($50m × 6%)	(3,000)
Profit before tax	118,000
Income tax expense (22,000 – 3,500 deferred tax)	(18,500)
Profit for the year	99,500

CHAMBERLAIN
STATEMENT OF FINANCIAL POSITION AS AT 30 SEPTEMBER 20X4

	$'000
Assets	
Non-current assets	
Property, plant and equipment (W2)	407,000
Development expenditure (W4)	15,000
	422,000
Current assets	
Inventories	38,500
Gross amount due from customers for contract work (W3)	25,000
Trade receivables	48,000
Cash and cash equivalents	52,500
	164,000
Total assets	586,000
Equity and liabilities	
Equity	
Share capital	200,000
Retained earnings (162,000 + 99,500 profit – 8,000 dividend)	253,500
	453,500
Non-current liabilities	
6% Loan Note	50,000
Deferred tax	14,000
	64,000
Current liabilities	
Trade payables	45,000
Accrued interest ($3,000 charge - $1,500 paid)	1,500
Income tax	22,000
	68,500
Total equity and liabilities	586,000

Workings

1   Cost of sales

	$'000
Opening inventory (from TB)	35,500
Purchases (from TB)	78,500
Depreciation (W2)	16,000
Construction contract costs (W3)	30,000
Closing inventory (from question)	(38,500)
Research expenditure (from question)	25,000
	146,500

2   Property, plant and equipment

Total depreciation ($6m + $10m = $16m)
Total carrying value ($337m + $70m = $407m)

Land & buildings	$'000	$'000
Cost		403,000
Depreciation b/f	60,000	
Charge [(403m – 163m) × $\frac{1}{40}$]	6,000	
		(66,000)
Carrying value		337,000
Plant and equipment		
Cost		124,000
Depreciation b/f	44,000	
Charge [(124m – 44m) × 12.5%]	10,000	
		(54,000)
Carrying value		70,000

3   *Construction contract*

Total expected profit (125 − 75)	$50m
Profit to date $(50 \times \frac{30}{75})$	$20m

Income statement

Revenue $(125 \times \frac{30}{75})$	$50m
Cost of sales (balancing figure)	($30m)
Profit to date	$20m

Statement of financial position

Costs to date	$30m
Attributable profit	$20m
Costs relating to future activity	$5m
Less progress billings	($30m)
Gross amount due from customer	$25m

4   *Research and development*

	$'000
Research (Charge to I/S as incurred)	25,000
Development (Capitalise in statement of financial position)	15,000
Total	40,000

Question 3 Boston

Text reference. Chapters 19 and 21.

Top tips. These financial statements may have looked a bit confusing to start with, which is why you must take time to go through the question carefully and make sure you understand it. Once you had found your way round the numbers, the statement of cash flows was fairly simple and more marks were available for the report in (b). In this case, the ratios were already provided, so you just had to analyse the information. As this is worth 15 marks, you should have taken time to analyse the information properly and come to some useful conclusions.

Easy marks. The statement of cash flows was easy but was only worth 10 marks. 15 marks were available for the report and there was no reason not to do well on this part. Make notes before you start and cover the issues methodically.

Examiner's comments. Overall, most candidates did well on the cash flow with many receiving full marks for this section, but interpretation of the company's performance was mixed. Some simply commented on whether a particular ratio had gone up or down. This is not interpretation and attracts few marks. It is necessary to suggest what the underlying causes of the changes might be.

Marks

(a)
Profit before tax	1
Depreciation	1
Loss on sale of hotel	1
Increase in current assets	1
Decrease in current liabilities	1
Interest paid	1
Income taxes paid	1
Purchase of non-current assets	1
Sale of non-current assets	1
Share issue	1
Issue of loan	1
Cash and cash equivalents b/f and c/f	1
Available	12
Maximum	10

(b) One mark per valid point to maximum — 15

Maximum for question — 25

(a) BOSTON STATEMENT OF CASH FLOWS FOR THE YEAR ENDED 31 MARCH 20X6

	$m
Net cash flow from operating activities	
Profit before tax	65
Depreciation	35
Loss on sale of non-current asset	12
Interest expense	10
Increase in current assets	(25)
Reduction in current liabilities	(7)
Cash generated from operations	90
Interest paid	(10)
Income tax paid	(30)
Net cash flow from operating activities	50

	$m	$m
Cash flows from investing activities		
Purchase of non-current assets (W)	(123)	
Proceeds of sale of non-current assets	28	(95)
Cash flows from financing activities		
Loan issue (65 – 40)	25	
Proceeds of share issue (120 – 80)	40	
		65
Increase in cash and cash equivalents		20
Cash and cash equivalents at beginning of period (bank overdraft)		(5)
Cash and cash equivalents at end of period (bank balance)		15

Working

PROPERTY, PLANT AND EQUIPMENT – CARRYING AMOUNT

	$m		$m
Bal b/f	332	Depreciation	35
		Property disposal	40
Additions (balancing figure)	123	Bal c/f	380
	455		455

(b)   **To: The Board, Boston**
       From: A N Accountant

       Report on financial performance and position for the year ended 31 March 20X6

All of Boston's profitability ratios have declined between 31 March 20X5 and 31 March 20X6. The overall ROCE has fallen from 25.6% to 18%. In spite of increased revenue and a small increase in gross profit, the operating profit has fallen. This is due to a rise in operating expenses of 8% above the rise in revenue, which should be investigated. The fall in the gross profit margin can be attributed to the $12m loss on sale of non-current assets, which was charged to cost of sales. Without this, the gross profit margin would have been 43.8%.

If ROCE were to be recalculated using the fair values of the segment net assets it would be 16.7% for 20X5 and 12.5% for 20X6. Although this is much lower overall, the gap between the ROCE for 20X5 and 20X6 is much reduced. The ROCE for 20X6 has been to some extent penalised by the addition of $64m assets to the hotels segment. These assets may not yet be producing much return.

If we look at the segments individually, carpeting is the most profitable segment and the hotel segment is the least profitable. However, if the loss on sale of non-current assets were not included in cost of sales, the hotel segment would show a gross profit of 36% - not far below house building. If we adjust the segment return on net assets for fair values, we get 36% carpeting, 8% hotels and 30% house building. This narrows the gap between carpeting and house building, but makes the hotel sector look unviable. However it is worth bearing in mind that the hotel sector currently holds $120m of unrealised profit in its net assets, which could be realised if needed.

Boston's current ratio has improved in the year to 31.3.X6, but this ignores the increase of $25m in loans. The statement of cash flows shows a decrease in cash before financing of $45m. This can be explained by the $123m capital expenditure in the year, mainly on hotel properties. The company's gearing has increased due to the new loans, partly offset by the share issue, and it will now be facing higher interest payments. However, its gearing level is still not high in absolute terms.

Question 4 Atomic Power

Text reference. Chapter 13.

Top tips. IAS 37 is an important 'anti-abuse' standard in the IAS repertoire. The definitions and recognition criteria you are required to discuss in (a) are fundamental to the standard; you will not be able to apply IAS 37 if you don't know them.

(a)   TECHNICAL NOTE
       IAS 37 PROVISIONS, CONTINGENT LIABILITIES AND CONTINGENT ASSETS

The use of provisions has created substantial opportunities for the **manipulation of reported profits**. One reason for this is that provisions are pervasive; they may arise in relation to almost all areas of a company's operations. Both the recognition and measurement of provisions rely to a great extent on the **judgement of management**. There is thus substantial scope for adjustment of provisions.

A particular issue is the way management use provisions to **'smooth' profits;** provisions are created for future expenditure in years when profits are healthy and then released to profit or loss as the expenditure arises, thus reducing the volatility of reported profits over time. IAS 37 is designed to prevent this.

Another difficult area is the use of **provisions for future losses** when one business acquires another. By creating provisions for **restructuring on acquisition** as part of the fair value exercise, the acquiring business can increase the future profitability of the acquired entity, again by releasing the provisions in future periods against the expenditure. This practice has the perverse effect of increasing goodwill the greater the restructuring charges! This has been largely prevented, not only by IAS 37, but also by IFRS 3 *Business combinations*.

Note the emphasis on a 'present obligation'; it is not sufficient to determine that there may or will be some obligation in the future. Where it is unclear as to whether there is a present obligation, IAS 37 states that it should be assumed that there is one if, on the available evidence, it is **more likely than not** that one exists.

Assuming the above definitions and recognition criteria are met, IAS 37 has rules regarding **measurement** of a provision. The amount recognised as a provision should be the **best estimate** of the expenditure required to settle the present obligation at the end of the reporting period. It is necessary to incorporate this notion because of the uncertainties surrounding the outcome of provisions.

(b) Atomic Power's current accounting policies regarding accounting for provisions is **no longer acceptable** under IAS 37. Where an entity has a present obligation that will (probably) lead to an outflow of resources embodying economic benefits as a result of past events, then a provision should be made of the full amount of the expected liability. Where that amount is expressed in future prices then these must be **discounted back** at a nominal rate. Atomic Power should thus recognise $360m as a liability, not $540m, for environmental costs on 1 July 20X0.

The credit side of the accounting entry is thus to non-current liabilities in the statement of financial position. The treatment of the corresponding debit entry required by IAS 37 is controversial; it must be **added in to the cost of the asset**, to be released as the asset is depreciated over its useful life. This effectively 'grosses up' the assets and liabilities of the statement of financial position and has called into question the nature of the assets recognised in this way in relation to how assets are defined in the IASB's *Framework*. In Atomic Power's case (barring the error in using $540m instead of $360m), the effects on profits will not be much different under IAS 37 than the previous policy. The value of the power station plus the provision for environmental costs will be written off over its 12 year life.

The treatment of the possible costs of contamination leaks is more problematic. If there is a leak then the company will have to pay for the clean-up costs, and each leak will cost between $60m and $120m to clean-up. The main issue is whether a **'past event'** has taken place. Is the past event the leak itself, or is it the generation of the electricity that could lead to a leak? There is also the question of the **probability** of a leak. Generally, if there is a greater than 50% chance of a liability occurring, it should be provided for, but it below 50%, then presumably the liability would be classed as contingent only, and disclosed in the notes rather than provided. The probability of a leak is only 30% in any year and indeed one did not occur this year. But over 12 years of generation of electricity, probability would suggest that a leak will occur about four times (ie one year in three). It would therefore be prudent to provide on this assumption. The cost of each leak is $60m – $120m; so taking the mid-cost, the cost of four leaks will be $90m × 4 = $360m. Over 12 years, therefore, the company would provide $30m per year.

Applying the above, the revised accounts extracts are as follows.

INCOME STATEMENT (EXTRACTS)

	$m
Non-current asset depreciation: 1/12 × (600 + 360)	80
Provision for clean-up costs: 1/12 × (90 × 4)	30
	110

STATEMENT OF FINANCIAL POSITION (EXTRACTS)

	$m
Non-current assets	
Power station at cost	960
Depreciation (as above)	(80)
	880
Provisions for liabilities and charges	
Provision for environmental and clean up costs (360 + 30)	390

An alternative view on the cost of cleaning up after leaks would be to say that at the end of the reporting period there have been no leaks and so there is no obligation to pay out any clean-up costs. Although there may be leaks in the future, these will be from future operations, and so they should not be provided for now.

(c) In the case put where there is no statutory requirement to clean up environmental damage, one might expect IAS 37 not to require a provision because there is no obligation the settlement of which will require an outflow of resources embodying economic benefits. However, IAS 37 also includes the notion of a **'constructive obligation'** as discussed in (a)(ii) above.

In Atomic Power's case, if the company has a **track record** for cleaning up environmental damage or pollution, or if it has stated its intention to do so in terms of specific or general commitment then the provisions should be made as in (b) above. However, if the company has not raised any expectations that it will clean up environmental damage, then no provisions would be required and the power station would simply be recorded at a cost of $600m and depreciated by $50m a year over 12 years.

Question 5 Errsea

> **Top tips.** This question requires really clear workings, to enable you to work methodically and to show the marker what you have done.

INCOME STATEMENT (EXTRACTS)

	$
Income from government grants (W2)	19,000
Loss on disposal of plant (30,000 – 12,000)	18,000
Depreciation (52,500 + 22,500 (W1))	75,000

OF FINANCIAL POSITION (EXTRACTS)

	$
Non-current assets	
Property, plant and equipment (W1)	165,000
Current assets	
Receivable-government grant	48,000
Non-current liabilities	
Government grants	39,000
Current liabilities	
Government grants	27,000

Workings

1   *Property, plant and equipment*

	Cost	Accumulated depreciation	Carrying value
	$	$	$
At 1.4.X6	240,000	(180,000)	60,000
Disposal 1.4. X6	(90,000)	60,000	(30,000)
Acquisition 1.7. X6	210,000		210,000
Depreciation on acquisition ((210/3) × 9/12)		(52,500)	(52,500)
Depreciation on assets on hand at 1.4.X6			
((240 – 90) × 15%)		(22,500)	(22,500)
	360,000	(195,000)	(165,000)

2   *Government grants*

	Current liability $	Non-current liability $	Income $
At 1.4.X6	10,000	30,000	
Grant repaid	(3,000)		
	7,000		
Transfer to income at 31.3.X7	(7,000)		7,000
Transfer to current liability	11,000	(11,000)	
Grant receivable *	16,000	20,000	12,000
	27,000	39,000	19,000

	$
*	
Total grant (192,000 × 25%)	48,000
Transfer to income ((48,000/3) × 9/12)	12,000
Current liability (48,000/3)	16,000
Non-current liability	20,000
	48,000

ACCA Fundamentals Level

Paper F7

Financial Reporting (Int)

Mock Examination 3 (December 2009 paper)

Question Paper	
Time allowed	
Reading and Planning Writing	15 minutes 3 hours
Answer all FIVE questions	

DO NOT OPEN THIS PAPER UNTIL YOU ARE READY TO START UNDER EXAMINATION CONDITIONS

ACCA Fundamentals Level

Paper F7

Financial Reporting (Int)

Mock Examination 3

(December 2009 paper)

Question Paper		
Time allowed		
Reading and planning	15 minutes	
Writing	3 hours	
Answer all FIVE questions		

DO NOT OPEN THIS PAPER UNTIL YOU ARE READY TO START UNDER
EXAMINATION CONDITIONS

Question 1

On 1 April 2009 Pandar purchased 80% of the equity shares in Salva. The acquisition was through a share exchange of three shares in Pandar for every five shares in Salva. The market prices of Pandar's and Salva's shares at 1 April 2009 were $6 per share and $3.20 respectively.

On the same date Pandar acquired 40% of the equity shares in Ambra paying $2 per share.

The summarised income statements for the three companies for the year ended 30 September 2009 are:

	Pandar $'000	Salva $'000	Ambra $'000
Revenue	210,000	150,000	50,000
Cost of sales	(126,000)	(100,000)	(40,000)
Gross profit	84,000	50,000	10,000
Distribution costs	(11,200)	(7,000)	(5,000)
Administrative expenses	(18,300)	(9,000)	(11,000)
Investment income (interest and dividends)	9,500		
Finance costs	(1,800)	(3,000)	nil
Profit (loss) before tax	62,200	31,000	(6,000)
Income tax (expense) relief	(15,000)	(10,000)	1,000
Profit (loss) for the year	47,200	21,000	(5,000)

The following information for the equity of the companies at 30 September 2009 is available:

Equity shares of $1 each	200,000	120,000	40,000
Share premium	300,000	nil	nil
Retained earnings 1 October 2008	40,000	152,000	15,000
Profit (loss) for the year ended 30 September 2009	47,200	21,000	(5,000)
Dividends paid (26 September 2009)	nil	(8,000)	nil

The following information is relevant:

(i) The fair values of the net assets of Salva at the date of acquisition were equal to their carrying amounts with the exception of an item of plant which had a carrying amount of $12 million and a fair value of $17 million. This plant had a remaining life of five years (straight-line depreciation) at the date of acquisition of Salva. All depreciation is charged to cost of sales.

In addition, Salva owns the registration of a popular internet domain name. The registration, which had a negligible cost, has a five year remaining life (at the date of acquisition); however, it is renewable indefinitely at a nominal cost. At the date of acquisition the domain name was valued by a specialist company at $20 million.

The fair values of the plant and the domain name have not been reflected in Salva's financial statements.

No fair value adjustments were required on the acquisition of the investment in Ambra.

(ii) Immediately after its acquisition of Salva, Pandar invested $50 million in an 8% loan note from Salva. All interest accruing to 30 September 2009 had been accounted for by both companies. Salva also has other loans in issue at 30 September 2009.

(iii) Pandar has credited the whole of the dividend it received from Salva to investment income.

(iv) After the acquisition, Pandar sold goods to Salva for $15 million on which Pandar made a gross profit of 20%. Salva had one third of these goods still in its inventory at 30 September 2009. There are no intra-group current account balances at 30 September 2009.

(v) The non-controlling interest in Salva is to be valued at its (full) fair value at the date of acquisition. For this purpose Salva's share price at that date can be taken to be indicative of the fair value of the shareholding of the non-controlling interest.

(vi) The goodwill of Salva has not suffered any impairment; however, due to its losses, the value of Pandar's investment in Ambra has been impaired by $3 million at 30 September 2009.

(vii)   All items in the above income statements are deemed to accrue evenly over the year unless otherwise
        indicated.

Required

(a)   (i)   Calculate the goodwill arising on the acquisition of Salva at 1 April 2009;   **(6 marks)**

      (ii)   Calculate the carrying amount of the investment in Ambra to be included within the consolidated
             statement of financial position as at 30 September 2009.   **(3 marks)**

(b)   Prepare the consolidated income statement for the Pandar Group for the year ended 30 September 2009.

                                                                                                  (16 marks)

                                                                                           (Total = 25 marks)

Question 2

The following trial balance relates to Sandown at 30 September 2009:

	$'000	$'000
Revenue (note (i))		380,000
Cost of sales	246,800	
Distribution costs	17,400	
Administrative expenses (note (ii))	50,500	
Loan interest paid (note (iii))	1,000	
Investment income		1,300
Profit on sale of investments (note (iv))		2,200
Current tax (note (v))	2,100	
Freehold property – at cost 1 October 2000 (note (vi))	63,000	
Plant and equipment – at cost (note (vi))	42,200	
Brand – at cost 1 October 2005 (note (vi))	30,000	
Accumulated depreciation – 1 October 2008 – building		8,000
– plant and equipment		19,700
Accumulated amortisation – 1 October 2008 – brand		9,000
Available-for-sale investments (note (iv))	26,500	
Inventory at 30 September 2009	38,000	
Trade receivables	44,500	
Bank	8,000	
Trade payables		42,900
Equity shares of 20 cents each		50,000
Equity option		2,000
Other reserve (note (iv))		5,000
5% convertible loan note 2012 (note (iii))		18,440
Retained earnings at 1 October 2008		26,060
Deferred tax (note (v))		5,400
	570,000	570,000

The following notes are relevant:

(i)   Sandown's revenue includes $16 million for goods sold to Pending on 1 October 2008. The terms of the sale
       are that Sandown will incur ongoing service and support costs of $1·2 million per annum for three years
       after the sale. Sandown normally makes a gross profit of 40% on such servicing and support work. Ignore
       the time value of money.

(ii)   Administrative expenses include an equity dividend of 4·8 cents per share paid during the year.

(iii) The 5% convertible loan note was issued for proceeds of $20 million on 1 October 2007. It has an effective
       interest rate of 8% due to the value of its conversion option.

(iv)   During the year Sandown sold an available-for-sale investment for $11 million. At the date of sale it had a
       carrying amount of $8·8 million and had originally cost $7 million. Sandown has recorded the disposal of the
       investment. The remaining available-for-sale investments (the $26·5 million in the trial balance) have a fair

value of $29 million at 30 September 2009. The other reserve in the trial balance represents the net increase in the value of the available-for-sale investments as at 1 October 2008. Ignore deferred tax on these transactions.

(v) The balance on current tax represents the under/over provision of the tax liability for the year ended 30 September 2008. The directors have estimated the provision for income tax for the year ended 30 September 2009 at $16·2 million. At 30 September 2009 the carrying amounts of Sandown's net assets were $13 million in excess of their tax base. The income tax rate of Sandown is 30%.

(vi) Non-current assets:

The freehold property has a land element of $13 million. The building element is being depreciated on a straight-line basis.

Plant and equipment is depreciated at 40% per annum using the reducing balance method.

Sandown's brand in the trial balance relates to a product line that received bad publicity during the year which led to falling sales revenues. An impairment review was conducted on 1 April 2009 which concluded that, based on estimated future sales, the brand had a value in use of $12 million and a remaining life of only three years. However, on the same date as the impairment review, Sandown received an offer to purchase the brand for $15 million. Prior to the impairment review, it was being depreciated using the straight-line method over a 10-year life.

No depreciation/amortisation has yet been charged on any non-current asset for the year ended 30 September 2009. Depreciation, amortisation and impairment charges are all charged to cost of sales.

Required

(a) Prepare the statement of comprehensive income for Sandown for the year ended 30 September 2009.

(13 marks)

(b) Prepare the statement of financial position of Sandown as at 30 September 2009.　　**(12 marks)**

Notes to the financial statements are not required.

A statement of changes in equity is not required.

(Total = 25 marks)

Question 3

(a)   The following information relates to Crosswire a publicly listed company.

Summarised statements of financial position as at:

	30 September 2009 $'000	30 September 2009 $'000	30 September 2008 $'000	30 September 2008 $'000
Assets				
Non-current assets				
Property, plant and equipment (note (i))		32,500		13,100
Development costs (note (ii))		1,000		2,500
		33,500		15,600
Current assets		8,200		6,800
Total assets		41,700		22,400
Equity and liabilities				
Equity				
Equity shares of $1 each		5,000		4,000
Share premium	6,000		2,000	
Other equity reserve	500		500	
Revaluation surplus	2,000		nil	
Retained earnings	5,700		3,200	
		14,200		5,700
		19,200		9,700
Non-current liabilities				
10% convertible loan notes (note (iii))	1,000		5,000	
Environmental provision	3,300		nil	
Finance lease obligations	5,040		nil	
Deferred tax	3,360		1,200	
		12,700		6,200
Current liabilities				
Finance lease obligations	1,760		nil	
Trade payables	8,040		6,500	
		9,800		6,500
Total equity and liabilities		41,700		22,400

Information from the income statements for the year ended:

	30 September 2009 $'000	30 September 2008 $'000
Revenue	52,000	42,000
Finance costs (note (iv))	1,050	500
Income tax expense	1,000	800
Profit for the year (after tax)	4,000	3,000

The following information is available:

(i)   During the year to 30 September 2009, Crosswire embarked on a replacement and expansion programme for its non-current assets. The details of this programme are:

On 1 October 2008 Crosswire acquired a platinum mine at a cost of $5 million. A condition of mining the platinum is a requirement to landscape the mining site at the end of its estimated life of ten years. The present value of this cost at the date of the purchase was calculated at $3 million (in addition to the purchase price of the mine of $5 million).

Also on 1 October 2008 Crosswire revalued its freehold land for the first time. The credit in the revaluation surplus is the net amount of the revaluation after a transfer to deferred tax on the gain. The tax rate applicable to Crosswire for deferred tax is 20% per annum.

On 1 April 2009 Crosswire took out a finance lease for some new plant. The fair value of the plant was $10 million. The lease agreement provided for an initial payment on 1 April 2009 of $2·4 million followed by eight six-monthly payments of $1·2 million commencing 30 September 2009.

Plant disposed of during the year had a carrying amount of $500,000 and was sold for $1·2 million. The remaining movement on the property, plant and equipment, after charging depreciation of $3 million, was the cost of replacing plant.

(ii)   From 1 October 2008 to 31 March 2009 a further $500,000 was spent completing the development project at which date marketing and production started. The sales of the new product proved disappointing and on 30 September 2009 the development costs were written down to $1 million via an impairment charge.

(iii)   During the year ended 30 September 2009, $4 million of the 10% convertible loan notes matured. The loan note holders had the option of redemption at par in cash or to exchange them for equity shares on the basis of 20 new shares for each $100 of loan notes. 75% of the loan-note holders chose the equity option. Ignore any effect of this on the other equity reserve.

All the above items have been treated correctly according to International Financial Reporting Standards.

(iv)   The finance costs are made up of:

For year ended:	30 September 2009	30 September 2008
	$'000	$'000
Finance lease charges	400	Nil
Unwinding of environmental provision	300	Nil
Loan-note interest	350	500
	1,050	500

Required

(i)   Prepare a statement of the movements in the carrying amount of Crosswire's non-current assets for the year ended 30 September 2009;   **(9 marks)**

(ii)   Calculate the amounts that would appear under the headings of 'cash flows from investing activities' and 'cash flows from financing activities' in the statement of cash flows for Crosswire for the year ended 30 September 2009.

Note: Crosswire includes finance costs paid as a financing activity.   **(8 marks)**

(b)   A substantial shareholder has written to the directors of Crosswire expressing particular concern over the deterioration of the company's return on capital employed (ROCE).

Required

Calculate Crosswire's ROCE for the two years ended 30 September 2008 and 2009 and comment on the apparent cause of its deterioration.

Note: ROCE should be taken as profit before interest on long-term borrowings and tax as a percentage of equity plus loan notes and finance lease obligations (at the year end).   **(8 marks)**

(Total = 25 marks)

Question 4

(a)   An assistant of yours has been criticised over a piece of assessed work that he produced for his study course for giving the definition of a non-current asset as 'a physical asset of substantial cost, owned by the company, which will last longer than one year'.

Required

Provide an explanation to your assistant of the weaknesses in his definition of non-current assets when compared to the International Accounting Standards Board's (IASB) view of assets.   **(4 marks)**

(b)   The same assistant has encountered the following matters during the preparation of the draft financial statements of Darby for the year ending 30 September 2009. He has given an explanation of his treatment of them.

   (i)   Darby spent $200,000 sending its staff on training courses during the year. This has already led to an improvement in the company's efficiency and resulted in cost savings. The organiser of the course has stated that the benefits from the training should last for a minimum of four years. The assistant has therefore treated the cost of the training as an intangible asset and charged six months' amortisation based on the average date during the year on which the training courses were completed.   **(3 marks)**

   (ii)   During the year the company started research work with a view to the eventual development of a new processor chip. By 30 September 2009 it had spent $1·6 million on this project. Darby has a past history of being particularly successful in bringing similar projects to a profitable conclusion. As a consequence the assistant has treated the expenditure to date on this project as an asset in the statement of financial position.

           Darby was also commissioned by a customer to research and, if feasible, produce a computer system to install in motor vehicles that can automatically stop the vehicle if it is about to be involved in a collision. At 30 September 2009, Darby had spent $2·4 million on this project, but at this date it was uncertain as to whether the project would be successful. As a consequence the assistant has treated the $2·4 million as an expense in the income statement.   **(4 marks)**

   (iii)   Darby signed a contract (for an initial three years) in August 2009 with a company called Media Today to install a satellite dish and cabling system to a newly built group of residential apartments. Media Today will provide telephone and television services to the residents of the apartments via the satellite system and pay Darby $50,000 per annum commencing in December 2009. Work on the installation commenced on 1 September 2009 and the expenditure to 30 September 2009 was $58,000. The installation is expected to be completed by 31 October 2009. Previous experience with similar contracts indicates that Darby will make a total profit of $40,000 over the three years on this initial contract. The assistant correctly recorded the costs to 30 September 2009 of $58,000 as a non-current asset, but then wrote this amount down to $40,000 (the expected total profit) because he believed the asset to be impaired.

           The contract is not a finance lease. Ignore discounting.   **(4 marks)**

Required

For each of the above items (i) to (iii) comment on the assistant's treatment of them in the financial statements for the year ended 30 September 2009 and advise him how they should be treated under International Financial Reporting Standards.

Note: the mark allocation is shown against each of the three items above.

                                                                                                  (Total = 15 marks)

Question 5

(a) The following figures have been calculated from the financial statements (including comparatives) of Barstead for the year ended 30 September 2009:

Increase in profit after taxation	80%
Increase in (basic) earnings per share	5%
Increase in diluted earnings per share	2%

Required

Explain why the three measures of earnings (profit) growth for the same company over the same period can give apparently differing impressions. **(4 marks)**

(b) The profit after tax for Barstead for the year ended 30 September 2009 was $15 million. At 1 October 2008 the company had in issue 36 million equity shares and a $10 million 8% convertible loan note. The loan note will mature in 2010 and will be redeemed at par or converted to equity shares on the basis of 25 shares for each $100 of loan note at the loan-note holders' option. On 1 January 2009 Barstead made a fully subscribed rights issue of one new share for every four shares held at a price of $2·80 each. The market price of the equity shares of Barstead immediately before the issue was $3·80. The earnings per share (EPS) reported for the year ended 30 September 2008 was 35 cents.

Barstead's income tax rate is 25%.

Required

Calculate the (basic) EPS figure for Barstead (including comparatives) and the diluted EPS (comparatives not required) that would be disclosed for the year ended 30 September 2009. **(6 marks)**

(Total = 10 marks)

Answers

DO NOT TURN THIS PAGE UNTIL YOU HAVE
COMPLETED THE MOCK EXAM

A plan of attack

What's the worst thing you could be doing right now if this was the actual exam paper? Sharpening your pencil? Wondering how to celebrate the end of the exam in about 3 hours time? Panicking, flapping and generally getting in a right old state?

Well, they're all pretty bad, so turn back to the paper and let's sort out a **plan of attack**!

First things first

You have fifteen minutes of reading time. Spend this looking carefully through the questions and deciding the order in which you will attempt them. As a general rule you should attempt the questions that you find easiest first and leave the hardest until last.

This paper has five compulsory questions. Therefore, you do not have to spend your 15 minutes reading time working out which questions to answer. So you can use it to read the paper and get some idea of what you need to do. At this stage you can make notes on the question paper but not in the answer book. So scribble down anything you feel you might otherwise forget.

It's a good idea to just start with Question 1. Once you have the consolidation question done, you will feel more relaxed. Question 1 will have lots of information and you should read it a second time before you start. Get really clear about % shareholdings and dates on which they were acquired. Get the formats down and then proceed methodically with the workings.

Question 2 is a single company accounts preparation question. This is where the examiner can bring in leases, construction contracts, fixed/non-current asset complications and other issues he wants to examine. In this case you have an intangible asset and financial instrument issues. Again, set the formats out and then tackle the workings. Make it very clear to the marker which workings belong to which question and cross-reference them.

Question 3 covers non-current assets, cash flows and ROCE. You should not have any trouble with the ratios, but you must be able to *interpret* them. Read the answer carefully to see what this means.

Question 4 is a discussion and scenario question on non-current assets. In part (b) make sure you read the scenarios carefully.

Question 5 is on EPS. This is a popular topic, so do not neglect it.

You've got spare time at the end of the exam.....?

If you have allocated your time properly then you **shouldn't have time on your hands** at the end of the exam. But if you find yourself with five or ten minutes to spare, check over your work to make sure that there are no silly arithmetical errors.

Forget about it!

And don't worry if you found the paper difficult. More than likely other candidates will too. If this were the real thing you would need to **forget** the exam the minute you leave the exam hall and **think about the next one**. Or, if it's the last one, **celebrate**!

Question 1

Marking scheme

			Marks
(a)	(i)	Goodwill of Salva:	
		Consideration	2
		Net assets acquired calculated as:	
		Equity shares	1
		Pre-acquisition reserves	2
		Fair value adjustments	1
			6
	(ii)	Carrying value of Ambra	
		Cost	1
		Share of post-acquisition losses	1
		Impairment charge	1
			3
(b)		Income statement:	
		Revenue	2
		Cost of sales	4
		Distribution costs and administrative expenses	1
		Investment income	2½
		Finance costs	1½
		Finance costs	1
		Share of associate's losses and impairment charge	1
		Income tax	2
		Non-controlling interests	1
		Domain name not amortised	16
		Total for question	25

(a) (i) Goodwill

	$'000	$'000
Consideration transferred (120m × 80% × 3/5 × $6)		345,600
Non-controlling interest (120m × 20% × $3.20)		76,800
FV of identifiable net assets acquired:		
Share capital	120,000	
Reserves (152,000 + ((21,000 + (W3) 2,000*) × 6/12))	163,500	
FV adjustments (W2)	25,000	
		(308,500)
		113,900

* Note that the interest on the loan note is a post-acquisition cost for Salva, so it is added back for the purpose of calculating pre-acquisition reserves.

Alternative working

	Group	NCI
	$'000	$'000
Consideration transferred/FV of NCI	345,600	76,800
FV of identifiable net assets		
Acquired (308,500) × Group/NCI share		
80%/20%	(246,800)	(61,700)
Goodwill	98,800	15,100
		113,900

(ii) *Investment in Ambra*

	$'000
Cost (40m × 40% × $2)	32,000
Share of post-acquisition loss (5,000 x 40% x 6/12)	(1,000)
Impairment loss	(3,000)
	28,000

(b) PANDAR GROUP
CONSOLIDATED INCOME STATEMENT FOR THE YEAR ENDED 30 SEPTEMBER 2009

	$'000
Revenue (210,000 + (150,000 x 6/12) – (W4) 15,000)	270,000
Cost of sales (W5)	(162,500)
Gross profit	107,500
Distribution costs (11,200 + (7,000 × 6/12)	(14,700)
Administrative expenses (18,300 + (9,000 × 6/12)	(22,800)
Investment income (W6)	1,100
Finance costs (W7)	(2,300)
Share of loss of associate ((5,000 × 40% × 6/12)+(3,000) impairment)	(4,000)
Profit before tax	64,800
Income tax expense (15,000 + (10,000 × 6/12))	(20,000)
Profit for the year	44,800
Attributable to:	
Owners of the parent	43,000
Non-controlling interest (W8)	1,800
	44,800

Workings

1. Timeline

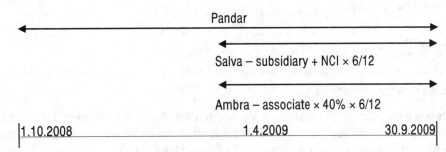

2. Fair value adjustments

	Acquisition 1.4.09		Movement	Year end 30.9.09
	$'000		$'000	$'000
Plant (17,000 – 12,000)	5,000	5000/5 × 6/12	(500)	4,500
Domain name	20,000		–	20,000
	25,000			24,500

3. *Intragroup interest*

Interest   50,000 × 8% × 6/12 = $2,000
Dr Finance income/Cr Finance costs

4. *Intragroup trading*

Cancel intragroup sales/purchases:
Dr Revenue 15,000/Cr Cost of sales 15,000

Unrealised profit 15,000 × 1/3 × 20%:
Dr Cost of sales 1,000/Cr Inventories (SOFP) 1,000

5. *Cost of sales*

	$'000
Pandar	126,000
Salva (100,000 × 6/12)	50,000
Intragroup (W4)	(15,000)
Depreciation on FVA (W2)	500
Unrealised profit (W4)	1,000
	162,500

6. *Investment income*

	$'000
Pandar	9,500
Intragroup interest (W3)	(2,000)
Intragroup dividend (8,000 × 80%)	(6,400)
	1,100

7. *Finance costs*

	$'000
Pandar	1,800
Salva ((3,000 − 2,000) × 6/12) + 2,000)	2,500
Intragroup (W3)	(2,000)
	2,300

8. *Non-controlling interest*

	$'000
Salva's post acquisition profit ((21,000 − 2,000(a)) × 6/12)	9,500
Depreciation on FVA (W2)	(500)
	9,000
× 20%	1,800

Question 2

Text references Chapters 3, 5 and 14

Top tips This was a time-pressured question. It was important to deal with it efficiently and not get bogged down. The question requirement tells you that there will be some other comprehensive income, so this makes it possible to get down the correct proformas and then go straight through the workings.

Easy marks The difficult issues here were the deferred revenue, the amortisation of the brand for the period after the impairment loss and the recycling of the gains on the available-for-sale investment to profit or loss. Being given the equity element of the convertible loan note may also have confused some students. There were easy marks on PPE, on transferring back the dividend and on deferred tax.

		Marks
(a)	Statement of comprehensive income	
	Revenue	1½
	Cost of sales	3
	Distribution costs	½
	Administrative expenses	1
	Investment income	½
	Profit on sale of investments	2
	Finance costs	1
	Income tax expense	1½
	Other comprehensive income	2
		13

		Marks
(b)	Statement of financial position	
	Property, plant and equipment	2
	Brand	1
	Investments	1
	Inventory/trade receivables	½
	Bank	½
	Equity shares/equity option	½
	Other equity reserve	1
	Retained earnings (1 for dividend)	2
	Deferred tax	1
	Non-current deferred revenue	½
	5% loan note	1
	Current deferred revenue	½
	Trade payables/current tax payable	½
		12
	Total for question	25

SANDOWN
STATEMENT OF COMPREHENSIVE INCOME FOR THE YEAR ENDED 30 SEPTEMBER 2009

	$'000
Revenue (380,000 – 4,000 (W5))	376,000
Cost of sales (W1)	(265,300)
Gross profit	110,700
Distribution costs	(17,400)
Administrative expenses (W1)	(38,500)
Investment income	1,300
Profit on sale of available-for-sale investments (W2)	4,000
Finance costs (W7)	(1,475)
Profit before tax	58,625
Income tax expense (16,200 + 2,100 – 1,500 (W8))	(16,800)
Profit for the year	41,825
Other comprehensive income:	
Gain on available-for-sale investments	2,500
Realised gain transferred to profit or loss (W2)	(1,800)
Total comprehensive income for the year	42,525

SANDOWN
STATEMENT OF FINANCIAL POSITION AS AT 30 SEPTEMBER 2009

	$'000	$'000
Non-current assets		
Property, plant and equipment (W3)		67,500
Intangible asset (W4)		12,500
Available for sale investments (W2)		29,000
Current assets		109,000
Inventory	38,000	
Receivables	44,500	
Bank	8,000	
		90,500
Total assets		199,500

	$'000	$'000
Equity		
Share capital 20c		50,000
Equity option		2,000
Other reserve (W2)		5,700
Retained earnings (26,060 + 41,825 − 12,000 (W6))		55,885
		113,585
Non-current liabilities		
Deferred tax (W8)	3,900	
Deferred revenue (W5)	2,000	
5% convertible loan note (W7)	18,915	
		24,815
Current liabilities		
Trade payables	42,900	
Deferred revenue (W5)	2,000	
Tax payable	16,200	
		61,100
Total equity and liabilities		199,500

Workings

1. Expenses

	Cost of sales	Distribution costs	Administrative expenses
	$'000	$'000	$'000
Per question	246,800	17,400	50,500
Depreciation (W3)	10,000	–	–
Amortisation (1,500 + 2,500 (W4))	4,000	–	–
Impairment loss (W4)	4,500	–	–
Dividend transferred (W6)	–	–	(12,000)
	265,300	17,400	38,500

2. Available-for-sale investments

   (a) Investment disposed of:

	$'000
Proceeds	11,000
Carrying amount	(8,800)
Gain on disposal	2,200
Gain previously recognised in equity (8,800 − 7,000)	1,800
Total gain recognised in profit or loss	4,000

(b)   *Remaining investments:*

	$'000
FV at end of reporting period	29,000
Carrying amount in TB	(26,500)
Gain – other comprehensive income	2,500

(c)   *Other reserve*

	$'000
Balance per TB	5,000
Reclassified gain (a)	(1,800)
Gain in year (b)	2,500
	5,700

3.   *Property, plant and equipment*

	Land	Buildings	Plant	Total
	$'000	$'000	$'000	$'000
Cost	13,000	50,000	42,200	105,200
Acc depreciation b/d	–	(8,000)	(19,700)	(27,700)
Carrying amount	13,000	42,000	22,500	77,500
Depreciation:				
Building (50,000/50 yrs*)	–	(1,000)	–	(1,000)
Plant (22,500 × 40%)	–	–	(9,000)	(9,000)
Carrying amount c/d	13,000	41,000	13,500	67,500

* $8m depreciation since 2000 = 8 years. Therefore 50-year life.

4.   *Intangible asset – brand*

	$'000
Cost	30,000
Accumulated amortisation b/d	(9,000)
	21,000
Amortisation to 1.4.09 (30,000/10 × 6/12)	(1,500)
	19,500
Impairment loss	(4,500)
Recoverable amount (higher of FV less CTS and VIU)	15,000
Amortisation to 30.9.09 (15,000/3 × 6/12)	(2,500)
Carrying amount at 30.9.09	12,500

5.   *Deferred revenue*

Per IAS 18 a proportion of the revenue from sales to Pending should be deferred to cover the ongoing service and support costs. The costs for the year to 30.9 09 will already have been accounted for, but revenue must be deferred to cover the costs for the remaining two years.

The total amount deferred should include the 40% profit, so will be calculated as:

	$'000
((1,200 × 2) × 100/60)	4,000

This will be deducted from revenue and split between current and non-current liabilities.

6.   *Dividend*

Shares in issue ($50,000 of 20c shares)	250,000 ×
Dividend per share	4.8 cents = $12m

This is added back to administrative expenses and deducted from retained earnings.

7.   *Convertible loan note*

	$'000
Balance per TB	18,440
Interest paid to 30.9.09	(1,000)
Effective interest (18,440 × 8%)	1,475
Balance at 30.9.09	18,915

Adjustment required: (1,475 − 1,000) = 475

Dr Finance costs/Cr Convertible loan note

8. *Deferred tax*

	$'000
Balance b/f	5,400
Balance to c/f (13m × 30%)	(3,900)
Adjustment	1,500

Dr Deferred tax (SOFP) / Cr Income tax expense

Question 3

Text references Chapters 4, 19 and 21

Top tips This was a mixed question, comprising calculation of movement on non-current assets, calculation of two elements of the statement of cash flows and calculation of and comment on ROCE. The only part that may have given some trouble was analysing the share issue to see how much cash was actually received. It is important in a question like this to allocate an equal amount of time to each part and note that the requirement in (a)(i) also includes intangible assets.

Easy marks There were plenty of easy marks in this question. Students should have had no trouble with the movement on non-current assets in part (a) or with 'cash flows from investing activities'. A careful re-reading of the question would have provided some sensible comments to make about the ROCE.

Marking scheme

				Marks
(a)	(i)	Property, plant and equipment		
		Mine		1½
		Land revaluation		1½
		Leased plant		1
		Plant disposal		1
		Depreciation		1
		Replacement plant		1
				7
		Development expenditure		2
				9
	(ii)	Investing activities:		
		Purchase of property, plant and equipment		2
		Disposal proceeds of plant		½
		Development expenditure		1
		Financing activities:		
		Issue of equity shares		1½
		Redemption of convertible loan notes		1
		Lease obligations		1
		Loan interest		1
				8
(b)		Calculation of ROCE		2
		Supporting components ratios		2
		Explanatory comments – up to		4
				8
			Total for question	25

(a)   (i)   Property, plant and equipment

	$'000
Balance at 30 September 2008	13,100
Addition – mine (5m + 3m restoration)	8,000
Plant obtained under finance lease	10,000
Revaluation surplus on land (2,000 × 100/80)	2,500
Plant disposal	(500)
Depreciation	(3,000)
Plant replacement (balance)	2,400
Balance at 30 September 2009	32,500

Intangible asset – development costs

	$'000
Balance at 30 September 2008	2,500
Additions	500
Impairment charge (balance)	(2,000)
Balance at 30 September 2009	1,000

(ii)   Cash flows from investing activities

	$'000	$'000
Purchase of PPE:		
Mine	5,000	
Plant	2,400	
		(7,400)
Development costs		(500)
Proceeds from sale of plant		1,200
Net cash used in investing activities		(6,700)

Cash flows from financing activities

	$'000
Proceeds of share issue (400 + 1,600 (W))	2,000
Loan notes redeemed (W)	(1,000)
Capital payments under finance lease (10,000 – (5,040 + 1,760))	(3,200)
Finance lease interest paid	(400)
Loan note interest	(350)
Net cash used in financing activities	(2,950)

Working:

	Share $'000	Shares premium $'000
At 30 September 2008	4,000	2,000
Issued on conversion:		
$4m × 20/100 × 75%	600	
Premium – ((100/20 x 600) – 600)		2,400
Issued for cash (balance)	400	1,600
At 30 September 2009	5,000	6,000

(b)   Loan notes redeemed for cash are therefore $4m x 25% = $1m

ROCE

	2008	2009
$\dfrac{4,300 \quad (3,000+800+500)}{14,700 \quad (9,700+5,000)}$	29.3%	
$\dfrac{5,750 \quad (4,000+1,000+400+350)}{27,000 \quad (19,200+1,000+5,040+1,760)}$		21.3%

We can see that profit before interest and tax has increased between 2008 and 2009 both in real terms and as a percentage:

2008 – (4,300/42,000) x 100 = 10.2%
2009 – (5,750/52,000%) x 100 = 11%

The decline is therefore due to changes in asset turnover:

2008 – 42,000/14,700 = 2.8 times
2009 – 52,000/27,000 = 1.9 times

This points to **capital being utilised less efficiently** in the year to 30 September 2009. This can be analysed further by looking at the nature of the additional capital.

During the year Crosswire spent $5m on a platinum mine which has an expected life of 10 years. It is possible that the mine was not running at full capacity for the first year.

$6.8m is owed on a finance lease for plant. The lease was not taken out until April 2009, so this equipment has only had 6 months to show a return.

$2m arises from a revaluation of freehold land. This will not give rise to any increase in return.

We are told that during 2009 Crosswire embarked on a **replacement and expansion programme** for its non-current assets. It is to be expected that such a programme would have a **temporarily adverse effect** on its ROCE. In future years it can expect to reap the benefit of this expenditure and see an improved ROCE.

Question 4

Text references Chapters 1, 5 and 6

Top tips It was important for this question to know the IASB definition. This made it possible to do a good answer to part (a) and know where you were going with part (b). It was important to spend time on all four parts of the question and read the scenarios carefully.

Easy marks This was all quite easy until you got to (b) (iii), which was a slightly confusing scenario. The clue was in 'the assistant *correctly* recorded the costs..', which would have told you that the point at issue was the impairment write-down.

Marking scheme

		Marks
(a)	1 mark per valid point	4
(b)	(i) to (iii) – 1 mark per valid point as indicated	11
	Total for question	15

(a) The IASB *Framework* defines an asset as 'a resource controlled by the entity as a result of past events and from which future economic benefits are expected to flow to the entity'. IAS 1 sets out the defining features of a current asset (intended to be realised during the normal operating cycle or within 12 months of the year end, held for trading or classified as cash or a cash equivalent). All other assets are classified as non-current.

The assistant's definition diverges from this in a number of ways:

(i) A non-current asset does not have to be physical. The definition can include intangible assets such as investments or capitalised development costs.

(ii) A non-current asset does not have to be of substantial cost. An item of immaterial value is unlikely to be capitalised, but this is not part of the definition.

(iii)   A non-current asset does not have to be legally owned. The accounting principle is based on 'substance over form' and relies on the ability of the entity to **control** the asset. This means for instance that an asset held under a finance lease is treated as an asset by the lessee, not the lessor.

(iv)   It is generally the case that non-current assets will last longer than one year. IAS 16 specifies that property, plant and equipment 'are expected to be used during more than one period'. However, if a non-current asset failed to last longer than one year, it would **still be classified as a non-current asset during its life**.

(b)   (i)   IAS 38 makes the point that 'an entity usually has **insufficient control** over the expected future economic benefits arising from a team of skilled staff..' This is the case in this situation. Darby's trained staff may stay with the company for the next four years or they may decide to leave and take their skills with them. Darby has no control over that. For this reason, the expenditure on training **can not be treated as an asset** and must be charged to profit or loss.

(ii)   The work on the new processor chip is research with the aim of eventually moving into development work. IAS 38 requires all research expenditure to be expensed as incurred. Even at the development stage, it **will not be possible to capitalise the development costs unless they satisfy the IAS 38 criteria**. When the criteria are satisfied and development costs can be capitalised, it will still not be possible to go back and capitalise the research costs. The company's past successful history makes no difference to this.

The research work on the braking system is a different case, because here the work has been commissioned by a customer and the customer will be paying, regardless of the outcome of the research. In this situation, as long as Darby has no reason to believe that the customer will not meet the costs in full, the costs should be treated as **work in progress**, rather than being charged to profit or loss.

(iii)   If we agree that the assistant was correct to record $58,000 as a non-current asset, the only question is whether it should be regarded as impaired.

An impairment has occurred when the recoverable amount of an asset falls below its carrying amount.

The projected results for this contract are:

	$
Revenue (50,000 × 3)	150,000
Costs (bal)	(110,000)
Profit	40,000

If we ignore discounting, the future cash flows are $150,000, less remaining costs of $52,000 ($110,000 - $58,000), which amounts to $98,000. This is well in excess of the $58,000 carrying amount, so **no impairment has taken place** and the non-current asset should remain at $58,000.

Question 5

Text references Chapter 18

Top tips The answer to part(a) may have seemed fairly obvious, but the question asked you to *explain* and allowed 4 marks for it, so clearly more than three sentences were required. It was worth spending a few moments thinking about this and writing a proper answer.

Easy marks Part (a) was easy with a bit of thought and (b) was easy for students who had revised EPS and knew what they were doing. Otherwise it would have been difficult to score much at all on (b).

Marking scheme

		Marks
(a)	1 mark per valid point	4
(b)	Basic EPS for 2009	3
	Restated EPS for 2008	1
	Diluted EPS for 2009	2
		6
	Total for question	10

(a) An increase in profit after tax of 80% **will not translate into a comparable increase in EPS** unless the number of shares in issue has remained constant. The disparity between the increase in profit and the increase in EPS shows that Barstead has obtained the resources it needed in order to generate higher profit through share issue(s). This may have been done as part of an acquisition drive, obtaining a controlling interest in other entities through share exchange. In this way, EPS is a more reliable indicator of performance than pure profit because **it matches any additional profit with the resources used to earn it**.

Diluted EPS takes into account the existence **of potential ordinary shares**, arising from financial instruments such as options, warrants and convertible debt. Diluted EPS shows what EPS would be if all of these potential shares came into existence in the current year. In the case of Barstead, the diluted EPS has increased by less than the basic EPS. This shows that some of the profit increase has been financed by the issue of financial instruments carrying future entitlement to ordinary shares. These instruments will carry a lower finance cost than non-convertible debt, which helps to boost current profits. But this means that the finance costs saved when these instruments are converted will probably be insufficient to offset the adverse effect of the additional shares, leading to dilution. This is an advance warning signal to investors.

(b) Theoretical ex-rights price will be:

4 shares at $3.80 –   15.2
1 share at $2.80 –   2.8
                      18.0 / 5 = $3.60

Weighted average calculation:

Date	Narrative	No. shares (m)	Time period	Bonus fraction	Weighted average (m)
1.10.2008	b/d	36	× 3/12	× $3.80/$3.60	9.5
1.1.2009	Rights issue	9			
		45	× 9/12		33.75
					43.25

Basic EPS for the year ended 30 September 2009 is therefore:

$15m/43.25m = 34.7c

Comparative EPS = 35c × 3.6/3.8 = 33.2c

Diluted EPS:

The additional earnings will be $800,000 ($10m × 8%) less 25% tax = $600,000
The additional shares will be (10m/100) × 25 = 2.5m
The net effect is therefore $600,000/2.5m = 24c
This is below basic EPS and therefore dilutive.

Earnings = $15.6m

Shares = 43.25 + 2.5 = 45.75

Diluted EPS = 34.1c

ACCA examiner's answers:
June and December 2009 papers

1   Consolidated statement of financial position of Pacemaker as at 31 March 2009:

	$million	$million
Non-current assets		
Tangible		
Property, plant and equipment (w (i))		818
Intangible		
Goodwill (w (ii))		23
Brand (25 – 5 (25/10 x 2 years post acq amortisation))		20
Investments		
Investment in associate (w (iii))		144
Other available-for-sale investments (82 + 37)		119
		1,124
Current assets		
Inventory (142 + 160 – 16 URP (w (iv)))	286	
Trade receivables (95 + 88)	183	
Cash and bank (8 + 22)	30	499
Total assets		1,623
Equity and liabilities		
Equity attributable to the parent		
Equity shares (500 + 75 (w (iii)))		575
Share premium (100 + 45 (w (iii))	145	
Retained earnings (w (iv))	247	392
		967
Non-controlling interest (w (v))		91
Total equity		1,058
Non-current liabilities		
10% loan notes (180 + 20)		200
Current liabilities (200 + 165)		365
Total equity and liabilities		1,623

Workings (all figures in $ million)
The investment in Syclop represents 80% (116/145) of its equity and is likely to give Pacemaker control thus Syclop should be consolidated as a subsidiary. The investment in Vardine represents 30% (30/100) of its equity and is normally treated as an associate that should be equity accounted.

(i)	Property, plant and equipment	
	Pacemaker	520
	Syclop	280
	Fair value property (82 – 62)	20
	Post-acquisition depreciation (2 years) (20 x 2/20 years)	(2)
		818

(ii)	Goodwill in Syclop:		
	Investment at cost – cash		210
	– loan note (116/200 x $100)		58
	Cost of the controlling interest		268
	Fair value of non-controlling interest (from question)		65
	Equity shares	145	
	Pre-acquisition profit	120	
	Fair value adjustments – property (w (i))	20	
	– brand	25	
	Fair value of net assets at acquisition		(310)
	Goodwill		23

13

(iii) Investment in associate:

	$million
Investment at cost (75 x $1·60)	120
Share of post-acquisition profit (100 – 20) x 30%	24
	144

The purchase consideration by way of a share exchange (75 million shares in Pacemaker for 30 million shares in Vardine) would be recorded as an increase in share capital of $75 million ($1 nominal value) and an increase in share premium of $45 million (75 million x $0·60).

(iv) Consolidated retained earnings:

Pacemaker's retained earnings	130
Syclop's post-acquisition profits (130 x 80% see below)	104
Gain on investments – Pacemaker (see below)	5
Vardine's post-acquisition profits (w (iii))	24
URP in Inventories (56 x 40/140)	(16)
	247

Syclop's retained earnings:	
Post-acquisition (260 – 120)	140
Additional depreciation/amortisation (2 + 5)	(7)
Loss on available-for-sale investments (40 – 37)	(3)
Adjusted post-acquisition profits	130

Gain on the value of Pacemaker's available-for-sale investments:	
Carrying amount at 31 March 2008 (345 – 210 cash – 58 loan note)	77
Carrying amount at 31 March 2009	82
Gain to retained earnings (or other components of equity)	5

(v) Non-controlling interest

Fair value on acquisition (from question)	65
Share of adjusted post acquisition profit (130 x 20% (w (iv)))	26
	91

2 (a) Pricewell – Statement of comprehensive income for the year ended 31 March 2009:

	$'000
Revenue (310,000 + 22,000 (w (i)) – 6,400 (w (ii)))	325,600
Cost of sales (w (iii))	(255,100)
Gross profit	70,500
Distribution costs	(19,500)
Administrative expenses	(27,500)
Finance costs (4,160 (w (v)) + 1,248 (w (vi)))	(5,408)
Profit before tax	18,092
Income tax expense (4,500 +700 – (8,400 – 5,600 deferred tax)	(2,400)
Profit for the year	15,692

14

(b) Pricewell – Statement of financial position as at 31 March 2009:

	$'000	$'000
Assets		
Non-current assets		
Property, plant and equipment (24,900 + 41,500 w (iv))		66,400
Current assets		
Inventory	28,200	
Amount due from customer (w (i))	17,100	
Trade receivables	33,100	
Bank	5,500	83,900
Total assets		150,300
Equity and liabilities:		
Equity shares of 50 cents each		40,000
Retained earnings (w (vii))		12,592
		52,592
Non-current liabilities		
Deferred tax	5,600	
Finance lease obligation (w (vi))	5,716	
6% Redeemable preference shares (41,600 + 1,760 (w (v)))	43,360	54,676
Current liabilities		
Trade payables	33,400	
Finance lease obligation (10,848 – 5,716) (w (vi))	5,132	
Current tax payable	4,500	43,032
Total equity and liabilities		150,300

Workings (figures in brackets in $'000)

	$'000
(i) Construction contract:	
Selling price	50,000
Estimated cost	
To date	(12,000)
To complete	(10,000)
Plant	(8,000)
Estimated profit	20,000

Work done is agreed at $22 million so the contract is 44% complete (22,000/50,000).

	$'000
Revenue	22,000
Cost of sales (= balance)	(13,200)
Profit to date (44% x 20,000)	8,800
Cost incurred to date materials and labour	12,000
Plant depreciation (8,000 x 6/24 months)	2,000
Profit to date	8,800
	22,800
Cash received	(5,700)
Amount due from customer	17,100

(ii) Pricewell is acting as an agent (not the principal) for the sales on behalf of Trilby. Therefore the income statement should only include $1·6 million (20% of the sales of $8 million). Therefore $6·4 million (8,000 – 1,600) should be deducted from revenue and cost of sales. It would also be acceptable to show agency sales (of $1·6 million) separately as other income.

	$'000
(iii) Cost of sales	
Per question	234,500
Contract (w (i))	13,200
Agency cost of sales (w (ii))	(6,400)
Depreciation (w (iv)) – leasehold property	1,800
– owned plant ((46,800 – 12,800) x 25%)	8,500
– leased plant (20,000 x 25%)	5,000
Surplus on revaluation of leasehold property (w (iv))	(1,500)
	255,100

15

	$'000
(iv) Non-current assets	
Leasehold property	
valuation at 31 March 2008	25,200
depreciation for year (14 year life remaining)	(1,800)
carrying amount at date of revaluation	23,400
valuation at 31 March 2009	(24,900)
revaluation surplus (to income statement – see below)	1,500

The $1·5 million revaluation surplus is credited to the income statement as this is the partial reversal of the $2·8 million impairment loss recognised in the income statement in the previous period (i.e. year ended 31 March 2008).

Plant and equipment	
– owned (46,800 – 12,800 – 8,500)	25,500
– leased (20,000 – 5,000 – 5,000)	10,000
– contract (8,000 – 2,000 (w (i)))	6,000
Carrying amount at 31 March 2009	41,500

(v) The finance cost of $4,160,000 for the preference shares is based on the effective rate of 10% applied to $41·6 million balance at 1 April 2008. The accrual of $1,760,000 (4,160 – 2,400 dividend paid) is added to the carrying amount of the preference shares in the statement of financial position. As these shares are redeemable they are treated as debt and their dividend is treated as a finance cost.

(vi) Finance lease liability	
balance at 31 March 2008	15,600
interest for year at 8%	1,248
lease rental paid 31 March 2009	(6,000)
total liability at 31 March 2009	10,848
interest next year at 8%	868
lease rental due 31 March 2010	(6,000)
total liability at 31 March 2010	5,716

(vii) Retained earnings	
balance at 1 April 2008	4,900
profit for year	15,692
equity dividend paid	(8,000)
balance at 31 March 2009	12,592

16

3 **(a)** Coaltown – Statement of cash flows for the year ended 31 March 2009:

Note: figures in brackets in $'000

	$'000	$'000
Cash flows from operating activities		
Profit before tax		10,200
Adjustments for:		
depreciation of non-current assets (w (i))	6,000	
loss on disposal of displays (w (i))	1,500	7,500
interest expense		600
increase in warranty provision (1,000 – 300)		700
increase in inventory (5,200 – 4,400)		(800)
increase in receivables (7,800 – 2,800)		(5,000)
decrease in payables (4,500 – 4,200)		(300)
Cash generated from operations		12,900
Interest paid		(600)
Income tax paid (w (ii))		(5,500)
Net cash from operating activities		6,800
Cash flows from investing activities (w (i))		
Purchase of non-current assets	(20,500)	
Disposal cost of non-current assets	(500)	
Net cash used in investing activities		(21,000)
		(14,200)
Cash flows from financing activities:		
Issue of equity shares (8,600 capital + 4,300 premium)	12,900	
Issue of 10% loan notes	1,000	
Equity dividends paid	(4,000)	
Net cash from financing activities		9,900
Net decrease in cash and cash equivalents		(4,300)
Cash and cash equivalents at beginning of period		700
Cash and cash equivalents at end of period		(3,600)

Workings	$'000
(i) Non-current assets	
Cost	
Balance b/f	80,000
Revaluation (5,000 – 2,000 depreciation)	3,000
Disposal	(10,000)
Balance c/f	(93,500)
Cash flow for acquisitions	20,500
Depreciation	
Balance b/f	48,000
Revaluation	(2,000)
Disposal	(9,000)
Balance c/f	(43,000)
Difference – charge for year	6,000
Disposal of displays	
Cost	10,000
Depreciation	(9,000)
Cost of disposal	500
Loss on disposal	1,500

	$'000
(ii) Income tax paid:	
Provision b/f	(5,300)
Income statement tax charge	(3,200)
Provision c/f	3,000
Difference cash paid	(5,500)

17

(b) **(i)** Workings – all monetary figures in $'000

(note: references to 2008 and 2009 should be taken as to the years ended 31 March 2008 and 2009)

The effect of a reduction in purchase costs of 10% combined with a reduction in selling prices of 5%, based on the figures from 2008, would be:

Sales (55,000 x 95%)	52,250
Cost of sales (33,000 x 90%)	(29,700)
Expected gross profit	22,550

This represents an expected gross profit margin of 43·2% (22,550/52,250 x 100)

The actual gross profit margin for 2009 is 33·4% (22,000/65,800 x 100)

(ii) The directors' expression of surprise that the gross profit in 2009 has not increased seems misconceived.

A change in the gross profit margin does not necessarily mean there will be an equivalent change in the absolute gross profit. This is because the gross profit figure is the product of the gross profit margin and the volume of sales and these may vary independently of each other. That said, in this case the expected gross profit margin in 2009 shows an increase over that earned in 2008 (to 43·2% from 40·0% (22,000/55,000 x100)) and the sales have also increased, so it is understandable that the directors expected a higher gross profit. As the actual gross profit margin in 2009 is only 33·4%, something other than the changes described by the directors must have occurred. Possible reasons for the reduction are:

The opening inventory being at old (higher) cost and the closing inventory is at the new (lower) cost will have caused slight distortion.

Inventory write downs due to damage/obsolescence.

A change in the sales mix (i.e. from higher margin sales to lower margin sales).

New (lower margin) products may have been introduced from other new suppliers.

Some selling prices may have been discounted because of sales promotions.

Import duties (perhaps not allowed for by the directors) or exchange rate fluctuations may have caused the actual purchase cost to be higher than the trade prices quoted by the new supplier.

Change in cost classification: some costs included as operating expenses in 2008 may have been classified as cost of sales in 2009 (if intentional and material this should be treated as a change in accounting policy) – for example it may be worth checking that depreciation has been properly charged to operating expenses in 2009.

The new supplier may have put his prices up during the year due to market conditions. Coaltown may have felt it could not pass these increases on to its customers.

(iii) Note – all monetary figures in $'000

Trade receivables collection period in 2008:

2,800/28,500 x 365 = 35·9 days

Applying the 35·9 days collection period to the credit sales made in 2009:

53,000 x 35·9/365 = 5,213, the actual receivables are 7,800 thus potentially increasing the bank balance by 2,587.

A similar exercise with the trade payables period in 2008:

4,500/33,000 x 365 = 49·8 days

Note the 33,000 above is the cost of sales for 2008. This was the same as the credit purchases as there was no change in the value of inventory. However, in 2009 the credit purchases will be 44,600 (43,800 + 5,200 closing inventory – 4,400 opening inventory).

Applying the 49·8 days payment period to purchases made in 2009 gives:

44,600 x 49·8/365 = 6,085, the actual payables are 4,200 thus potentially increasing the bank balance by 1,885.

Inevitably a shortening of the period of credit offered by suppliers and lengthening the credit offered to customers will put a strain on cash resources. For Coaltown the combination of maintaining the same credit periods for both trade receivables and payables would have led to a reduction in cash outflows of 4,472 (2,587 + 1,885), which would have eliminated the overdraft of 3,600 leaving a balance in hand of 872.

18

4 **(a)** Events after the reporting period are defined by IAS 10 *Events after the Reporting Period* as those events, both favourable and unfavourable, that occur between the end of the reporting period and the date that the financial statements are authorised for issue (normally by the Board of directors).

An adjusting event is one that provides further evidence of conditions that existed at the end of the reporting period, including an event that indicates that the going concern assumption in relation to the whole or part of the entity is not appropriate. Normally trading results occurring after the end of the reporting period are a matter for the next reporting period, however, if there is an event which would normally be treated as non-adjusting that causes a dramatic downturn in trading (and profitability) such that it is likely that the entity will no longer be a going concern, this should be treated as an adjusting event.

A non-adjusting event is an event after the end of the reporting period that is indicative of a condition that arose after the end of the reporting period and, subject to the exception noted above, the financial statements would not be adjusted to reflect such events.

The outcome (and values) of many items in the financial statements have a degree of uncertainty at the end of the reporting period. IAS 10 effectively says that where events occurring after the end of the reporting period help to determine what those values were at the end of the reporting period, they should be taken in account (i.e. adjusted for) in preparing the financial statements.

If non-adjusting events, whilst not affecting the financial statements of the current year, are of such importance (i.e. material) that without disclosure of their nature and estimated financial effect, users' ability to make proper evaluations and decisions about the future of the entity would be affected, then they should be disclosed in the notes to the financial statements.

(b) **(i)** This is normally classified as a non-adjusting event as there was no reason to doubt that the value of warehouse and the inventory it contained was worth less than its carrying amount at 31 March 2009 (the last day of the reporting period). The total loss suffered as a result of the fire is $16 million. The company expects that $9 million of this loss will be recovered from an insurance policy. Recoveries from third parties should be assessed separately from the related loss. As this event has caused serious disruption to trading, IAS 10 would require the details of this non-adjusting event to be disclosed as a note to the financial statements for the year ended 31 March 2009 as a total loss of $16 million and the effect of the insurance recovery to be disclosed separately.

The severe disruption in Waxwork's trading operations since the fire, together with the expectation of large trading losses for some time to come, may call in to question the going concern status of the company. If it is judged that Waxwork is no longer a going concern, then the fire and its consequences become an adjusting event requiring the financial statements for the year ended 31 March 2009 to be redrafted on the basis that the company is no longer a going concern (i.e. they would be prepared on a liquidation basis).

(ii) 70% of the inventory amounts to $322,000 (460,000 x 70%) and this was sold for a net amount of $238,000 (280,000 x 85%). Thus a large proportion of a class of inventory was sold at a loss after the reporting period. This would appear to give evidence of conditions that existed at 31 March 2009 i.e. that the net realisable value of that class of inventory was below its cost. Inventory is required to be valued at the lower of cost and net realisable value, thus this is an adjusting event. If it is assumed that the remaining inventory will be sold at similar prices and terms as that already sold, the net realisable value of the whole of the class of inventory would be calculated as:

$280,000/70% = $400,000, less commission of 15% = $340,000.

Thus the carrying amount of the inventory of $460,000 should be written down by $120,000 to its net realisable value of $340,000.

In the unlikely event that the fall in the value of the inventory could be attributed to a specific event that occurred after the date of the statement of financial position then this would be a non-adjusting event.

(iii) The date of the government announcement of the tax change is beyond the period of consideration in IAS 10. Thus this would be neither an adjusting nor a non-adjusting event. The increase in the deferred tax liability will be provided for in the year to 31 March 2010. Had the announcement been before 6 May 2009, it would have been treated as a non-adjusting event requiring disclosure of the nature of the event and an estimate of its financial effect in the notes to the financial statements.

19

5 Flightline – Income statement for the year ended 31 March 2009:

	$'000
Depreciation (w (i))	13,800
Loss on write off of engine (w (iii))	6,000
Repairs – engine	3,000
– exterior painting	2,000

Statement of financial position as at 31 March 2009

Non-current asset – Aircraft	cost	accumulated depreciation	carrying amount
	$'000	$'000	$'000
Exterior (w (i))	120,000	84,000	36,000
Cabin fittings (w (ii))	29,500	21,500	8,000
Engines (w (iii))	19,800	3,700	16,100
	169,300	109,200	60,100

Workings (figures in brackets in $'000)

(i) The exterior of the aircraft is depreciated at $6 million per annum (120,000/20 years). The cabin is depreciated at $5 million per annum (25,000/5 years). The engines would be depreciated by $500 ($18 million/36,000 hours) i.e. $250 each, per flying hour.

The carrying amount of the aircraft at 1 April 2008 is:

	Cost	accumulated depreciation	carrying amount
	$'000	$'000	$'000
Exterior (13 years old)	120,000	78,000	42,000
Cabin (3 years old)	25,000	15,000	10,000
Engines (used 10,800 hours)	18,000	5,400	12,600
	163,000	98,400	64,600

Depreciation for year to 31 March 2009:	$'000
Exterior (no change)	6,000
Cabin fittings – six months to 30 September 2008 (5,000 x 6/12)	2,500
– six months to 31 March 2009 (w (ii))	4,000
Engines – six months to 30 September 2008 (500 x 1,200 hours)	600
– six months to 31 March 2009 ((400 + 300) w (iii))	700
	13,800

(ii) Cabin fittings – at 1 October 2008 the carrying amount of the cabin fittings is $7·5 million (10,000 – 2,500). The cost of improving the cabin facilities of $4·5 million should be capitalised as it led to enhanced future economic benefits in the form of substantially higher fares. The cabin fittings would then have a carrying amount of $12 million (7,500 + 4,500) and an unchanged remaining life of 18 months. Thus depreciation for the six months to 31 March 2009 is $4 million (12,000 x 6/18).

(iii) Engines – before the accident the engines (in combination) were being depreciated at a rate of $500 per flying hour. At the date of the accident each engine had a carrying amount of $6 million ((12,600 – 600)/2). This represents the loss on disposal of the written off engine. The repaired engine's remaining life was reduced to 15,000 hours. Thus future depreciation on the repaired engine will be $400 per flying hour, resulting in a depreciation charge of $400,000 for the six months to 31 March 2009. The new engine with a cost of $10·8 million and a life of 36,000 hours will be depreciated by $300 per flying hour, resulting in a depreciation charge of $300,000 for the six months to 31 March 2009. Summarising both engines:

	cost	accumulated depreciation	carrying amount
	$'000	$'000	$'000
Old engine	9,000	3,400	5,600
New engine	10,800	300	10,500
	19,800	3,700	16,100

Note: marks are awarded for clear calculations rather than for detailed explanations. Full explanations are given for tutorial purposes.

20

1 (a) (i)

		$'000	$'000
Goodwill in Salva at 1 April 2009:			
Controlling interest			
Shares issued (120 million x 80% x 3/5 x $6)			345,600
Non-controlling interest (120 million x 20% x $3·20)			76,800
			422,400
Equity shares		120,000	
Pre-acquisition reserves:			
At 1 October 2008		152,000	
To date of acquisition (see below)		11,500	
Fair value adjustments (5,000 + 20,000)		25,000	308,500
Goodwill arising on acquisition			113,900

The interest on the 8% loan note is $2 million ($50 million x 8% x 6/12). This is included in Salva's income statement in the post-acquisition period. Thus Salva's profit for the year of $21 million has a split of $11·5 million pre-acquisition ((21 million + 2 million interest) x 6/12) and $9·5 million post-acquisition.

(ii)

	$'000
Carrying amount of investment in Ambra at 30 September 2009	
Cost (40 million x 40% x $2)	32,000
Share of post-acquisition losses (5,000 x 40% x 6/12)	(1,000)
Impairment charge	(3,000)
	28,000

(b) Pandar Group

Consolidated income statement for the year ended 30 September 2009

	$'000	$'000
Revenue (210,000 + (150,000 x 6/12) – 15,000 intra-group sales)		270,000
Cost of sales (w (i))		(162,500)
Gross profit		107,500
Distribution costs (11,200 + (7,000 x 6/12))		(14,700)
Administrative expenses (18,300 + (9,000 x 6/12))		(22,800)
Investment income (w (ii))		1,100
Finance costs (w (iii))		(2,300)
Share of loss from associate (5,000 x 40% x 6/12)	(1,000)	
Impairment of investment in associate	(3,000)	(4,000)
Profit before tax		64,800
Income tax expense (15,000 + (10,000 x 6/12))		(20,000)
Profit for the year		44,800
Attributable to:		
Owners of the parent		43,000
Non-controlling interest (w (iv))		1,800
		44,800

Workings (figures in brackets in $'000)

(i)

Cost of sales	$'000
Pandar	126,000
Salva (100,000 x 6/12)	50,000
Intra-group purchases	(15,000)
Additional depreciation: plant (5,000/5 years x 6/12)	500
Unrealised profit in inventories (15,000/3 x 20%)	1,000
	162,500

As the registration of the domain name is renewable indefinitely (at only a nominal cost) it will not be amortised.

(ii)

Investment income	
Per income statement	9,500
Intra-group interest (50,000 x 8% x 6/12)	(2,000)
Intra-group dividend (8,000 x 80%)	(6,400)
	1,100

		$'000	$'000
(iii)	Finance costs		
	Pandar	1,800	
	Salva post-acquisition ((3,000 – 2,000) x 6/12 + 2,000)	2,500	
	Intra-group interest (w (ii))	(2,000)	
		2,300	
(iv)	Non-controlling interest		
	Salva's post-acquisition profit (see (i) above)	9,500	
	Less: post-acquisition additional depreciation (w (i))	(500)	
		9,000	
		x 20%	= 1,800

2 (a) Sandown – Statement of comprehensive income for the year ended 30 September 2009

	$'000
Revenue (380,000 – 4,000 (w (i)))	376,000
Cost of sales (w (ii))	(265,300)
Gross profit	110,700
Distribution costs	(17,400)
Administrative expenses (50,500 – 12,000 (w (iii)))	(38,500)
Investment income	1,300
Profit/gain on sale of available-for-sale investments (w (iv))	4,000
Finance costs (w (v))	(1,475)
Profit before tax	58,625
Income tax expense (16,200 + 2,100 – 1,500 (w (vi)))	(16,800)
Profit for the year	41,825
Other comprehensive income	
Gain on available-for-sale investments (w (iv))	2,500
Realised profit reclassified (recycled) to income on available-for-sale investment	(1,800)
Total other comprehensive income	700
Total comprehensive income	42,525

(b) Sandown – Statement of financial position as at 30 September 2009

Assets	$'000	$'000
Non-current assets		
Property, plant and equipment (w (vii))		67,500
Intangible – brand (15,000 – 2,500 (w (ii)))		12,500
Available-for-sale investments (at fair value)		29,000
		109,000
Current assets		
Inventory	38,000	
Trade receivables	44,500	
Bank	8,000	90,500
Total assets		199,500
Equity and liabilities		
Equity		
Equity shares of 20 cents each		50,000
Equity option		2,000
Other reserve (w (viii))		5,700
Retained earnings (26,060 + 41,825 – 12,000 dividend (w (iii)))		55,885
		113,585
Non-current liabilities		
Deferred tax (w (vi))	3,900	
Deferred income (w (i))	2,000	
5% convertible loan note (w (v))	18,915	24,815
Current liabilities		
Trade payables	42,900	
Deferred income (w (i))	2,000	
Current tax payable	16,200	61,100
Total equity and liabilities		199,500

Workings (figures in brackets in $'000)

(i) IAS 18 *Revenue* requires that where sales revenue includes an amount for after sales servicing and support costs then a proportion of the revenue should be deferred. The amount deferred should cover the cost and a reasonable profit (in this case a gross profit of 40%) on the services. As the servicing and support is for three years and the date of the sale was 1 October 2008, revenue relating to two years' servicing and support provision must be deferred: ($1·2 million x 2/0·6) = $4 million. This is shown as $2 million in both current and non-current liabilities.

(ii) Cost of sales

Per question	246,800
Depreciation – building (50,000/50 years – see below)	1,000
– plant and equipment (42,200 – 19,700) x 40%))	9,000
Amortisation – brand (1,500 + 2,500 – see below)	4,000
Impairment of brand (see below)	4,500
	265,300

The cost of the building of $50 million (63,000 – 13,000 land) has accumulated depreciation of $8 million at 30 September 2008 which is eight years after its acquisition. Thus the life of the building must be 50 years.

The brand is being amortised at $3 million per annum (30,000/10 years). The impairment occurred half way through the year, thus amortisation of $1·5 million should be charged prior to calculation of the impairment loss. At the date of the impairment review the brand had a carrying amount of $19·5 million (30,000 – (9,000 + 1,500)). The recoverable amount of the brand is its fair value of $15 million (as this is higher than its value in use of $12 million) giving an impairment loss of $4·5 million (19,500 – 15,000). Amortisation of $2·5 million (15,000/3 years x 6/12) is required for the second-half of the year giving total amortisation of $4 million for the full year.

(iii) A dividend of 4·8 cents per share would amount to $12 million (50 million x 5 (i.e. shares are 20 cents each) x 4·8 cents). This is not an administrative expense but a distribution of profits that should be accounted for through equity.

(iv) The profit reported on the sale of the available-for-sale investment has two parts:

gain in current year (11,000 proceeds – 8,800 carrying amount)	2,200
reclassified past revaluation gains (from other equity reserve):	
(8,800 carrying amount – 7,000 original cost)	1,800
	4,000

The remaining investments of $26·5 million have a fair value of $29 million at 30 September 2009 which gives a fair value increase (credited to other reserve) of $2·5 million.

(v) The finance cost of the convertible loan note is based on its effective rate of 8% applied to $18,440,000 carrying amount at 1 October 2008 = $1,475,000 (rounded). The accrual of $475,000 (1,475 – 1,000 interest paid) is added to the carrying amount of the loan note giving a figure of $18,915,000 (18,440 + 475) in the statement of financial position at 30 September 2009.

(vi) Deferred tax

credit balance required at 30 September 2009 (13,000 x 30%)	3,900
balance at 1 October 2008	(5,400)
credit (reduction in balance) to income statement	1,500

(vii) Non-current assets

Freehold property (63,000 – (8,000 + 1,000)) (w (ii))	54,000
Plant and equipment (42,200 – (19,700 + 9,000)) (w (ii))	13,500
Property, plant and equipment	67,500

(viii) Other reserve (re available-for-sale investments)

at 1 October 2008	5,000
'reclassified' gain (w (iv))	(1,800)
increase in year ((w (iv))	2,500
	5,700

3 (a) (i) Non-current assets

Property, plant and equipment	$'000
Carrying amount b/f	13,100
Mine (5,000 + 3,000 environmental cost)	8,000
Revaluation (2,000/0·8 allowing for effect of deferred tax transfer)	2,500
Fair value of leased plant	10,000
Plant disposal	(500)
Depreciation	(3,000)
Replacement plant (balance)	2,400
Carrying amount c/f	32,500

Development costs	
Carrying amount b/f	2,500
Additions during year	500
Amortisation and impairment (balance)	(2,000)
Carrying amount c/f	1,000

(ii) Cash flows from investing activities:

Purchase of property, plant and equipment (w (i))	(7,400)
Disposal proceeds of plant	1,200
Development costs	(500)
Net cash used in investing activities	(6,700)

Cash flows from financing activities:

Issue of equity shares (w (ii))	2,000
Redemption of convertible loan notes ((5,000 – 1,000) x 25%)	(1,000)
Lease obligations (w (iii))	(3,200)
Interest paid (400 + 350)	(750)
Net cash used in financing activities	(2,950)

Workings (figures in brackets in $'000)

(i) The cash elements of the increase in property, plant and equipment are $5 million for the mine (the capitalised environmental provision is not a cash flow) and $2·4 million for the replacement plant making a total of $7·4 million.

(ii) Of the $4 million convertible loan notes (5,000 – 1,000) that were redeemed during the year, 75% ($3 million) of these were exchanged for equity shares on the basis of 20 new shares for each $100 in loan notes. This would create 600,000 (3,000/100 x 20) new shares of $1 each and share premium of $2·4 million (3,000 – 600). As 1 million (5,000 – 4,000) new shares were issued in total, 400,000 must have been for cash. The remaining increase (after the effect of the conversion) in the share premium of $1·6 million (6,000 – 2,000 b/f – 2,400 conversion) must relate to the cash issue of shares, thus cash proceeds from the issue of shares is $2 million (400 nominal value + 1,600 premium).

(iii) The initial lease obligation is $10 million (the fair value of the plant). At 30 September 2009 total lease obligations are $6·8 million (5,040 + 1,760), thus repayments in the year were $3·2 million (10,000 – 6,800).

(b) Taking the definition of ROCE from the question:

Year ended 30 September 2009	$'000
Profit before tax and interest on long-term borrowings (4,000 + 1,000 + 400 + 350)	5,750
Equity plus loan notes and finance lease obligations (19,200 + 1,000 + 5,040 + 1,760)	27,000
ROCE	21·3%

Equivalent for year ended 30 September 2008	
(3,000 + 800 + 500)	4,300
(9,700 + 5,000)	14,700
ROCE	29·3%

To help explain the deterioration it is useful to calculate the components of ROCE i.e. operating margin and net asset turnover (utilisation):

	2009		2008
Operating margin (5,750/52,000 x 100)	11·1%	(4,300/42,000)	10·2%
Net asset turnover (52,000/27,000)	1·93 times	(42,000/14,700)	2·86 times

From the above it can be clearly seen that the 2009 operating margin has improved by nearly 1% point, despite the $2 million impairment charge on the write down of the development project. This means the deterioration in the ROCE is due to poorer asset turnover. This implies there has been a decrease in the efficiency in the use of the company's assets this year compared to last year.

Looking at the movement in the non-current assets during the year reveals some mitigating points:

The land revaluation has increased the carrying amount of property, plant and equipment without any physical increase in capacity. This unfavourably distorts the current year's asset turnover and ROCE figures.

The acquisition of the platinum mine appears to be a new area of operation for Crosswire which may have a different (perhaps lower) ROCE to other previous activities or it may be that it will take some time for the mine to come to full production capacity.

The substantial acquisition of the leased plant was half-way through the year and can only have contributed to the year's results for six months at best. In future periods a full year's contribution can be expected from this new investment in plant and this should improve both asset turnover and ROCE.

In summary, the fall in the ROCE may be due largely to the above factors (effectively the replacement and expansion programme), rather than to poor operating performance, and in future periods this may be reversed.

It should also be noted that had the ROCE been calculated on the average capital employed during the year (rather than the year end capital employed), which is arguably more correct, then the deterioration in the ROCE would not have been as pronounced.

4 (a) There are four elements to the assistant's definition of a non-current asset and he is substantially incorrect in respect of all of them.

The term non-current assets will normally include intangible assets and certain investments; the use of the term 'physical asset' would be specific to tangible assets only.

Whilst it is usually the case that non-current assets are of relatively high value this is not a defining aspect. A waste paper bin may exhibit the characteristics of a non-current asset, but on the grounds of materiality it is unlikely to be treated as such. Furthermore the past cost of an asset may be irrelevant; no matter how much an asset has cost, it is the expectation of future economic benefits flowing from a resource (normally in the form of future cash inflows) that defines an asset according to the IASB's *Framework for the preparation and presentation of financial statements*.

The concept of ownership is no longer a critical aspect of the definition of an asset. It is probably the case that most non-current assets in an entity's statement of financial position are owned by the entity; however, it is the ability to 'control' assets (including preventing others from having access to them) that is now a defining feature. For example: this is an important characteristic in treating a finance lease as an asset of the lessee rather than the lessor.

It is also true that most non-current assets will be used by an entity for more than one year and a part of the definition of property, plant and equipment in IAS 16 *Property, plant and equipment* refers to an expectation of use in more than one period, but this is not necessarily always the case. It may be that a non-current asset is acquired which proves unsuitable for the entity's intended use or is damaged in an accident. In these circumstances assets may not have been used for longer than a year, but nevertheless they were reported as non-currents during the time they were in use. A non-current asset may be within a year of the end of its useful life but (unless a sale agreement has been reached under IFRS 5 *Non-current assets held for sale and discontinued operations*) would still be reported as a non-current asset if it was still giving economic benefits. Another defining aspect of non-current assets is their intended use i.e. held for continuing use in the production, supply of goods or services, for rental to others or for administrative purposes.

(b) (i) The expenditure on the training courses may exhibit the characteristics of an asset in that they have and will continue to bring future economic benefits by way of increased efficiency and cost savings to Darby. However, the expenditure cannot be recognised as an asset on the statement of financial position and must be charged as an expense as the cost is incurred. The main reason for this lies with the issue of 'control'; it is Darby's employees that have the 'skills' provided by the courses, but the employees can leave the company and take their skills with them or, through accident or injury, may be deprived of those skills. Also the capitalisation of staff training costs is specifically prohibited under International Financial Reporting Standards (specifically IAS 38 *Intangible assets*).

(ii) The question specifically states that the costs incurred to date on the development of the new processor chip are research costs. IAS 38 states that research costs must be expensed. This is mainly because research is the relatively early stage of a new project and any future benefits are so far in the future that they cannot be considered to meet the definition of an asset (probable future economic benefits), despite the good record of success in the past with similar projects.

Although the work on the automatic vehicle braking system is still at the research stage, this is different in nature from the previous example as the work has been commissioned by a customer, As such, from the perspective of Darby, it is work in progress (a current asset) and should not be written off as an expense. A note of caution should be added here in that the question says that the success of the project is uncertain (which presumably means it may not be completed). This does not mean that Darby will not receive payment for the work it has carried out, but it should be checked to the contract to ensure that the amount it has spent to date ($2·4 million) will be recoverable. In the event that say, for example, the contract stated that only $2 million would be allowed for research costs, this would place a limit on how much Darby could treat as work in progress. If this were the case then, for this example, Darby would have to expense $400,000 and treat only $2 million as work in progress.

(iii) The question suggests the correct treatment for this kind of contract is to treat the costs of the installation as a non-current asset and (presumably) depreciate it over its expected life of (at least) three years from when it becomes available for use. In this case the asset will not come into use until the next financial year/reporting period and no depreciation needs to be provided at 30 September 2009.

The capitalised costs to date of $58,000 should only be written down if there is evidence that the asset has become impaired. Impairment occurs where the recoverable amount of an asset is less than its carrying amount. The assistant appears to believe that the recoverable amount is the future profit, whereas (in this case) it is the future (net) cash inflows. Thus any impairment test at 30 September 2009 should compare the carrying amount of $58,000 with the expected net cash flow from the system of $98,000 ($50,000 per annum for three years less future cash outflows to completion the installation of $52,000 (see note below). As the future net cash flows are in excess of the carrying amount, the asset is not impaired and it should not be written down but shown as a non-current asset (under construction) at cost of $58,000.

Note: as the contract is expected to make a profit of $40,000 on income of $150,000, the total costs must be $110,000, with costs to date at $58,000 this leaves completion costs of $52,000.

5 (a) Whilst profit after tax (and its growth) is a useful measure, it may not give a fair representation of the true underlying earnings performance. In this example, users could interpret the large annual increase in profit after tax of 80% as being indicative of an underlying improvement in profitability (rather than what it really is: an increase in absolute profit). It is possible, even probable, that (some of) the profit growth has been achieved through the acquisition of other companies (acquisitive growth). Where companies are acquired from the proceeds of a new issue of shares, or where they have been acquired through share exchanges, this will result in a greater number of equity shares of the acquiring company being in issue. This is what appears to have happened in the case of Barstead as the improvement indicated by its earnings per share (EPS) is only 5% per annum. This explains why the EPS (and the trend of EPS) is considered a more reliable indicator of performance because the additional profits which could be expected from the greater resources (proceeds from the shares issued) is matched with the increase in the number of shares. Simply looking at the growth in a company's profit after tax does not take into account any increases in the resources used to earn them. Any increase in growth financed by borrowings (debt) would not have the same impact on profit (as being financed by equity shares) because the finance costs of the debt would act to reduce profit.

The calculation of a diluted EPS takes into account any potential equity shares in issue. Potential ordinary shares arise from financial instruments (e.g. convertible loan notes and options) that may entitle their holders to equity shares in the future. The diluted EPS is useful as it alerts existing shareholders to the fact that future EPS may be reduced as a result of share capital changes; in a sense it is a warning sign. In this case the lower increase in the diluted EPS is evidence that the (higher) increase in the basic EPS has, in part, been achieved through the increased use of diluting financial instruments. The finance cost of these instruments is less than the earnings their proceeds have generated leading to an increase in current profits (and basic EPS); however, in the future they will cause more shares to be issued. This causes a dilution where the finance cost per potential new share is less than the basic EPS.

(b) (Basic) EPS for the year ended 30 September 2009 ($15 million/43·25 million x 100)   34·7   cents

Comparative (basic) EPS (35 x 3·60/3·80)   33·2   cents

Effect of rights issue (at below market price)

100 shares at $3·80	380
25 shares at $2·80	70
125 shares at $3·60 (calculated theoretical ex-rights value)	450

Weighted average number of shares

36 million x 3/12 x $3·80/$3·60	9·50	million
45 million x 9/12	33·75	million
	43·25	million

Diluted EPS for the year ended 30 September 2009 ($15·6 million/45·75 million x 100)   34·1   cents

Adjusted earnings

15 million + (10 million x 8% x 75%) $15·6   million

Adjusted number of shares

43·25 million + (10 million x 25/100)   45·75   million

Review Form & Free Prize Draw – Paper F7 Financial Reporting (International) (1/10)

All original review forms from the entire BPP range, completed with genuine comments, will be entered into one of two draws on 31 July 2010 and 31 January 2011. The names on the first four forms picked out on each occasion will be sent a cheque for £50.

Name: _____   Address: _____

_____

_____

How have you used this Kit?
(Tick one box only)

☐ Home study (book only)

☐ On a course: college _____

☐ With 'correspondence' package

☐ Other _____

Why did you decide to purchase this Kit?
(Tick one box only)

☐ Have used the complementary Study text

☐ Have used other BPP products in the past

☐ Recommendation by friend/colleague

☐ Recommendation by a lecturer at college

☐ Saw advertising

☐ Other _____

During the past six months do you recall seeing/receiving any of the following?
(Tick as many boxes as are relevant)

☐ Our advertisement in *Student Accountant*

☐ Our advertisement in *Pass*

☐ Our advertisement in *PQ*

☐ Our brochure with a letter through the post

☐ Our website www.bpp.com

Which (if any) aspects of our advertising do you find useful?
(Tick as many boxes as are relevant)

☐ Prices and publication dates of new editions

☐ Information on product content

☐ Facility to order books off-the-page

☐ None of the above

Which BPP products have you used?

Text	☐	*Success CD*	☐	*Learn Online*	☐
Kit	☑	*i-Learn*	☐	*Home Study Package*	☐
Passcard	☐	*i-Pass*	☐	*Home Study PLUS*	☐

Your ratings, comments and suggestions would be appreciated on the following areas.

	Very useful	Useful	Not useful
Passing ACCA exams	☐	☐	☐
Passing P1	☐	☐	☐
Planning your question practice	☐	☐	☐
Questions	☐	☐	☐
Top Tips etc in answers	☐	☐	☐
Content and structure of answers	☐	☐	☐
'Plan of attack' in mock exams	☐	☐	☐
Mock exam answers	☐	☐	☐

Overall opinion of this Kit	Excellent ☐	Good ☐	Adequate ☐	Poor ☐

Do you intend to continue using BPP products?   Yes ☐   No ☐

The BPP author of this edition can be e-mailed at: marymaclean@bpp.com

Please return this form to: Lesley Buick, ACCA Publishing Manager, BPP Learning Media Ltd, FREEPOST, London, W12 8BR

Review Form & Free Prize Draw (continued)

TELL US WHAT YOU THINK

Please note any further comments and suggestions/errors below.

Free Prize Draw Rules

1   Closing date for 31 July 2010 draw is 30 June 2010. Closing date for 31 January 2011 draw is 31 December 2010.

2   Restricted to entries with UK and Eire addresses only. BPP employees, their families and business associates are excluded.

3   No purchase necessary. Entry forms are available upon request from BPP Learning Media Ltd. No more than one entry per title, per person. Draw restricted to persons aged 16 and over.

4   Winners will be notified by post and receive their cheques not later than 6 weeks after the relevant draw date.

5   The decision of the promoter in all matters is final and binding. No correspondence will be entered into.